Rights on Trial

How Workplace Discrimination Law Perpetuates Inequality

ELLEN BERREY, ROBERT L. NELSON,
AND LAURA BETH NIELSEN

THE UNIVERSITY OF CHICAGO PRESS   CHICAGO AND LONDON

The University of Chicago Press, Chicago 60637
The University of Chicago Press, Ltd., London

Published 2017
Printed in the United States of America

26 25 24 23 22 21 20 19 18 17   1 2 3 4 5

ISBN-13: 978-0-226-46671-2 (cloth)
ISBN-13: 978-0-226-46685-9 (paper)
ISBN-13: 978-0-226-46699-6 (e-book)
DOI: 10.7208/chicago/9780226466996.001.0001

The publication of this work was supported by the American Bar Foundation.

Library of Congress Cataloging-in-Publication Data

Names: Berrey, Ellen, author. | Nelson, Robert L., 1952– author. | Nielsen, Laura Beth, author.
Title: Rights on trial : how workplace discrimination law perpetuates inequality / Ellen Berrey, Robert L. Nelson, Laura Beth Nielsen.
Description: Chicago ; London : The University of Chicago Press, 2017. | Includes bibliographical references and index.
Identifiers: LCCN 2016049356 | ISBN 9780226466712 (cloth : alk. paper) | ISBN 9780226466859 (pbk. : alk. paper) | ISBN 9780226466996 (e-book)
Subjects: LCSH: Discrimination in employment—Law and legislation—United States. | Discrimination in employment—Law and legislation—Economic aspects—United States.
Classification: LCC KF3464 .B477 2017 | DDC 344.7301/133—dc23 LC record available at https://lccn.loc.gov/2016049356

♾ This paper meets the requirements of ANSI/NISO Z39.48–1992 (Permanence of Paper).

TO ELI AND ADELA, THAT YOU KNOW JUSTICE AND WORK FOR PEACE
—EB

TO MY CHILDREN AND TO GRANDBABY NELSON (FORTHCOMING)
—RLN

FOR TYLER PARSONS, WHO LOVED JUSTICE AND PRACTICED KINDNESS WHEREVER HE WENT
—LBN

Contents

Tables and Figures

TABLES

FIGURES

Online Appendix

press.uchicago.edu/sites/rightsontrial/

1. Coding Form for Case Filing (Quantitative) Data
2. Interview Schedules (Part I with open-ended questions, Part II with closed-ended questions)
   - 2.1 Plaintiffs Interview Schedule, Part I
   - 2.2 Plaintiffs' Lawyers Interview Schedule, Part I
   - 2.3 Defendant Representatives Interview Schedule, Part I
   - 2.4 Defendants' Lawyers Interview Schedule, Part I
   - 2.5 Plaintiffs Interview Schedule, Part II
   - 2.6 Lawyers Interview Schedule, Part II
   - 2.7 Defendant Representatives Interview Schedule, Part II
3. Online Audio Recordings (Throughout this book we note when an audio recording of a quote is available online with the symbol . These quotes are available at the authors' website for this book at http://www.rightsontrial.com.)

Authors' Note

For more than a decade, we have been considering the relationship between workplace discrimination, inequality, and law's capacity to remedy injustice and promote social change. This has included writing grants to support the extensive empirical work reported here, collecting and analyzing (and reanalyzing) our data, and writing reports, articles, and this book. In that time, the prevailing argument in academic research has been that animus-based discrimination is *not* the primary mechanism perpetuating inequality in the workplace. Rather, implicit bias, structural mechanisms held over from the past, subtle favoritism toward white people, and a few "bad apples" have been identified as the major challenges for antidiscrimination law to address.

Much of this book is an argument that—in addition to the less visible mechanisms that produce workplace discrimination and inequality—overt racism, sexism, ableism, and ageism must remain part of the scholarly and activist agenda.

As our data demonstrate, and as the United States and the world are now seeing, racial hatred, discrimination, and animus have not been eliminated; they were merely deemed inappropriate for "polite conversation" in many contexts. As this book goes to press, Donald Trump takes office (he has been the US president for five days at the time of this writing), but the 2016 presidential election itself was one long demonstration that dehumanization, racism, sexual assault, and mockery of people with disabilities can still serve as a rallying cry to unify enough of the American voters to elect a president. Hate crimes are on the rise. We see the emergence of overt white supremacy rebranded as the "alt-right," and explicit appeals to racism to stoke anti-immigrant, xenophobic isolationism. These events reveal the renewed importance for empirical research about discrimination in the workplace and the capacity of our regulatory and judicial systems to effectively prevent and punish it. We hope this book is a constructive part of that effort.

PART I

Introduction

CHAPTER ONE

Introduction

Putting Rights on Trial

Plaintiffs' Stories

Gerry Handley's Case against Manufacturing, Inc.

Gerry Handley (P14),[1] a thirty-four-year-old African American computer operator, had worked for a large manufacturing company for nine years when, after being assigned to a new unit, he began to receive what he perceived as racial harassment from his supervisor and coworkers. He told us:

> We worked in this big computer, like a lab. They had these big computers and every day, you know, we would run and maintain these computers like 24 hours, 7 days a week, and they had like a main console. And these guys that were like our supervisors, you know, you'd come in and they might, almost like on the board. . . . They'd have a picture of a black man eating like ribs, and he'd have like all types of sauce on his face, you know. And they would just all the time say stuff like the KKK, and just to me it was like a poisoned environment.

Mr. Handley said he suffered such treatment for three years before he complained to the Equal Employment Opportunity Commission (EEOC). We asked what finally led him to file a formal complaint:

> GH: They would like always bring up these racial conversations and make these racial jokes. What I would do is I'd just ignore them. I wouldn't laugh or I wouldn't listen in, I would just sit there and they would try to pull me

> into the conversation asking me questions. They started talking about incest, and they started talking about blacks from slavery time, you know, they bred them and sold them, and they inbred them down in the south. And I'm from down south, and so they asked me, they told me a lot of the blacks had sex with their daughters and stuff like that, way back from the Caribbeans. And I would just sit there listening like, "Oh my God, I know they're not saying this." And the guy asked me, he said, did I ever have sex with my daughter. And so . . .
>
> LBN: He asked you if you had sex with your daughter?
>
> GH: Yeah.
>
> LBN: And this is your boss or your manager?
>
> GH: He was like my lead.

Mr. Handley's case is unusual among employment discrimination lawsuits along several dimensions. First, he was joined by two other plaintiffs. Among federal discrimination claims, 90% are made by a single plaintiff. Second, Mr. Handley experienced overtly racist harassment that was well documented by fellow workers; his own records provided an unusually strong legal claim. Third, he ended up, according to official records, a "winner" at law. He settled with the manufacturer for $50,000, substantially higher than the median settlement ($30,000) in employment civil rights cases. Finally, Mr. Handley's case is unusual in that he maintained his job with his employer and even won back the position from which he had been transferred when he complained.

Yet in other respects, Mr. Handley's case was typical. He suffered many of the harms that other plaintiffs have incurred over the course of litigation. Tensions surrounding the lawsuit led to a divorce from his wife (who was white), and Mr. Handley lived out of his car during the course of the lawsuit. He did not trust his lawyer and felt shortchanged in the settlement, but he felt he had no choice but to accept it. Mr. Handley had to pay 20% of his settlement to his attorney, and his ex-wife claimed one-half of the remainder. While he regained his old job, he suffered a loss in job seniority, which may have contributed to his layoff just a year later during a major "downsizing."

We asked whether Mr. Handley felt like anyone in the company supported him:

> GH: These ten people that were supporting me in the department, they like ruined their lives. They like had to move and lost their jobs and had

to relocate, and I could tell you, it was just horrible. It poisoned the whole environment. If I had to do it over again, I wouldn't do it because I lost everything.

LBN: So what would you do if you had to do it over again?

GH: I would have took it. When he said that, you know, about my daughter, I would have just took it and kept my mouth shut and not tell anybody. Keep your mouth shut and just take it, you know, because if you fight back, it ain't worth it. The legal system and the justice, it ain't there.

Gerry Handley exemplifies the burdens that many plaintiffs bear in employment civil rights litigation. Despite several advantages, the Handley case illustrates plaintiffs' personal risks in the contemporary American approach to workplace discrimination. The United States' employment civil rights system is extensive and complex. It rests on constitutional protections, as well as on statutory prohibitions of discrimination. Those prohibitions were elaborated first by Title VII of the US Civil Rights Act of 1964—which prohibited discriminatory employment decisions based on race, sex, color, religion, or national origin—and later extended to include, significantly, disability and age as well as sexual harassment. Enforcement of these rights depends on regulation and litigation brought by those who believe they have been the targets of discrimination. These rights are intended to dismantle workplace discrimination across multiple hierarchies, the most notable of which, today, are race, sex, disability, and age.

As evident in Mr. Handley's experience, the adversarial character of the antidiscrimination regime imposes considerable personal and financial costs upon individual plaintiffs. These costs appear to be especially high for African Americans and other people of color who bring claims of racial discrimination. Ironically, then, the groups for whom civil rights legislation was first and most urgently sought may now experience a unique form of inequality within the system of employment civil rights litigation.

Kristen Baker's Case against GCo

Kristen Baker (P34), a thirty-three-year-old white woman, worked as an assistant buyer in the sales division of GCo, a relatively small, family-owned company that manufactures components for cars and other machinery. As Ms. Baker told us, in her first four years of employment she worked hard, took classes, and earned a certificate of expertise relevant to the work. In her fifth year, Daniel Miller, a male employee with six months longer tenure in the same job, was promoted to salesman despite the extra efforts Ms. Baker believed Mr. Miller had not undertaken. Ms. Baker approached the vice president with whom she had been working. As she recalled, he told her, "'Daniel is a guy and he's got three kids and a wife, and you are a girl and you married a doctor, so you obviously don't need the income.'" Although she thought this was not fair, she made the best decision for her and her family, which was to continue working at the manufacturing plant.

Ms. Baker says she knew from the moment she was hired that the work environment might be, in her words, somewhat "salty." She remembered being told that "'the salesmen are *men*, and they are busy people and there is some cussing and stuff that goes on.' And I said, 'Well that's fine, I can handle that. I can dish it out too.' . . . It didn't bother me, because it wasn't about me."

According to Ms. Baker, the workplace was increasingly professionalized when GCo was sold to a larger company. Ironically, though, the introduction of more formal human resources (HR) practices resulted in a rise of unprofessional behavior. The norms that were carefully policed when the company was family-run were harder to enforce in the new bureaucratic structure. Soon, the salesmen generally, and Mr. Miller in particular, were swearing more. And it was not just about venting frustration; what once could be explained away as rude or bawdy became obscene. Ms. Baker came to believe that the sexualized teasing was ruining her credibility with her vendors and clients.

Mr. Miller began bringing pornographic magazines and movies to work, Ms. Baker told us. He facilitated and even charged admission for pornography viewing sessions in the conference room at lunch. He showed Ms. Baker pictures of pornography depicting bestiality. She utilized the new HR policies and complained to her manager, documenting multiple complaints. There were other women in the department, but the ethic was one of gendered toughness and, while they would express frustration privately to Ms. Baker, they did not make formal complaints. Ms. Baker described what led her to take formal action outside the company:

> There were two final straws. One of them was when he [had] a pornographic picture of a woman who had a watermelon shoved into her vagina. And [the woman in the photograph] was on a bed, and [she] had stiletto heels

> on. . . . Daniel took it in front of a group of my peers and said, "Oh, look Kristen, we would recognize you anywhere with those heels on." I was humiliated, just humiliated and then reported it.

Shortly thereafter, in front of a client:

> Daniel went in a room and pulled out this tray of chocolate dildos and took out one, a big one, and stuck it in my face, in my mouth, and said, "Here I know you like to suck on these. Suck on this." And I just [said], "I can't do this anymore."

The facts of Ms. Baker's situation are extreme. Although blatant discrimination may be more common than a number of modern commentators and scholars suggest, this case is one of the more outrageous examples of obvious sex discrimination in our data. Ms. Baker took all of the appropriate steps to stop the discrimination, making repeated reports to the appropriate workplace representatives, but nothing happened. After the chocolate dildo incident, she told us that she told her boss:

> "Look: if this does not stop, if some action is not taken, I will file a lawsuit." What wound up happening is that I just kept threatening and threatening and threatening. . . . I said, "You know, I keep talking to you about what is going on, he is now the vice president, nothing has changed, and I am going to talk to an attorney." I really wasn't going to at that time. I just wanted him to stop so that I could just do my job without having to be nervous about staying late, about being there alone with him because he was a sexual pervert.

The company did nothing to try to remedy the situation, and a friend encouraged Ms. Baker to speak with an attorney. As she recounted, her attorney told her, "You know, I don't normally take noncorporate clients . . . [but] I have to take this case, because you really were treated inhumanely." Ms. Baker said her attorney informed her "that it wasn't a million dollar case." This was not important to her, she told us: "It was never about money, so we [demanded] a simple [settlement] of just $100,000 . . . and then an apology." And she wanted to keep her job because it provided her family's health insurance (her husband had a chronic illness that required ongoing medical attention).

Ms. Baker described how the new owner of the company reacted to notice of the suit: "[He] just laughed and said to my face, 'I've had numerous lawsuits against me in companies that I have owned.' And he is a very rich, pompous man, and he said, 'I have never lost one yet.'" Ms. Baker recalled:

> The owner truly believed that I made all of this stuff up just to get money. And because I could get no one—literally no one—to corroborate any of my stories except my manager, they really believed that the two of us were trying to rip off the company.

As the case proceeded, Mr. Miller eventually was forced to give a deposition in which he denied the most outrageous accusations and sugar-coated others. Shortly after his deposition, the company's owner asked a respected former employee, Tim Fligstein, what he saw when he worked with Mr. Miller and Ms. Baker. With nothing to lose now that he worked for another company, Mr. Fligstein answered honestly. In Ms. Baker's words, he told the owner what happened, "word for word." Ms. Baker cried as she told us, "That is when they decided to drop the suit because they knew that they were wrong."

After the owner heard the truth from someone he apparently valued (a man), GCo decided to settle the lawsuit. The company's first offer was $10,000 for Ms. Baker's attorney's fees and a confidentiality clause. She would not receive health insurance, and she was bothered that the settlement "would have to go down in [*sic*] record that I lost the lawsuit and I said, 'No. I can't do that.'" After a month of negotiations, she would have settled for a public apology, one dollar, and to keep her job. GCo wanted a private apology, some cash settlement, and for Ms. Baker to leave the company. She recounted her feelings:

> I am not leaving the company. I didn't do anything wrong. If I leave at this point then I am the guilty party because then it looks like I just wanted it for the money. . . . And it had absolutely not one thing to do with the money. It had to do with my integrity and who I am.

Ms. Baker dropped the lawsuit, keeping her job and benefits in exchange for the following concessions: apologies from Mr. Miller, as well as from the past and current presidents of GCo in front of all of GCo's executive management; one dollar (that was not recorded in any settlement documents); a stipulation that the case would neither be characterized as a "loss" for Ms. Baker nor could GCo's owner ever claim that he "always won lawsuits"; that Mr. Miller could never advance in management; and that the company start a sexual harassment program that month. Ms. Baker enjoyed a seventeen-year career at GCo after the lawsuit. Mr. Miller eventually was fired or quit (no one we interviewed was exactly sure which).

It may be difficult to believe that discrimination this blatant and offensive still occurs in American workplaces every day, but it does. It may be surprising that those who suffer this kind of treatment often are abandoned and even persecuted by the very HR departments that are supposed to help resolve such matters, but they are. And it may be shocking that the legal system is so difficult to navigate and so loaded with steep personal costs, but it is. Finally, it may be alarming to believe, in the era of media accounts that portray "greedy plaintiffs," "runaway juries," and a litigation "explosion," that even proverbial "winners" in the employment discrimination system receive only modest awards, if any. But they do.

The system of employment civil rights litigation reflects a paradox in American society. At some level, America's commitment to workplace fairness has never seemed so obvious. As Berrey, Dobbin, and Skrentny each suggests, government, business, universities—indeed, a whole professional subgroup of equal employment officers—articulate a normative commitment to equal opportunity and inclusion across a range of traditionally disadvantaged groups.[2] For over five decades, employment civil rights litigation has been seen as an instrument to achieve greater workplace opportunity—first for people of color and women, and more recently for the aged and those with disabilities. The 1991 Civil Rights Act reflected this ongoing commitment to litigation as a vehicle for change. The 1990s saw a dramatic increase in the number of discrimination lawsuits filed in federal court, before the number of lawsuits flattened and declined in the 2000s. Recent calls to expand employment discrimination protection to lesbian, gay, bisexual, transgender, and queer individuals are another indication of at least some groups' faith in legally enforceable rights as a tool to bring about social change.

Yet we also see stalled progress (if not retrenchment) on the ladder to more influential and better paying jobs for disadvantaged groups, as well as signs of growing economic inequality in the American workplace. We continue to see attacks on employment civil rights litigation from critics who decry such litigation as a frivolous, costly, excuse factory.[3]

A paradox posed by this system is that American society reveres rights and considers some individuals who have asserted their rights heroes—Rosa Parks, Martin Luther King, Jr., and César Chávez, to name a few. But psychological literature demonstrates that in the workplace, we regard those who claim to be the victim of discrimination with suspicion and tend to denigrate them.[4]

What, then is the role of employment civil rights litigation in dismantling barriers to equal employment opportunity for traditionally disadvantaged groups? To address that fundamental question, we must look at how employment civil rights litigation works in practice. Despite considerable research on various aspects of employment discrimination and its treatment by law, there has been no comprehensive analysis of this system and its consequences for parties to litigation.

Rights on Trial

This book puts rights on trial in two ways. First, we document the process through which plaintiffs in employment civil rights cases put forth their claim in law. Plaintiffs literally must put their rights on trial. As their relationships with their employers change from employees to litigants, the workers are put on trial. Their loyalty, credibility, and competence are scrutinized and often attacked. Defendants, too, have rights—namely, to defend themselves against charges of violating civil rights laws through the legal process. We ask: What is the experience of litigation for these parties and their attorneys? How do they understand litigation and its outcomes?

Second, we put the system of employment civil rights litigation on trial, or at least under empirical scrutiny, by examining how it works. We ask: What does it mean to have civil rights at work? Are these rights meaningful if exercising them is expensive and difficult? What is the role and obligation of the legal profession in ensuring these rights? How has law helped or hurt the struggle for workplace equality? If rights are the lynchpin to fairness in the workplace, who bears the burden of exercising the right to help us all achieve that social goal?

Using an original, comprehensive mixed-methods research design that combines a large quantitative sample of almost 1,800 court filings across the country with one hundred in-depth interviews of parties and their attorneys, we investigate how rights-based litigation actually operates. Our approach enables us to explore both the general dynamics of an adversarial legal system of employment civil rights and the system's consequences for the ordinary citizens, corporate representatives, and lawyers who navigate it. Our analysis exposes the strengths and weaknesses of the system and the complex ways that the *vindication* of rights—necessary in any system of rights—is perceived by those who use the structures and processes necessary for enforcing employment civil rights.

Although antidiscrimination law holds employers legally accountable by forbidding workplace discrimination, we find that the system of employment civil rights litigation is substantially controlled by employers. The law functions to preserve managerial authority on personnel matters in ways both subtle and direct. Government data make abundantly clear that the American workplace consists of organizational hierarchies that are raced, gendered, abled, and aged. Despite four decades of antidiscrimination enforcement and some modest gains by women and minorities, white men predominate in management positions.[5] The ostensibly neutral policy of deferring to managerial authority, sustained throughout the legal system, functions to reproduce these status hierarchies. Such deference is part of the broader phenomenon of *reinscription* that we elaborate throughout this book: the processes by which the ascriptive hierarchies that the law is intended to disrupt are reified and rearticulated through law in the workplace and in court.

The broad theoretical question we engage in this book is about the utility of rights, as a form of law, for dismantling hierarchies of unearned privilege in the United States. Though we remain close to the empirical example of employment civil rights, the questions that animate this research emerge from the theoretical, empirical, and critical study of rights across various decades, disciplines, and locales. We see the role of antidiscrimination law in the American system of inequality as deriving from the relationships between rights, law, and hierarchy.

Rights

This book builds on the scholarship that demonstrates that, in the United States, we use rights—often conferred as individual rights—to achieve important social goals.[6] Rights are significant sources of power because we construe them to (at least formally) be available equally to everyone, neutral, and backed by the legitimate authority of the state.[7] When rights are vindicated in courts, social actors are expected to take notice and implement changes (for example, in workplace policies) to achieve social change. Yet both empirical social scientists and theoretically minded critical legal scholars note many problems in relying upon rights-based litigation to effect social change: many people whose rights have been violated do nothing to vindicate them, rights are not self-enforcing, rights are enforced differently based on the relationships of the parties involved, and rights may inappropriately introduce politics into law.[8]

These critiques have generated new interest in theoretical and empirical studies of rights among scholars in various disciplines. The renewed interest, which focuses as much outside as inside the context of litigation, shows how rights can be mobilized formally and informally in very different ways. This focus shows much to be optimistic about in the study of rights because in addition to the material effects that rights may have, symbolic effects can be similarly meaningful.[9] Rights can affect social movements and social movement actors' strategic decisions.[10] Rights discourse may not have material effects but, even without resorting to litigation, simply knowing one *has* rights can dramatically improve the lived experience of individuals.[11] Law is a rhetorical toolkit, a source of symbolic power, and a bargaining chip that can determine whether people who need family leave can actually keep a job and meet the caregiving needs of their family.

Further decentering litigation, some scholars demonstrate that, even in the absence of lawsuits, decisions by administrative and bureaucratic experts who act to enforce rights in society contribute to systems of "legalized accountability" or "managerialized authority."[12] And finally, we know that rights can shape legal consciousness, which forms the essential backdrop to how individuals relate to the law.[13]

Other scholars are more skeptical about the capacity of rights discourses, litigation, and rights awareness to redress inequalities in the workplace. They note that the antidiscrimination law model requires targets of discrimination to define themselves as "victims";[14] they fear that recourse to law using the current "discrimination frame" will create more problems than it will solve,[15] and they argue that the current model of discrimination focuses on individual harms rather than on more fundamental inequalities of race and gender. Many suggest that more fundamental social interventions are required to address those inequalities.[16] Some scholars decry the increasing tendency to treat inequality and discrimination as "interpersonal problems" or questions of "mismanagement" because it recasts employer-organizations as mere onlookers to discrimination or even victims themselves, rather than as sources of discrimination that should be held legally accountable.[17]

These are just some of the contrasting assessments of rights and rights-based models with which this book converses. We look not just to court outcomes but to the personal, social, and financial costs of fully enforcing a right. We also examine how representatives of employer organizations think of these disputes, the costs for business, and the legal consciousness of the parties post dispute.

Law and society scholarship illuminates how law-in-action, as opposed to law-on-the-books, shapes the realization of rights. Our findings on employment civil rights litigation as a system of dispute resolution echo the general findings of the law and society literature. For example, we estimate in chapter 2 that only a tiny fraction of possible targets of workplace discrimination take formal action before the EEOC, the federal agency charged with investigating discrimination, and the courts. When targets do sue, they are likely to settle or lose. Only a small percentage of cases (6%) reach trial. And plaintiffs, as "one-shotters," challenge defendant employers, "repeat players." This disparity in legal experience puts plaintiffs at a distinct disadvantage at virtually every stage of the dispute. Many plaintiffs do not get lawyers. If they do, the lawyer generally controls how the case is litigated and often insists on settlement. Defendants, by contrast, always have legal representation and considerable control over litigation decisions. In short, the formally neutral system of adversarial justice in the United States favors the haves over the have-nots.[18]

Our data on employment civil rights litigation go much deeper than just to show *how* the law works in this particular institutional context where law, the workplace, and social hierarchies intersect. Our data reveal that employment civil rights law *reinscribes* hierarchies by challenging and containing discrimination claims. We elaborate specific mechanisms of reinscription, including employers' tactics for preventing workplace disputes from transforming into legal disputes, the often-failed attempts by plaintiffs to get legal representation, the dramatic differences in lawyer-client relationships for plaintiffs and defendants, employers' strategy of settling at modest costs, and the persistence of nefarious stereotypes of disadvantaged groups. At the intersection of rights, law and hierarchy, we find the conflicting ideologies that plaintiffs and defendant employers bring to these cases and their outcomes. At this intersection, from these grounded analyses of law-in-action, we see the myriad ways that the adversarial system exacerbates workplace conflicts.

Law

Rights are defined by law and shaped by the features of the bureaucratic, regulatory, and judicial systems through which rights are asserted. Employment civil rights, in the contemporary era, have been formed both by changes in formal law and regulatory practice and by general aspects of the American adversarial process.

In recent decades, statutory law and judicial interpretations have both expanded and restricted possibilities for using the law to advance employment civil rights. The passage of the Age Discrimination in Employment Act of 1967 and the Americans with Disabilities Act in 1990 added two major groups to those legally protected in employment. The Supreme Court recognized sexual harassment as a form of sex discrimination in 1986, establishing a new theory of liability under Title VII.[19] Congress also has sometimes acted to overrule Supreme Court rulings that limit the scope of discrimination law. The Civil Rights Act of 1991 was a congressional response to the *Wards Cove* case, a ruling that limited the application of the disparate impact theory of discrimination.[20] The 1991 act not only restored disparate impact as a theory of discrimination; it also expanded the right to jury trials and the possibility of punitive damages in Title VII cases.

The Civil Rights Act of 1991 resulted in a brief but substantial increase in filings. But the number of discrimination filings receded quickly. By allowing punitive damages in employment civil rights cases, the 1991 act had the unintended effect of undercutting the likelihood of plaintiffs' obtaining class certification in discrimination cases, because punitive damages necessarily vary by individual. Thus, courts have been less willing to grant class certifications when punitive damages are sought. Congress also expanded employment civil rights with the Lilly Ledbetter Fair Pay Act of 2009, which overturned the 2007 *Ledbetter* decision.[21] As a result, pay discrimination claims can reach back to the time that discrimination took place, rather than being limited to the time when discrimination was discovered by the plaintiff.

Yet court rulings also have limited the pursuit of employment civil rights claims in court. As Burbank and Farhang demonstrate, many of these rulings have come in the form of procedural rulings that do not garner much media attention.[22] In chapter 3 we demonstrate the importance of collective action—including class action cases—to the success of employment discrimination claims. In *Wal-Mart v. Dukes* the Supreme Court rejected the certification of what would have been the largest class ever certified in an employment discrimination lawsuit.[23] Other Supreme Court cases have made it easier for defendants to win motions for summary judgment, which, we will see, are a key strategy that employers use to limit their exposure in employment discrimination litigation. Edelman and colleagues document a trend in which courts have excused employers from liability if employers have adopted policies designed to prevent discrimination from occurring, even when the policy may not actually be effective.[24] As we have argued elsewhere, the courts over the past two decades have embraced a perpetrator model that construes discrimination as purposeful and discrete acts of animus, looking for the proverbial smoking gun as acceptable evidence.[25]

We detail many of these changes in chapters 2 and 3, but a broad perspective shows that courts have narrowed the basis for plaintiffs seeking systemic remedies (through class action lawsuits and disparate impact claims) and made it more difficult for employers to use affirmative action to redress systemic unbalances in the demographic composition of their workforces. What results is a system of employment civil rights litigation overwhelmingly dominated by disparate treatment claims by individual plaintiffs. Only 1% of cases today seek class action certification, 93% of claims are made by one plaintiff, and 93% of claims only involve an allegation of disparate treatment (rather than or in addition to disparate impact). We argue that the courts have moved in the direction of treating employment discrimination as a set of individual cases of intentional misbehavior, while the social science literature on discrimination increasingly points to the widespread, systemic character of bias in the organization of workplaces.[26]

Hierarchy

Social hierarchies are the foundation of social stratification. In the United States, race, gender, and class—as well as statuses such as (dis)ability, age, ethnicity, and sexual orientation—are profoundly salient and pervasive social categories.[27] So-called majority groups, such as men or white people, are deemed normal, typical, and desirable. Those in the minority are stigmatized and degraded. The pervasiveness of shared norms can render these hierarchies barely visible,[28] even as these distinctions shape groups' access to wealth, opportunities, prestige, and other goods of society.[29] The ability to impose an external category on someone and withhold or provide resources based on that category is an exercise of power.

Race, sex, disability, and age are all categories that form the basis of ascriptive hierarchies, as they are all beyond an individual's control, and in one form or another, they are all embodied. Yet they do not operate the same way in daily life or in the workplace.[30] Race serves primarily as an explanation for racist economic, political, and legal relationships. Behaviors, attitudes, and assumptions involving race are layered onto objectively arbitrary physical characteristics such as skin color and, in turn, organize racial hierarchies.[31] Sex—or, really, the expression of gender—is articulated foremost through sexist norms of acceptable behavior for women and men, particularly the division of labor. These norms are justified by specious claims about social conditions of sexual reproduction and separate spheres.[32] Disability is characterized by physical, intellectual, emotional, or behavioral conditions that impair one's activities within social contexts that limit or cut off full participation in mainstream social life.[33] A disability embodies categorization and stigmatization, but only if an individual's disability is known to others. Some disabilities can remain invisible, though, whereas more visibly evident categories, such as gender, are more difficult to conceal. Thus, people with disabilities often experience overt discrimination during the interview process and on the job if and when potential employers learn of their disability.[34]

Aging, for its part, is widely viewed as a social problem in the United States. Age is a unique basis of ascriptive hierarchy in that most people will eventually join the purportedly lower-status category of older people.[35] Yet age hierarchies are variable and extraordinarily context-specific. In the workplace, employees over the age of forty face unique disadvantages in hiring and promotions. However, when rules of seniority are in place, as in many unionized workplaces, older workers are more likely to have greater job protections than their younger counterparts.

Each of these ascriptive hierarchies is made more complicated when multiple axes of subordination are involved.[36] Hierarchies of sex and age intersect, for example, in that people commonly define "age appropriate" behavior differently depending on whether the individual assessed is female or male.

Antidiscrimination law is among the few institutions that proactively attempts to *minimize* ascriptive hierarchies through legal means.[37] Depending on the basis of discrimination (such as race or age), antidiscrimination laws have distinctive jurisprudential histories shaped by constitutional law and the nature of civil rights protections, as well as the extension of employment discrimination laws to the aged and those with disabilities and new theories of discrimination such as sexual harassment.

For example, in constitutional litigation, racial distinctions are subject to the most stringent standard, strict scrutiny, while categorization on the basis of sex is subject only to intermediate scrutiny.[38] While race discrimination law protects people of color and white people alike and sex discrimination law protects both women and men, age discrimination law draws a bright line around what constitutes a protected class: those forty years of age and older. Antidiscrimination law on disability also draws such a line and uniquely concerns standards of appropriate accommodation.

Ascriptive hierarchies of race, sex, age, and ability and the inequalities that spring from them persist in US workplaces. For example, in the workforce—if a worker can find a job (something that is itself racialized)—the median weekly wage for African American workers is about 78% that of similarly situated white workers, and Latino/a workers earn about 73%.[39] By the same token, white women, on average, receive weekly wages at 82% of their white male counterparts' pay. Considerable research demonstrates that these disparities remain after controlling for several possible explanations.[40] Social hierarchies permeate the American workplace and job market.

And yet, scholars debate how much of workplace inequality in hiring, promotion, wages, and salaries results from illegal discrimination. Some economists, most notably James Heckman, believe that only a very small percentage (1%–2%) of the gap can be explained by discrimination.[41] Most labor market economists, sociologists, and statisticians who have carefully studied the problem believe that a much greater proportion (some 35%–50%) of the gap is due to workplace discrimination itself.[42] Banaji and colleagues tell us that some of the disparity likely is due to unconscious bias (as opposed to animus-based discrimination).[43] Meanwhile, critical race and feminist scholars observe that both blatant hate and more subtly institutionalized discrimination remain a very important source of disadvantage in the workplace.[44]

Our review of the literature indicates that significant, obvious, animus-based discrimination is still far more prevalent than we want in the United States. A growing body of work also indicates that discrimination routinely now occurs through implicit biases, norms, and assumptions that fall outside the purview of law.[45] Insofar as any part of workplace inequality is due to discrimination, Americans share an increasing consensus that the state has a legitimate duty to eliminate discrimination.

In addition to the hierarchies of ascribed status characteristics, workplace conflict necessarily embodies workplace hierarchy as well. Managerial prerogatives, workers' rights, income and status differences, and other kinds of hierarchies in the workplace environment all play a role in workplace conflict.[46] In the workplace, a worker/management hierarchy is implicated in these conflicts (unlike race, sex, age, and disability, worker status is not a protected category). Class-based hierarchies affect the very ability of plaintiffs to pursue viable cases, most notably in whether they can afford an attorney. And they advantage defendant employers, who have far more training and experience in litigation and far more resources to manage a defense. All of the people we study are embedded in these hierarchies, which influence how they make sense of their situation.[47]

This theoretical framework of rights, law, and hierarchy guides our thinking as we put rights on trial. It raises critical questions about employment discrimination litigation: is our regulatory and court system of primarily individually driven civil rights working to eliminate illegal discrimination? At what cost?

Our answer, based on systematic quantitative and qualitative data, is that law is deeply implicated in and affected by the very hierarchies of race, sex, disability, and age that employment civil rights law was created to address. Our analysis shows that law's capacity to disrupt illegitimate workplace hierarchies is undermined by three intertwined factors, all of which tend to disadvantage plaintiffs relative to employers and attorneys: structural asymmetries in power in workplaces and the courts; the adversarial nature of the conflict; and the individualization of the dispute. These factors result in the reinscription of ascriptive hierarchy rather than its dismantling, as we show in chapter after chapter. Managerial prerogatives, workplace structures, agency rules, and the courts that appear bias-neutral actually function to obfuscate bias themselves.

Most plaintiffs not only lose or gain small settlements in the process of litigation; they are vilified by their employer (or former employer) during the EEOC complaint process and litigation. Contrary to the ideal model of civil rights law effecting social change by correcting discriminatory behavior at work, we find that seldom is the outcome of a case implemented in a way that promotes equal opportunity. Instead, most outcomes are sealed off from the workplace. When plaintiffs settle their claims, they typically sign a confidentiality agreement that encapsulates the results of litigation, preventing it from resulting in meaningful change.

In addition, we see the influence of social hierarchies in the litigation process itself. Chapter 9 systematically investigates how stereotypes are invoked both by workplace actors and in legal accounts. During litigation, African American men are characterized as dangerous, lazy, and incompetent; African American women are referred to as overbearing ("bitchy"). All African Americans are less likely to gain legal counsel, which has disastrous consequences for their case outcomes. Female plaintiffs are characterized as "hysterical"—even by their own lawyers—or as being overly sensitive to sexual innuendo in the workplace. Plaintiffs with disability cases are labeled slackers. Plaintiffs charging age discrimination are said to be resistant to change or out of touch with the modern workplace.

At the same time, the litigation system routinely flattens the differences *across* these groups, particularly through its privileging of managerial authority. With the exception of a few key patterns, including African Americans' reduced access to legal representation, we do not find major discrepancies in how different claims fare in court. Time and again, plaintiffs told us very similar stories of how they were treated, regardless of whether their claim was based on race, sex, disability, age, or some combination thereof.

As we show, law—in the form of employer responses to claims of employment discrimination and the administration of complaints and lawsuits by the EEOC and the courts—reinscribes the invidious hierarchies it was created to ameliorate. These findings suggest the need for a reexamination of the system of employment civil rights litigation as a policy matter. Can it be effectively reformed? Are there plausible alternatives to the current system of rights litigation? Or is the system so flawed that it must be remade from scratch? We take up this discussion in the final chapter of this book.

The Design of the Study: A Mixed-Methods, Multi-perspectival Approach

Most empirical scholarship about employment civil rights litigation has studied the relatively small proportion of cases that lead to published judicial opinions or otherwise become visible through media coverage.[48] While valuable, these approaches have limited generalizability and can miss legal participants' nuanced, complex, often contradictory accounts of litigation. We devised our mixed-method, multi-perspectival approach to pursue core concerns in the sociology of law: moving from law in the books to law in action to how law is experienced and perceived by the actors within it. We also designed our methodology to capture the stories of plaintiffs such as Gerry Handley and Kristen Baker, whose cases represent the promise and perils of pursuing employment civil rights in the post–Civil Rights era American courts. Our combination of quantitative datasets and in-depth qualitative interviews supports a more comprehensive treatment of the relationship between the system of employment civil rights litigation and hierarchies of race, gender, disability, and age in the American workplace.

Specifically, our project draws on three datasets. The first is an expanded replication of Donohue and Siegelman's groundbreaking research on employment discrimination case filings from 1972 to 1987—a project that, like ours, was conducted under the auspices of the American Bar Foundation.[49] We collected a random sample of employment civil rights cases filed in federal courts between 1988 and 2003 in seven regionally diverse federal districts: Atlanta, Chicago, Dallas, New Orleans, New York City, Philadelphia, and San Francisco. These are the same seven federal district courts included in Donohue and Siegelman's research. These districts contain about 20% of all filings, capture variation in legal and social context, and, for cost considerations, are located close to federal records depositories. In each of these districts we drew three hundred cases from the list of all civil employment discrimination cases (classified as nature of suit code "442") compiled by the Administrative Office of the US Courts (AOUSC) , yielding a sample of 2,100 total cases. We derived sampling weights by district based on the total number of employment discrimination case filings in each district. Some of the sampled cases were missing key variables and were discarded, resulting in a final sample for analysis of 1,788. For some analyses we include only closed cases, of which there are 1,672.

We developed an extensive, thirteen-page coding form (see online appendix at press.uchicago.edu/sites/rightsontrial/) and established coding operations with trained teams of coders for each site. The same data collection manager supervised and trained coders in each location. Ten percent of the cases were coded independently by different coders to allow tests of intercoder reliability. In 94% of those cases there was agreement between coders on case outcome, the key dependent variable. Manually coding a random sample of case filings provides far more valid and representative data, but the approach presents some limitations: publicly available files can be incomplete due to misfiling or poor record keeping. These quantitative data frame our study and are the focus, in particular, of chapter 3.

A second dataset consists of one hundred in-depth interviews with parties and their legal counsel. We selected these individuals first by constructing a four-by-four table with the most common bases of discrimination in the national data (race, sex, age, and disability) cross-tabulated with the outcomes of greatest theoretical interest (dismissed, early settlement, late settlement, and trial).[50] Each of the sixteen cells represented a possible case, such as discrimination based on age and settled early. The purpose of the interviews was to better understand the process of employment civil rights litigation that we documented at the macro level.[51]

Then, from our filings sample in two districts, we drew a random subsample within each of the sixteen cells for willing participants. Specifically, we interviewed forty plaintiffs (and one adult child of a deceased plaintiff), nineteen plaintiff lawyers, twenty HR officers and inside counsel representing defendant employers (whom we refer to as defendant representatives), and twenty lawyers serving as outside counsel to employers. We did not try to interview any named individual defendants, such as a manager accused of sexual harassment.

We then conducted interviews with plaintiffs, their lawyers, and, when feasible, with defendants' representatives and lawyers in the same case. When this was not feasible, we selected defendants' representatives and lawyers from other cases in the random subsample.

Our response rate for the interviews (after locating a potential informant) was 51%, with defense attorneys agreeing to interviews at the highest rate (68%) and plaintiffs at the lowest (44%). The greatest challenge in this respect was locating plaintiffs. Despite extensive sleuthing, we were unable to find and make personal contact with 149 (58%) of the randomly selected plaintiffs. This difficulty raises the possibility that our subsample of plaintiffs is not representative of the sample overall, particularly of low-wage workers who would be less likely to have phone records, but we do not believe it compromised the quality of our data. The plaintiffs we did locate and interview represent a range of occupations, workplace contexts, and litigation experience. The appendix (table A.1) contains a listing of interviewees by pseudonym, age, and race. The age of plaintiffs referred to throughout this book is at time of filing. For all other interviewees we report age in 2007.

Our interview protocols consisted of open-ended, semi-structured questions about closed employment discrimination cases involving the interviewee. The plaintiffs' interviews covered their personal experiences of job discrimination, workplace dispute resolution, legal authorities, and case resolution. Defendant representatives discussed a specific closed case and their organization's general strategies for managing discrimination complaints and lawsuits. Each interview lasted about one hour and ended with forced-choice demographic and attitudinal questions that replicated questions used in previous studies.[52] The appendix (table A.2) contains a brief summary of demographic and attitudinal data we obtained through interviews. We coded interview transcripts using NVivo qualitative analysis software. We developed the coding scheme inductively, with codes identified through data analysis, and deductively, with codes based on secondary literature.[53] Throughout this book we use pseudonyms for the names of interviewees and the private employers and government agencies for which they worked.

We use rich, textured data to identify social mechanisms and general processes at work in the system of employment civil rights litigation.[54] Because we asked interviewees to "tell us their story," the data can be viewed as narrative.[55] Respondents provide a personal account, or a "plot," with a beginning, middle, and end.[56] Such narrative studies are sometimes criticized as overly individualistic, but we locate these narratives within larger structures and social processes that are intertwined with employment civil rights litigation: the workplace, the dispute claim system, the life course, and membership in identity groups.[57]

Our interviewees' plots are necessarily retrospective. Nonetheless, interviewees' reconstructions of their closed cases are important in their own right, even if necessarily different from their *in situ* experiences. Through memories of salient events, legal actors continually reconstruct their faith, or lack of faith, in the law.

Our project is unusual in that it includes both plaintiffs and defendants,[58] in order to reveal the subjective and relational experiences that create each side's assessments of litigation. We do so by putting dynamic social relationships and social processes at the center of analysis and by staying attuned to the interplay of social structure and culture at the macro and micro levels.[59] Most of the chapters in this book are based on interviewees' narratives, contextualized with the national case filings data and interviewees' answers to close-ended questions. To some extent, we foreground plaintiffs' perspectives, opening the qualitative chapters with plaintiffs' narratives relevant to the chapter themes. We integrate attorneys' and defendants' perspectives into those case studies whenever possible. In this respect, plaintiffs' actions and interpretations drive the narrative, just as they drive the legal cases through court.

A relatively unique aspect of our qualitative data is the voice recordings of interviews made available online. With few exceptions, interviewees gave us permission to record their interviews and use the audio in publications and presentations. As we saw above, in the quotes from the interview with Gerry Handley, throughout this book we note when an audio recording of that quote is available on our website with the symbol 🎧 (available at press.uchicago.edu/sites/rightsontrial/).[60] The audio recordings provide further richness to our data. They reveal the race, gender, age, class, emotion, education, and legal sophistication of our interviewees. They help bring our respondents and our observations to life.

We also make limited use of the confidential charge data file obtained from the EEOC for the years 1991–2002, which contains all complaints made to the EEOC or state fair-employment agencies.[61] In some 85% of cases in the court filings dataset we were able to match to the EEOC charge file. For cases from 1995 on, we are able to use the EEOC priority handling code contained in the EEOC charge file.

Our research design offers several important innovations. By systematically coding a representative sample of discrimination complaints, from the least visible and most routine cases to the blockbuster trials and settlements that dominate media coverage, we attempt to more comprehensively assess law's role in processing claims of discrimination.[62]

The quantitative portion of the research, together with the findings from Donohue and Siegelman's research, provides an historical perspective on litigation over time. Further, rather than analyze litigation outcomes in binary terms (i.e., as a plaintiff's win or loss), we conceptualize case outcomes as a sequential variable. This approach better captures the dynamic character of the litigation process and the dilemmas that parties and courts face in adjudicating claims. By including distinct categories of outcomes that are largely unmeasured and therefore invisible in other research, our analysis more clearly reveals the social organization of discrimination litigation.

Interviewing all sides in a subset of cases affords insight into the multiple, conflicting perspectives on workplace events and the transformation of those events in litigation. Our interest is in contested constructions—an interest that aligns with an emergent theoretical orientation toward relational conceptions of discrimination and stratification.[63] Our intervention captures the constitutive interplay of institutions, lived experience, and interaction through both our conceptualization of the litigation system and our use of mixed methods.

This combination of quantitative results and interviews with opposing sides and their lawyers is significant for the empirical study of law and the social sciences more generally. As one of the authors, Nielsen, has written in a handbook on empirical legal research, this particular combination of quantitative and qualitative data offers three important payoffs.[64] First, the quantitative data informed how to select cases for in-depth interviewing, making case selection more rigorous and systematic. Second, the in-depth interviews revealed that even experts in employment civil rights litigation harbor perceptions about the system that are disproved in quantitative data. Finally, the mixed methods used in this book provide multiple vantage points on basic facts of each case, shedding light on both those facts and participants' experiences and perceptions of them in ways that quantitative or qualitative data could not do alone.

For example, one plaintiff-interviewee featured later in this book, Sam Grayson (P4), reported that he thought the settlement he received was a loss—he had hoped to get his job back. We know from the quantitative data, however, that the settlement he received was much higher than the median settlements in cases like his. The quantitative data revealed his settlement as substantial, whereas the qualitative data revealed that it was personally unsatisfactory and why.[65]

For all the strengths of this combination of methods, our research often cannot answer what is often posed as the core legal question in these cases: *did discrimination happen?* Because most cases settle or are decided on technicalities, there is usually no official adjudication of the facts of the case. During data collection, we initially asked the research assistants who read and coded the case files to try to assess the merits of the cases, but they rarely agreed about the validity of any particular case. Some were clear instances of "frivolous" cases and a few seemed to have "smoking guns," but the vast majority fell in between. As such, the qualitative data are interviewees' *accounts* of what occurred in the workplace and in court, not our own first-hand observations or even adjudicated "facts."[66] Because they are not definitive statements of what transpired, but represent plausible interpretations, we incorporate multiple viewpoints on the same events wherever possible.

More fundamentally, while lawyers, judges, and human resource professionals understandably want to know whether or not discrimination "happened" in any given case, from a socio-legal perspective, this emphasis is misplaced. As one of the anonymous reviewers of the manuscript observed, "Discrimination is a contested event, told from multiple perspectives. These stories carry different weight and legitimacy depending on who is telling them, in what venue, and with what support. Thus the question of 'what happened' is itself a variable, subject to much interference from social factors," such as the social position and resources of the target and the employer. In fact, whether the target has legal support, social networks, and knowledge of the law can influence both formal and informal determinations that discrimination did or did not occur.

Indeed, this poses a central quandary for our analysis and for the system of employment civil rights litigation. If the problem of discrimination is as much structural as intentional, then finding evidence of it in individual cases is fraught with difficulty. As many of our narrative accounts reflect, individual claims of discrimination often are complicated and ambiguous. This in itself is an important aspect of the American regime of antidiscrimination law.

Overview of the Book

This book is organized into three parts with ten chapters. Part I of the book includes the Introduction (chapter 1) along with two other chapters. Chapter 2 establishes the legal context of our study. It highlights major legislative, regulatory, and judicial trends over fifty years of employment civil rights. The chapter covers additional ground by examining public data on trends in discrimination claims and filings, outlining a model that estimates the likelihood that a target of discrimination will bring a lawsuit, and reviewing research on the media (mis)treatment of employment civil rights cases. Chapter 3 presents key findings from our quantitative dataset on case filings from 1988 to 2003. It provides a quantitative portrait of case filings and outcomes previously unavailable. This chapter reveals several social facts of significance to theoretical and policy discussions about the system of employment discrimination litigation.

Chapters 4 through 8 constitute the second part of the book. Each presents narrative analyses of litigation based on our in-depth interviews with parties and lawyers. In chapter 4, we consider the beginnings of the workplace dispute that eventually leads to the filing of an EEOC charge of discrimination and a federal lawsuit. In chapter 5, we examine who gets legal representation and why, and we consider at length why African American plaintiffs have a lower rate of legal representation than other racial/ethnic groups. Chapter 6 discusses the relationships between litigants and their attorneys and demonstrates the sharp contrast in the nature of this relationship for plaintiffs and defendants. In chapter 7, we analyze the adversarial process in employment civil rights cases and make sense of the conflicting views of plaintiffs and defendants in these disputes. Defendants accept the tenets of antidiscrimination law, but almost always reject the validity of the claims brought by particular plaintiffs. In chapter 8, we examine the outcomes of litigation and how the parties view those outcomes.

The narrative chapters of the book show how law fails to live up to its ideals in practice. They illustrate the reinscription of hierarchy by analytically attending to adversarialism, structural asymmetry, and individualization in employment civil rights cases. These processes show up in different ways at different stages of the litigation process, but they provide the critical link between rights, law, and hierarchy. With this theoretical framing, we see how workplace discrimination occurs and how biases operate not only in the institutional setting of the workplace but also as actors move into the institutional setting of the law. We see inequities in access to justice and differences in the perceived legitimacy of the various actors' stories throughout the disputing process—from the search for counsel, to the experience in early and later stage settlements, and occasionally in going to trial. We see that nearly all plaintiffs encounter ascriptive biases in the legal realm.

Chapters 9 and 10, which constitute the third and concluding part of the book, present theoretical and policy conclusions. Chapter 9 elaborates our theory of the reinscription of hierarchy through employment civil rights litigation by foregrounding one notable and measurable manifestation of social hierarchies: stereotypes about disadvantaged groups. By centering our analysis on stereotypes, we fully illustrate a key mechanism by which ascriptive hierarchies of race, gender, age, and disability are mobilized in the workplace and reinforced through the legal process. The book concludes with a discussion of the policy implications of our results and the theoretical implications of our analysis for models of rights-based social change.

Throughout these chapters, we develop the concept of *the legal reinscription of hierarchy*. We suggest that reinscription occurs both directly in the litigation process and indirectly, given that challenges to workplace hierarchies in the form of discrimination lawsuits typically are insulated from the workplace through legal decisions that settle claims and make the terms of settlement confidential. We also attend to the importance of voice in employment civil rights law. We consider the various voices we have made heard in this project: from conservative critics of litigation, to the voice of management in the workplace, to the voices of plaintiffs who sought justice through law, to the voices of their lawyers and adversaries.

Conclusion

Mr. Handley and Ms. Baker's experiences, introduced at the outset of this chapter, reveal the deep contradictions that characterize the American system of employment civil rights regulation and enforcement. The Civil Rights Act gave these plaintiffs the right to challenge egregious discriminatory treatment in the workplace. Yet as they pursued their legal claims, they were subjected to hostile treatment by their employers and defense counsel—the plaintiffs were put on trial.

This book explores the realities of the system of employment civil rights litigation and critically assesses the relationship between this system and patterns of illegitimate hierarchies in the American workplace.

Our analysis suggests that the system is widely viewed as unfair by both plaintiffs and defendants. It is shaped by and likely amplifies the asymmetry of power between plaintiffs and defendants. And yet the system is entrenched in regulatory politics, the legal system, and the personnel systems of employers. It functions to legally reinscribe ascriptive status hierarchies. As such, it must be seen as a fundamentally flawed aspect of the American system of justice and an inadequate institutional response to persistent patterns of illegal discrimination.

CHAPTER TWO

Fifty Years of Employment Civil Rights

It shall be an unlawful employment practice for an employer:

(1) to fail or refuse to hire or to discharge any individual, or otherwise to discriminate against any individual with respect to his compensation, terms, conditions, or privileges of employment, because of such individual's race, color, religion, sex, or national origin; or

(2) to limit, segregate, or classify his employees or applicants for employment in any way which would deprive or tend to deprive any individual of employment opportunities or otherwise adversely affect his status as an employee, because of such individual's race, color, religion, sex, or national origin. —Title VII of the US Civil Rights Act of 1964

With the passage of the US Civil Rights Act of 1964, the United States embarked on fifty years of enforcing workplace rights in the courts. This chapter provides context from social science, law, and publicly available data to examine the history of employment civil rights litigation and how it operates today.

Like much social science research on rights in general and employment civil rights in particular, this book takes a "litigation centric" approach in that we primarily analyze what happens when someone files a lawsuit. Work in this vein often is critiqued because it typically begins with the published opinions of courts, ignoring the case filings that never generate an opinion. Such research designs lead to misinterpretations of how the law operates by "studying the iceberg from the tip."[1] While our research design avoids that flaw by beginning with case filings, we also are cognizant that case filings themselves are not the beginning of the story. Most disputes never reach a lawyer, much less a courthouse.[2] Critical determinants of whether a dispute is transformed into a lawsuit include the relationship between the parties, social context, and the law itself.[3]

Before we analyze the original quantitative and qualitative data that make up *Rights on Trial*, this chapter looks at key aspects of the system of employment civil rights litigation to examine such factors and frame our inquiry. Using legislative, doctrinal, social science, and public data, we review the past fifty years in three ways. First, we summarize what social science teaches us about the role of law in ameliorating workplace discrimination, asking: What do we know about trends in workplace inequality, the role of workplace discrimination in those trends, and the implications for antidiscrimination law? We show that there is scholarly agreement that the law substantially reduced employment discrimination in the early period of Title VII. Despite evidence of persistent workplace discrimination, scholars have more divided views about the role of law in combating workplace discrimination today.

Second, we briefly assess the patterns of expansion and retrenchment in antidiscrimination law in the legislature and in the courts to demonstrate the decidedly contradictory history of statutory expansion of and the (often less-visible) judicial restriction of civil rights. We also consider the organizational responses to these legal developments. Finally, this chapter uses publicly available data to analyze fifty years of employment civil rights claims in the EEOC, in the federal courts, and in the media. We demonstrate that a relatively small number of claims proceed from a perceived grievance through the filing of a lawsuit despite media reports on employment civil rights cases that dramatically inflate the odds for plaintiff success and the amount of awards. Media reports may feed broader cultural misunderstandings about discrimination lawsuits and their effects.

Declining Discrimination? Social Science on Law's Role in Ameliorating Discrimination

In 1964, barriers to employment for white women and people of color were blatant. Some work organizations were openly segregationist. Textile mills in South Carolina employed either African American or white workforces.[4] Employers continued to post separate "help wanted" ads for men and women until 1972.[5] In 1966, when the EEOC began to collect data on the race and gender composition of workplaces (EEO-1 reports), half of private establishments had no African American male employees and almost two-thirds had no African American female employees.[6] White men were dramatically overrepresented in desirable positions (management, craft jobs, and professional occupations), while African American men and women and white women were dramatically underrepresented in these positions in proportion to their presence in the labor force.[7]

Title VII struck down these barriers and courts clarified employers' responsibilities in the first years after its passage. In 1972 Congress gave the EEOC the power to sue directly under Title VII. Personnel professionals began to develop systems to advance equal opportunity, not just ending the Jim Crow era of gender and racial exclusion in employment, but creating new best practices to recruit and promote minorities and women in large private employers.[8] Doctrinal innovation,[9] as well as mobilization by the National Organization for Women (NOW), led the EEOC to begin to prosecute sexual harassment as sex discrimination in 1972.[10]

These changes brought tangible gains for protected groups from 1966 to 1980, as demonstrated in a major study by Stainback and Tomaskovic-Devey. African American men gained access to craft employment. White women made rapid progress in achieving both managerial positions and professional occupations. African American women also registered gains in managerial positions and professional jobs, although well below that of white women.[11] The gains were significant, but white men retained a very strong advantage in the American private sector workforce. Although some scholars suggested that the economic progress of the minority groups was not the product of the civil rights laws,[12] the weight of social science research points to law's impact in removing barriers to equal opportunity in the early period.[13]

Despite relative consensus about law's efficacy in the early period of civil rights, some social scientists now disagree about the role of discrimination in perpetuating continued inequalities in the workplace. These scholars cite public opinion data showing a decline in bias against African American and women workers, arguing that the rise in the number of discrimination lawsuits could not, therefore, be due to increasing discrimination.[14] Still others argue that the main source of economic inequality for African Americans now is not labor market discrimination but pre-labor-market disadvantages in early education and noncognitive development.[15] As Heckman wrote in 1998, labor market discrimination is "the problem of an earlier era."[16]

While there is little doubt that overt racist, sexist, ablest, and ageist attitudes are less prevalent now than in the 1970s, and that premarket factors are important determinants of individual economic success, considerable scientific evidence of the persistence of workplace discrimination is evident in audit studies, grounded labor market analyses, social psychological research using experimental designs, and surveys of ordinary citizens.

Audit studies, in which testers of different races and genders apply for the same jobs, consistently demonstrate that employers *behave* in discriminatory fashion.[17] A meta-analysis of some thirty-two audit studies of hiring discrimination published between 1974 and 2014 found that white testers received 44% more positive responses to job applications and interviews than did African American testers and 18% more positive responses than Latino/a testers.[18] Moreover, this differential neither declined over time nor varied by education level or type of occupation involved. The authors of this study conclude by saying, "Discrimination continues, and we find little evidence that it is gradually diminishing to nothing. Instead, we find the persistence of discrimination at a distressingly uniform and unchanged rate."[19] Perhaps more dramatically, employers are more likely to offer a job interview to a white applicant *with* a criminal record than a similarly situated African American applicant with *no* criminal record, a pattern that holds even when employers express a willingness to hire ex-offenders and African American workers.[20] Audit studies consistently reveal bias along gender, race, and sexual orientation.[21]

Grounded labor market studies provide another method for analyzing workplace discrimination, one that controls for premarket skills and labor market experience. Using a novel dataset on the labor market experiences of African Americans and whites in New Jersey, including a rich set of controls, Fryer, Pager, and Spenkuch find that one-third of the observed wage gap in starting wages for whites and African Americans is due to labor market discrimination.[22]

In addition to these real-world studies of workplace decisions, there is a substantial body of experimental psychological research showing that implicit (or unconscious) bias is a pervasive phenomenon in society and in the workplace. Given the often unconscious tendencies of organizational decision makers to favor traditionally advantaged groups over other workers, this research suggests that without carefully conceived debiasing approaches to hiring, pay, and promotion, workplace discrimination will persist.[23] And finally, as we examine in more detail below, surveys of workers about perceptions of workplace discrimination show a striking disjuncture between the perceptions of white women and people of color in the workplace versus their white male colleagues and supervisors.[24]

Despite this compelling interdisciplinary evidence of the persistence of discrimination, political consensus about the significance of labor market discrimination began to weaken at the beginning of the 1980s. As politically conservative Republicans assumed control of the executive and judicial branches, progress on workplace equality began to wane. As Tomaskovic-Devey and Stainback document, between 1980 and 2003 white women made steady progress in achieving managerial and professional jobs but African American men largely stalled in advancing their representation in craft, managerial and professional positions in the private sector.[25] African American women made modest progress achieving management and professional positions, but at a markedly slower pace than white women. White men maintained a clear advantage in holding managerial and craft positions during this period. Only in the professions did their dominance decline, but not disappear, compared to white women.

Our own analysis of EEO-1 reports for 2013 demonstrates the resilience of this pattern.[26] Based on labor market presence, white men are significantly overrepresented in management positions and all other groups are underrepresented, with white women slightly below what would be expected. African American workers are more than 50% below expectations and white men are almost twice as likely to hold craft positions as we would expect by their numbers in the workforce. Although African American men are almost a quarter more likely to hold craft positions, both white and African American women remain largely shut out of craft jobs. White women now slightly outdo white men in holding professional jobs. African American men are substantially underrepresented in professional jobs (61% below expectation). African American women also are underrepresented in professional jobs (35% below expectation).

Reflecting disparities in occupational position, we find significant earnings disparities among racial/ethnic and gender groups. The census reports that in 2014 Asian American men led all groups in earnings with a median income of $59,766, followed by white men with $58,712, Asian American women with $48,419, white women with $44,236, African

American men with $41,167, African American women with $35,212, Latino men with $35,114, and Latinas with $30,289.[27]

In fifty years of employment civil rights litigation and enforcement, we see some progress in achieving workplace equality, especially during the early period after the passage of the 1964 Civil Rights Act and especially for white women. Yet throughout this history, despite popular perceptions that equal opportunity law has lowered the relative standing of white men, white men retain the most desirable positions in private sector employment. Asian Americans have gained parity in earnings with white Americans, but African Americans and Latino/as lag well behind these two groups.

Despite tangible gains for white women, social psychological research demonstrates that women face continued discrimination when they pursue both a career and a family.[28] While there is less publicly available data concerning unequal outcomes for workers with disabilities and older workers, research suggests that these employees also continue to face workplace discrimination as well.[29]

The persistence of workplace inequality fifty years after passage of the Civil Rights Act of 1964 reflects the entrenched character of workplace hierarchies. Social science research suggests that discrimination may not be the leading source of these continuing disparities, but it plays an impactful role in workplace inequality.

Expansion and Retrenchment in Employment Discrimination Law: Legislative and Judicial Patterns

Employment discrimination law has been a dynamic and contentious field in legislative, judicial, and regulatory arenas for fifty years.[30] A series of Supreme Court decisions in the 1970s and 1980s and new legislation in the 1990s significantly expanded rights and protections for employees. And yet, the conservative turn in the federal judiciary from the 1980s onward resulted in significant retrenchment in what constitutes an actionable employment discrimination claim. Expansion of rights through legislation and landmark judicial innovations is perhaps the most visible change in the system, whereas judicial retrenchment can be a more technical and invisible process, what some have referred to as the procedural attack on civil rights.[31] We conclude this section by looking at some of the social science on these judicial trends and employers' managerial responses.

Expansion: Major Statutory and Judicial Developments Encouraging Litigation

After a period of uncertainty immediately following the passage of the Civil Rights Act of 1964, when it was still unclear what legal effect the courts would give to the law's broad but ambiguous proscriptions, Supreme Court decisions and legislative acts gave real teeth to employment civil rights law. In this early period, the Supreme Court expanded workers' rights by holding that plaintiffs did not need to prove discriminatory intent to prove discrimination;[32] discrimination could be presumed if qualified minority candidates were passed over in favor of white candidates;[33] "substantially similar work" between male and female workers required equal pay;[34] and that back pay[35] and retroactive seniority[36] were appropriate remedies when discrimination was proven. The Court also leaned in favor of employees' rights by holding that the use of local labor market data could support an inference of discrimination.[37] Perhaps the most significant judicial intervention by the courts, however, was the emergence of sexual harassment as a cause of action under Title VII, reasoning that quid pro quo sexual harassment constitutes discrimination "on the basis of sex."[38]

In the early period, Congress too appeared to be the champion of plaintiffs in discrimination cases. In 1967, it passed the Age Discrimination in Employment Act (ADEA), with extensions in 1974 and 1978 protecting more workers. By 1972, Congress gave the EEOC power to file lawsuits on behalf of aggrieved workers. In the late 1980s and 1990s, as the Supreme Court issued a number of pro-employer decisions restricting protections for employees, Congress responded with the Civil Rights Act of 1991, which overrode three prodefendant decisions.[39] The Civil Rights Act of 1991 overrode damage limitations to equitable relief which provided only back pay for most plaintiffs (unless they could also file a §1981 claim)[40] and allowed all workers to claim compensatory damages in employment civil rights lawsuits (though claims are capped according to the size of the organization/defendant).[41] This not only allowed plaintiffs greater potential awards, but also triggered the Seventh Amendment right to a jury trial in a civil action.[42]

In addition to expanded remedies, Congress also passed laws expanding categories of protected workers. President George H. W. Bush signed the Americans with Disabilities Act (ADA) into law in 1990.[43] The ADA protects employees from discrimination based on disability (with damages similar to those provided under the Civil Rights Act of 1991) and requires employers to make "reasonable accommodations" for employees with qualifying disabilities.[44] President Clinton signed the Family and Medical Leave Act in 1993.[45] This provides employees of qualifying organizations with up to twelve weeks of unpaid leave due to their own illness, a close family member's medical need, and/or birth or adoption of a child.[46] Both represent significant expansions of employee rights in the workplace.

Retrenchment: Evolving Limitations on Antidiscrimination Litigation

Despite the early legislative and judicial expansion of protected groups, increased available remedies, and broader understandings of what constitutes discrimination outlined above, the last thirty years also have seen the Supreme Court and other appellate court decisions begin to limit the scope of antidiscrimination law, often in invisible ways. Judicial retrenchment has limited what constitutes discrimination, increased the difficulty of a discrimination claim getting to trial, and made discrimination more difficult to prove in court.

Perhaps the most significant doctrinal development limiting antidiscrimination law is the Supreme Court's relatively new interpretation of the Eleventh Amendment, which bars (or at least chills) Congress from enacting antidiscrimination legislation. This resurgence of federalism began with decisions that did not affect employment discrimination at all,[47] but the erosion of nearly one hundred years of Supreme Court deference to congressional power via the Commerce Clause eventually was used to strike down Congress's extension of the ADEA to state and federal employees[48] and the application of the ADA to the states.[49]

In addition to binding Congress's authority, courts also have made it more difficult for public and private employers to practice affirmative action, which is a form of decision making that intentionally considers race and gender for the purposes of expanding opportunities for disadvantaged groups. Established in 1965 by President Johnson's Executive Order 11246, affirmative action programs require government contractors to set up proactive interventions, with federal oversight, to increase the representation of people of color and women in the workplace. Subsequent judicial decisions have restricted such programs. The reasoning is that racial distinctions—whether or not designed to favor a traditionally underrepresented group—now trigger strict scrutiny and may not be used to remedy general or societal discrimination or inequality[50] absent a formal finding of past discrimination by the organization.[51] The courts also have interpreted Title VII to limit the discretion of private employers in designing affirmative action programs. Employers must make a showing of past discrimination, propose a plan to remedy a "manifest imbalance" along race or gender lines in a "traditionally segregated job category," and not employ quotas or otherwise unnecessarily "trammel the rights" of the majority group.[52] Recent Supreme Court decisions on affirmative action in education reveal that the Supreme Court is unlikely to allow racial classification to remedy inequality. Chief Justice John Roberts famously observed that "the best way to stop discriminating on the basis of race is to stop discriminating on the basis of race."[53]

Courts have also retreated from antidiscrimination laws through statutory interpretations that limit what constitutes discrimination. For example, courts have narrowly construed what constitutes a disability, rejecting protection for many disabled workers and creating low thresholds for what constitutes a "reasonable accommodation."[54]

Disparate impact and class action lawsuits are increasingly difficult to argue because of Supreme Court rulings. As we demonstrate in chapter 3, civil rights cases that employ collective action are far more likely to result in plaintiff victories. Despite Congress's attempt to restore disparate impact theories through the Civil Rights Act of 1991, more recent decisions have limited its influence in employment civil rights litigation because of the required showing of animus.[55] The scope of the disparate impact theory of discrimination has not just been limited in Title VII,[56] but also in ADEA claims.[57]

Similarly, class action certification has become more difficult to achieve under new interpretations of the "commonality" requirement in the Federal Rules of Civil Procedure to bring a class action.[58] Although the *Wal-Mart* case was unusual in terms of the size of the proposed class and the media coverage it received, it was typical of the anticlass action trend in court decisions since 1994.[59] In fact, the estimated probability of a proclass action outcome dropped from 59% in the late 1980s to 26% in 2013.[60]

If a plaintiff can make a cognizable claim that gets to court, they are confronted with changes in standards that favor defendants in winning motions to dismiss and for summary judgment. In a trilogy of cases in 1986 the Supreme Court encouraged the granting of such motions.[61] Recent rulings further encouraged that trend. In *Bell Atlantic Corporation v. Twombly*[62] and *Ashcroft v. Iqbal*,[63] the Supreme Court ruled that plaintiffs' pleadings must be factually plausible even if plaintiffs have not yet had an opportunity to collect evidence through discovery. These rulings have been shown to tilt the playing field in favor of defendants with pronounced impact in employment cases (compared to contract and constitutional tort cases) and in *pro se* cases.[64]

Sexual harassment under Title VII has become easier to defend against as a result of decisions from the late 1990s to the present allowing generous affirmative defenses for companies.[65] In *Faragher* the Supreme Court announced that employers may be held vicariously liable for the actions of employees who create a hostile work environment, but the employer may offer an affirmative defense that they, the employer, had a reasonable policy on sexual harassment, and that the target of the harassment failed to act reasonably to end the harassment.[66] And lower courts have begun to interpret nearly any policy as a "reasonable" one.[67] In a 2013 case, the Supreme Court may have further eased the threat of liability for employers by articulating different standards for harassment by coworkers and supervisors.[68]

Organizational Perspectives on the History of Employment Civil Rights

Organizational sociologists have written extensively on the rise of equal employment opportunity policies and programs within employing organizations in response to the law summarized here and the emergence of the modern personnel profession.[69] Those histories and analyses demonstrate the crucial role of personnel professionals in the evolution of equal opportunity policies, from ending blatant forms of discrimination and creating equal opportunity offices in the 1960s, to promoting affirmative action hiring and outreach in the 1970s, to redefining equal opportunity as diversity in the 1990s and 2000s. Dobbin's important analysis demonstrates that the law was not always the first mover as the agent of change. For example, Dobbin reads *Griggs v. Duke*, the landmark Supreme Court case creating disparate impact analysis, as the court adopting personnel professionals' definition of best practices for job requirements.[70]

As the courts began to turn against affirmative action through reverse discrimination cases, personnel officials shifted from the use of quotas to diversity programs.

Dobbin and other scholars, notably Lauren Edelman, agree that since the 1980s and continuing through the present period many large employers have had well-developed equal opportunity structures that seek to achieve compliance with the law. And yet, the widespread presence of these structures is not equivalent to the end of employment discrimination. Courts increasingly defer to defenses based on employers' assertions that they have compliance structures in place, without probing as to whether these systems amount to anything more than symbolic compliance or whether these systems in fact prevent the discrimination alleged in a particular case.[71] Dobbin is at least agnostic about whether the rise of the equal opportunity edifice has had practical effect in eliminating discrimination. This is not entirely surprising because, as he writes, "if what matters is protecting yourself in court, and if the courts accept the argument that the defendant is doing what everyone else is doing, then the ultimate irony of the history of equal opportunity is that compliance is a self-fulfilling prophecy."[72]

Social science also demonstrates that judges increasingly deferred to employer compliance structures beginning in the 1980s and 1990s with the result that plaintiffs lost at higher rates in employment civil rights cases.[73] Edelman and colleagues refer to this phenomenon as legal endogeneity.[74] As courts began to develop doctrine that limited employer liability for discrimination (described in greater detail in the next section), including sexual harassment, federal district and appellate courts increasingly accepted the employer's having any EEO compliance programs in place to prevent such discrimination as evidence of nondiscrimination. This had the effect of explicitly encouraging employers to create these structures, symbolic as they may be, since courts seldom investigated whether the programs were effective in practice. According to Edelman, this began a spiral of judicial deference to employment "best practices," which in turn led to the further diffusion of those practices. Edelman has found this trend to accelerate after 2000.[75]

Recent scholarship underscores the importance to employment civil rights of who controls the executive branch, including the enforcement agencies of the US Civil Rights Commission, the Office of Federal Contract Compliance Programs, and the EEOC. Woodward documents legal mobilization as it took place during the first years of the EEOC.[76]

Without successful mobilization of the agency by the National Association for the Advancement of Colored People (NAACP) and, somewhat later, NOW, the EEOC may not have been as much of a force for social change in the early years of civil rights enforcement.[77] In periods of Republican control, the agency was far more passive in outreach efforts than was the case when Democrats held the White House. These studies bring home the fact that the number of EEOC charges received and the number of charges that turn into lawsuits are affected by the politics of the executive branch.

Some socio-legal scholars offer a somewhat more optimistic reading of the possibilities for redressing current forms of discrimination in the workplace through the use of law. They argue that deference can encourage new forms of governance within organizations to embrace egalitarian values and fight the more subtle forms of bias that operate against historically protected groups—an approach they refer to as structural.[78] Some structural approaches seek better compliance through regulatory structures rather than judicial rulings, while other structural approaches seek more effective internal mechanisms of enforcement by assigning specific organizational positions with responsibility for less intentional forms of bias.[79] Some of these scholars argue that structural approaches provide new opportunities for employment civil rights attorneys and organizational insiders to make real change on the ground in organizations. Still others decry such approaches because they are vulnerable to cooptation and because they demonstrate that neither the courts nor legislatures are willing to expand antidiscrimination law in the ways necessary to fundamentally redress workplace inequality.[80]

Public Data on Trends in EEO Charges and Federal Lawsuits

The broad contours of federal employment civil rights claiming can be observed from data published by the federal courts and the EEOC.[81] While publicly available data have limitations that demand the kind of original data collection that supports the remainder of this book, the public data are valuable by providing a complete time series of fifty years and by validating some of the patterns revealed in our sample data. The public data demonstrate in quantitative terms the expansion and retrenchment in employment civil rights litigation that we described in the previous section.

Figure 2.1 displays forty years of data on employment discrimina-

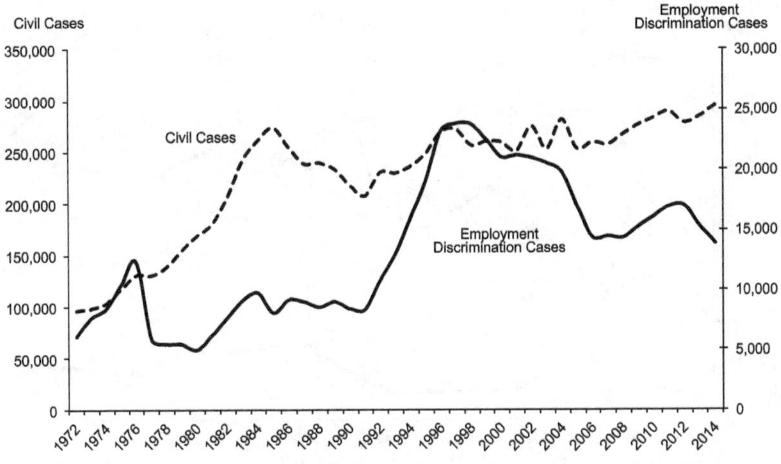

FIGURE 2.1. Total number of civil cases and employment discrimination cases filed in federal court, 1972–2014. Source: Administrative Office of the US Courts. Annual. *Civil Master File.*

tion filings compared to the total number of federal civil case filings. The number of discrimination cases filed in federal district court grew from 336 in 1970, to some 9,000 in 1983, and then declined to 7,613 in 1989.[82] The early 1990s saw a marked increase in the number of filings, more than doubling from under 10,000 in 1991 to 23,735 in 1998. The year 1998 was the high water mark for filings and led to doomsday predictions about the growth in employment civil rights claiming, similar to the alarms sounded about the growth in the total number of civil filings in the early 1980s.[83]

But the doomsday predictions proved wrong. From 1998 to 2004 filings declined by 15% to about 20,000 and went on to dip significantly between 2004 and 2008 before recovering somewhat to 17,000 in 2011. In 2014, the most recent year for which data are available, 13,831 lawsuits were filed.

Prior to filing a lawsuit in federal court, parties must make a charge with the EEOC and/or a Fair Employment Practices Agency (FEPA) at the state or local level. Some charging parties receive relief through the EEOC conciliation process, making a lawsuit unnecessary. Most EEOC complaints do not receive definitive resolution and the agency later provides a right to sue letter. As figure 2.2 shows, only a fraction of charging parties file suit.[84] The ratio of lawsuits to charges (sometimes referred to

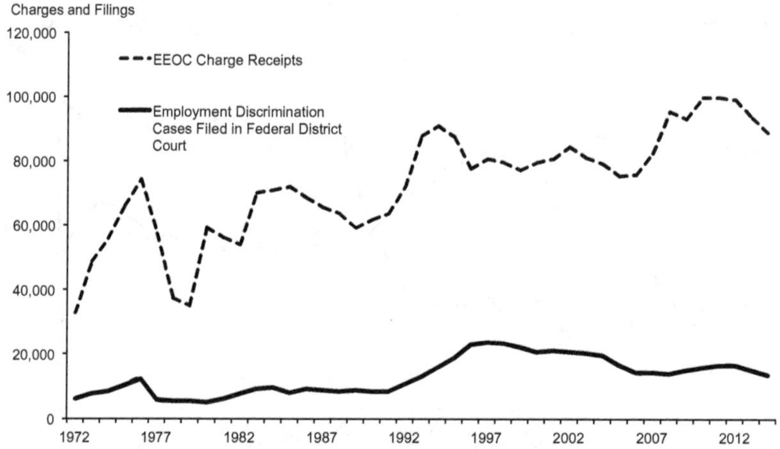

FIGURE 2.2. EEOC charge receipts and employment civil rights cases filed in federal court, 1972–2014. Source: Administrative Office of the US Courts. Annual. *Civil Master File*; EEOC Annual Reports, 1972–2014; EEOC *Enforcement Statistics* 1992–2014.

as the conversion rate) fluctuates between 15% and 30% for most years in this series. Beginning in 1994 there were steady increases in the percentage of charges leading to lawsuits—from 15% in 1993 to 18% in 1994, and almost 30% in the years 1996 through 1999, and then receding to an average of roughly 17% between 2007 and 2014.

The trends in charges and filings are different across Republican and Democratic presidential administrations. The Clinton years (1993 through 2000) brought a rise in charges, filings, and the rate of filing due to the new protection for workers with disabilities and the early effects of the Civil Rights Act of 1991. As figure 2.2 reveals, in 1992, 77,302 charges of discrimination were filed with the EEOC. In 1993 this jumped to 87,942 complaints, including 15,274 disability charges. During the years of the George W. Bush administration the number of EEOC charges declined slightly but remained largely stable at around 80,000 charges per year. But the number of lawsuit filings declines from 21,157 in 2001 to 14,314 in 2008. During the Obama administration, which begins after the great recession of 2008, the number of EEOC charges increases sharply to over 90,000 per year, but the number of lawsuit filings increases only slightly to an average of around 16,000 per year. Hence the conversion rate remains well under 20%.

As figures 2.1 and 2.2 display, since 2000 there has been a decline and leveling off of lawsuit filings, which could be attributable to several factors we cannot definitively address. It may reflect the increased difficulty for plaintiffs established by the judicial decisions discussed in the previous section. Or, after a period of optimism about greater available damages under the Civil Rights Act of 1991, plaintiffs' lawyers may have learned that the odds of success and the likely size of awards make such claims not worth pursuing. The decline may also be due to employers requiring arbitration of employment claims, though the evidence of that is mixed.[85]

Prior to our study, employment discrimination filings were thought to follow economic cycles, with difficult economic times predicting an increase in lawsuits.[86] The more recent data on trends complicate that hypothesis. Although there is an increase in the number of EEOC charges and filings from 2008 as the theory predicts, the dramatic rise in claims and lawsuits during the Clinton years defies the prediction that claims fall during good economic times.

Key to understanding these trends is to understand what types of claims are being made in EEOC charges and in lawsuits. Unfortunately, the Administrative Office of the US Courts data on Title VII filings does not categorize claims by type or issue of discrimination (race vs. sex vs. religion, etc.). Thus, we do not know the relative growth or decline in certain kinds of discrimination filings. The charge statistics of the EEOC do contain this information, although annual reports are not entirely consistent in what they report.

Figure 2.3 presents data on the four major types of discrimination alleged to the EEOC between 1966 and 2014. Early on, racial discrimination claims predominate, making up over half of charges until the late 1970s. Sex discrimination claims attain a consistent presence at 30% and stay there through 2014. Age discrimination charges begin at 10% of charges in 1979, more than double by 1986, and average slightly above 20% of charges through 2014. Disability discrimination charges first appear in 1992 after the passage of the ADA, quickly rise to 20% or more of charges until 2007, and then rise to 30% of charges by 2014. By 1993 the system of employment civil rights had matured and all four major bases for discrimination charges appear in EEOC reports. Types of charges not shown here make up a small percentage of charges overall. National origin charges make up about 10% of EEOC charges while religion and equal pay are only 1% to 3% respectively.

These data reveal a notable trend in the rise of retaliation charges

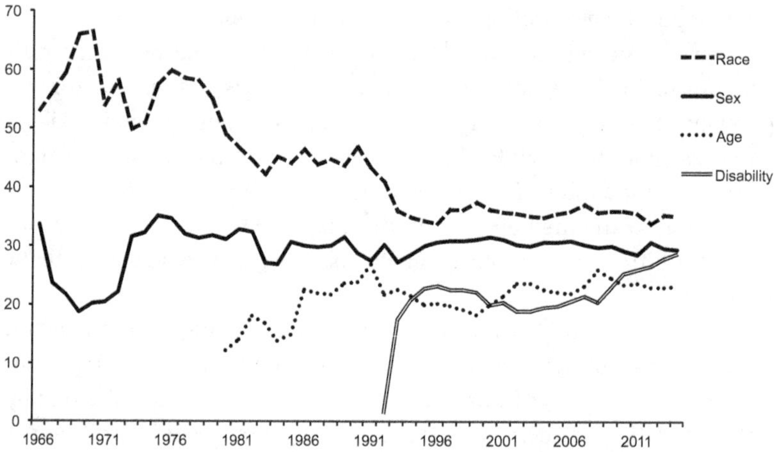

FIGURE 2.3. Percent of EEOC charge receipts containing discrimination on the basis of race, sex, age, and disability, 1966–2014. Source: EEOC Annual Reports, 1966–2014; EEOC *Enforcement Statistics* 1992–2014.

over time. They rose from 15.3% of charges in 1992 to 42.8% by 2014. The growth in retaliation charges may reflect the rising proportion of charges that involve dismissal, a finding documented by Donohue and Siegelman for the 1965–87 period and in our data for the 1988–2003 period.[87] It may also reflect an increasing tendency for plaintiffs (and their lawyers) to add retaliation as a claim in discrimination disputes. It may reflect more retaliatory behavior by employers. Without in-depth analysis of claims over time and the employment contexts that produce them, we are left to speculate about the reasons for this shift.

Data on outcomes in discrimination charges at the EEOC are less comprehensive than data on the demographics of those charges. For 2014, the modal EEOC charge resolution was a finding of "no reasonable cause" (57%), which means the agency does not find the case meritorious and the individual may pursue a private cause of action (file a lawsuit in federal court). Fifteen percent of cases are closed administratively, which means the case was closed without any remedy or finding for the charging party. Slightly more than 7% were resolved by "settlements," meaning the charging party received some compensation, and 5.2% were "withdrawn with benefits," presumably also favorable to the complaining individual. In just 2.8% of cases, the EEOC made a finding of "reasonable cause" that discrimination occurred, which is followed by efforts at conciliation. Of the 2,745 charges that year in which reconciliation was attempted, it succeeded less than half the time (1,031 successes and 1,714 failures).

In 2014, the EEOC reported obtaining $296.1 million in monetary benefits for charging parties (not including monetary benefits won through litigation)[88] for an average of about $24,524 per charge for which monetary benefits were obtained by the EEOC. The EEOC itself litigates a relatively small number of cases per year. Between 1992 and 2013, the EEOC acted as plaintiff in between 148 and 481 cases per year. As such, most EEOC complainants (73% in 2014) obtain no relief from the EEOC and very few (0.2% in 2014) are directly represented by the agency in court.

The plateauing number of lawsuits undercuts the assertion of some critics of antidiscrimination law that at the beginning of the 1990s we were witnessing an explosion of litigious behavior. But it does not resolve questions about the propensity to sue of workers who perceive their rights have been violated. To illuminate that question we turn to an analytic exercise drawing on a classic concept from the law and society literature: the pyramid of disputes.

A Litigation Explosion? The Pyramid of Employment Civil Rights Disputes

The metaphor of a pyramid often is used to provide an overview of the processes that lead from perceived injuries to formal claiming behavior in a variety of areas of litigation.[89] At the base of the dispute pyramid are *perceived injurious experiences*: the broad mass of injuries that people recognize.[90] Some proportion of these experiences becomes *grievances*: injuries that involve a violation of right or entitlement.[91] Only some grievances become *claims*: when an individual contacts the party responsible for the grievance.[92] Fewer still are *disputes*: when the party allegedly responsible for an individual's claim initially denies its responsibility.[93] Some number of disputes results in *filings*: a formal complaint (in a litigation model, or an EEOC charge). The smallest category of all is made up of *trials*: cases that are adjudicated.

In all areas of litigation, we know that as disputes advance through the claiming process, cases drop out of the dispute pyramid at a rapid rate.[94] In medium-size civil cases only 70% of people with grievances press them to a claim, only 46% pursue a grievance to the level of dispute, only 5% of grievances lead to filing a lawsuit, and only .06% of grievances end up in trial.[95] We also know that the wealthier and better educated are more likely to make claims and pursue them to court, as are those individuals who have terminated their relationship with the party with whom they have a grievance.

A comprehensive understanding of trends in employment discrimination litigation requires comprehensive data on *all* stages of the dispute pyramid. That is, what is the likelihood that individuals will have grievances stemming from perceived employment discrimination, complain about discrimination, engage in disputes with employers, file formal complaints outside the organization (with the EEOC, an equivalent state agency, or a federal or state court), and adjudicate their claim?

The base of the dispute pyramid—whether one perceives oneself as injured and thus as someone who might have a legal claim—is the most difficult to analyze and the least understood. A baseline rate of injury is difficult to determine in all areas of law, but is especially vexing in efforts to determine personal experiences with discrimination because a target of discrimination may not even know they have been discriminated against.[96] Individuals may be uncertain as to what qualifies as employment discrimination (e.g., epithets, jokes, verbal assaults),[97] and they may have different propensities to report that they feel discriminated against. Some may "over-report" discrimination because, in race matters, they attribute their frustrations to racial disadvantage,[98] while others "under-report" perceived discrimination for a variety of reasons. They may have a sense of shame, or they may reject victimhood, because friends, family, and coworkers discourage them from thinking they were victims of discrimination, or they may perceive the interpersonal costs associated with making a discrimination claim.[99] Responses about experience with discrimination vary with question formats, depending on whether the question is explicitly race-focused or open-ended, venue-specific or general, time-specific or not, and the like.

Despite these difficulties establishing a baseline frequency of discrimination, a considerable body of empirical research on experiences with discrimination exists.[100] Using survey data and self-reports, scholars find self-reports to be meaningful measures of experience with discrimination.[101] There are several clear patterns in the survey data that inspire confidence about the validity and reliability of the data, including that some 95% of respondents reporting discrimination could provide highly specific descriptions of the circumstances in follow-up questions.[102]

With that methodological background, what do the survey data on personal experiences with employment discrimination indicate? African Americans consistently report the highest levels of discrimination, white people report the least, and Asian Americans and Latino/as fall in between.[103] The percentage of African Americans reporting that they were discriminated against "at [their] place of work" within "the last 30 days" varied between 21% and 18% for years 1997 through 2001 in national Gallup polls,[104] and the percentage rises with longer time horizons. Some 33% of African Americans and Latino/as reported that they "ever" were "not offered a job that went to a white" because of racial discrimination, while 31% reported being "passed over for a promotion which went to a white" because of racial discrimination.[105] The data also show that better-educated and more race-conscious respondents report higher levels of experience with discrimination than other respondents.[106]

A study of discrimination in the workplace conducted by researchers at Rutgers University deserves special consideration, given its focus on employees, the detailed nature of the questions it employed about the experience of workplace discrimination, and its nationwide sample.[107] That study found that 10% of respondents said they had been "treated unfairly at [their] workplace because of their race or ethnicity."[108] Over half of the African American workers surveyed "knew of" discrimination in the workplace in the last year and more than one-quarter (28%) had themselves experienced discrimination due to race in the last year.[109] In contrast, only 6% of white workers had themselves been treated unfairly due to their race in the previous year.[110] More generally, when asked if the practice of determining promotions is unfair, only 6% of white workers said yes, while almost half (46%) of African American workers and 12% of workers of other racial groups answered yes.[111] Those who report being treated unfairly most commonly report being passed over for promotion (28%), being assigned undesirable tasks (21%), and hearing racist comments (16%).

In the Rutgers study more than a third (34%) of those who reported unfair treatment in the workplace opted not to do anything.[112] Although they also may have complained to friends, family members, or even coworkers, some 29% said they "reported the incident to a supervisor," 19% "filed a complaint according to company procedures," 10% "avoided certain areas or people in the office," 4% "quit," and 2% "confronted the person." Only 3% said they "sued" the company or their coworker.[113]

Using these data, we consider just one category of protected employees, African American workers. The surveys described above contain different estimates of how many African Americans experienced discrimination at work in the last year. The high estimate was 46%, the average was 33%, and the low figure, in the Rutgers study, was 28%.[114] Using this most conservative measure, we analyze the pyramid of disputes for African Americans. According to the Bureau of Labor Statistics, the number of African Americans working full-time, year-round in the United States in the year 2014 was 12,245,000.[115] Although the Rutgers study found that most African American employees reported two incidents of discrimination in the last year, we conservatively assume that individuals will file only one discrimination claim. Using the 28% figure from the Rutgers study, we estimate that 3,428,600 African American workers perceived that they were the targets of workplace race discrimination in 2014. This number of perceived discrimination surely includes misperceptions (when the target attributes a decision to discrimination when that is not the motivation of the decision maker) and unfair treatment that does not meet the legal standard for employment discrimination. It also excludes discrimination that goes unnoticed by its targets. Nonetheless, 3.42 million serves as a rough approximation for the pool of African American workers who think they have been a target of discrimination and therefore reside at the base of the dispute pyramid.

What percentage of this group starts a claiming process? The EEOC reported that 31,073 individuals filed race discrimination charges in 2014. Of course, an EEOC charge is only one avenue of formal complaint, yet it probably is the most common nationally. Using this estimate, less than 1% (0.91%) of African American workers who felt they were discriminated against filed an EEOC complaint.

As we noted above, this 1% faces further attrition before receiving any remedy. In 2014, 12,074 charges or about 15% of charging parties received some kind of positive relief in the EEOC. We estimate that 35% of the favorable EEOC outcomes, or 4,226, were awarded to race discrimination charges. To estimate the number of disputes remaining after the EEOC charging process, we subtract the number of cases with positive relief (4,226), which leaves 26,847 potential race discrimination disputes after the EEOC process.

Here we reach a disjuncture in official statistics. Publicly available data do not include what proportion of employment discrimination lawsuits allege racial discrimination in employment. The best estimate we can make from public data of the number of race-based claims is to assume that the proportion of race cases filed in federal court is the same as the proportion of race charges in the EEOC charge statistics or to estimate from our own sample of federal lawsuits described in greater detail in the next chapter.

Both the EEOC charge data and our own data indicate that 35% of federal employment civil rights lawsuits include a race claim. Thus of the 13,831 employment civil rights lawsuits filed in 2014, we estimate that 4,841 alleged racial discrimination. Figure 2.4 depicts the part of the dispute pyramid through filing in federal court. Note that "pyramid" is a misnomer for this figure. Given a base of over 3.4 million potential grievances, 31,043 EEOC charges, 26,847 disputes, and 4,841 lawsuits filed, the figure looks less like a pyramid and more like a radio tower on the deck of an aircraft carrier. Less than 1% of potential grievants complain to the EEOC. Only 0.13%, or 13 in 10,000, potential grievants sue.

We take up the remainder of the disputing period, from the point of filing suit to ending a case, in the next chapter. Although there has been some research published on case outcomes in employment civil rights cases using federal court data, they lack the detailed data we collected.[116]

This analytic exercise is somewhat crude. A more precise estimate would require survey data from larger samples and data from state agencies and courts. And this estimate treats cases as though only one individual plaintiff was involved. While this is largely correct, we do know that at least some cases (1% of the sample of filings we discuss in chap-

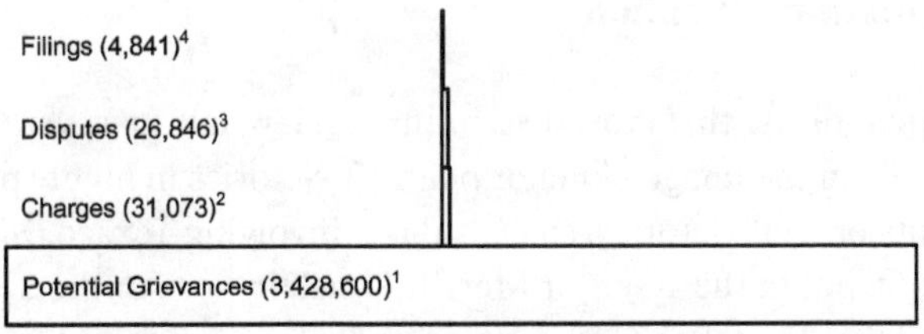

FIGURE 2.4. Dispute pyramid of estimated employment discrimination claims by full-time African American workers, 2014. For details of calculations, consult the preceding text. Notes: (1) Estimate of full-time African American workers who experienced employment discrimination in last year. Based on Dixon, Storen, and Van Horn (2002); US Bureau of Labor Statistics (2014). (2) Race charges filed with EEOC in 2014. EEOC (2014). (3) Race charges filed that were not positively resolved by EEOC. EEOC (2014). (4) Estimate of federal employment civil rights lawsuits alleging race discrimination filed in 2014. Based on Administrative Office of the US Courts, annual, *Civil Master File*, Table C-2 12-month period ending September 2012; and EEOC *Enforcement Statistics* (2014).

ter 3) include classes of plaintiffs. And yet this exercise reveals the miniscule percentage of African Americans who feel they are discriminated against in the workplace and make a charge with the EEOC or in court. If larger percentages of workers took action it would have a dramatic impact on caseloads. After looking at these numbers, we are inclined to ask not why there are so many discrimination claims, but why there are so few?

The answer to that question may also be suggested in the statistics we have reviewed here, as well as data we present in chapter 3. Only about 15% of those who complain to the EEOC receive some kind of positive outcome. The average monetary benefit for those winners is under $25,000. As we will see in the next chapter, we see a similar pattern for those who file in court. When these awards are weighed against the difficulties of bringing a complaint, and the social opprobrium such an action typically provokes, it is hardly surprising that so few targets of discrimination take formal action to obtain redress.[117]

Given these data it is difficult to understand why there appears to be a widespread perception in the general public, and certainly among employers, that workers are likely to file discrimination lawsuits and that many of these claims are inflated or even frivolous. Research on media coverage of employment civil rights litigation provides insights into why this is the case.

Media Reports: Inflating the Risk of Employment Discrimination Litigation

These data indicate that most discrimination lawsuits have very different outcomes from the image of major plaintiff victories in highly publicized settlements or trial victories, such as those involving Texaco, Mitsubishi, or Home Depot in the 1990s or Merrill Lynch in 2013 or the $20 million settlement that Gretchen Carlson reportedly received from Fox News for her sexual harassment claim in 2016. Most plaintiffs who file a federal lawsuit never reach trial. If they do go to trial, they lose more than 60% of the time. If they win, they get relatively modest awards. Perhaps what we know the least about are settlement figures in the large number of lawsuits settled each year.

Yet the number of cases and the size of some awards have generated considerable fear among employers and spawned a new line of insurance against employment liability.[118] The US Chamber of Commerce's Institute for Legal Reform advocates on behalf of employers, sounding the alarm that "our nation's litigation addiction hurts families, businesses, communities, and America's ability to compete for jobs and investment in a global economy."[119] It runs FacesOfLawsuitAbuse.org, a website portal with regular press announcements such as an "Annual List of Ten Most Ridiculous Lawsuits" and video interviews with those who believe they have been "abused" by aggrieved plaintiffs and plaintiff's attorneys. A leading employment law firm publishes an annual report on workplace class actions that is critical of such litigation. It reported that in 2015 there were 11,550 discrimination class actions filed in federal and state court and that the top ten settlements in class action suits cost more than $295.57 million.[120]

These insurance industry and employment counsel assertions seem dubious, but are interesting because they frame employment civil rights litigation as a system that poses substantial risk to employers. This perspective, while inflated, is echoed in the media treatment of this system of disputes, as Nielsen and Beim document.[121] National and local media coverage of employment cases report an overall plaintiff win-rate nearly three times the actual win-rate of 32%. Moreover, this analysis shows that newspaper accounts of awards in such cases have a median value well over $1 million, a figure nearly six times greater than the actual median award of $150,000.

The popular image of a plaintiff-oriented system stands in marked contrast to how most targets of discrimination and most plaintiffs' lawyers view the system. They think the system heavily favors employers. A survey of employers, defense attorneys, and plaintiffs' lawyers found that employer defendants have considerable advantages in contests over discrimination claims, especially in the area of dismissals.[122] Employers, human resource professionals, and defense lawyers report that they have developed techniques for minimizing the legal threat posed by discrimination lawsuits. Plaintiffs' lawyers also recognize the distinct advantages that employer defendants possess, and hence are reluctant to take cases unless they contain particularly powerful evidence of discrimination.

All of these data confirm Edelman's now decades-old thesis—there is in HR and popular conception a dramatically inflated threat of employment litigation compared to what actually happens in the litigation system.[123] For example, in the area of wrongful termination claims, employment lawyers and HR professionals have exaggerated the threat of such litigation in professional journals, which has prompted many employers to revise their employee manuals and management practices to prevent any suggestion that the manuals alter employment-at-will relationships. In employment litigation, as in other areas of litigation, the biased character of media reports has led to a hardening of business attitudes toward rights of injured parties and to political and public relations campaigns to define litigation as a problem in its own right.

Conclusion

This brief review of fifty years of employment civil rights sets the context for the analysis of data from the current study. Here we relied on existing research and public sources to begin to dispel some myths about the current system of employment civil rights. First, employment discrimination is not a thing of the past, but remains a significant factor in inequalities of race, gender, disability, and age in the workplace. Second, while the scope of antidiscrimination law now embraces a broader set of types of discrimination than when it was initially passed into law, race discrimination remains the most frequent type of alleged discrimination, followed closely by sex discrimination. The current regime of rights protection is broader than in 1964 and supports a significant amount of federal litigation. Yet the growth in the amount of litigation we observed in the 1980s and 1990s has ended. We have seen significant declines in the number of lawsuit filings since the turn of the century. Third, despite the continuing emphasis on class action litigation and direct government intervention in reports by the employment defense bar and the insurance industry, employment civil rights litigation is overwhelmingly prosecuted by sole plaintiffs. The reduction in class action litigation and in the total number of lawsuits may well be the result of procedural rulings by the Supreme Court that have undercut the opportunity for plaintiffs to file as a class and proceed past the early stages of litigation. Fourth, contrary to the image of a highly litigious workforce, we see that but a fraction of potential targets of discrimination either complain to the EEOC or file in federal court. Fifth, contrary to the image projected from media reports, most employment civil rights plaintiffs do not succeed in court and very few receive significant financial awards.

What prior research and public data begin to suggest is that fifty years of employment civil rights has led to a regime of workplace rights that may have a larger symbolic presence in society than it has a practical impact in court and in the workplace. To assess whether that is true, it is necessary to examine original data on the dynamics of employment civil rights litigation. In the next chapter we examine quantitative data on claims and outcomes. In subsequent chapters we turn to the narratives of plaintiffs and defendants who have been cast as adversaries in this system of rights on trial.

CHAPTER THREE

A Quantitative Analysis of Employment Civil Rights Litigation

Case Characteristics, Plaintiff Characteristics, and Legal Outcomes

The previous chapter described the claiming system in employment civil rights based on publicly available data from the federal courts and the EEOC. Public data leave much unknown about discrimination litigation, including such basic questions as whether federal court filings contain the same proportions of race, sex, age, and disability claims as do EEOC charges. Nor do these data describe the characteristics of plaintiffs and their claims. While researchers have analyzed cases that generate published opinions, such research is at serious risk of sample selection bias and fails to capture the majority of lawsuit filings: those that generate no opinion.[1]

Our quantitative dataset consists of detailed coding of a random sample of 1,788 cases filed in federal court from 1988 to 2003. As noted in the introductory chapter, our project builds on seminal research by Donohue and Siegelman, which studied 1,200 cases filed in federal court between 1972 and 1987.[2] We extend their analysis into the contemporary era and expand its scope. After describing case characteristics, we present a multivariate analysis of case outcomes. The quantitative analysis we present here is an essential backdrop to the narratives of the parties we analyze in later chapters.

Our analysis offers important corrections to common misperceptions about employment civil rights litigation, as well as new insights into the determinants of case outcomes. The most significant feature we identify is the overwhelming predominance of cases involving a solitary plaintiff. Class actions constitute less than 1% of cases. Another key finding is that the most important predictor of a successful outcome is legal representation. Plaintiffs who do not have a lawyer have their cases dismissed at a 40% rate, compared to 11% for plaintiffs with lawyers. We also show that settlement is the most common outcome of cases, and most settlements are modest in amount, with an estimated median of $30,000. Trials are exceedingly rare and return a victory for the plaintiff one time in three. But even while the contours of the system are clear, our analysis suggests it would be difficult to predict the outcome in specific cases at the outset of a case.

These data portray a system of individualized claims processing embedded in an adversarial process. Contrary to media images of litigation delivering significant awards to a high percentage of plaintiffs, our data reveal a system that dismisses or summarily terminates a significant portion of cases or that offers small settlements without authoritative determinations of the validity of claims.

General Characteristics of Employment Civil Rights Cases, 1988–2003

Our full dataset of cases contains 1,788 cases drawn from 1988 to 2003 from the master civil file of the Administrative Office of the United States Courts, case category 442, employment civil rights. The dataset includes a small number of cases that were still open at the end of this time period. We begin with a description of all cases, including open cases. The analysis of case outcomes in the second part of this chapter is limited to closed cases.[3]

Types of Discrimination

The four major types of cases are race, sex, age, and disability. As depicted in figure 3.1, race and sex claims are the most common types of employment civil rights litigation cases. About 40% of cases involve a race claim, while 37% of all cases involve a sex claim. Claims based on age and disability are the next most common, making up about 22% and 20%, respectively, of all cases. A third tier of claims involve discrimination because of national origin, accounting for about 12% of all cases.

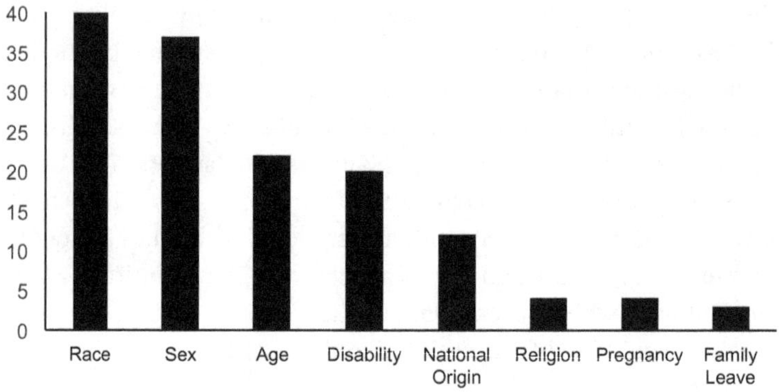

FIGURE 3.1. Percent of cases by discrimination type

Claims based on the remaining types of discrimination—because of religion (4%), pregnancy (4%), and family leave (3%)—are considerably rarer. A significant minority of cases (35%) include multiple claims of discrimination.[4]

Discriminatory Issues

The data on discriminatory issues tell a straightforward story. Discriminatory firing is far and away the most prevalent claim made in employment civil rights litigation cases, followed by claims of unlawful retaliation (fig. 3.2). Claims of discrimination in promotion (19%), sexual harassment (17%), and pay (14%) are the next most common challenged issues. Somewhat less common are claims of discriminatory hiring and demotion (9% each). Claims of unlawful seniority practices are extremely rare (2% of all cases). A complainant may make claims based on more than one issue (pay *and* promotion, for example). And indeed, a majority of all sampled cases (55%) include multiple issue claims. Complainants are more likely to make multiple issue claims in cases involving promotion (85%), pay (89%), and sexual harassment (83%), than in cases involving hiring or firing, although the latter two issues each have about a fifty-fifty likelihood of including at least one additional issue claim (48% and 54%, respectively).

We see substantial uniformity in the breakdown of cases by type and issue. Race, age, disability, and national-origin discrimination cases follow a strikingly similar pattern in the proportion of issue claims: unlawful firing is the most prevalent across these types of cases, followed (in order) by claims of discriminatory retaliation, promotion, pay, and hiring. One major exception to this pattern is sex discrimination cases, in which the proportion of retaliation claims (54% of all sex cases) is slightly higher than that for firing claims (50%). Discriminatory firing and employer retaliation are, by substantial margins, the two greatest concerns of *all* plaintiffs, regardless of their race, sex, age, disability, or national origin.

Individual vs. Collective Litigation

The filings dataset reveals even more clearly than the public data that the system of employment civil rights litigation overwhelmingly pits an individual plaintiff against an organizational defendant. As noted in chapter 2, there are two theories of discrimination available to employment civil rights plaintiffs: disparate treatment and disparate impact. Disparate treatment cases require a showing of discriminatory *intent.* Disparate impact cases, by contrast, involve facially neutral employment practices that have a *statistically disproportionate effect* on a protected group; the employer's motivation or intent is largely irrelevant in disparate impact cases. Disparate treatment cases overwhelmingly predominate among discrimination claims (see fig. 3.3). Of the cases in our national study, 98% of cases allege disparate treatment. Only 4% of cases brought a disparate impact cause of action. Although plaintiffs may invoke both causes of action, they do so in less than 3% of cases. Plaintiffs largely challenge how they are treated by the employer as individu-

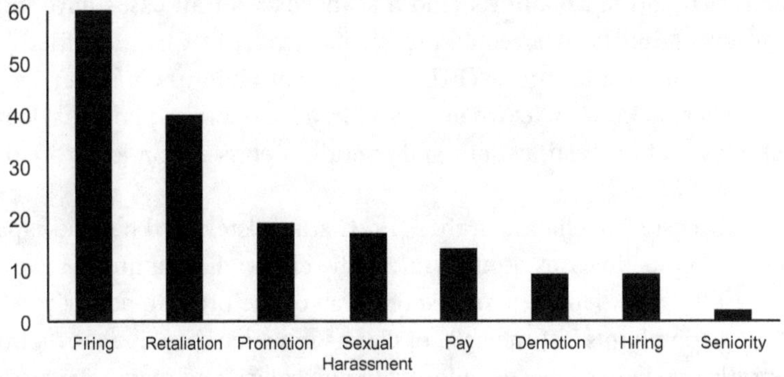

FIGURE 3.2. Percent of cases by discrimination issue

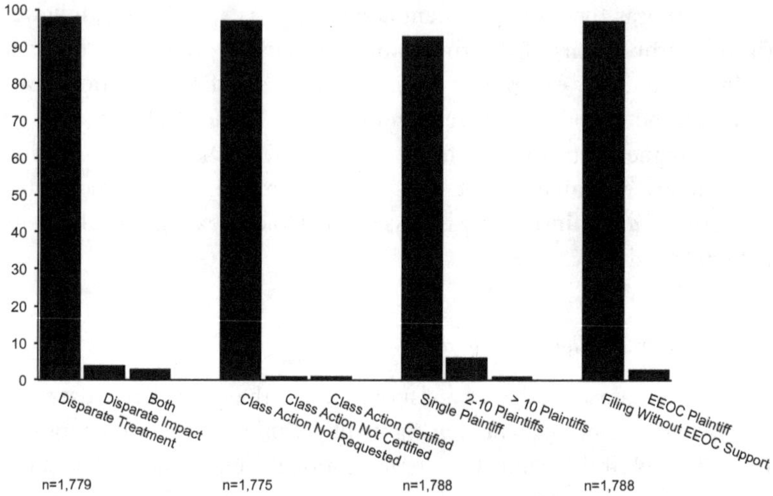

FIGURE 3.3. Percent of cases by measures of collective versus individual litigation

als rather than employment practices that may have a disparate impact on a group of workers.[5]

Employment civil rights complaints may involve a single individual, multiple individuals, or a class action. Donohue and Siegelman found a dramatic decline in class action lawsuits as a proportion of lawsuits filed between 1972 and 1987. In 1975 there were 1,106 class action filings. By the end of the 1980s the number had dropped 96% to only 51 cases.[6] As we see in figure 3.3, in the 1988 to 2003 period, over 93% of all sampled cases are brought by a sole individual. Only 6% of cases include between two and ten plaintiffs, and a scant .05% of all cases have more than ten plaintiffs. A sizeable proportion (23%) of cases are filed *pro se*. Public interest law firms (PILFs) represent plaintiffs in under 1% of cases. Class actions are extremely rare. In 97% of cases, plaintiffs do not seek class action certification, and overall, a class action is certified in just 1% of all cases.

As discussed in chapter 2, the EEOC administers and has the capacity to intervene in cases brought under the civil rights statutes. However, the EEOC fails to make a finding one way or the other in nearly 77% of all filed complaints. Of the 23% of claims in which they do make a finding, only one in five have been found to have merit and therefore warrant conciliation. The EEOC intervened as a plaintiff in just 3% of cases.

Plaintiff Characteristics

Case files do not disclose all the data that social scientists would like to know about plaintiffs, but they provide information on their racial status, gender, and occupation. Forty-four percent of the plaintiffs are African American, while 33% are white. All other racial categories make up the remaining 23% of cases.[7] We find essentially equal numbers of female and male plaintiffs (51% female, 49% male). The plurality of cases (48.5%) are filed by plaintiffs who work in sales, service, or administration, followed by those in managerial or professional occupations (32.5%). The smallest percentage of cases (19%) come from blue collar and/or workers in other occupations.

Although federal law protects people of any racial background from employment discrimination, African Americans account for the overwhelming proportion of plaintiffs in cases alleging racial bias (80%). By contrast, 8% of race discrimination cases are filed by white people; so-called "reverse discrimination" cases are relatively rare. All remaining racial groups make up just 11% of race-based claims. Men are substantially more likely to allege racial discrimination than are women (58% compared to 42%).

White women are most likely to allege sex discrimination (41% of cases), followed somewhat closely by African American women (35%). Occupational status differs in a fundamental respect in sex discrimination cases from racial discrimination cases: the largest proportion of sex allegations are brought by those in management or professional occupations compared to those in sales, service, or administration (50% versus 37%). Like race discrimination cases, however, sex discrimination cases filed by blue collar or other workers make up the smallest percentage of plaintiffs (13%).

By a wide margin, white people make up the largest proportion of age discrimination plaintiffs (49%). African American, Latino/a, and Asian American plaintiffs combined account for 30% of age discrimination cases. Also, male plaintiffs outnumber female plaintiffs by about a two-to-one margin. Those in managerial or professional jobs slightly outnumber those in sales, service, and administration (45% to 39%). Meanwhile, blue collar or other workers make up just 16% of such cases.

Plaintiff characteristics in disability discrimination cases show a similar pattern as age cases, at least with respect to the plaintiff's race and sex. White men and women (49%) and men of all racial backgrounds

(59%) are most likely to allege disability discrimination. The highest proportion of disability cases (43%) involve plaintiffs in sales, service, or administration, while about equal percentages of plaintiffs are in managerial/professional (29%) and blue collar or other jobs (28%).

These data demonstrate that the four major types of discrimination claims are employed by groups of plaintiffs that vary not just in the particular characteristic protected by law but by race, gender, and occupation. In succeeding chapters of this book, particularly chapter 9, we will explore the significance of these differences among groups of plaintiffs. In some respects, different groups of plaintiffs fare differently in the system of employment civil rights litigation. In most respects, though, as individual claimants filing individual charges, they receive similar treatment by their employers and by the law.

Explaining Outcomes of Employment Civil Rights Litigation

Understanding the resolutions of discrimination cases is crucial to understanding the relationship between rights, law, and hierarchy.[8] We know from previous research that employment discrimination litigation cases are treated more harshly by the courts, with lower levels of settlement rates, higher rates of summary judgment motions against plaintiffs, higher plaintiff loss rates, and higher appellate reversal rates of plaintiff awards than is the case for other kinds of civil litigation.[9] Yet prior to our analysis, it was not known what factors explain when a case closes and who wins.

In addition to providing new, representative data on case outcomes, our quantitative analysis enhances our understanding of discrimination litigation by treating case outcomes as a sequential variable. This departs from much socio-legal scholarship and popular thinking, which conceptualizes legal outcomes in binary terms: did the plaintiff win or lose? Our approach better captures the dynamic character of the litigation process and the dilemmas that parties and courts face in adjudicating claims. By including distinct categories of outcomes that are largely unmeasured and therefore invisible in other research, we more accurately explain the social organization of discrimination litigation.

To identify the distinct outcomes of cases and other variables in our national sample of cases, we use our originally coded data on case filings. For cases after 1995, we also are able to match case filings data with

EEOC charge data, allowing us to look at the impact of various EEOC variables on court outcomes. The means and standard deviations for all independent variables are shown in appendix table A.3.

A Sequential Model of Litigation Outcomes

As any lawyer knows, litigation is a dynamic process. We will see in chapter 4 that the filing of a discrimination lawsuit in federal court often comes at the end of much disputing behavior in the workplace and after the required filing of a charge with the EEOC.

Once a lawsuit is filed, the parties engage in strategic behavior concerning the lawsuit itself. We coded six mutually exclusive formal outcomes that occur as a sequence in litigation: (1) dismissed, (2) early settlement, (3) summary judgment loss for plaintiff, (4) late settlement, (5) trial win for plaintiff, and (6) trial loss for plaintiff. Figure 3.4 diagrams the sequence and frequency of case outcomes from our data. Here we describe the legal process that leads up to these outcomes and our methodology for analyzing outcomes.

As noted in the previous chapter, individuals filing a claim of employment discrimination in federal court must first file a charge with the

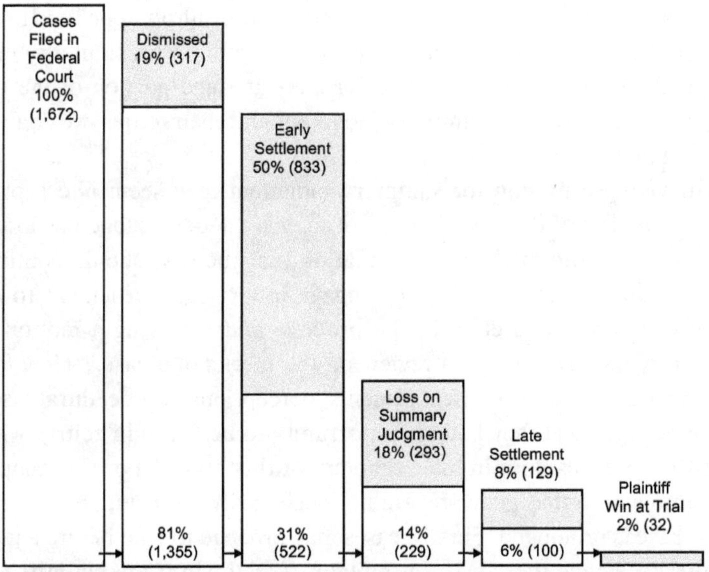

FIGURE 3.4. Percent of cases by sequential outcome

EEOC or state fair employment practice administration (FEPA) and obtain a right-to-sue letter.[10] Once in federal court, a plaintiff's case is classified as "dismissed" if it is involuntarily disposed of without trial of the issues.[11] Such cases typically are dismissed for the plaintiff's failure to state a claim, failure to serve the defendant, or for want of prosecution. These fundamental legal flaws often result from plaintiff misunderstanding. If the plaintiff has counsel and the case is dismissed, the plaintiff recovers nothing and may bear attorney's fees and court costs.[12]

The next three outcomes—early settlement, plaintiff loss on all counts of summary judgment, and late settlement—are defined in reference to the motion for summary judgment.[13] During the discovery period (when the parties request, acquire, and analyze the opposing party's evidence), the defendant organization makes a decision about whether to file a motion for summary judgment. In such a motion, the defendant argues that there is no material issue of fact to be adjudicated and the judge should rule in favor of the defendant as a matter of law. If a case resolves through settlement prior to the motion for summary judgment, we code it as an early settlement. If the defendant organization files and wins on all counts of the motion for summary judgment, the plaintiff loses and bears attorney's fees and court costs and is coded as the plaintiff losing all counts on motion for summary judgment. Plaintiffs may appeal the summary judgment ruling, but they seldom prevail on appeal.[14] If even one part of the plaintiff's complaint survives motion for summary judgment, the case continues forward for trial. If some portion of the case survives the motion for summary judgment and then settles, we code the case a late settlement.

Surviving a motion for summary judgment may seem like a proxy for the quality of the case, because it means a federal judge has looked into the case and made a determination that the case should continue. But we know parties sometimes engage in strategic settlement to dispose of strong cases early in the process, and surviving a motion for summary judgment is not a review on the merits of a case.[15] How far a case proceeds may also affect litigants' perceptions of procedural justice (whether they feel they had an opportunity to be heard in court), which is a theme we explore in later chapters of this book.[16] For this chapter, we simply note that plaintiffs are not necessarily uniformly better off if their case is prolonged. Finally, cases may proceed to trial before a judge or jury. We code these cases as a plaintiff trial win if the plaintiff wins any part of a verdict.

A significant proportion of cases (some 19%) are dismissed. By far the most frequent outcome is early settlement, which makes up one-half of the entire sample of closed filings (50%). Most parties seek to avoid the risks associated with investing in a motion for summary judgment and resolve their claims prior to the filing of a motion. Of the cases that do not settle early, plaintiffs lose the motion for summary judgment in more than one-half the cases (57% of remaining cases or 18% of filings overall). In the 14% of cases that remain active after the disposition of the motion for summary judgment, more than one-half (57%, or 8% of filings overall) settle before a trial outcome. In the 6% of filings that result in trial outcomes, plaintiffs win 33% of the time (2% of filings overall).

Because settlement is the modal outcome, it is important on both theoretical and policy grounds to know the size of settlements, yet data on the details typically are unavailable because of confidentiality agreements that often accompany settlement. Of the 945 cases in our sample that settled, we obtained settlement amounts for only seventy-five cases from court records. The median settlement was $30,000, the twenty-fifth percentile was $11,500, and the seventy-fifth percentile was $92,458. In the very small number of cases ($N = 14$) in which a plaintiff survived a motion for summary judgment—coded as a late settlement—the median award rises to $40,000 and the seventy-fifth percentile to $110,000. Three settlements in our sample, all for class actions, were very large: one for $110 million, one for $29 million, and one for $8.1 million.[17]

Cases that proceed to trial produce larger awards for plaintiffs on average than those reached in settlement. The data on trial verdicts in our dataset are more complete, given the recording of the amount in case files, but the number of plaintiff trial victories is small ($N = 32$). The median award amount at trial is $110,000, with a twenty-fifth percentile of $23,000, and a seventy-fifth percentile of $403,098. The largest trial award in our data is almost $3 million.

The sequential model of case outcomes provides a more realistic assessment of the prospects for plaintiffs in these cases than previous research suggests. If the measure of plaintiff success were winning "something," the plaintiff win rate would be approximately 60%. Yet many of those "wins" come in the form of small settlements with a median value of $30,000, of which a considerable portion goes for legal fees. Some 40% of plaintiffs formally win nothing. This pattern by itself has significant implications for understanding the role that litigation might play in redressing workplace discrimination. The fact that most plaintiffs gain modest settlements or nothing at all suggests that such litigation may be a relatively weak engine for social change, both because potential plaintiffs and their attorneys will lack the incentives to pursue their claims and because defendants typically face limited risk from litigation.

Explanatory Variables

Our coding of case files not only carefully classified cases by outcome, it also captured as much detailed information about the lawsuit and its parties as can be gleaned from a document file. Explanatory variables include (1) plaintiff characteristics, including race, gender, occupational status, and age; the industry and public or private status of the employing organization; the tenure of plaintiffs in their position and their union status; (2) the legal theories invoked in a case, as measured in a variable that combines statute and type of discrimination involved; (3) case characteristics, including the issue raised in the case (hiring, firing, etc.); an index of legal effort that ranged from zero to three (one point each was awarded if a file contained depositions, expert testimony, and/or statistical evidence; the variable was only computed for cases that proceeded to motions for summary judgment); whether the case alleged discriminatory actions by specific individuals; and whether the case alleges a disparate impact theory of discrimination; (4) the treatment of the charge that preceded the lawsuit by the EEOC, as well as the EEOC priority code for cases filed after 1995; (5) legal representation, including whether plaintiffs were represented by a lawyer throughout the litigation, were *pro se* (i.e., they represented themselves) throughout, or filed *pro se* and obtained counsel during the course of litigation; (6) measures of collective legal mobilization, including whether a case was a certified class action, whether there were multiple plaintiffs, whether the EEOC joined the lawsuit as a party, and whether the plaintiff was represented by a public interest law firm; (7) jurisdiction: the seven federal districts in which we coded case filings; (8) year: 1988–2003; and (9) the political party of the presiding judge, as measured by the party of the appointing president.

As noted in chapter 1, we made an effort in the coding of case files to construct valid measures of what can be conceived of as a latent or unmeasured variable of the "quality" of a case. Several of our measures might capture aspects of this variable, including the index of legal effort, the outcome of a case in the EEOC, and the EEOC priority code, but none is definitive. We tried, without success, to have coders provide a subjective rating of the strength of a case. As we expected, we found that there are inherent limitations to case files as a source of indicators of the "merits" of a case. Unlike some medical malpractice research in which medical records can be sent to medical professionals to assess, the merits of the case in employment discrimination depend on subjective assessments of job performance and the meaning of employer actions. Even where such records are included in the file, there is no standard for keeping employment records that would allow us to evaluate personnel files as a medical professional can do using agreed-upon standards of care. We coded sets of documents constructed by the adversarial process of which they are a part. The relationships between those documents and a "good" or "bad" case are difficult to discern. Accordingly, our study does not attempt to adjudicate *which* side is the most meritorious. Rather, our quantitative findings here outline *what* are the contours and the results of case filings while our qualitative analyses in later chapters explain *how* the parties arrive at their understandings of a case.

Statistical Models

We use discrete-time event-history models with a random-effects term to estimate the probability that a case will end at a particular stage as a function of the effects of independent (explanatory) variables, net of the odds that a case has survived to that point. The use of an event-history model captures the sequential nature of the litigation process and allows us to vary the coefficients for each stage of the litigation process. In this sense, it is an improvement over simple logistic or probit models that do not allow for multiple litigation outcomes.[18] Because we are concerned with the likelihood that a case will end at each given stage, we use each stage as the time period. This implies that we model the hazard rate that a case will end at each stage or continue on to the next stage. The event-history model also allows us to introduce a random-effects term, which controls for case-specific variation in the error term. Given the small number of cases to survive to trial, it was necessary to limit our analysis to the first four sequences of litigation: dismissal, early settlement, plaintiff loss on summary judgment, and late settlement.

Table 3.1 summarizes this model. It contains 3,778 observations, which equals the total number of cases at risk of concluding in the first

TABLE 3.1 **Discrete-Time Random Effects Event History Model of Litigation Outcomes**

	Dismissal		Early Settlement		Summary Judgment Loss		Late Settlement	
	ß	Robust Z-score	ß	Robust Z-score	ß	Robust Z-score	ß	Robust Z-score
Plaintiff Characteristics								
Other nonwhite	0.044†	(1.91)	0.172	(0.99)	0.402	(1.29)	−0.528	(0.96)
Black	0.335	(1.27)	−0.056	(0.24)	0.901*	(2.42)	−0.772	(1.17)
Male	0.303†	(1.66)	−0.087	(0.53)	0.38	(1.34)	−0.322	(0.67)
Manager/professional	0.018	(0.08)	−0.593**	(3.15)	−0.176	(0.50)	−0.509	(0.71)
Sales, services, office	−0.212	(1.08)	−0.137	(0.76)	−0.095	(0.28)	−0.564	(0.83)
Age	−0.023*	(2.14)	−0.023**	(2.65)	−0.005	(0.31)	−0.022	(0.83)
Job tenure	−0.018	(1.57)	−0.029**	(3.43)	0.031*	(2.14)	−0.073*	(2.53)
Member of union	−0.459	(1.46)	−1.126**	(4.61)	0.298	(0.85)	0.111	(0.16)
Private defendant	−0.452*	(2.29)	0.250	(1.41)	0.600+	(1.95)	1.894**	(3.17)
Statutory Basis/Type of Discrimination Alleged								
Title VII—race	0.351†	(1.63)	−0.045	(0.21)	−0.753*	(2.23)	−0.089	(0.15)
Title VII—sex	0.502*	(2.29)	−0.405*	(2.08)	0.488	(1.51)	−0.844	(1.38)
Title VII—retaliation	−0.303	(1.55)	−0.053	(0.31)	−0.635*	(2.17)	−0.322	(0.65)
Title VII—other	−0.114	(0.51)	−0.461*	(2.25)	−0.121	(0.40)	−0.288	(0.40)
ADEA—age	0.045	(0.16)	0.267	(1.13)	0.209	(0.53)	−0.255	(0.36)
ADEA—retaliation	0.501	(1.30)	−0.119	(0.38)	0.576	(1.31)	2.149*	(2.25)
ADA—disability	−0.191	(0.78)	−0.511*	(2.43)	−0.287	(0.78)	0.869	(1.21)
ADA—retaliation	−1.070*	(2.32)	0.161	(0.48)	−0.881	(1.51)	−1.385	(1.31)
42 USC 1981	−0.076	(0.35)	−0.287	(1.56)	0.400	(1.27)	−0.121	(0.20)
42 USC 1983	0.286	(0.80)	−0.601†	(1.88)	−0.315	(0.67)	1.235	(1.52)
Constitutional case	−0.006	(0.01)	−0.136	(0.37)	0.269	(0.52)	−1.394	(1.31)
Other statute	0.244	(1.22)	−0.040	(0.24)	−0.320	(1.02)	−0.478	(0.98)

Alleged Discriminatory Practice								
Hiring	−0.244	(0.77)	0.230	(0.90)	−0.630	(1.35)	1.232	(1.39)
Firing	0.040	(0.23)	0.040	(0.26)	−0.291	(1.08)	−0.541	(1.13)
Sexual harassment	−0.354	(1.19)	0.300	(1.17)	−0.238	(0.49)	0.393	(0.49)
Conditions of employment	0.129	(0.66)	0.344*	(2.10)	0.013	(0.05)	1.041†	(1.76)
Pay	0.113	(0.46)	0.422†	(1.88)	−0.865*	(2.50)	1.119†	(1.92)
Other Case Characteristics								
Index of legal effort					0.066	(0.34)	−0.409	(1.02)
Specific individual perp.	−0.138	(0.78)	−0.155	(1.00)	−0.128	(0.48)	0.117	(0.22)
disparate impact theory	−0.701†	(1.71)	−0.510	(1.31)	0.053	(0.10)	0.426	(0.48)
EEOC Treatment								
EEOC A categorization	−0.167	(0.49)	0.331	(1.19)	0.414	(0.94)	0.020	(0.02)
EEOC B categorization	0.137	(0.55)	0.428*	(2.03)	0.250	(0.66)	0.416	(0.47)
EEOC C categorization	−0.077	(0.29)	0.254	(1.08)	0.176	(0.42)	0.875	(0.97)
EEOC supported	−0.088	(0.21)	−0.215	(0.62)	−0.365	(0.69)	0.435	(0.44)
EEOC not supported	−0.172	(0.76)	−0.398†	(1.86)	0.161	(0.48)	−0.936	(1.17)
Legal Representation								
Only *pro se*	2.632**	(11.60)	−0.889**	(3.44)	2.116**	(4.65)	−0.660	(0.48)
Gained counsel	0.081	(0.25)	−0.755**	(3.04)	0.488	(1.20)	−0.265	(0.33)
Collective legal mobilization	−1.045*	(2.40)	−0.038	(0.16)	−1.167**	(3.14)	0.132	(0.22)
Constant	−0.889	(1.37)	2.32**	(4.00)	−0.194	(0.21)	1.362	(0.77)
Observations	3778							
Chi^2	1193.77**							
Pseudo-R^2	0.300							

† $p < .10$, * $p < .05$, ** $p < .01$

Note: Effects for city and year were estimated, but not reported. Reference categories for categorical variables with multiple categories are for race, white; for occupational status, blue collar and other; for EEOC outcome, no findings; for EEOC categorization, no categorization; for legal representation, lawyer throughout. All cases were weighted by the sampling weight.

four sequences. That is, all 1,672 cases were at risk of ending in dismissal; plus the 1,355 which survived dismissal and were at risk of ending in early settlement; plus the 522 cases that progressed past early settlement which might have ended in a loss on summary judgment; plus the 229 cases that survived past the motion for summary judgment and might have ended in late settlement. For the final stage, we model those cases that ended in a late settlement against the 100 cases that continued to trial. While discrete-time event-history models are appropriate for estimating the probability of sequenced events, levels of significance for coefficients will be affected by how many cases survive to a given stage.[19] The coefficients presented in table 3.1 estimate the effect of each variable on the hazard rate of a case ending at each specific stage, given that it has already reached that stage.

Results

SIGNIFICANCE OF LEGAL REPRESENTATION AND COLLECTIVE LEGAL MOBILIZATION. By far the most significant effects on outcome are legal representation and collective legal mobilization. One in five plaintiffs acts as his or her own lawyer, operating *pro se* over the course of their lawsuit. These plaintiffs are almost three times more likely to have their cases dismissed, are less likely to gain early settlement, and are twice as likely to lose on summary judgment. If *pro se* plaintiffs survive beyond summary judgment, they are not significantly different from other plaintiffs in terms of their odds of obtaining a late settlement. Another 8% of plaintiffs file *pro se* but obtain counsel during their case. Table 3.1 reveals that, controlling other variables, these plaintiffs are still less likely to settle early than plaintiffs who had counsel throughout.

These dramatic effects of legal representation are demonstrated when we run a logit model predicting dismissals. The pseudo R^2 for the model before adding the legal representation variables is 0.09 (model not shown); in other words, the independent variables explain 9% of the variation in outcome.[20] By adding legal representation, the independent variables explain 22% of the variation in outcomes. At the first, perhaps least visible, aspect of the litigation process, legal representation is crucial to continuing, and representation remains critical for plaintiffs to obtain early settlement and avoid loss on summary judgment.

Why would plaintiffs who have the benefit of counsel be more likely to exit at the early settlement stage? Why do they choose not to pursue their cases? As succeeding chapters will show, the statistical results are consistent with what our interviews with plaintiff and defense lawyers suggested. Settlement offers at this stage typically include attorney fees, which offer a direct incentive to plaintiffs and their attorneys to settle. This is a stage when sophisticated parties come to recognize that they can minimize cost and risk, even if the settlement amounts involved are modest. Plaintiffs' lawyers obviously are pivotal in persuading their clients to accept early settlement, as one-half of filings are resolved at this stage.

The powerful effect of legal representation might be explained as a selection effect. That is, obtaining legal representation reveals an otherwise unmeasured variable of quality of case. A considerable amount of research, some involving random assignment of counsel, finds an independent effect for legal representation for a range of problems facing individuals regardless of the strength of the case.[21] As we discussed above, included in our model are several measures that should tap the strength of a case. Yet the presence of counsel had a significant effect on outcome net of those variables. Thus we are not persuaded that the effect of counsel can be attributed to unmeasured aspects of the strength of a case. We offer a detailed analysis of obtaining representation in chapter 5.

In addition to legal representation, collective legal mobilization (cases involving multiple plaintiffs, certified class actions, and representation by a public-interest law firm or the EEOC) is an important predictor of case outcomes. Of the 152 cases in which collective legal mobilization was employed, 108 involved a lawsuit by multiple plaintiffs, which may consist only of two plaintiffs; forty-six were cases in which the EEOC intervened as a party; eighteen were certified class actions; and in only nine cases were plaintiffs represented by a public interest law firm. As we saw in the descriptive statistics presented in the first part of this chapter, collective legal mobilization is rare in the system of workplace discrimination litigation (less than 10% of all cases). Most cases are brought by individual plaintiffs, without the support of other plaintiffs, the EEOC, a class, or a public interest law firm.

Yet table 3.1 shows that plaintiffs in cases with collective legal mobilization are far more successful. They are less likely to be dismissed and less likely to lose on motion for summary judgment. In simplified analyses of trial outcomes (not shown), we found that plaintiffs in collective cases had an even chance of winning at trial, compared to only three in ten chances for plaintiffs overall.

PLAINTIFF CHARACTERISTICS: RACE, GENDER, OCCUPATIONAL STATUS, JOB TENURE. Early in the litigation process, plaintiffs' racial status and gender matter significantly for the treatment of their cases. Plaintiffs are more likely to survive the dismissal phase if they are white than if they are a person of color and if they are a woman rather than a man (see table 3.1). After surviving the dismissal phase, white plaintiffs have similar experiences to plaintiffs of color in later stages and female plaintiffs' outcomes are similar to their male counterparts. The race effect is not explained by reverse discrimination cases (i.e., when white people file a race discrimination claim).[22] The gender effect, in contrast, *is* attributable in part to the lack of success enjoyed by men filing gender claims.[23]

Other plaintiff characteristics that are associated with outcomes suggest more "staying power" and may reflect greater resources or a different kind of attachment to the employer. Managerial and professional employees, older plaintiffs, employees with more time on the job, and plaintiffs working at unionized establishments are less likely to be dismissed or to settle early. Not only are these plaintiffs more likely to have lawyers, they may be more persistent in seeking redress. Tenure may also strengthen a plaintiff's claim that a negative employment action results from discrimination.

EEOC ACTIONS. Finally, we explore the effect of EEOC action, short of intervening as a plaintiff, on case outcomes. As we observed in our discussion of collective action, when the EEOC becomes a plaintiff in a case it has a significant effect. However, EEOC priority codes and merit determinations, which the agency adopted in an effort to reduce case backlog by dedicating resources to the strongest cases, have little explanatory effect. The EEOC established a priority case-handling process (PCHP) in 1995 that requires an EEOC complaint processing specialist (who is not a lawyer) to assign each case an A, B, or C priority code. The specialist decides if further investigation will "probably" result in a cause finding (an A case), will "likely" result in a cause finding (a B case), or has "uncertain merit" (a C case). The parties are not allowed to know the priority code their case receives. Some 20% of EEOC charges are classified as A cases, 58% as B cases, and 22% as C cases.[24] We matched the EEOC data to case filings in 815 of our cases. There is a filtering effect by priority code on cases with A, B, and C priority codes because they receive different treatment and outcomes in the EEOC. Nonetheless, the matched cases in the filings dataset roughly matched the proportion of A, B, and C cases in the EEOC. Of the matched cases, 20.4% (179) were A cases, 47.3% (416) were Bs, and 32.3% (384) were Cs. Thus, despite the EEOC's differential efforts in A, B, and C cases, the proportion of each case that makes it to federal court is similar to the proportion at EEOC intake, leaving a credible subset of cases with which to evaluate the effect of priority code on case outcome.

Table 3.1 shows that the only statistically significant effect that EEOC priority codes have is that B cases are more likely to obtain early settlement than other cases. The absence of significant effects holds both in models that included legal representation variables and those that did not. Moreover, the explanatory value of the model (R^2) does not change when the variables for EEOC priority codes are included.

In addition to the EEOC's PCHP code, we analyzed information on the disposition of the EEOC (or FEPA) charge in the case. As noted above, in 80% of the lawsuits in our sample, the EEOC made no finding and provided the plaintiff with a right-to-sue letter. In the 20% of cases in which there was an EEOC finding, the EEOC supported the plaintiff's charge 21% of the time and did not support on the merits 79% of the time. These EEOC administrative decisions also have relatively little effect on litigation outcomes. Table 3.1 reports that when the EEOC supports a plaintiff's charge, there are no significant differences from cases with no EEOC finding. When the EEOC issues a finding that does not support the plaintiff, cases are less likely to settle early. Employers apparently take the EEOC ruling in these cases as an indication they should continue to litigate rather than settle.

The other variables we included in the multi-variate models were not statistically significant or did not present patterns that warrant discussion here. Our quantitative analysis of case outcomes sheds new light on who wins employment discrimination litigation (measured in formal legal terms) and how they win. Whatever uncertainty may exist about possible outcomes when a case is filed, we know in the aggregate that the more resourceful parties—those who have legal representation or are supported through collective mobilization—obtain superior results in law. Given the relative prevalence of individual cases within an adversarial system, we see a system that conforms to predictions from law-and-society classics: many one-shot litigants, who are typically outgunned, lose or obtain small settlements without ever obtaining a day in court in which they present their grievance and bring evidence to support it.[25] These results are the product of institutional forces that treat the cases as though they involve small stakes. Social advantages play a role in case processing such that more privileged social groups obtain better results. This pattern is especially ironic in a subfield of law intended to protect traditionally disadvantaged groups. And while these more resourceful plaintiffs may have stronger cases, we must be skeptical about the ability of lawyers, courts, and regulators to draw neat lines between weak and strong cases. We can explain such results in terms of resources without making assumptions about the strength of the case.

Conclusion: Rights, Law, and Hierarchy in a System of Individualized Justice

When we study a random sample of cases, and include what typically is excluded in research that looks only at published opinions, an image of discrimination litigation emerges that is very different from media representations of highly successful and consequential outcomes.[26] The image also is different from many social scientific accounts that emphasize high-impact class action litigation.[27] Employment discrimination litigation is a system dominated by individual cases bringing claims of disparate treatment, rather than cases that attack policies that have a widespread disparate impact on protected groups. As we will see in succeeding chapters, in this system of individualized justice plaintiffs and defendants come to court seeking a vindication of their respective positions, but typically they leave with a settlement they feel they must accept, even if it is not "just." Plaintiffs who come to the process with legal representation or the strength of collective legal mobilization fare significantly better than other plaintiffs. It is a system characterized by considerable indeterminacy about the outcome of a particular case, even though the overall distribution of outcomes is remarkably stable over the time we analyzed.

Our quantitative results suggest that the law fails to seriously address discrimination, not because it excuses discriminatory behavior, but because of how it organizes the enforcement of legal rights. Similar to findings on the relationship between law and inequality in other domains, these data demonstrate that employment civil rights law takes jurisdiction over a set of potential rights claims.[28] But unlike comparable worth or hate speech, in which the courts authoritatively rejected a species of rights claims, in this system the process of marginalizing rights claims is less formal and less visible. The courts largely deflect rights claims without authoritative resolution: they dismiss, they orchestrate settlement, they reject on summary judgment. In only a very limited portion of cases—the collective legal mobilization cases and a small number of individual cases—are plaintiffs able to deviate from the normal pattern of case processing. Those relatively rare cases sustain the myth of a responsive system of employment civil rights.

We see in our quantitative results the three processes that limit law's capacity to vindicate rights: individualization, structural asymmetry between parties, and adversarialism. The predominance of individual claims makes it possible for employers to recast inherently legal issues as individual problems or personality conflicts. The statistical results suggest that the best path to success is to move from an individual to a collective case. But that occurs in less than one case in ten. The asymmetry of power between parties is reflected in the imbalance of representational resources. A significant proportion of plaintiffs lack legal representation. While unrepresented plaintiffs face dismal prospects, plaintiffs with lawyers also typically lose or receive a small settlement. The influence of adversarialism is made manifest in the sequential pattern of case outcomes. The costs of litigation, coupled with the possibility of losing before a judge or jury, drive both sides to settle. These processes can support the reinscription of ascriptive hierarchies in the workplace and in law. While neither plaintiffs nor defendants receive an authoritative ruling on their case, the absence of strong remedies tends to leave workplace discrimination in place.

To understand more fully the interplay between law, the workplace, and ascriptive hierarchies, it is necessary to take the inquiry into the arena of social action. How do the actors in this system deal with conflicts around claims of discrimination? In the next part of the book we hear from plaintiffs, defendants, and their lawyers about how they experience employment civil rights litigation and the impact of litigation—or lack thereof—on their lives, their work, and their workplace.

PART II

Narratives of Employment Civil Rights Litigation

CHAPTER FOUR

Workplace Wars

The Origins of Employment Civil Rights Lawsuits in the Workplace

Employment civil rights claims emerge from workplace conflicts. Plaintiffs come to see negative working conditions or adverse personnel actions taken against them as violations of their civil rights. By complaining of discrimination, plaintiffs challenge the legality of their treatment by management and begin a personal battle to vindicate their rights, typically on their own as individuals. Management and its legal representatives react defensively to these claims. Given that many defendant organizations have developed personnel practices meant to eliminate discrimination, to prevent disputes from entering the legal system, and to minimize legal risks to the organization, they tend to see the source of the problem as the employee. Rather than see a violation of rights, they see a lack of fit between the individual employee and the organization.

In this chapter we examine these two very different perspectives on the workplace conflicts that give rise to the filing of civil rights lawsuits. Even in the workplace at this stage, we see power asymmetries and early dynamics of legal reinscription, particularly in the efforts by HR personnel and inside counsel to head off disputes before they become legal claims. We begin with the stories of two plaintiffs, Catherine Harris and Daris Barrett, who experienced a long series of conflicts with their supervisors before eventually reaching the conclusion that they were being subjected to illegal discrimination. Their stories are in part supported and in part challenged by the plaintiffs' and defense lawyers we interviewed for these cases.

Plaintiffs' Stories

Catherine Harris's case against the City of Allendale

Catherine Harris (P12), a middle-aged white lesbian, filed a case against the City of Allendale after what she perceived as a long period of harassment by her boss. She was represented by a well-established employment discrimination attorney, and her federal court filing charged discrimination on the basis of sex, race, sexual orientation, and religion. Her case settled "early," that is, before a hearing on a motion for summary judgment. She was awarded $160,000, considerably more than the median settlement in employment civil rights cases.

Ms. Harris had worked for the City of Allendale for more than seven years as an employment manager with responsibility for hiring and classification when a coworker was promoted and became her immediate supervisor. Ms. Harris told us he "had no background at all in personnel or my area." Her coworkers told her that this new boss, an African American man named William Painter, had immediately started to bad mouth her. In their first face-to-face interaction, he snapped at her. She remembered, "I went and I shook his hand and I said, 'Congratulations, I hear you're the new boss.' He says, 'I hate being called boss. Don't ever use that word to me again.' It seemed like a slap. I got a slap in the face." She also recalled what Mr. Painter said during his very first meeting with the staff: "'Well, the first thing I want to tell you is I'm a Christian. I'm going to run this place on Christian values.' And a lot of people turned to look at me [for my response]." As one of two managers below Mr. Painter, Ms. Harris supervised a large division of people whom she described as loyal to her. "I was stunned. . . . I didn't realize the implications for me at that time yet, but it made quite an impression."

Ms. Harris suspected that Mr. Painter disliked the fact that the two managers directly under her were both white, despite the fact that she had hired only one of them and the rest of the staff were "very diverse." She told us that Mr. Painter "started meeting with exclusively African American people on the staff, including my subordinates, and asking 'What should we do to change Catherine's unit?' . . . Like he was prejudiced." He continued to be rude to her, too. "And he would sort of bark out what seemed to me to be orders that just weren't grounded in good thinking or reality. He would have these emotional outbursts." She found Mr. Painter's directions to be "stuff that was against my years of experience, against my judgment, against what made sense." For example, he refused to pay the cost of catering lunch for a full-day meeting during which the city was recruiting someone for an executive position.

Ms. Harris described a series of actions that led to the deterioration of their relationship. She was trained in employment civil rights law and was responsible for responding to employees when they reported allegations of discrimination in the department. She described herself as committed to fair working conditions for women and minorities, but also willing to challenge "bogus" complaints by employees. She began to have conflicts with Mr. Painter on the legality of employment decisions. She told us:

> I can be very flexible, but where there's laws. Sometimes he'd tell me stuff that was illegal. Like do this, throw away the employment list. I would say, "You know, we can't throw away the employment list. You can't do that. It's illegal." He'd say, "If it's not completely diverse, just throw it away." I'm like, "Can I, can we get a legal opinion on that?" "No. You're going against me." In fact, two or three weeks before I finally decided to call a lawyer, he had just told me, "Don't you ever call a lawyer for a legal opinion again," and up to that time, I used to routinely call for advice. And he told me, "I don't want them sticking their nose in my business. You don't ever talk to the lawyers unless I ask you to." So I was feeling more cornered and cornered and cornered because he kept asking me to do more things that were borderline legal.

Ms. Harris described the turning point when she decided that his actions were discrimination. It happened at a private meeting she had arranged with him to discuss their working relationship. She recounted that she had said,

> "William, we've got to get along for the sake of the staff and sake of work, I really want things to work out, and I just, there's so much tension, I want to know what's going on. . . . What *is* it? What can I do?"

When he explained that *she* was the problem, she asked,

> "Well, what is it about me then?" And he was like, "I don't know." And I said, "Well, is it my race? Is it because I'm a woman? Is it because of my lifestyle, because I'm gay?" And he didn't answer. He just, it was sort of a stare down. So it left me wondering.

Other troubling events followed. After one conflict, Mr. Painter called her into his office. She remembered him putting his hand on the Bible—"He always kept the Bible open on his desk"—and telling her, "'You know, I've prayed on this, and I just think your staff is out of control. You're out of control. . . . I'm going to write a negative evaluation about you because of this.'"

She concluded it was "racial stuff" because she saw Mr. Painter favoring African Americans;

> He was making these remarks about, "I'm going to blow up the silos of racial isolation" or something like that. What was ironic is he was only having black advisers, and he was accusing me of being the one that was having racial issues. And he did it in front of the entire staff.

She also saw him favoring men, calling one of her male subordinates for advice when she was the appropriate person to consult.

> I knew there was racial stuff. I knew there was the man stuff, and everybody knew that. And then the Bible thing. . . . Even though I wasn't like real vocal about being gay, I know people knew . . . I thought well, with the Bible, he just, he must hate me in the worst way. Because it was so personal.

Ms. Harris finally reported Mr. Painter to his supervisor, an assistant city manager, and things improved for a month or two. Then, Mr. Painter started to write her up "just for nonsensical stuff, in my opinion. Just bogus stuff, and stuff that was not true. And I could just see it was a losing situation because whether it was true or not true, he didn't want to work with me. He didn't want life to be good for me." Ms. Harris's health worsened. Her blood pressure got much worse, and she would get dizzy. Members of her staff were getting mad at her and siding with Mr. Painter because of conflicts he had created.

Before finding a lawyer, Ms. Harris consulted the city's internal EEO officer. "Oh, I went to the affirmative action guy and talked to him, and he made it pretty clear it was his job first, you know, he worked for [Mr. Painter]. And he did. He worked directly for him." She found the officer's response especially troubling. "At times I confided in him and so on. He privately agreed that the situation as it arose was just horrible, but also said 'If you quote me on that, I'll call you a liar or something.' And sadly that's what happened."

Looking back on the experience many years later, Ms. Harris wished she had tried harder to resolve things at work without going to court, but also recalled that she had lost the resolve to do so.

> I had gotten beaten down to the point where I hardly had any energy to make the one phone call to the lawyer and say, "Guess what just happened." I was very willing then to just be told [what to do]: "Tell me what to do and I'll just do it because I'm so tired."

In Ms. Harris's case we have the benefit of interviews with her attorney, the defense attorney for the City of Allendale, and the EEO officer for the City (although he took his position well after Ms. Harris's case and discussed an alternative case he knew about personally). Ms. Harris's attorney, Joseph Shapiro (PL12), a white, middle-aged man, took the case based on Ms. Harris's relatively high salary, which provided "a chance for a significant recovery," and his perception that Allendale "run[s] their operation and their legal operation and their personnel operation in shockingly amateurish fashion." Moreover, he was impressed by Ms. Harris's story about her supervisor openly expressing fundamentalist Christian values that "seemed to express an orientation that would be hostile to gay people. Catherine's gay." Further confounding the case was an allegation that Ms. Harris had been involved in a physical altercation with a subordinate (which would, of course, be legitimate grounds for termination).

The defense attorney (DL12), Cindy Abbott, a Latina in her forties, suggested that the case was brought in federal court, despite more favorable state law, because the plaintiff's lawyer worried about bringing the case before a jury, given strong community sentiment that might support the manager named as an individual defendant in the case. Ms. Abbott perceived Ms. Harris as not that "likeable of a person," and thought her attorney shared that view. "I think the plaintiff's attorney rightfully evaluated his client as someone who . . . wasn't that likeable. And so it made sense for both of us to try to dispose of the claim quickly." As Mr. Shapiro told us, he was able to persuade Ms. Harris, after "a lot of drama around the wording of the agreement," to accept the settlement. She took her large monetary settlement, but regretted having lost her job. She has not regained employment of similar stature or remuneration since the lawsuit concluded.

Daris Barrett's case against Retail Stores, Inc.

Daris Barrett (P24), a forty-five year-old African American woman, worked as an assistant store manager for Retail Stores, Inc., a discount clothing store chain, before she developed heel spurs, a sometimes painful condition in which a bony growth forms on normal bone. After surgery to remove the spurs, she asked for accommodations. Her manager refused, she was not allowed to return to the store, and she was terminated. She filed a case alleging disability discrimination. The case was dismissed on summary judgment for the defendant. Ms. Barrett appealed, but the appellate court affirmed the lower court's ruling.

As Ms. Barrett recalled during our telephone interview, personality conflicts with her management snowballed into what she perceived as discriminatory action:

> I had a district manager that was kind of temperamental, but he had picks and chooses. I wasn't one of the "chosen ones" . . . I didn't challenge his authority, but I would ask questions. And everything that he was doing was not right and I would ask questions. . . . I had a manager that was one of his chosen ones and she wouldn't answer a question. She would tell me, "read the book." Due to the fact that I had no one that would tell me anything, I had to read the policy and procedure book a lot. So I had acquired a nickname. They used to call me Miss P&P.

When one of us filled in the abbreviation as "policy and procedure," Ms. Barrett replied, "Exactly."

Ms. Barrett took leave to have her heel spurs removed because, she told us, "I had trouble standing. I was an assistant manager and the position required standing. And I just couldn't do it on a regular basis, and it was necessary for me to have surgery." Ms. Barrett followed the policy to take her leave and did not anticipate trouble returning to work after surgery, although she had some problems on the job prior to that and suspected her managers—all of them white—were mad at her.

In a departure from normal procedure, she was evaluated by the district manager rather than by her store manager. He gave her a negative evaluation, including a reprimand for not recruiting new employees. "I wouldn't recruit because I wasn't happy with the company. And I stated that." The evaluation also rebuked Ms. Barrett for failing to train anyone, which Ms. Barrett denied. Ms. Barrett contacted a woman in the HR Department about the negative evaluation. As she explained:

> I spoke to her because I was really adamant about that I never, ever worked anywhere and received a bad evaluation. This was the first one I ever received in my life. I was really upset about it. I spoke to her and she asked me, she said, "Well, what do you want me to do?" I said just like, "You can rescind [the negative evaluation]. There's a procedure for everything. . . . I never worked under him. He never knew what I was capable of doing. He was not the person who was supposed to give me my evaluation." So they did rescind it.

Another incident contributed to workplace tension before her surgery. Ms. Barrett had been injured at work while setting up a display. A shelf fell on her hand and thumb. The injury required treatment by a doctor, but she returned to work the following day. Her manager told her to take a few days off, because she was unable to continue hanging shelves. Ms. Barrett took the days off, but insisted on being paid. "I knew—policy and procedure once again—that they had to pay me. It was an on-the-job injury." But she thought that management was angry with her for insisting on the paid leave. "You're not supposed to be an independent thinker. . . . And you definitely don't use [the rules], even if you know them."

Ms. Barrett had already witnessed situations in which "they discriminated on a lot of different things." She described seeing the company treat African American customers differently than white customers. They allowed white people to return merchandise for cash back, while African Americans were only allowed store credit.

After the surgery for her heel spurs, Ms. Barrett informed the company that she was coming back to work and required accommodation. She did not specify what she needed: to use a cane and to continue wearing orthopedic shoes at work. The district manager had long complained about Ms. Barrett's inability to wear high heels, and she received a letter from the company in response. "They told me they couldn't accommodate me. If I came back with a disability, I'd be fired." Ms. Barrett told us that she knew about the issues of accommodations and firing because "I knew they had a disability act." She contacted the EEOC and was advised that she still had her job and should return to it. When she contacted management, however, she was told she no longer had a position.

Ms. Barrett worked with a lawyer whom she later evaluated as ignorant of the law. The Americans with Disabilities Act defines a disability as "a physical or mental impairment that substantially limits one or more major life activities of such individual." As she eventually learned, her heel spurs did not qualify. She recalled that she was surprised when she learned that the ADA did not cover the kind of minor accommodation she needed (i.e., a cane and orthotic shoes to be worn during her work shifts). After a period of unemployment, she found another, more satisfying job but filed for bankruptcy, primarily so she could avoid paying the attorney due to financial need.

As she reflected on her case, Ms. Barrett recalled what she had wanted most: "To be able to come back to work. . . . I didn't feel that it was fair, and the accommodations that I was requesting were minor."

In Ms. Barrett's case, we interviewed her lawyer and opposing counsel. Her attorney, Aaron Edlington (PL24), a white man in his forties, recognized that at the time of the lawsuit there was ambiguity in case law about whether her physical problem would be covered by the ADA. As Mr. Edlington recalled:

> 🎧 This came . . . not long after the ADA was enacted. . . . At that time the courts were not crystal clear as to what was a "substantial limitation." . . . She had mentioned . . . people were making fun of the shoes she wore . . . and there was a statement made to her that "we don't accommodate." The employer said, "We don't accommodate people with disabilities." So that was enough to definitely get her in the door and pursue the case as far as we did.

Mr. Edlington thought the statement "we don't accommodate" was the smoking gun in this case. Meanwhile, the defense attorney, Mitch Weiss (DL24), a fifty-four year-old white man, thought the filing was frivolous:

> 🎧 I think I probably said, well this is a BS [bullshit] kind of claim and we should be able to win. . . . [She] was a fundamentally healthy person who didn't have what I considered to be a disability. . . . I probably had an unsympathetic view of the plaintiff's case.

Moreover, Mr. Weiss said, the defendant employer "took a very hard line on a lot of these things. . . . It was a client that said, 'Hey, we'd rather spend a lot more money to vindicate ourselves than spend less money and throw something [meaning, present a less vigorous defense].'" In addition to ambiguity about the coverage of the ADA for the kinds of problems Ms. Barrett faced, the defense lawyer thought that her case was weaker because she raised questions about her treatment after being terminated rather than during her period of employment.

Introduction

The extended narratives of Catharine Harris and Daris Barrett reveal the interaction of rights, law, and hierarchy at the very origins of employment civil rights disputes in the workplace. As Ms. Harris, Ms. Barrett, and other employees challenge their treatment based on their conception of rights and law, they encounter a workplace hierarchy that rejects their claim and prepares to use law to defend the employing organization.

Both Ms. Harris and Ms. Barrett experienced escalating conflicts with new managers. Both invoked law or organization policy to object to management decisions. Both were subjected to negative performance evaluations that foreshadowed termination. Both came to perceive their identities—membership in legally protected groups—as the cause of their mistreatment. Both said they observed race and/or gender bias operating in the workplace, either against employees or against customers. Both attempted to resolve the issue through their employer's internal EEO channels. And both came to a breaking point that led them to turn to law. Ms. Harris contacted a lawyer while still employed. Ms. Barrett contacted the EEOC and obtained counsel after she was terminated.

The defense narratives in these cases reveal that employers and their lawyers view these conflicts very differently. Both employer organizations reported facts that made the claims seem ambiguous at best and frivolous at worst. Both employers reported that the employee had serious performance issues or misbehavior unrelated to an EEO claim. Both companies' HR departments were unable to resolve the conflict and indeed came to support the management interpretation that the plaintiffs deserved adverse personnel actions. Both employers eventually terminated the complaining employees. And both employers utilized outside legal counsel to minimize the effects of the plaintiffs' rights claims—one by strategic settlement, one by aggressive lawyering that led to the dismissal of the case on summary judgment and the successful defense of that judgment upon appeal. Both defense lawyers disparaged the respective plaintiffs, characterizing Ms. Harris as "not very likeable" and

Ms. Barrett as filing a frivolous claim. In the end neither case resulted in a serious legal challenge to the existing workplace structure.

This chapter examines the workplace origins of employment civil rights lawsuits from both the plaintiff and the defendant perspective. We first analyze the process from the plaintiffs' perspective—how the conflict grew out of the workplace situation, how they came to define their experience as discrimination, how they first sought redress inside the organization, and the chilly reaction they received from their employer when they raised the prospect of a legal claim. We then examine these conflicts from the defendants' perspective. The paramount objective of defendants and their representatives is to prevent litigation and to minimize legal risk to the organization. The way in which defense representatives see themselves as agents of legal compliance colors their view of employees who bring legal claims. In their eyes, conflicts that become claims are, literally, deviant cases. Defendants thus tend to view the claimants as "problem employees" who are, themselves, deviant.

Plaintiffs' Perspective on the Workplace Wars

The workplace situations that plaintiffs come to see as discrimination are often components of broader problems at work. That is, plaintiffs rarely experience discrimination as a singular, distinct event or process. For many, what they come to consider discrimination is not all that different from many other conflicts with management. Discriminatory treatment is different because there is an outside authority—the law—that can provide recourse. Yet the law may not recognize the dynamic, contextual nature of the plaintiff's emerging sense of having been discriminated against. Lawyers and courts look for specific proof, not just of conflict, but of invidious treatment. In the messy world of workplace relationships, a plaintiff's claim may appear legally naïve or incomplete.

Defining Discrimination

Plaintiffs' narratives of discrimination reference a range of workplace situations. Some are complicated and messy; others are clear-cut. This section describes some of the variation in how cases of perceived discrimination present themselves.

While they are on the job, sometimes these individuals are not sure if they are going through a rough patch at work or if they are being discriminated against; sometimes they aren't sure on which basis they are discriminated against. For example, Rick Nolls (P3), a white man in his sixties who had a serious chemical imbalance and eventually won his disability discrimination lawsuit, felt mounting pressure to retire and believed that his age was the reason for negative performance reviews and the company's failure to accommodate his disability. Mr. Nolls had requested accommodations to manage his chemical imbalance, but he felt that the company simply used his condition as a pretext to terminate him because of his age. As his chemical imbalance worsened, someone in the company started a rumor claiming that Mr. Nolls was missing work for psychiatric problems. Personnel officers questioned his ability to carry out his duties, labeling him "crazy" and referring him to a program usually reserved for employees with drug and alcohol problems. All of this amounted to an attack on Mr. Nolls' authority as a supervisor and on his credibility as an aggrieved employee. To Mr. Nolls, it seemed the company saw a relationship between his age and his illness. "They were probably going to start on me anyway because of the age. I was fifty-seven, but because of [my condition] and being sick and weakened, 'Here's an old guy who's already sick and shouldn't be here, get rid of him,' you know."

Evan Oliver (P40), a forty-four year-old white environmental scientist, was similarly being mistreated for various reasons. Mr. Oliver believed that his supervisor, Verna Jackman, resented that he was hired under the company's Excepted Appointment program. He said, "It was just purely a matter of this woman didn't like me being on a handicap program. . . . In one of her depositions she says, 'Well, he was on the handicap, there are a lot of other people who have handicaps but don't claim handicap.'" At another point, Ms. Jackman said Mr. Oliver was "'using the system.'"

Catherine Harris (P12), the hiring and classification manager whose narrative began this chapter, had a slower realization. She verbalized for us her thinking at the time: "Here I am, writing a laundry list. . . . And honestly I don't know if it was one [identity category] more than the other, but I knew that some elements were there for each and I didn't feel like I was making it up or stretching or anything."

Employees like Mr. Nolls, Mr. Oliver, and Ms. Harris define their negative workplace events as discrimination even though they often cannot pinpoint the precise reason they became a target. Confusion about the source of workplace hostility can lead plaintiffs to delay making a claim inside the workplace. In these cases, the different reasons for mistreatment may be illegal, but plaintiffs generally wanted to understand the source of the animus before they were willing to claim discrimination. Other plaintiffs told us they knew right away that they were experiencing discrimination that was prohibited by law (whether we think they are correct or could prove discrimination are different questions). This immediate certainty usually came in cases that lawyers would later call "smoking gun" cases—those in which a manager used sexually explicit or racially hostile language. Lois Smith (P19), for example, knew right away that she was experiencing sexual harassment when she was propositioned by her supervisor after six months on the job. This harassment "happened all the time," Ms. Smith recalled, with the manager telling her, "You know you're attracted to me. You know we're going to do it eventually. I do it with everybody you know who works for me." Gerry Handley (P14), the computer operator whose story of racial harassment began this book, quickly realized he was working in a "poisoned environment" when he transferred into a new department: racist jokes, nicknames, and even signs reading "KKK" appeared in his work area. Kristin Baker (P34), whose narrative followed Mr. Handley's in chapter 1, had no doubt that the sexual harassment she was undergoing was illegal.

We also encountered stories in which the plaintiff clearly perceived mistreatment, but it was not necessarily around a status protected by law. Laila Walter (P33), a forty-year-old white police officer, noticed that her supervisors began to treat her differently after she began a relationship with a fellow police officer. Both had been well liked by superior officers and had strong performance records, but "as soon as we hooked up, that's when our problems began. [Officers] started literally making things up about us. . . . They were trying to get rid of us." Although Ms. Walter and her partner claimed discrimination on the basis of race and sex, it was the unfair treatment stemming from their relationship that caused them to see their situation as discrimination.

Precipitating Events

In all of the discrimination stories we were told, specific events occurred that clarified for our subjects that they were the target of discrimination. Each story is unique, but some precipitating events occur more frequently than others. The primary precipitating event recognized in this research is the arrival of a new manager who begins to treat the plaintiff differently than did their predecessor. Management changes were noted as "part of the problem" in the cases of twenty-one of the plaintiffs we interviewed.[1] Ms. Harris, Ms. Barrett, and Mr. Oliver all indicated a change in supervision as the start of their troubles. Mr. Oliver told us a supportive manager retired. After that,

> No one would step in and say, "This guy's a scientist," you know? "We could use scientists . . . we could either change his job around. . . ." They wanted absolutely no part of that. They were just hell bent on getting me out of there.

Mr. Oliver was terminated shortly before his one-year probationary period expired.

New management and perceived elitism changed Christopher Coker's workplace (P27). Mr. Coker was a middle-aged African American attorney who was the graduate of a night law school and worked in a government law department. In what Mr. Coker described as an effort "to upgrade [the department] by getting more attorneys who had finished from top law schools to replace those who had been there," a new supervisor arrived. Mr. Coker and his colleagues perceived "they were being attacked, pushed out. So we all were accused of [poor] performance and were being replaced." The stress of the changing environment led some of the old guard to go on workmen's compensation and others to leave for other jobs. Mr. Coker and two of his coworkers eventually decided to file an age discrimination lawsuit.

New management and the changed expectations and styles of work that come with reshuffled teams are by no means the only precipitating events. Sometimes there is a particular event, such as a surprise firing or the revelation of information that suggests the employer has been engaging in discrimination. Billy Deeds (P2), a forty-nine year-old African American machine operator, filed for race, disability, and religion discrimination. Mr. Deeds was fired shortly after returning from a leave of absence for mental health issues. Having become a devout Christian in the months before his termination, Mr. Deeds often read the Bible during his lunch breaks. His supervisors allowed it so long as it did not interfere with his work. Mr. Deeds was surprised when he was called into a meeting with the personnel supervisor.

> [The factory manager] had my supervisor come and get me, turn my machine off. . . . Everybody that runs [the company] was in that office. "Have a seat." They tell me to sit down. . . . So [the personnel supervisor] started lecturing me . . ."I'm sick of you, I'm tired of you, I'm just sick of everybody staring at you." . . . I said, ". . . What? My Bible, laying over there by the machine? I'm not saying anything to anybody." . . . I'm shocked and all, trying to wonder, "Who did this?"

Mr. Deeds was fired and escorted out of the factory.

After she was injured in a car accident, Murielle Byrd (P37), an African American accounting clerk, requested her workplace medical records. She planned to use them in a claim about the accident. She told us:

> I showed [the medical records] to my mother, who was a retired nurse. And she said, "Do you know what they were doing?" I said, "No." She said, "[W]ell, this test is for syphilis, and this one"—which I could read myself—"tested . . . for sickle cell anemia." And they did a pregnancy test.

Ms. Byrd later learned that other women and African American employees in her workplace were subject to the same battery of tests without their consent. The tests were administered ten years earlier during required pre-employment physicals.

The Slow Burn

Most often, discrimination claims arise from multiple encounters and evolve over time, escalating in such a way that the workplace becomes very uncomfortable for the employee. Recall the series of episodes that Ms. Harris reported about her relationship with her new manager or the ongoing conflicts that Ms. Barrett reported with her employer. Other plaintiffs shared similar stories of complicated and drawn-out negative encounters with management.

Matthew Brown's "workplace war" began with management after his promotion. Mr. Brown (P9), an African American retail account manager in his forties, faced continued hostility from his supervisors, all of whom were white men. The position normally required an undergraduate degree, but Mr. Brown was given the job before he finished his degree, which he was completing at night. Rumors began to circulate that Mr. Brown had been promoted on the basis of his race, rather than his qualifications, and he began to have frequent conflicts with his new manager, who aggressively criticized his work. When Mr. Brown would seek a second opinion to confirm that he was in fact performing his duties and producing good work, the manager would respond with insults and, in one instance, by throwing things. These tantrums stopped after Mr. Brown took the issue to the HR office. The manager resigned shortly after. After a second manager quit, coworkers began to accuse Mr. Brown of pushing talented people out of the company and of enjoying "special protection" against termination because the company feared a race discrimination suit. Although he saw the increasingly racialized nature of these accusations, Mr. Brown felt reluctant to, in his words, "play the race card," since the messages being sent to him were, "'How dare you. You're African American. You've been given an opportunity. You should play ball.'"

Looking for Allies and Support

Regardless of how the determination is made that a workplace conflict has reached the level of discrimination, when plaintiffs become embroiled in a workplace conflict, they often reach out for support. This may be within their employing organization or among outside professionals and advocacy groups. In a small number of cases, employees organize in the workplace or in litigation.

COWORKER SUPPORT. Some plaintiffs reported coworker support either because some of their coworkers were coplaintiffs or because they were part of a group of workers seeking redress of grievances. As we detailed in chapter 3, having coplaintiffs or being part of a class makes a difference for how cases are likely to conclude. Those who had coworkers in the action with them included Mr. Handley (P14), the African American computer operator, who spoke of the coworkers who joined him in fighting racial harassment. Floyd Kelly's (P7) case stemmed from his role as spokesperson for a group of African American employees who complained of unfair promotion practices. Christopher Coker (P27) was part of a group of old-guard lawyers who joined together in filing a lawsuit. Laila Walter (P33) filed suit along with her coworker/fiancé. Denise

Slayton (P36) was a member of a class action against a retail chain. And Sal DeLuca (P39) was among a group of employees who challenged the elimination of their department and their jobs with an age discrimination lawsuit.

The other thirty-five plaintiffs we interviewed pursued their legal claims alone, but many spoke of their efforts—often disappointing—to gain support from others in the course of their workplace dispute.

HUMAN RESOURCES PERSONNEL. In many cases, employees turn to management before a lawyer or the EEOC. This may come in the form of a supervisor or, more often, the HR or equal employment office. However, these actors often support other managers in the organization and, rather than providing the plaintiff help, may begin to regard the complaining employee as the problem. Some plaintiffs we interviewed reported an "a-ha" moment when they realized their company's HR department was ultimately loyal to the organization's needs, not to theirs.[2]

HR personnel seemed helpful, particularly in their initial interactions. Mitchell Collins (P6), a white skilled tradesman in his forties, told us:

> They were acting like they were very helpful [but] they never actually offered to contact anybody. But they seemed to be very helpful, which, of course, they were not. . . . I truly believed that their job was to help the employees! [Now] people tell me, "Well, their number one job is the company."

For numerous plaintiffs HR professionals were privately supportive but would not advocate for the employee to others in the company. For example, Matthew Brown met with the director of HR who, as Mr. Brown recalled, told him, "'Look man, I've got a wife and kids and a house in Beverly Hills,'" which Mr. Brown took to mean, "'I'm not in the fight with you. . . . I get what you're saying, because I'm black and you're black, but I gotta keep this job, and it's not going to work out in accounting for you.'"

Ms. Harris's narrative, with which we began this chapter, includes a similar anecdote about the city EEO officer. In Ms. Harris's terms, it became clear that he would not risk his job to support her allegations, even if he believed they were valid. Within the formal channels that were ostensibly there to address employee grievances, discrimination complaints were rarely adequately addressed from the plaintiffs' perspective.

OTHER POTENTIAL ALLIES: UNIONS AND DOCTORS. A few of our plaintiffs worked in unionized organizations. While the unions were helpful in securing certain benefits, such as workmen's compensation, none of the unions played a significant role in supporting the plaintiffs' assertions of discrimination. Plaintiffs generally agreed (and their lawyers confirmed) that unions were not motivated to use their power in a one-off kind of dispute. Peter Nichelson (P56), a white police officer in his fifties who alleged age and race discrimination, reported that his union liaison gave him the names of a few union attorneys, but "nobody wanted to touch it because it's 'reverse discrimination' against [the city]." He seemed to think union lawyers saw the case as possibly harmful to future union negotiations and that a race discrimination charge brought by a white man was politically unpopular.

Plaintiffs in disability and medical leave cases depend on the medical opinions of doctors, but sometimes plaintiffs are embroiled in a battle of medical opinions, as when an employer requires that a physician the company retains evaluate the employee. In some of the cases, our plaintiffs saw doctors as heroic, in that they provided objective medical opinions that cut against the interest of the employer. In other cases, the plaintiff perceived a negative medical report as evidence of a pro-employer bias. We return to this topic of the medicalization of disability discrimination cases in chapter 9.

After the Complaint

After the employee's complaint became known to others in the organization (especially if it was revealed that the worker was defining the problem as possible discrimination), things moved quickly. Employees told us they were told not to go forward, warned of negative consequences, and often terminated.

Mr. Collins's problems with HR went beyond their refusal to help; having discovered that he had consulted an attorney, HR personnel seemed to actively undermine his reputation. Mr. Collins told us, "I had excellent reports on what a good employee I was for the two years, and then, of course, when they wanted to terminate me, well, I was a very poor employee." According to Mr. Collins, a personnel manager told him he "had no right" to contact an attorney.

Sometimes HR or other internal supporters did not have power in the dispute between management and employee. Rick Nolls talked to a personnel officer who was embarrassed by the company's failure to accommodate but did not try to intervene in Mr. Nolls's situation: "He didn't know what to say. I said, 'Well, why, what's with it?' He spun around and walked away from me, because he was so embarrassed he didn't want to say."

A number of plaintiffs told us their termination came shortly after meeting with HR. This included Evan Oliver, who reported that he had "seen his termination coming" and "went and tried to fight through every channel." Mr. Oliver went on, "I went and spoke to the handicap coordinator. . . . I tried to see if he would go to bat for me, and apparently he didn't . . . or no one listened to him." Annie Daley (P18), who we will meet in depth in chapter 7, was terminated two weeks after consulting HR about her supervisor.

Defendants' Perspectives on the Workplace Wars

Defendants perceive the origins of employment civil rights claims in very different terms. Defendants and their attorneys are aware of the tremendous asymmetries in the disputes. As Donald Bryant (DL71), a forty-seven-year-old white attorney with a large law firm, explained:

> The emotion is on the plaintiff's side of the equation in these cases. Another favorite expression of mine is that "Employment law is the family law of business law." And what I mean by that is people spend so much time in their jobs in America today and associate themselves so much with what they do. . . . If you terminate somebody's employment, you've not just taken away their livelihood, their ability to pay their mortgage, send their kids to school, put food on the table, forget all those issues. More important than that almost is what it does to their psychological makeup. You've taken away what they *are* . . . . That's what fuels a lot of this employment litigation. It's an emotional reaction. And there is no other catharsis for it. So, it has to go somewhere.

What is a *war* for plaintiffs is more often a *problem* for defendants. The persons we interviewed on the defendant side of these cases (inside counsel, HR or EEO officers, and outside defense counsel) are far less personally involved in the circumstances leading up to a case. While all of our plaintiff interviewees remember their cases, often in great detail, those on the defendant side generally remember the plaintiffs' cases only vaguely, if at all. If we had gained access to the managers who directly worked with the plaintiffs, we might have gained a far more personal account. The fact that we seldom gained such access is a feature of employment civil rights litigation. The lawyers and EEO/HR professionals take over these disputes when a charge or lawsuit is filed. Their task is to manage the response to the individual case and to implement programs that prevent workplace conflicts from escalating into charges of discrimination at the EEOC or in federal court. Indeed, to understand how these professionals treat plaintiffs in filed cases, it is necessary to look at their broader role in administering EEO policies.

The Legalized Workplace: Bringing Law In and Keeping Law Out

HR professionals and in-house attorneys attempt to manage workplace disputes in ways that maximize the employer's organizational interests, tempered by a professed (and perhaps actual) commitment to discrimination-free workplaces. Doing so involves two seemingly contradictory goals: bringing law *to* the workplace and keeping law *out* of the workplace.

Elsewhere, two of the authors of this book have argued that lawyers in business occupy three ideal-typical roles in organizations: cop, counsel, and entrepreneur.[3] Lawyer-cops limit their advice to legal matters without interjecting much, if any, business advice. Lawyer-counsel mix business and legal advice, and lawyer-entrepreneurs give more weight to business analysis than to lawyering. These ideal-types map neatly onto the behavior of the lawyers we interviewed, as well as their HR counterparts. Here, we emphasize the roles of those people in organizations who hope to defuse employment discrimination claims before they rise to the level of an EEOC complaint or lawsuit.

Our sample of defendant interviewees includes twenty interviews with inside counsels and HR/EEO officers and twenty with outside defense counsels. These representatives work for a range of defendant organizations. Although the sample is relatively small, it has the great virtue of being a random sample of a larger random sample. Six of the defendant organizations are in the public sector, ranging from a state government unit to a research institute to a branch of the US military. Most of the private-sector defendants are large, for-profit corporations, but the sample includes some smaller, privately held businesses. A range of industries is included in the defendant organizations.

These organizations vary on a continuum of the legalized workplace, as that concept has been developed in the literature on employment civil rights and organizations.[4] Some defendant-employers (usually larger ones, such as the federal government) have fully developed internal complaint processing systems for employment civil rights claims. Many employers also have complaint hotlines and ombudsmen. Smaller organizations often are on the other side of the continuum, with little evidence of legalized accountability in the workplace. They may have no formal EEO structures or distinct HR departments. These different organizational environments affect how claims originate and how they are dealt with in the early phases of the dispute.

The position of the respondent in the defendant organization shapes their views around the origins of claims. Many inside counsel and HR/EEO officers acknowledged that, in organizations as large as theirs, they could not guarantee that discrimination never took place. A small number of defendant respondents recounted instances in which their investigations uncovered discriminatory behavior, and they explained that they took actions to redress these incidents. Several respondents made observations on how the employer organization, often through their leadership, had improved its fidelity to law. Thus, the defendant representatives are less patient with plaintiff employees.

BRINGING LAW TO THE WORKPLACE. Both inside and outside counsel portray themselves as bringing law to the workplace. These lawyers describe themselves and their departments' roles in very entrepreneurial terms. They have instituted trainings, processes, and, more broadly, norms of fairness and equality into their workplaces.

Many told us that, when they were consulted "early enough," they were able to intervene and halt discriminatory actions. One such "success story" was recounted by Jim Schultz (DL22), an eighty-one-year-old law firm attorney who acted as general counsel for several small municipalities. Mr. Schultz's advice was dispositive in both the hiring and firing of one of the plaintiffs in this study, Officer Stern. Mr. Schultz told us:

> 🎧 I got a call from the chief of police. He said, "We have a young man who has passed the physical, has passed the mental, gone through the Board of Fire and Police Commissioners, highly recommended for an opening, but he has [a chemical imbalance]. Can we hire him?" I said, "Well, first of all, I have to tell you that we cannot discriminate because of his health as long as

> we can reasonably accommodate him." And I said, "Does he self-medicate? How does he handle his [condition]?" And the chief said, "Well, I believe that he takes [medication] every morning himself." I said, "Well, I will advise you that if he's otherwise qualified, you ought to hire him." So he did.

By bringing the law to the process (or more aptly, by the chief's recognizing he needed to go to the law), Mr. Schultz was able to prevent hiring discrimination. He quoted the exact legal requirements to the chief, and they engaged in a cursory analysis of the facts in a very lawyer-cop kind of way.

What started as a set of decisions to bring law *into* the workplace ended with the termination of Officer Stern on a rationale of keeping law *out* of the workplace. After six months of good service, but still within the one-year statutory probationary period, Officer Stern was found unconscious in his patrol car, crashed in a ditch. At that point, Mr. Schultz said:

> I felt strongly, and I advised the Police Department, that he should be terminated. The man is out on the street in a squad car with a gun. . . . There is nothing we can do to accommodate him. . . . We couldn't take a chance of having a police officer have that recur again.

Here the good employment decision to not discriminate on the basis of a disability ran into the fear of legal liability if such an incident occurred again and resulted in harm to civilians. Officer Stern filed suit under the ADA. Mr. Schultz said he was not surprised, but he was sure terminating Officer Stern was the right decision for the municipality: "If a court imposed [rehiring him] upon us, so be it, but we did not want to be responsible, because God forbid if something happened."

We see in Mr. Schultz's version of his role in the case a commitment to legality. By his telling, he virtually orders his client not to discriminate on the basis of a disability. But then when a risk is realized, he is equally clear in advising that the safety of the public demands the firing of Officer Stern.

The most frequent and entrepreneurial way in which inside counsel and EEO officers bring law to the workplace is not by responding to claims, then, but through the training of managers and employees about what constitutes discrimination. These trainings and workshops serve the dual purpose of helping employees understand what they should not be doing in the workplace and, as defense lawyers told us, contributing to future legal defense strategies as proof that the organization takes antidiscrimination mandates seriously.

The most entrepreneurial lawyers spoke energetically of service to their "clients" (who, for internal defense counsel, were different departments of the same organization in which they worked) and talked about reaching out to be proactive about education and training. After the passage of the ADA, for example, Kate Duffy (D63), a white in-house counsel in her fifties, told us that the legal department in which she worked

> went out . . . to various clients and we would talk to them about the provisions of the act. . . . It took a long time for the EEOC to come out with regulations, and so we were sort of left without a lot of guidance for a period of time. But . . . we tried to be proactive.

This example shows commitment to law even when the organization is not completely sure what the law requires. For entrepreneurial lawyers seeking to make the cost-case for the legal department, this kind of training is a tangible way to promote their services in the organization. It not only informs and puts managers on notice, but it also serves to bolster the role of the HR or legal department within the company.

Another preventive measure reported by lawyers and HR officers in defendant organizations is systematically analyzing where the discrimination claims are coming from so as to tackle them at the source. Elena Mendoza (D21), a Latina fifty-four-year-old HR/EEO officer in the US military, described such an approach. Ms. Mendoza's staff had EEO responsibility for large numbers of military bases and defense-contracting operations around the country. Where they found a concentration of complaints, they would investigate and conduct training to attempt to ameliorate the problem.

Marilyn Cole (DR71), a fifty-five-year-old white inside counsel to a finance corporation, explained that when she is referred to a case, she directly contacts the managers involved in order to avoid—in her words—"a spin" HR officers might put on the facts: "I prefer—rather than just simply rely on what human resources is telling me—to actually get the manager in the room and hear from the manager. . . . Our human resources department—they're well trained and they're good. [But] they filter the information a little bit." Ms. Cole's approach indicates a potential tension between HR and law departments, where the lawyers feel they have special expertise evaluating legal risk for the company.

Defendant informants see their role as evaluating whether other actors in the organization might have discriminated. One tool they use are ethics hotlines. Joyce Mason (D62), a white inside counsel in her forties, told us that her company has "omnibus lines [that] give you an opportunity to make changes that you need to make."

Whether through her investigation or calls to the omnibus line, Ms. Mason and all of the lawyers told us that their company would absolutely deal with discrimination if they found it. It's just that they almost never do.

Some defense representatives commented on their role in protecting employees from discrimination. Nicole Price (D64), a white forty-seven-year-old inside counsel for a large nonprofit health care organization, spoke of this concern whenever a charge is brought to her attention.

> I always think of it from the perspective of, "Is there something going on that we need to be aware of and to investigate?" And to ensure there isn't discrimination. I mean, obviously, with 1,300 employees, I don't know what's going on in every single pocket of the organization, and yet we are committed to our employees, you know. They're one of our great resources, and so we don't want to have discrimination going on.

In addition to ethics hotlines that allow employees to make confidential complaints about employment problems, defense representatives described how they encouraged employees to bring potential discrimination problems to them right away. Bernard Farkas (D72), a white seventy-one-year-old senior HR officer in a product manufacturing company, said: "We pride ourselves on doing the right thing in terms of meeting with the employees constantly and letting them know their rights, let them know they have someone that they can talk to, let them know if they have a complaint that rather than going to the EEOC they have an avenue to pursue."

Note that in several of the plaintiffs' narratives discussed in the previous section, plaintiffs reported being surprised that they received cool to hostile reactions from the HR department when they raised the possibility of an employment civil rights claim. We initially thought this reflected naiveté on the part of plaintiffs, but while doing our analysis, we could see that HR may be responsible for (mis)leading employees to think they will be receptive to such complaints. The reality for at least some employees may prove very different.

Lawyers and HR professionals import rules from legislatures, courts, and regulatory agencies and implement them in company practices, structures, and policies. In so doing, these management professionals have a lot of power to define organizational practices *and* discrimination. Although many hold a commitment to the ideals of workplace antidiscrimination law, the stories we heard reveal that they are actively managerializing the workplace by redefining incidents as productivity, communication, and training problems, but only rarely as discrimination.

LEGAL RISK MANAGEMENT: KEEPING LAW OUT OF THE WORKPLACE. Law is a double-edged sword for employment civil rights in the workplace. A major HR personnel concern is that they ensure organizational compliance with antidiscrimination law; a closely related, even predominant concern is with limiting legal risk to the organization. These professionals deploy their knowledge of antidiscrimination law to protect the employer—indeed, to protect managerial hierarchy.

Arbitration is perhaps the most significant tool organizations use to avoid discrimination lawsuits.[5] After experiencing several threatened lawsuits, Krista Hewick, the white, fifty-something general counsel for a large retailer, reported that her company had decided to prevent federal lawsuits with a mandatory arbitration clause for all employees: "I said, 'I am done with the bologna!' And we put an arbitration clause in our agreements." Similarly, Ms. Mason (D62) told us that, since the company added an arbitration clause, "they've already seen a big drop off [in lawsuits], and will see even more of a drop off as they hire more employees."

If It's Wrong We Fix It. If Not, We Fight It. In his interview, Harold Ward (D67), a white inside counsel and HR officer in his sixties, firmly articulated a message that came through in many of the interviews with defendant lawyers and HR professionals:

> HW: Our philosophy is if we're wrong, we fix it. And we do things wrong. [W]e have fifty-six plants, fifty-six facilities, and we screw up. We do things we shouldn't do. Or they do the right thing, but they don't do it the right way. . . . And we fix those things, but we don't settle very often and we don't lose. . . . We've gotten costs five times in the last four years.

I: Wow. Can you actually recover them?
HW: I have liens on two houses.

Mr. Ward acknowledges the probability that his company occasionally does "things we shouldn't do" with respect to employment civil rights law or that they fail to document that they did things properly. In those instances, the organization "fixes" its errors, apparently by settling with the complaining employee. But if the company thinks they are right, they fight back. His reference to "costs" means that after the company won the primary lawsuit, they sued the plaintiff for costs incurred by the company in defending against the lawsuit. "Getting costs" means the company won those suits and, in trying to recover the costs, Mr. Ward claims he has put liens on the former employees' homes.

Training as Risk Reduction, Not Rights Realization. Daniel Jain (D12), a biracial EEO officer in the city government involved in the Catherine Harris case, started with the city after the Harris case was resolved. Mr. Jain spoke of his intense efforts to expand training for city managers and employees. Now the training is mandatory, but Mr. Jain also believes training people about discrimination may lead to more claims:

> I'm telling the managers, "I'm trying to protect you and the City, and the more we work together, the more likely it is we can reduce litigation . . . and obviously with people getting more educated, well, they'll take a few more chances [at making discrimination claims]. . . . We don't want 'em all to understand what their rights are."

Mr. Jain wants the managers to learn how to avoid risk and consult the EEO office when questions arise, but he believes that training may encourage claiming behavior among employees. Later in the interview, he describes how he tries to discourage employees from making discrimination charges by having them fill out a form detailing the evidence for their claim.

> Most of the people that bring complaints in here—I'm saying 3, 4, 5 % of the workforce—we're not talking about the smartest . . . nails in the box or anything. These are folks that sometimes they have attitude and/or conduct and/or behavioral problems. Sometimes they mix discrimination and stuff. They try and mask their performance issues. . . . Me, it's "show me a

> *prima-facie* case. Show me you met the legal threshold." If they don't understand that when they first come in, my job and my staff's job is explain to 'em what . . . their burden is. . . . I don't want 'em leaving here not understanding [what it means to] have met their burden [of proof].

In most defendant organizations in which we conducted interviews, training and other systems result in a tiny fraction of potential charges being filed. Ms. Hewick described how, in her retail chain organization of two hundred thousand employees, her office had opened three hundred "situation files"—employee "situations" that might result in a formal complaint. Of these, she reported that only five or so produced EEOC or federal court filings. We asked how they had achieved such a low rate of formal complaints given the number of their employees:

> We work really hard. . . . When I started, we got on the road and we trained people. We had a lot of training . . . basic EEO law . . . red flags, [and] things to watch for. "If you see this, you call us. . . ." . . . It's easier to get out of the way of the train if you see it as a little tiny headlight a mile away as opposed to [when] it's already on you.

Ms. Hewick went on to explain that she helps supervisors manage with relatively little obvious input from her department (although her department is running the show from behind the scenes):

> [W]e try to resolve the thing and help the supervisor resolve it. Help the supervisor see his or her managerial responsibilities and obligations, but also his or her managerial rights. . . . We don't allow employees to walk all over a supervisor or walk all over a team. [We] expect everyone to show up and do the best they can, understanding that the best you can do some days is not as good as somebody else given maybe some kind of medical situation. . . . Basically it's walking people—supervisors—through how to respond at the very, very beginning. . . . It's easier to blow out a match than it is to extinguish a conflagration.

Informants occasionally referred to the litigation benefit of training programs. Troy Pedlow (D9), the fifty-three-year-old white inside counsel in the company sued by Matthew Brown, suggested that training "may not reduce the number of filings," but "it would be more effective in establishing defenses when those charges come."

The process of keeping law out of the workplace is accomplished by identifying problems as early as possible, by helping potential plaintiffs understand the difficulty of pursuing their case, by transitioning the problem from a legal one to a miscommunication, and by empowering managers to "know their rights."

Pre-Emptive Efforts: Early Involvement, Planning for Terminations, Severance Packages, and Waivers

Both our quantitative data and the observations of defendant representatives demonstrate that most employment civil rights claims begin with a termination. As such, terminations involve focused attention on limiting legal risks. For example, some organizations require the legal department be given advance clearance of a termination.

HR and legal departments prefer to be involved in a workplace dispute early on and to oversee the permission to terminate. Early intervention by HR and legal department personnel are important for defusing conflict, and they often are considered the key to an effective "termination" (meaning a firing that does not result in a lawsuit). We had the following exchange with Mr. Pedlow:

I: And so, if you're involved at the get-go, you know right from the beginning, what are the steps you're going to take to ensure that everything is done properly before a termination?

TP: We are going to speak with the employee's immediate superior (and very often that superior's superior) and find out what their perspective is on what the problems are and why it is they want to take whatever employment action it is they want to take. . . . [We ask them], "How is [Matthew] Brown different from anybody else? Have you had the same problem with anybody else? How have you addressed this problem with that somebody else? Have you been consistent? Have you documented it? Have you spoken with the employee? Is he aware of your view that there are some deficiencies? Have you given him a chance to correct or improve on those deficiencies?"

If the answers to any of these questions raise the risk of legal liability, Mr. Pedlow will not allow the "employment decision" to go forward. He will instruct the supervisor about how to meet conditions for a successful termination.

Similarly, at the health care nonprofit in which Nicole Price is inside counsel, the law department reviews terminations. She said,

> Before anyone is terminated . . . we have a discussion within my office. . . ." Is there sufficient documentation? Is there sufficient evidence? Have we examined this to ensure that that there has been no discrimination?"

In addition to individual terminations, companies conduct "reductions in force" or "reorganizations" that mean terminating many employees at once. In those situations, attorneys try to predict the "potentially litigious" employees. Mr. Ward told us how he protects against such employees" by taking special measures to prepare for winning a motion for summary judgment if it comes to litigation:

> I'd rather spend the money up front and get everything right and then win at summary judgment. . . . That's . . . another reason we prevail at summary judgment. We do a lot of work up front. . . . Lucas Steidley, for example . . . and two other employees were the high-risk of litigation, but we terminated three hundred eighty some people . . . and he was the only one that sued us out of the whole group. The rest of them signed, took their severance pay, and went away.

Marilyn Cole, inside counsel to a financial corporation, described her company's "generous severance pay plan" that helped employees "land on their feet . . . but we also [do so because] it resolves a lot of disputes early on, puts things to rest.'" Occasionally Ms. Cole's company "will sweeten the severance offer" if her team believes the "situation is dicey and perhaps the manager hasn't crossed all the T's and dotted all the I's." The result is a very small number of charges and even fewer lawsuits.

Employer strategy around termination means few potential claims ripen into formal charges. Toward this goal, lawyers take additional precautions to document the basis for the employment action. If the facts are "dicey," they can provide a somewhat larger settlement offer to preempt litigation. As we see below and in future chapters, the small number of plaintiffs who complain often are seen as greedy, misinformed, or irrational.

Interestingly, in identifying who might be "litigation prone," the lawyers and HR personnel continue to think of employees in categorical terms according to prohibited categories. Although they say "litigation prone," this routinely is code for racial minorities, women, people with disabilities, and older employees.

Explaining the Rare Lawsuit

Given their efforts to avoid litigation, how do defendant representatives explain cases that lead to lawsuits? While some informants acknowledged there may have been a management failure, more often they blame the plaintiff or the plaintiff's lawyer.

MISMANAGEMENT THAT IS NOT ILLEGAL. In interviewing, sometimes the most interesting comments are made after the recorder is turned off. This occurred in the interview with Ms. Duffy, the inside counsel for a county government. What follows is the verbatim recall by one of us:

> Okay, so after I turned off the tape recorder, she said, and these are very close to direct quotes, if not direct quotes, "You know, when I was practicing employment discrimination law, I had the sense that most often what happened had been a breakdown in personal relationships. So there's a worker who'd been doing a good job for a lot of years that got a new supervisor. The supervisor decided they weren't doing such a good job, and if we had just treated them better on the way out or explained their demotion better, we wouldn't have had as many lawsuits as we've had."

A frequent theme in interviews with defendant representatives is that management may mistreat employees, but not in ways that violate antidiscrimination law. Alexandra Parker (D65), a fifty-year-old white inside counsel for a finance corporation, supported this view:

> There's always something we could have done better in terms of management. I don't think most of the cases involve discrimination, but I do think most of them involve some kind of mismanagement . . . and the employee may perceive [that] as discrimination.

A particular form of mismanagement occurs in unexpected termination. Mr. Pedlow suggested that most cases were frivolous, but singled out surprise terminations as a cause of litigation:

> Based on my experience, 80 to 85% of the cases have little or no merit. . . . The biggest reason employees file discrimination charges or employment lawsuits, generally, is because they are truly and sincerely surprised at the action being taken and don't understand why. They just don't see it. I mean [the employee perspective is], "I've been here fifteen years, everybody's been telling me I've been doing such a great job. All of a sudden, the last six months, I'm toxic waste. Nobody ever told me."

ILL-INFORMED, UNREASONABLE, AND CRAZY PLAINTIFFS. A recurrent theme is that employees misunderstand the law and are ill-informed in filing a charge. Ms. Price explains:

> Oftentimes it's somebody may have made a remark to somebody that that person took offense to. . . . We have tended to be very successful on [cases like that], because a lot of people don't understand. They take it to extremes. They hear one remark and . . . get very upset or they feel like they can't tell their supervisor, so they'll actually file a complaint, but those typically aren't going to be found to be discriminatory. We may need to do some work with that area and figure out what's going on, but they aren't discrimination. . . . Yelling at an employee is not discrimination, but . . . some people believe that it should be.

Defendant representatives also often see plaintiffs as out of touch with reality. For example, Troy Pedlow said Matthew Brown "was a nut." In future chapters we examine in greater depth the denigration of plaintiffs.

GREEDY PLAINTIFF, GREEDY PLAINTIFF'S LAWYER. Defendant representatives attribute the filing of a lawsuit to greedy plaintiffs or greedy plaintiffs' lawyers. We return to Harold Ward's description of Lucas Steidley, the employee who filed a claim after a major round of layoffs:

> The VP of sales, who had never met Lucas Steidley, said, "I don't need this level, I can get rid of this level and go direct to the salespeople." Boom, Lucas got fired. We offered Lucas severance, as we do everybody. Lucas made an outrageous demand. He wanted five years of pay or something like that.

Mr. Ward characterizes Mr. Steidley as an outlier: every other terminated employee took the severance and left, but Mr. Steidley was "outrageous."

When a senior manager tried to persuade Mr. Steidley to take the employer's offer, they did not succeed. Mr. Ward continued:

> By then, Lucas was convinced that he got fired because he was black. He got fired because he was the only account manager, national account manager, in the whole division. Yes, he was the only black one. That was a true statement. He was the only one over age sixty. That was also a true statement. But what I've found is people get, they are so convinced that it couldn't be just an objective business decision, somebody had it out for them, and we call it "playing [the] race card."

In similarly racialized language, Mr. Pedlow recalled his reaction to Mr. Brown's lawsuit:

> TP: I remember my initial reaction—not in particularly artful terms—was, "Oh, this guy's a nut. This is going nowhere. . . ." Certain cases that are absolutely meritless, even though it's not the right cost benefit analysis, you'll fight. Whatever it takes, you'll fight because sometimes you just need to send the message. Brown's was one of those.
>
> LBN: Your view was that it was absolutely meritless, so. . . . ?
>
> TP: He was holding us up. Our view was he was holding us up, and, you know, if you have a legitimate grievance, we can discuss it. We'll address it. We're not unreasonable. We're not bad people. We'll try to get close to where everybody wants to get, but if you're going to hold me up, it's not going to happen.

In associating Mr. Brown's race discrimination claim with a hold-up, Mr. Pedlow, probably unconsciously, invoked the stereotype of African American male criminality. In saying the defendant was not unreasonable or bad and would listen to legitimate grievances, he implies the reverse of the plaintiff.

Defendant representatives often accuse plaintiffs of trying to exploit their protected status for illegitimate financial gain. Mr. Jain, the advocate of EEO law training for his city government employer, was frustrated by a worker claiming disability, then discrimination. Jain suggested that "the guy really didn't want to come back to work." When the disability period expired, the employee claimed discrimination. Mr. Jain was furious at what he saw as the employee's audacity.

Conclusion

From their origins in the workplace, we can see the problematic and contested character of employment civil rights claims. As employees come to see themselves as the targets of invidious discrimination, it often is too late to achieve an amicable resolution that protects their rights. As they begin to challenge management decisions about whether they have been sexually harassed, whether they have a disability that can be reasonably accommodated, about whether they are being treated unfairly due to their age or gender or race, a circle already has begun to close against them. The professionals who administer policies to eliminate workplace discrimination already and invisibly are working with management to minimize the legal risk to the organization that might be posed by their claim if it enters the legal system.

While potential plaintiffs see the law as a source of rights from which they can argue for fair treatment, they may not be aware of the asymmetry of power they will confront in trying to use the law to effect those rights. The initial skirmishes in workplace wars are between employees in legally protected categories and their coworkers and supervisors. Inside lawyers and HR professionals see themselves upholding antidiscrimination law in the workplace and managing the legal risks posed by the potential claiming behavior of employees. It is not surprising, as we show in future chapters, that they take a combative view of employees who "cross the line" to invoke the outside legal system. They typically join with management to treat the employee claimant as a maladjusted individual who misunderstands the law and who must be treated as a potential adversary in a legal contest.

For most plaintiffs, the workplace war results in their termination. Unprepared for what happens when they cross the line from being an employee to being a litigant, they soon learn they are leaving one battle zone for another, entering the world of lawyers and litigation.

CHAPTER FIVE

Representation and Race

Finding a Lawyer, Screening Clients, and the Production of Racial Disparities

A critical step for plaintiffs who file an employment civil rights lawsuit is finding an effective attorney. As we saw in chapter 3, almost one in four plaintiffs fail to obtain counsel, and these plaintiffs have far worse case outcomes than represented plaintiffs. In this chapter we return to our quantitative dataset to demonstrate that people of color are far less likely to obtain legal representation. We then examine possible explanations, using interviews with plaintiffs about their search for a lawyer and interviews with plaintiffs' lawyers about their client selection processes. It appears that racial inequality has an unspoken but pervasive influence on the search for lawyers and the selection of clients.

This process ultimately disfavors African American employees dramatically, and so the production of racial disparities is a major focus of this chapter. Specifically, African Americans' experiences are characterized by racialized disadvantages that stem from racial inequality in society at large, not necessarily from the merits of their cases. Meanwhile, attorneys voice many criticisms of potential clients in seemingly neutral language, but their views may be race-coded or at the very least can be disproportionately consequential for African Americans. In short, there are indications of institutional and interpersonal racism in the dynamics of obtaining legal representation. We open with the story of one African American plaintiff's disheartening experience of pursuing his legal case without representation.

Plaintiff's Story: Philip Jacobson's Case against the US Military

Philip Jacobson (P21) was a thirty-four-year-old African American production administrator in a government printing plant. After several failed attempts to gain a promotion and friction with managers, he went to HR, internal EEO officers, his union, the Fair Labor Relations Board, then finally to the EEOC. He filed a Title VII race discrimination claim in federal court in 1991 after receiving a negative finding from the EEOC. His case was dismissed for want of prosecution—meaning that he failed to take specific administrative actions stipulated by the court.

Mr. Jacobson came from a modest, working-class family; his mother was a church pianist and his father a longshoreman. He had completed high school and some college, earning an associate's degree in paralegal studies. At the time of his case, he was making about $30,000 a year and was married to a woman with disabilities caused by multiple sclerosis. Together, they had five children.

Mr. Jacobson was not a stranger to law or lawyers. He had used an attorney to deal with his mother's probate, and later he saw lawyers for his own probate matters, worker's compensation, and a problem with his home loan.

Mr. Jacobson initially tried to find a lawyer for his discrimination claim using the phonebook. He found what he believed to be the only lawyer in the area handling federal cases like his, but that attorney "wanted $500, and I didn't have any money. I had five children and a disabled wife." The discrimination lawyer suggested that there was little to do unless Mr. Jacobson got fired, at which point he could claim lost wages. When asked if he had looked for pro bono options, he said, "I didn't. I was looking. I tried. I thought maybe the union but there was just so many things going on my life. I had to work." Financially strapped and time-bound, Mr. Jacobson decided to file *pro se*. His case was terminated when he missed a hearing.

When we interviewed Mr. Jacobson, he was unaware that he had lost his case. Instead he recalled:

> I never heard anything from them. I don't think I ever heard anything from the federal court either. It was like I just filed and that was it. No, they didn't even acknowledge it. It was like, okay fine.

Mr. Jacobson experienced a dismissal for want of prosecution without even understanding it. His experience illustrates some of the many difficulties plaintiffs have obtaining adequate legal representation, the dire consequences if they do not, and the challenges disproportionately experienced by African Americans.

Introduction

In this chapter we locate Mr. Jacobson's story in our statistical data and then seek to make sense of why he and other plaintiffs fail to get a lawyer. After reviewing the data on the significance of legal representation to case outcomes from our large sample of filings, we analyze variations in the likelihood of representation across categories of plaintiffs and cases. These data demonstrate that there is significant racial disparity in plaintiffs' legal representation, with African American, Latino/a and Asian American plaintiffs being significantly less likely to have lawyers than white plaintiffs. We then turn our attention to the barriers plaintiffs report in their search to secure representation, which include high cost, inadequate information and networks, and a lack of trust in the legal profession. We also analyze whether the "merits' of the case play a role in plaintiffs' ability to retain counsel.

We draw on secondary data to identify factors that can influence plaintiffs' lawyers' selection of clients. Some factors working against African Americans may stem from their relative lack of opportunities to secure the economic, social, and human capital that would help them navigate the process of securing legal representation.[1] In addition, plaintiffs' lawyers' prejudicial assessments of potential clients may be a salient, if unspoken, factor. Although plaintiffs' lawyers never mentioned the racial identity of a potential client as a consideration, their discussions of "credibility," "demeanor," and "ability to pay" for services may be resting on stereotypical and unfounded assumptions and can function to disadvantage African Americans. Social psychologists and cognitive neuroscientists describe this as implicit bias: pervasive attitudes that shape people's perceptions and actions in an unconscious manner, to the disfavor of marginalized groups.[2] Critical race scholars characterize such language as colorblind racism; seemingly neutral terms are in fact racist code words that stigmatize and degrade their targets, particularly when mobilized within institutions.[3]

Our analysis reveals troubling racial disparities in legal representation in employment civil rights cases. It also casts new light on mechanisms that produce these disparities. First, plaintiffs and defendant employers have asymmetrical access to resources for managing law. All defendants have legal representatives. Second, the decisions that plaintiffs make about hiring a lawyer and that plaintiffs' lawyers make about accepting a case are made in reference to the adversarial process. While plaintiffs may initiate litigation to pursue justice, they and their potential lawyers have to make a cost-benefit analysis about whether the effort will be worth the cost. Third, as lawyers are assessing whether to take a case, they are themselves drawn into the individualization of civil rights claims. It is not enough that a plaintiff's lawyer perceives workplace discrimination. He or she must determine that this individual plaintiff and their particular claim can withstand the trial on their rights claim.

The Impact of Legal Representation

Before we turn to questions of who gets legal representation and how lawyers and clients work together, it is worth repeating how important legal representation is for case outcomes. In chapter 3, we saw that one of the main determinants of a plaintiff's case outcome is whether she or he has a lawyer. Table 5.1 displays the cross-tabulation of representation status by outcome. *Pro se* plaintiffs have dramatically higher levels of dismissal, lower rates of settlement, and higher rates of loss on motions for summary judgment than plaintiffs who have lawyers throughout their cases. The multivariate models we presented in chapter 3 demonstrated that these effects hold when controlling for other variables. Indeed, the

TABLE 5.1 **Case Outcome by Representation Status of Plaintiffs in Filings Sample**

Independent Variable	Dismissal	Early Settlement	P Loss on SJ	Late Settlement	P Trial Win	P Trial Loss	Total
*Representation****							
Lawyer throughout	12%	57%	15%	9%	2%	4%	100% (1296)
Pro se throughout	59%	15%	22%	1%	0.4%	3%	100% (247)
Gained counsel	13%	40%	31%	5%	2%	9%	100% (129)

*** $p < .001$

explanatory power of multivariate models of dismissals more than *doubled* with the addition of the legal representation variable.

As with plaintiffs in other areas of litigation,[4] employment civil rights plaintiffs' chances of success are dramatically increased if they have counsel.[5] Indeed, the presence or absence of counsel is the most significant predictor of case outcome.[6] And yet, our data reveal systematic differences in rates of representation among groups of plaintiffs.

As reported in an earlier article,[7] there are significant differences in representation by race, sex, and occupational status with systematic and statistically significant differences in who obtains legal representation. Controlling for relevant characteristics of the plaintiff, the defendant, and the case itself, we found African American plaintiffs were estimated to be 2.5 times more likely to be *pro se* than white plaintiffs; other people of color (chiefly Asian Americans and Latino/as) were 1.9 times more likely than whites to be *pro se*; and plaintiffs claiming racial discrimination are 1.8 times more likely to be *pro se*.

Similarly (but perhaps not surprisingly), legal claims requiring more sophisticated training to mount, such as §1981 claims, are more likely to be filed with legal representation. Managerial and professional workers with higher salaries (and therefore higher potential damages) are more likely to enjoy legal representation, as are workers with longer job tenure. Where the EEOC issued a negative finding on the merits, plaintiffs are significantly more likely to file *pro se*. There is no significant difference in representation across gender. Even considering these other factors that predict whether a plaintiff will be represented by counsel in an employment civil rights case, racial status itself is the most significant predictor.

Plaintiffs' Experiences: Barriers to Securing Counsel and the Production of Racial Disparities in Representation

Given that the plaintiff's racial status is the strongest predictor of whether a plaintiff has a lawyer—even when controlling for other seemingly relevant variables—we probed issues of lawyer and client selection at length in our interviews. This section uses these qualitative data to analyze the factors that affect how clients and lawyers evaluate and eventually enter into an employment arrangement with each other. As shown in table 5.2, of the forty-one plaintiffs we interviewed, eight filed *pro se*. Six of those

TABLE 5.2 **Race, Gender, and Representation Status of Interviewed Plaintiffs**

	Pro Se Entirely	Represented for at Least Part of Case	Total
African American men	5 (50%)	5 (50%)	10 (100%)
African American women	1 (14%)	6 (86%)	7 (100%)
White men	1 (8%)	12 (92%)	13 (100%)
White women	1 (8%)	10 (91%)	11 (100%)
Total	$N = 8$	$N = 33$	$N = 41$

were African American: five men and one woman. The qualitative data thus exactly mirror the large random sample of case filings used in the model above: 20% of respondents were *pro se*; of these, 75% were African American and 25% were white.

The interviews illustrate many of the factors that, according to existing research on *pro se* representation, are important determinants of getting a lawyer. They provide a "bottom-up" picture of the challenges that *pro se* plaintiffs face in seeking counsel, from their own perspectives and in their own voices. Despite the small numbers, because these interviews were selected as a random sample of a random sample, they are more likely to accurately represent the experiences of *pro se* plaintiffs than if the sample were opportunistic (nonrandom). We gain additional insights by considering the accounts of represented plaintiffs. The dataset includes thirty-three interviews with represented plaintiffs, including eleven African Americans.

As our interviews demonstrate, many of the reasons plaintiffs fail to obtain lawyers are a product of structural barriers that stem from the institutional dynamics of litigation. They are not merely a product of plaintiffs' unique life circumstances or their idiosyncratic personalities. Nonetheless, plaintiffs experience these barriers in personalized, acute ways. Our qualitative data reveal four primary hurdles to obtaining legal representation: plaintiffs' lack of information and connections, the economic costs they face, their distrust of lawyers, and plaintiffs' attorneys' assessments of the "merits" of potential cases.

Information and Connections

Plaintiffs' lack of information about the legal process coupled with no connections to lawyers or others who know more about these processes is the most significant barrier we find. In this, our work resonates with existing research that demonstrates how perceptions of legal complexity affect whether litigants obtain representation. We lack recent surveys regarding how legal knowledge differs across demographic groups, but earlier work suggests reasons that African American plaintiffs and potential plaintiffs may be less knowledgeable about the law. Social science research shows definitively that African Americans receive less education than whites at every level from high school graduation to graduate degrees;[8] are more likely to be segregated in low-status jobs, with lesser access to training and advancement opportunities;[9] and receive less positive socialization and fewer opportunities to build human capital even when they are in better jobs.[10] If, on average, African American plaintiffs have lower levels of knowledge and information about the law because of these systemic disparities in education and personal development opportunities, they may be more likely to file cases on their own.

For example, Billy Deeds (P2), a forty-nine-year-old *pro se* African American plaintiff, did not understand his situation as a legal one when he went to file for unemployment benefits. He was convinced his "human rights" had been violated and mistakenly believed that the EEOC would represent him.

Because plaintiffs must first file with the EEOC, the EEOC itself can (and sometimes should) work as a barrier to litigation, but overcoming this barrier is easier for more knowledgeable plaintiffs. The EEOC typically produces a "right to sue" letter, which informs the complainant that the agency is not making a discrimination finding and that the plaintiff may proceed to federal court to pursue their claim. And yet, even the right to sue letter can be misunderstood. Mitchell Collins (P6) misinterpreted his right to sue letter from the EEOC, believing it meant his case was invalid.

If a claimant makes it this far and understands how to file a claim in federal court, he or she may do so and, of course, may do so even if without representation. They may not understand the importance of finding a lawyer or they may be unable to retain one, but *pro se* African American plaintiffs like Chris Burns (P5) and Marjorie Turner (P25) clearly lacked information about these aspects of the legal process.

Conversely, the litigants we interviewed who obtained legal representation were far more likely to have a basic understanding of their legal issues, even if that understanding was only that the law is complicated and they needed help. They also were more likely to have prior connections in the legal world or the capacity to conduct some basic investigation of the bar. Joe Palmer (P20), a forty-five-year-old African American manager who filed a race claim, chose a law firm that his father had worked with professionally, while Jack Stern (P20), a twenty-six-year-old white police officer filing for disability discrimination, chose the law firm where a fellow officer cum law student was interning.

Some represented plaintiffs without personal knowledge about law or contacts with lawyers were resourceful enough, and resourced enough, to find lawyers through directories or other publicly available sources. Floyd Kelly (P7), a fifty-seven-year-old African American professional filing a racial discrimination claim, took advantage of a group plan through his American Express account that offered him access to a list of participating lawyers at reduced rates, and he ultimately selected a lawyer who charged an up-front fee that he could afford. Robert Lester (P16), a forty-nine-year-old white professional claiming age discrimination, obtained a list from the American Bar Association (ABA) and "just went down the list and . . . just selected four of them. And basically, then, I went out and I interviewed them and discussed my case." These plaintiffs both had financial resources as well as the stores of knowledge and confidence that make up human capital to help secure their lawyers through impersonal processes.

Of course, searching for a lawyer is complicated and time-consuming. Plaintiffs who have jobs and family obligations, like Mr. Jacobson, may lack the material and emotional resources to invest in calling multiple lawyers and organizations. This is especially true for plaintiffs whose personal networks do not include lawyers and who must turn to directories or legal aid providers. Because African American workers generally have smaller professional networks, they may be less likely to find a lawyer.[11] Racial differences in care obligations and household organization, all well documented in the social science literature, impede the search in the way that Mr. Jacobson described.[12] Even transportation is less accessible to urban minority populations because of suburbanization and its effects on public transit policy.[13] Given the resource-intensive nature of the search, racial disparities in access to social and material resources could further compound the disparity.

Even plaintiffs who *did* get a lawyer described the search as arduous. Plaintiffs with lawyers reported consulting with several attorneys before finding the "right" one, meaning one who would take the case, made the plaintiff feel comfortable, and agreed to an acceptable pay arrangement. Some plaintiffs said they were initially rejected by lawyers who told them to seek second opinions. This forced them to decide whether to persist and, if they persisted, to shore up their confidence in the strength of their case. Peter Nichelson (P1), a fifty-six-year-old white police officer filing a race discrimination case, received a referral from his police union. Instead of following it, he contacted the Pacific Legal Foundation, a conservative advocacy group he thought might sympathize with his "reverse discrimination" claim. When they rejected his case, Officer Nichelson talked to a friend who had used a lawyer for his own employment case and ultimately selected this attorney. Rick Nolls (P3), a sixty-four-year-old white warehouse manager filing an age and disability discrimination case, similarly started by going to an advocacy group focused on the rights of people with disabilities. He did not pursue becoming a client there, but instead obtained three referrals from the ABA. The referrals led to meetings with several lawyers and he chose the one with the most desirable fee plan. Sociological research shows that white men are more likely to have a strong sense of self-efficacy—meaning, a positive sense of control over their lives.[14] This appears to hold true for these plaintiffs, both white men, who shrugged off initial rejection and used additional resources to pursue different paths to representation.

In sum, getting a lawyer requires resources that—in the aggregate—African Americans may be less likely to possess due to systemic social inequality. The taxing process of meeting with multiple lawyers, some of whom are discouraging or unaffordable, requires time, a tolerance for rejection of one's views, and a firm conviction in the validity of one's case. Personal connections, public directories, and court appointment programs can all be more effectively used by plaintiffs with resources (whether financial or in the form of social capital). The search process seems to favor confident professional negotiators (including managers, as our multivariate analysis indicates) and people with background knowledge about the law and legal profession. Successfully gaining representation also requires a belief that a prolonged search is preferable to filing alone.

Financial Costs

Although there are lawyers who take employment civil rights cases on a contingency-fee basis, several plaintiffs—both those who eventually secured a lawyer and those who did not—mentioned the cost of a lawyer as a significant barrier to obtaining representation.

Cost is not a *straightforward* barrier, though. Plaintiffs must make decisions about how to spend their resources based on how they view the law, the legal profession, and their chances of success. A low-income plaintiff might decide to pay for a lawyer, at serious hardship, if she or he thought it crucial, while a plaintiff who could afford a lawyer might forgo one if she or he was confident in his or her self-representation ability. Cost matters and our findings are in line with other access-to-justice research that complicates the role finances play in use of legal services (making it clear that plaintiffs' views of those services are part of the equation).[15] Racial differences might interact with income disparities to explain why African American plaintiffs are less likely to have lawyers.

Franklin Williams (P11), a thirty-eight-year-old African American railroad laborer who filed *pro se*, recalled that, at the time of his case, he and his wife preferred not to mortgage their home in part because they had confidence in their own abilities and in part because they intended to ask for court-appointed counsel. Chris Burns and Philip Jacobson said they filed their cases *pro se* because they could not afford the fees lawyers quoted to them ($2,700 and $500, respectively). Based on their knowledge of the legal process and the perceived value of representation, these plaintiffs made a cost-benefit calculation.

Plaintiffs who secured lawyers generally seemed to have access to more resources of the kind that the *pro se* plaintiffs in our sample lacked, such as personal connections, which they could use to offset some of the economic costs of representation. Kristin Baker (P34), the sex discrimination plaintiff whose story appeared in chapter 1, had a friend in the insurance business who convinced a lawyer at a large law firm to take her case at a discount because of the heinous nature of the discrimination, even though he did not normally represent individuals. Because she had a lawyer in her personal network, she was able to negotiate lower fees.

Represented plaintiffs were not very specific about how they paid for their lawyers. Several talked about shopping around for an option that they could afford, but they knew that they had a budget to work with, in contrast to *pro se* plaintiff Mr. Jacobson, who obtained a single quote and decided representation was unaffordable. Rick Nolls, who contacted legal clinics and followed up on referrals from the ABA, specifically said his financial resources allowed him to persist. The more flexible tone with which represented plaintiffs talked about money is itself a difference from some of our *pro se* plaintiffs, who felt immediately that they could not afford a lawyer and did not seriously consider shopping around.

At least two plaintiffs said they used their ability to acquire and demonstrate legal knowledge to compensate for a lack of financial resources. Matthew Brown (P9), a forty-seven-year-old African American manager filing for race discrimination, consulted with many attorneys, but he realized early on that none would take his case without immediate payment. Mr. Brown persisted, because "every time I met with one of these lawyers, I'd try to squeeze a question in," thereby learning more about his case. Ultimately, Brown learned that if he filed *pro se* he could request a court-appointed lawyer, which he did successfully. Kristin Hamilton (P15), a forty-two-year-old African American supervisor working on her master's degree, filed a race claim *pro se* and persistently attended hearings and asked questions about her case until the judge appointed an attorney who happened to be in the courtroom. Unlike some of our *pro se* plaintiffs, Ms. Hamilton did not feel hesitant about asserting herself to members of the legal profession. Mr. Brown and Ms. Hamilton were well-educated professionals who had the skills to build and use a stock of legal knowledge that made them good candidates for court-appointed lawyers.

Cost may be related to the significant racial disparity in securing counsel, because the racial wage and wealth gap between African American and white workers is a persistent problem in the United States. In 2014, the average annual earnings for a male African American full-time worker was $52,236 and for a female, $40,495.[16] Their white, non-Latino/a counterparts, by contrast, averaged $74,108 (males) and $52,300 (females). On the whole, African Americans have far fewer financial resources than whites, face barriers to obtaining credit, and are paid less than their white worker counterparts.[17] Since our data do not include measures of wealth or income, part of the race effect we observe may be caused by the extent to which African Americans are, on average, poorer than whites.

Trust in Lawyers

Studies have shown racial differences in trust regarding counseling professionals and criminal defense lawyers. In our interviews, "trust" manifested itself in interesting ways. Chris Burns, for example, contacted at least ten attorneys, legal clinics, and law schools, eventually determining that no lawyer would take his case because they were unwilling to take on the government, not because his claim lacked merit. Once he came to this conclusion, Mr. Burns was no longer interested in trying to obtain a lawyer. He was convinced the lawyers were not really assessing the merits of his case.

Marjorie Turner (P25), a forty-six-year-old African American administrative assistant, had mixed feelings about lawyers, although she reported believing them when they said her case was frivolous and said she withdrew it as a result. Mr. Jacobson lost faith in attorneys when a lawyer told him that filing while he was still employed would accomplish little, so he proceeded on his own.

At the group level, if African American plaintiffs are less trusting of civil lawyers and their advice, they will be more likely to forgo representation even if they do not forgo the dispute. Though we cannot definitively make this claim from our interviews, it is in line with substantial research on how people's racialized experiences shape their views of legal actors and institutions as supportive of or opposed to their interests.[18]

The "Merits" of the Case

What about the *merits?* Is it possible that, as a group, African American plaintiffs have weaker cases that lawyers reject, forcing them to file *pro se?* If this were the case, lawyers would be performing a "gate keeping" function in an effort to keep weak claims out of court.

Our data do not allow an objective assessment of case merits, either statistically or through interviews. Cautiously, we can report that one of the interviewees—Chris Burns—seemed to have problematic claims, which would deter lawyers from accepting him as a client. Mr. Burns said he contacted multiple lawyers but none would take his case nine years after the fact, so his decision to file alone may have bypassed their gate keeping. His earlier efforts to find a lawyer seem to have failed because of his perception of the cost. Two other respondents—Franklin Williams, who advanced to trial despite substantial efforts by defense attorneys, and Marjorie Turner, who obtained a positive finding from a state review commission—appear to have had viable cases, but lacked representation for other reasons.

Acknowledging the limits of our data, unmeritorious cases do not seem to be the main reason that African American plaintiffs are less likely to have lawyers. Instead, the resources required to find and retain a lawyer are unequally distributed.

In sum, plaintiffs with and without legal representation told us that securing a lawyer depended on their resources, connections, effort, their ability to pay, education, and the plaintiff attorneys' perceptions of the merits of their case. While none said they thought lawyers discriminated against them on the basis of racial status or socioeconomic status, it is easy to see how, on average, these many barriers would systematically select against legal representation for African Americans, who are more likely to live in poverty, work low-wage jobs, have less education, and presumably have fewer lawyers in their networks than their white counterparts.

Plaintiffs' Lawyers' Decisions: The Invisibility of Racial Bias in Screening and Selecting Clients

Plaintiffs attributed their (in)ability to obtain representation in part to how they thought lawyers made decisions about clients and cases, so we asked the lawyers. Twenty plaintiffs' attorneys representing a range of practice specialties, firm sizes, and prestige levels—from solo practice generalists, to lawyers engaged in *pro bono* work through large firms, to an elite, national class action specialist[19]—spoke extensively about how they screen and select clients.[20] We asked both how the lawyers came to represent the clients in the particular case we drew randomly and a series of questions about how they assess potential clients in general. It is important to note that all but three of these attorneys were non-Latino/a whites.

Plaintiffs' lawyers often are characterized as taking any and every case that comes their way, but all of the plaintiffs' attorneys we interviewed stressed that they accept a very small fraction of potential discrimination clients. Several estimated an acceptance rate of less than 10%. Assuming their estimates are accurate, then only one in ten individuals who believe they have a discrimination claim and seek out an attorney secure representation from that lawyer. This high selectivity drove plaintiffs' attorneys' client selection process.[21] In-person and phone screening processes were designed to determine the level of a client's seriousness, their demeanor (how would they "play" to a judge or jury), and their ability to pay.

Thus, for most lawyers, the screening process began even before a face-to-face meeting with a potential client or a discussion of the details of the workplace dispute.[22] Joseph Shapiro (PL12), a fifty-six-year-old white plaintiffs' attorney with years of experience, said his office conducted in-depth phone screenings by an on-call intake attorney. That weeded out most would-be clients. If a client was referred directly, however, either Mr. Shapiro or his partner would personally perform the initial assessment. Dan Franco (PL22), a forty-six-year-old white specialist who connected with clients through referrals from lawyers, former clients, and professionals (such as accountants), as well as through mass advertising, said all potential clients were screened over the phone. About 10% of those calls resulted in an invitation to a meeting, at which clients were required to fill out an extensive questionnaire and pay a consultation fee starting at seventy-five dollars. The fee was designed to deter casual inquiries. Karen Green (PL40), a sixty-two-year-old white attorney, used phone screenings in which she probed for specific details that suggested discrimination, rejecting clients if they did not mention key points. If the client survived the phone screening, she charged a consultation fee for the first meeting.

Lawyers reported being intentionally pessimistic in their assessment of the likelihood of a successful outcome in order to eliminate individuals who were not serious enough about pursuing their case. One stated:

> I will say to people, "From what you tell me, I don't think I can help you. If you really want a consultation, I'll give it to you." And so sometimes people say, "Well, you mean I don't have a case?" Then I say, "I'm not telling you that, because you're not my client" (PL40).

Lawyers claimed they could almost instantly assess the merits of a case and their initial screening methods favor some clients. Those (potential) clients who know how to quickly "sell" a compelling story (demeanor), who have a personal vouching connection (trust), who are prepared, and who have the social capital to read discouraging assessments as tests of commitment and professional disclaimers, rather than rejection, were all likely to "pass" initial lawyer's screens.

Charging fees for initial assessments likely worked against some African American plaintiffs, who are statistically poorer and—as a correlate of educational disparities and segregation in low-level jobs (as elaborated above)—might be less experienced at making compelling presentations of self in person or on the phone or simply unable to counteract an attorney's prejudices.[23]

Demeanor

Most plaintiffs' attorneys said a large part of their decision about whether to accept a client after an initial phone call was based on his or her mannerisms or demeanor at the initial meeting.[24] Some attorneys said they assessed demeanor in terms of personal interaction as an indicator of how well the lawyer/client team would function. Harry Morgan (PL15), a prominent, seventy-five-year-old African American civil rights lawyer, said he had a "sixth sense" for those "difficult" clients who become "accusatory" or "whine[y]" in the course of the lawyer-client relationship. In his view, "a personal relationship with a client means a lot." Mark Lewis (PL34), a fifty-six-year-old white attorney and another experienced specialist, agreed: "First of all, a piece of whatever you do if you have any sense as a lawyer is, you know, is there chemistry? Is this somebody that you feel like you can work with? Are you able to communicate effectively with that person?"

Attorneys said that demeanor related to client credibility.[25] Ellis Barry (PL18), a fifty-year-old white male attorney who represented Annie Daley (whose narrative begins chapter 7) felt Ms. Daley was a "quality person." He said that "whatever the case is . . . if I personally don't get a sense of the honesty of the person or if I don't feel like what I'm hearing is what's really there, I generally don't get involved." Margaret Cottle (PL51), a thirty-eight-year-old white attorney, referred more directly to the "smell test" that, prior to discovery, she depended upon to determine whether a client was "trying to work the system" instead of having a "morally right" conviction that he or she had been discriminated against.

Finally, some attorneys assessed demeanor in terms of whether a client would interact favorably with a judge or jury. After all, the ultimate determination of a case is made by judges and juries (or the threat of appearing before a judge or jury). Some attorneys noted that this type of demeanor "test" is distinct from whether a potential client is persuasive about their claims. Joseph Shapiro explained that "we assess both the plaintiff in terms of our view of her and how she might be perceived [by the court]." Timothy George (PL30) said that, after deciding whether he "believed" a client, he focused on his "confidence in their ability to communicate their story and to be believed, to be likable, be sympathetic figures, and so forth, because so many times even people with good stories to tell, if they can't tell it well, just are not going to survive the process."[26]

"Top-down" lawyer preferences might interact with "bottom-up" client beliefs, as research shows that some African Americans have lower trust in counselors and lawyers in other contexts[27] and are often hesitant to describe themselves as "victims" of discrimination for fear of confirming stereotypes.[28] Because discussing sensitive events requires the trust of the attorney, instant screening processes may deter African Americans.

Predictably, none of the attorneys explicitly made a connection between their determinations of "credibility" and the race of the individuals who approached them. Yet such determinations do not happen in a vacuum. Extensive social science research confirms that implicit bias operates in interracial interactions.[29] These observations might help explain the underlying pattern of underrepresented African American plaintiffs in Title VII cases alleging race discrimination. If lawyers tend to unfavorably assess the demeanor of racial minority plaintiffs, viewing them as "difficult" to work with, not credible, or unlikely to present well to a judge or jury, then African American plaintiffs will be less able to obtain representation.

All but three of the attorneys in our sample were non-Latino/a whites, and thus are likely to be less cognizant of racial bias and anti-black treatment.[30] There likely also are parallels between how plaintiff's attorneys interview clients and how employers do that influence African Americans' lack of legal representation. These attorneys very well may reproduce the class and racial biases that pervade the hiring process, specifically through their definitions and evaluations of "fit" and "merit" and their personal contact and identification with people similar to them (i.e., homophily), all of which works overwhelmingly to the disadvantage of people of color.[31]

Seriousness and Preparedness

Apart from demeanor, several attorneys said they were more likely to accept clients who came to their initial meetings with documents or background work, or who seemed likely to be willing and able to assist with their case preparation. Mr. Shapiro said that a good client "was someone who's responsible and follows instructions, whether it's depo[sition], prep[aration], or getting the documents and responding to the document requests," and that he typically instructed potential clients to obtain documents prior to their first meeting. A few lawyers recalled cases they would have rejected had it not been for background work a client had already done to develop his claim. Doug Schwartz (PL52), a sixty-two-year-old white specialist who said he only represented plaintiffs, recalled a client for whom "the facts of the case were, as he told them . . . pretty outrageous, but he had some documents [obtained from his work] which made it all make sense, so I agreed to take his case." An attorney at a public interest firm said she accepted a case largely because the client had already organized other employees at her workplace to request medical files, thereby showing that discrimination was widespread and laying the groundwork for a class action claim (PL37).

These lawyers responded positively to clients' foresight in requesting and assembling documentary evidence. The preference some lawyers showed for prepared clients might also be expected to work to the disadvantage of African American plaintiffs, who are, statistically, likely to have less education, more likely to work in jobs with less access to documents or opportunities to request them, and perhaps more likely to have less general knowledge about law and the litigation process. Given that many plaintiffs' attorneys viewed racial discrimination cases as among the most ambiguous and dependent on "he said, she said" accounts, it is possible that some disfavored African American clients because of their presentation styles. At the aggregate level, these factors might make it difficult for African American clients to create the succinct, supported presentations that lawyers prefer.

Ability to Pay

There was wide variation as to how plaintiffs' lawyers in our sample negotiated payment. A few operated on a contingency-fee basis, expecting the bulk of payment only when and if a client prevailed. Others operated on a contingency-fee-plus, where the "plus" was an up-front fee (designed to screen out clients who were not "serious") and/or an hourly fee to be "topped up" with funds from the award if the case prevailed. Many lawyers reported no longer being willing to work on contingency and said they billed entirely by hourly rate. Some took *pro bono* cases. Most importantly, most lawyers used a variety of payment plans, having shifted between payment modes over the course of a career or according to the strength of each individual case. Notably, the payment scheme an attorney followed influenced how he or she evaluated potential clients.[32]

CONTINGENCY FEES. Attorneys who worked on contingency-based client choices on the projected recovery of the cost of their services. For these lawyers, liability was separate from and less relevant than potential damages. Since damages recovered in employment civil rights cases are often determined by calculating back pay, the potential plaintiff's salary was very important for determining whether to take a particular case. Similarly, lost wages figure into the recovery, which means that a plaintiff who found a new job immediately after being fired (effectively mitigating lost wages) would be less likely to secure legal representation, even when the client had a strong claim of discrimination. One lawyer said that he was generally unwilling to "invoke the heavy machinery of the law," even for "somebody who kind of seems to have the facts to support a case," if the client found a new job "two weeks" after being fired (PL34).

Another lawyer said he used a formula to determine whether one-third of anticipated recovery would equal his goal hourly billing rate because he would only take cases that made "economic sense." Given that recovery depends largely on a clients' salary, this lawyer said that, regardless of merits, "if [plaintiffs] were like low-wage earners, like $3,000 a month, I would not be interested in filing a lawsuit or anything like that" (PL8).

This cutoff, equivalent to $36,000 per year, would exclude many African American workers, given their average annual earnings. Our data suggest that lawyers ask about salary as part of the client screening process, sometimes in an initial phone call. Because African American workers are disproportionately likely to have lower income and fewer benefits, this practice would disparately impact African Americans' ability to retain counsel. In addition, the contingency lawyers in our sample reported conducting a cost-benefit analysis to assess the amount of work and immediate financial investment required to obtain a given award. Several said that racial discrimination cases were "difficult" and lengthy to litigate because of savvy employers and the frequent absence of "smoking gun" evidence (PL15; PL18; PL26; PL34). Race cases, to the extent that they promised low damages, substantial work, and delayed recovery, were thus disfavored by contingency lawyers.

HOURLY FEE STRUCTURE. Lawyers with hourly billing practices were less directly concerned with predicting the value of a claim because they are guaranteed payment regardless of outcome. These lawyers saw hourly billing arrangements as a way to represent clients who wanted to pursue cases that might not prevail or that promised to be extremely labor-intensive.[33] Aaron Erlington (PL24), a forty-eight-year-old white attorney, said he used an up-front retainer fee to force clients "to decide whether it's worth it" to proceed with a case and to give them an "awakening" regarding the risk of losing. When the retainer was spent, he continued at an hourly rate, avoiding contingency in almost all cases, because recovery is unpredictable. Other lawyers agreed that hourly fee structures only worked when the case appeared to have some merit and the client both understood the risks and could afford the expense.

Hourly-fee payment plans with up-front retainers would be out of reach for plaintiffs lacking substantial financial assets, among them most African American plaintiffs. Most lawyers described hourly-fee arrangements as an option for plaintiffs who could not convince contingency lawyers to accept their cases. In other words, they expanded the representation prospects for plaintiffs—but only for those with financial resources. Financial constraints probably limit some African American plaintiffs' access to these "auxiliary" lawyers, forcing many to return to looking for a contingency lawyer or forgo representation.

PRO BONO AND INFORMAL REPRESENTATION. Most lawyers said payment prospects were important to client evaluation, but there were some exceptions. Some lawyers with personal ideological commitments to plaintiffs described for us their indifference to financial gain. Valerie Lane (PL37), a fifty-eight-year-old white lawyer who worked for a public interest organization before transitioning to a firm, said she preferred clients who had "public interest goals" and were not "money driven." Ms. Lane reduced her fees considerably in order to help sympathetic plaintiffs and repeated that she "wasn't willing to do a case [simply] to make money," rejecting clients who appeared motivated only by financial gain. Another lawyer said that he felt it was typical to count on "mak[ing] up . . . for the weak cases by the strong cases" (PL34), while another said his firm took about one-third of their cases *pro bono* due to their commitment to helping plaintiffs, writing off these costs, and hoping that "at the end of the year [I] have some money left over after we pay everybody" (PL52). This minority of lawyers who reported taking cases without regard for payment generally said they selected cases based on legal interest or sympathy for a client.

To summarize, plaintiffs' attorney's calculations of potential clients' ability to pay are consequential for who gains representation. Contingency-fee structures would mean low-wage workers (disproportionately minority workers) were more likely to be turned down, too. Hourly-fee lawyers likely also contributed to the racial disparity, if white clients used them to advance questionable cases, even after having been advised of the risks.[34] *Pro bono* and ideologically sympathetic practitioners offer some prospects for such clients, but because many operate quietly and without advertising for "business," plaintiffs might have difficulty in reaching them. Thus, from the lawyers' side, the racial disparity in legal representation appears to stem from a combination of African American plaintiffs with legally-viable cases failing to secure lawyers *and* from white plaintiffs of sufficient means electing to pursue cases with lawyers they were able to hire out-of-pocket.

Thus, despite claims that plaintiffs' lawyers fuel "excessive" and frivolous litigation in employment civil rights cases,[35] our data demonstrate a highly selective process that ultimately results in only about 10% of people inquiring about a case becoming clients. That assessment involves intangible assessments about things like clients' truthfulness, demeanor, and work ethic, as well as a complicated formula accounting for likely damages (a function of pay), discounted by the probability of winning. Among the factors in this complex calculation, all disfavor (and perhaps even completely disenfranchise) people living in poverty or working for low wages, almost all have racially unequal consequences, and many appear to rest on implicit antiblack bias. Therefore, African American workers are disproportionately screened-out of representation from the very start.

Conclusion

Access to justice research has not looked systematically at racial patterns of lawyer use, but our research reveals a troubling disparity. Minority plaintiffs, especially African Americans, are much less likely than white plaintiffs to have lawyers in employment civil rights cases. Given the critical role of legal representation in case outcomes, this disparity has serious consequences.

At the systemic level, racial disparities in representation mean that the groups most affected by discrimination may be the least likely to have the resources to mount effective challenges in court. It is ironic that the Civil Rights Act—enacted largely to help minorities—ends up better serving nonminority groups who are more successful in obtaining legal representation.

Second, disparities in representation suggest that minorities, more than whites, will have a negative litigation experience that fails to meet their needs and leaves them disillusioned with the courts. Several of the *pro se* plaintiffs we interviewed stated that the legal system was operating over their heads; the law viewed them as irrelevant or incompetent and denied them respect. These plaintiffs felt disparaged when they asked questions in court. They sometimes believed that court personnel and judges secretly favored employers' attorneys because they knew them personally. For these plaintiffs, the experience of going to court was confusing and degrading. Afterward, their accounts show major, persistent misunderstandings about their cases. This pattern is problematic whether or not these plaintiffs have "good cases." Even if plaintiffs are in court *pro se* because they misunderstand the law, the legal system's legitimacy relies on consumers of justice being treated with respect and fairness.

CHAPTER SIX

Representing Rights

Lawyer-Client Relationships

In chapters 3 and 5, we demonstrated that legal representation is all but essential if a plaintiff is to have any chance of success in the system of employment civil rights litigation. In chapter 5 we examined which plaintiffs obtain counsel and why and discovered that African American plaintiffs are significantly less likely to gain counsel. Here we turn to the relationships between lawyers and clients on both sides of the dispute (on the plaintiff's side, for those who gained legal representation). The data reveal stark contrasts in lawyer-client relationships, with plaintiffs having far less control over and receiving much less support from their attorneys compared to defendant employers.

The differing patterns of lawyer-client relationships between plaintiffs and defendant employers reflect and reinforce the key processes that transform law from an instrument that protects those most vulnerable to discrimination to an institution that legitimates ascriptive hierarchies in the workplace: asymmetrical access to quality legal representation, the individualization of rights-based claims, and the intensification of adversarial conflict. The asymmetry in legal representation is made palpable in the comparison between the plaintiffs and defendants. The individualization of claims pervades the discussions of all four groups of actors about their cases, clients, and organizations. The social organization of lawyer-client relationships reinforces adversarialism, as the parties and lawyers on opposing sides see each other not as respected adversaries but as socially and professionally different. We open with the divergent stories of two plaintiffs, one who worked with a lawyer for only a portion of her case and another who had legal representation as part of class action litigation.

Plaintiffs' Stories

Pamela Richardson's Case against a Federal Government Agency

A high-school-educated, white, single parent, Pamela Richardson (P13) was employed by the same large federal government agency in which her brother and mother had spent their working lives. After more than ten years of seniority and upward movement, Ms. Richardson struggled with extreme premenstrual syndrome (PMS) that led her to miss two to three days of work each month.

Trouble began when Ms. Richardson moved to a new work site with a new manager, who rejected her efforts to gain accommodation for her condition, either under the Americans with Disabilities Act or the recently passed Family Medical Leave Act (FMLA). Despite doctors' documentation of her physical problems, her manager refused to accede to requests for medical leave and treated some missed days as unscheduled leave, possibly in violation of the collective bargaining agreement. This upset Ms. Richardson, who recalled "I was so angry . . . that I was making myself sick." The conflict came to a head when Ms. Richardson sought an excused absence from work based on a health evaluation by the agency's medical unit. The nurse recommended FMLA leave, but Ms. Richardson's manager put her on a forty-day suspension. The facts thereafter are in dispute.

Ms. Richardson said she kept her manager informed about when she would return to work after the suspension. Management alleged that Richardson was absent without permission after the suspension. According to Theodore Wilde (P13), an attorney Ms. Richardson later hired, his client resigned because she knew she was going to be fired—an action he viewed as weakening the legal case. Ms. Richardson never returned to work. Instead she began a protracted effort to regain her job through employment civil rights litigation.

Ms. Richardson began her federal court litigation *pro se* because she "could not afford" representation and ended it *pro se*, although along the way she worked with Mr. Wilde. With support from her brother, Ms. Richardson spent four years working through the government's

EEO procedures. She failed to obtain administrative relief but was given a right-to-sue letter. Despite her lack of legal counsel, she survived three government motions for summary judgment. (Alan Chin [DL13], who represented the government agency, suggested that the summary judgment decisions may have reflected the judge's liberal tendencies toward *pro se* plaintiffs.) As Ms. Richardson recounted, Mr. Wilde, an elderly white attorney, approached her after one of her court appearances and suggested, in her words, that "he could help." Because she and her brother did not know how to subpoena documents for trial, she retained Mr. Wilde on a contingency-fee basis for a portion of her case.

For his part, Mr. Wilde regarded his acceptance of the case as both charitable and conditional. We asked him why he took the case:

> Well, when she first came in I thought well she had some things going for her. She had a couple of medical reports. And I'm very sympathetic to these people. Not just black, but women and people, you know, employees that I think are not getting treated right. And so I looked at it. And oftentimes you get into what is kind of a legal or law practice trap: to get records, you have to state that you represent the client. So you almost have to have her sign an agreement whether you want the case or not. So this way I was able to get the medical records because they wanted a release and proof of my representation. And so I was stuck with the case whether I wanted or not. And I told her, "I'm going to look at it and I'll tell you frankly." . . . I said, "If I don't like it, I'm going to cut you loose."

Interestingly, it was typical in our interviews that lawyers remembered the case only after reading supporting documents, but this was the only example of a plaintiff's attorney not remembering the client's name. He also thought she was African American. These cases, remembered in vivid detail by plaintiffs, really are just one of many to the lawyers.

As preparations for trial proceeded, the defense demanded that Ms. Richardson undergo a medical and a psychiatric examination by defense-retained experts. When we asked whether her lawyer objected, Richardson reported that he did not. She said Mr. Wilde, initially "gung ho" about her case, wanted her to settle, but she insisted that she wanted her day in court: "What they did to me was illegal. I didn't care about the money. I really didn't care about the money. I wanted my job."

The government's expert reports proved damaging and insulting to Richardson. They referred to Ms. Richardson as "narcissistic" and cast doubt about her physical problems. In Ms. Richardson's view, her own attorney suddenly turned on her, saying, "'Pamela, they will hate you [in court].'" In a pretrial conference, Mr. Wilde reportedly made fun of her case in front of the judge: "It really got me," she cried. "I told the Judge, "'I'm sorry, it makes me angry. It makes me angry because the one person that I trusted to help me to get there thought it was a joke, do you understand?'" When Mr. Wilde requested another extension, postponing the trial, he and Ms. Richardson argued, and he resigned from the case. He told us that he estimated he had worked about twenty hours on the case, all unpaid as it had been a contingency-fee arrangement, and had spent about $1,000 on "copies of records, filing fees, whatever."

On her own, Ms. Richardson was badly outgunned at trial. Over the four or five days of the trial, the only witness she called was herself and, since she was not properly prepared to submit trial exhibits, she could put into evidence only a few documents. The jury took only forty minutes to reject all of Ms. Richardson's claims. In retrospect, she felt her case was worth the effort, although she believed her own "shyster" lawyer proved to be a significant obstacle to her success.

Denise Slayton's Case against Chain Stores

Compared to Ms. Richardson, Denise Slayton (P36) had a dramatically different experience with her legal representation. As a married, high-school-educated, white parent of four, Ms. Slayton began working for Chain Stores, a large retail chain in the early 1970s. Of the discrimination, she said, "It was just obvious. It took a couple of months to realize that the males were favored." She recalled that men were quickly moved into positions with promotion opportunities, women were limited to largely dead-end positions. The few women who were promoted were relatives of male workers or those who "rolled over." Once, when she worked in the retail unit, she asked a manager about job openings in the better-paying warehouse and trucking unit of the company. As she remembered, "I had been told by a supervisor that I could 'become a Chain Stores driver when you learn how to use a men's urinal.'" At this time, there was no formal system of posting new openings, so employees learned about promotion possibilities through word of mouth or directly from management. The limited networks opened to women kept them from even knowing about such possibilities.

Upon hearing of a discrimination lawsuit concerning Chain Stores' trucking unit, Ms. Slayton passed along her story about the men's urinal comment to the plaintiff's lawyer for that case and suggested they might look into the retail arm of Chain Stores. A year later Ms. Slayton contacted the attorney again, who assisted her with filing an EEOC charge. This launched a ten-year period in which she was both an employee and a named plaintiff in a class action involving thousands of female employees, what would be one of the largest class action employment civil rights cases of the time.

Bob Siegel (PL36–2), a white man who was one of Ms. Slayton's attorneys, spoke about the unique considerations in deciding whether an individual is appropriate as one of five or six named plaintiffs in a class action. To meet the requirement of typicality, the group of named plaintiffs needs to occupy the range of positions that are the target of the case. Mr. Siegel said it is also "absolutely critical . . . [to find] plaintiffs who had both the intestinal fortitude and the willingness to take on the fiduciary responsibility of being class rep, and not sell out the class for themselves." Mr. Siegel described very frank discussions with plaintiffs about becoming a named plaintiff in a class action: on the one hand, career employees see the possibility "of really changing the company." On the other hand, named plaintiffs will be walking into "litigation that is very intense" and the defense lawyers "will go gunning for you" and "try to dig up dirt," in a very public manner. Mr. Siegel recollected, "Denise remained employed through that whole litigation, as did several other plaintiffs. . . . Now she's a tough bird, she is."[1]

After filing the EEOC charge, Ms. Slayton received mixed messages from management: first a promotion, then a reassignment to her previous entry-level job. Working with her attorneys, she deflected attempts to ease her out. At the time, she understood "this is a game" and she had to play it. Management, she thought, "did not realize how hard-headed I can be." Other plaintiffs could not stand the pressure and left for jobs with other companies. Ms. Slayton asked her attorneys if she could quit and the suit could continue, they told her "'No, no, no'"—her continued employment at Chain Stores was critical to the lawsuit.

Despite the fact that the case was a class action, Slayton did not have solid support for her case at work. Other women told her she was wrong. The all-male union leaders did not help. Ms. Slayton said, "Part of the problem was they were just little boys themselves."

Although the plaintiffs had arguably strong claims and were represented by expert counsel, Chain Stores was largely unwilling to settle.

The company, Ms. Slayton recalled, defended the lawsuit on the basis that women were "not interested" in promotions, that women employees were often married and only working for supplemental income for their families, and that women did not want to work at night. Its initial settlement offer to one of the named plaintiffs was $1,000. On the eve of the filing, the defendant employer raised that offer to $40,000. According to Mr. Siegel, the individual plaintiff rejected what she had called "blood money. He described how the case became highly adversarial, "even bitter," with numerous letters from defense counsel threatening to seek sanctions against plaintiffs' counsel. The case went to trial for three months on liability issues, then to determine damages.

Finally, senior officials at Chain Stores intervened to begin settlement negotiations. The negotiations dealt with injunctive relief, the overall damage award for the class, and the awards for individual, named plaintiffs. Ms. Slayton received a substantial award (about three times the median amount for a late settlement) and a severance package for leaving her job at Chain Stores. While Slayton thought she deserved more than her individual award, she was realistic about her alternatives. She also was gratified that, after receiving their settlement awards, some of the female coworkers who had criticized her during the lawsuit told her they were wrong and thanked her for what she had done. She shared a story about how, after the settlement, an upper-level HR officer came in town to talk about the implications of the lawsuit for new procedures mandated by the consent decree. After hearing some resistance from local managers, the officer cut short the disagreement: "'What part of 100 million dollars do you not understand?'" And she described herself as "happy with the lawyers for most of the time," although she said that she and the other plaintiffs believed the attorneys inappropriately pressured them to accept the settlement.

The attorneys who represented Ms. Slayton and the class largely confirmed her account of the settlement negotiations. Damon Beim (PL36–1), another of Slayton's lawyers, acknowledged that the named plaintiffs were not happy with the initial proposal for their awards. As a result, there were separate settlement negotiations presided over by a settlement judge. When we asked whether the plaintiffs were satisfied in the end, Mr. Beim suggested defensively that, under current law, the named plaintiffs would have received significantly less than their ultimate award. Both Mr. Beim and Mr. Siegel spoke of the difficulties that some plaintiffs have "letting go" at the end of protracted class action litigation. But they also described the impact that this kind of class action litigation can have. As a result of Ms. Slayton's case and other similar sex discrimination class actions, women have seen dramatically more opportunities in various industries.

Introduction

Although Pamela Richardson and Denise Slayton represent polar opposites in the nature and quality of legal representation, even in Ms. Slayton's case the named plaintiffs were ambivalent about their representation and considered changing counsel at one point. This chapter reveals that such problematic experiences with lawyers form the predominant pattern among employment civil rights plaintiffs. The relationships between lawyers and their clients are critical to the operation of a rights-based system of employment civil rights, both in the workplace and in litigation. Lawyers are a resource, as a rich tradition of law and society research demonstrates. They are gatekeepers for the use of law, and they help to define the meaning of law, rights, and fair process.[2] According to Kagan, American law and politics are a system of adversarial legalism, and lawyers have a particularly important role therein.[3] As disputes are inserted into the legal process, adversarial approaches polarize the parties. Even if disputes settle, they have been transformed into a legal contest.

The legal representation that "repeat players" and "one shot" litigants have is perhaps the most important difference between them.[4] Structural asymmetries are fundamental to this dynamic. Repeat players such as corporate employers have representation across matters. They can game the legal system, from the legislative process through the adjudication of disputes. Lawyers embedded in an employing organization, either as inside counsel or as counsel on retainer, can devise systems to minimize legal risk—what Bisom-Rapp refers to as "bulletproofing the workplace."[5] This activity was abundantly clear in chapter 4 and is seen in this chapter as well. One-shotters have to rely on the market or on institutional sources of legal services (such as appointed counsel or EEOC representation) and then must summon the resources to pay for counsel. As we saw in chapter 5, plaintiffs often fail to obtain lawyers, although planned litigation campaigns (typified by the NAACP Legal Defense Fund's successful effort to dismantle state-sponsored racial segregation in *Brown v. Board of Education*) and a specialized plaintiffs' bar around a set of claims, such as in mass tort or potentially employment civil rights, may level the playing field somewhat for plaintiffs.[6]

There also are fundamental differences in lawyer-client relationships across this divide. A *corporate client hemisphere* is made up of lawyers who represent corporate clients and who have high social and law school status.[7] Corporate clients, like the defendant employers in our sample, call the shots in their relationships with lawyers, and lawyers come to strongly identify with the views of their clients.[8] Meanwhile, the *personal client hemisphere* is made up of lawyers representing individual clients and who graduate from lower status law schools and more often have lower status social origins. Personal clients are heavily reliant on their lawyer for information and decision making over the course of litigation. Although assertive clients can potentially shape the treatment of their case, their attorneys typically dominate their cases.[9] These attorneys play a gate-keeping role throughout the strategic choices parties make over the course of litigation, such as the extent of discovery, whether to move for summary judgment, and at what stage to settle.

Perhaps the most significant role of lawyers in employment civil rights is in defining the meaning and parameters of law, rights, and fair process. Edelman and colleagues observe that antidiscrimination law is ambiguous, leaving substantial room for lawyers and HR professionals to interpret what laws mean and how they are to be applied.[10]

Our interviews with parties and their lawyers shed new light on these insights into lawyer-client relationships. As we show, lawyers act simultaneously as resources, gatekeepers, *and* interpreters of rights in ways that shape the promise of employment civil rights law.

Plaintiffs' Perspectives on Their Legal Representation

We systematically coded plaintiffs' assessments of their lawyers. Given the semistructured nature of our interviews and our inductive approach to analysis, we did not always obtain a global assessment of how plaintiffs evaluated their legal representation. Yet we were able to analyze and assemble detailed comments about lawyers. Taken together, these provide a compelling portrait along three themes: the predominance of negative and ambivalent views about plaintiffs' lawyers; plaintiffs' experience of a power imbalance in their relationship with their lawyer and vis-à-vis defense attorneys; and emotional and psychological harms that some plaintiffs suffered at the hands of their attorneys.

Plaintiffs' Negative and Ambivalent Assessments of Plaintiffs' Lawyers

Some thirty-six plaintiffs in our sample offered at least general comments about experiences with attorneys (thirty-two included explicit evaluative comments); among these, seven were wholly positive and seven negative. Sometimes determining whether the client's overall assessment was positive or negative was easy, as in this exchange with Travis Winters (P38), an African American man who worked for a school district:

> I: "Did you feel that your lawyer did the best job he could?"
> TW: "Yes, I did."
>
> LBN: "So, you were satisfied with his . . ."
> TW: "I was totally satisfied with him. Yes, ma'am."

Laila Walter (P33), a white female police officer in her forties, had a starkly different assessment:

> I made the bad mistake of going through the phone book. And we found this attorney, and her name was Lisa and I don't remember her last name. She just sold us out. She was outrageous. . . . We'd call her office and we could never talk to her. It was always, "Who is this?" "This is so and so." "Oh, she is not in. She is in a meeting. She is on the phone." Never ever could we get a hold of her. . . . I don't think she put any time or effort into the case.

In most interviews, plaintiffs' assessments of their lawyers were more complex. In the thirty-two interviews containing explicit evaluative comments, we identified 150 different plaintiff assessments of lawyers. Table 6.1 reports detailed categories of comments.[11] Positive comments totaled fifty-three; negative comments totaled ninety-seven.

The categories in table 6.1 suggest that plaintiffs' main concerns about lawyers are commitment, competence, and honesty. Eight directly comparable categories appear on both the positive and negative sides of the table. For five of those categories, negative assessments outweigh positive ones. Thirty-three percent more plaintiffs reported that their law-

TABLE 6.1 **Frequency of Positive and Negative Comments by Plaintiffs about Plaintiffs' Lawyers**

Positive Categories		Negative Categories	
Category	Respondent Count	Category	Respondent Count
Believed me	2	Coercive	3
Cared about case	4	Could have done more	16
Competent	9	Criminal	1
Did something well	12	Did something bad[ly]	16
Honest	2	Didn't care about case	3
Kept me informed	8	Didn't keep me informed	10
On my side	7	Didn't understand story	2
Trustworthy	4	Dishonest	5
Understood story	5	Incompetent	9
		Law firm too small	4
		Not on my side	10
		Not trustworthy	9
		Too much money	5
		Withheld information	4
Total	53	Total	97

yer did something badly than reported that he or she did something well (16:12). Respondents were more than twice as likely to describe their lawyers as dishonest (5:2) and not trustworthy (9:4) than the opposite. More respondents also said they felt that their lawyer was not on their side (10:7). In the context of communication and information sharing, respondents were somewhat more likely to say that their lawyer did not keep them informed (10:8), with an additional four respondents reporting that their lawyers actively withheld information.

Across the comments, we find a predominance of ambivalent and negative assessments of lawyers. Only six of thirty-two plaintiffs (19%) offered *only* positive comments about lawyers. Thirteen plaintiffs (41%) had *only* negative things to say about their lawyers. Another thirteen (41%) offered at least one negative and one positive comment. One-quarter explicitly referred to feeling ambivalent. Three of those had different representation at different stages in the litigation process and reported that their attitudes varied between lawyers; two of the three were happier with their later representation than their earlier representation. The six others had distinctly mixed feelings about a single lawyer over the course of their case, with three becoming more dissatisfied over time. Although we are dealing with very small numbers, the results suggest that plaintiffs may be better off if they switch from unsatisfactory counsel than trying to stick it out. Likewise, plaintiffs are likely better off if they can join collectively with other plaintiffs, rather than bear the challenges and costs of working with an attorney as lone individuals.

Unpacking Plaintiffs' Attitudes

Among the thirty-two plaintiffs who offered explicit evaluations of their lawyer, we can identify a number of recurrent themes. Of these, ethics arose most frequently. Of the sixteen plaintiffs who spoke to ethics, more than two-thirds (11 of 16) spoke negatively about their lawyers' ethics, while five praised ethical behavior. Almost as many plaintiffs (15) commented on how well their lawyer communicated, mostly in the negative. Nine of these reported less than satisfactory communications and explanations from their lawyer, and six had only negative things to say about their representation overall.

Another common theme among dissatisfied plaintiffs was that lawyers had acted more in their own interests (generally, economic interests) than on behalf of their clients' interests. Twelve respondents out of the thirty-two (38%) reported that their lawyers' actions were unduly guided by self-interest. Eight had only negative things to say about their lawyers on the whole, and their attorneys' acting out of self-interest as a significant component of the problem. A smaller group of respondents (5) praised their lawyers for prioritizing their clients' interests, although three of these expressed a mix of positive and negative attitudes.

Ten plaintiffs from the thirty-two person subsample (31%) evaluated the extent to which their lawyers worked efficiently toward a timely resolution to their case. A number were dissatisfied with the perceived slowness of the case's progress, yet a few referenced a lawyer who moved *too aggressively* toward a speedy resolution, outstripping their own preferred pacing. One client said the case moved so quickly at the end that there was no sense of closure, laughing, "I was like, 'Wait a minute.' I was unsettled. I think the way it ended so quickly, and I just wasn't really prepared to settle that day, and yet it was like, 'Do it now or we'll never get offered it again'" (P12).

Nine among the subsample reported that their lawyers demonstrated significant failings in emotion management and self-presentation. Here, Ms. Walter describes how her lawyer's inappropriate self-presentation precipitated a complete breakdown in the attorney-client relationship and, ultimately, a premature termination of the case:

> Well, she was a strange woman. . . . When we first met her, she wasn't dressed like the typical . . . She had a very short skirt and high heels. She put her legs up on the desk, like kind of flirting with my husband, almost trying to entice him. And she would call me and literally get into arguments with me and yell at me, and I just couldn't deal with her. She was just outrageous, so we just kind of backed off. And I told my husband, "You deal with her, you seem to be able to deal with her. I can't." And then it went from, "You have a good case," to we get this phone call and it's over.

Plaintiffs repeatedly invoked failures in lawyers' emotional labor and self-presentation in explaining their overall dissatisfaction with the litigation process. For some, these drawbacks in a lawyer's "style" served to compound shortcomings in "substance" (his or her ethics and technical prowess in handling the case). Ron Reynolds (P35), a white salesperson, felt the lawyer "didn't do very much" and said:

> He wasn't very aggressive. . . . I think he was lying to me. Things like reading depositions. When he'd send it back to me, he would send back something else. I was not important enough for him to really give any attention and besides the misrepresentations on what he was doing and feeding me the wrong thing. That's my anger as much as anything else.

Other plaintiffs reported that their lawyers were technically proficient and morally upright, but their failure to connect emotionally undermined their relationship. One plaintiff described feeling satisfied up through the settlement negotiations, but that his lawyer's lack of enthusiasm made him uncomfortable with the idea of taking the case to trial. It was a major factor in his decision to take a settlement.

Six plaintiffs linked their dissatisfaction with the resolution of their case to the fact that their lawyers were working outside their area of experience or expertise. Marla Riteman (P32), an African American machine operator in her fifties, stated directly that her lawyer failed to live up to her expectations of professional expertise and authority by not making it clear that she was taking on both the workmen's compensation and civil rights aspects of her lawsuit:

> Maybe she didn't know better, I don't know, but I think she should have. But she handled both portions, which was not fair to me . . . I knew it was racial discrimination, and the act that he [my superior] did was a sexual harassment act, so there was two cases. I found out at the end of the trial and everything it was two different cases. So, I don't think that I got rewarded for punitive damages that I should have, because she [my lawyer] wasn't equipped to handle the discrimination part of it.

Finally, four of the thirty-two in the subsample (13%) advanced the view that their attorneys failed to maintain an appropriate—or at least an expected—distance from defense counsel. The clients felt there may have been some collusion or backroom horse-trading between the two sides of the case. Floyd Kelly (P7), an African American market analyst, described himself as "angry" because "I'm thinking maybe something was done under the table. . . . That could not have happened, but that's my opinion and I would die with that opinion."

Power Imbalances

Lawyers' power relative to clients is a critical dimension of attorney-client relationships, in the scholarly literature as well as in the experience of plaintiffs in employment civil rights cases. This theme arose in almost half (17 of 36, 47%) of the interviews in which plaintiffs made a comment about lawyers. Peter Nichelson (P1), a white police officer in his fifties, expressed the widely felt sense of dependence upon, and subordination to, his lawyer's authority:

> We just didn't think the same. . . . What's that old saying? . . ."The lawyer for himself . . . has a fool for a client," or something like that. So, I had to say, "You know what, either I'm going to hire him and let him do his job . . . and become the victim . . . or do my own, in which case, you know, I'm lost anyhow." So I had to just let him go [forward with the case].

Even plaintiffs with family connections to lawyers expressed feelings of powerlessness and forced deference to their lawyers, but they felt having a lawyer was crucial to their case's success.

In a particularly nuanced discussion of the attorney/client power dynamic, Floyd Kelly (P7) identified power imbalances cutting *both* ways. According to Mr. Kelly, despite their unequal positions, lawyers and their clients should ideally work as a partnership, unified in pursuit of shared goals: "I said, 'If you're my attorney, and you're working for me and *with* me supposedly. The reason I hired you in the first place is because I don't know legal things. . . . You and I are supposed to be partners. Even though you work for me, we're still partners."

Unfortunately, Mr. Kelly did not experience this ideal attorney/client relationship. As one of the nine plaintiffs who discussed the topic of attorney power, he described an experience in which his representation failed to live up to an expected level of professional authority and expertise. He—like others in the sample—explained that he retained counsel specifically to deal with the aspects of legal procedure and terminology with which he was unfamiliar, but then he found their attorneys unable to adequately handle that responsibility. Mr. Kelly said:

> When he asked me [about a settlement offer], I said, "Well, I don't know." Then I'm thinking, "You're the attorney, you tell me what's fair and what I should get." . . . I think he said something like, "How can you determine what is fair?" In other words, fair could be ten dollars. I said, "Well, and I'm saying that's what you guys are for."

Plaintiffs' feeling that their attorneys failed to exercise their expert power responsibly may help explain whether they are dissatisfied with their lawyer overall. Of the nine plaintiffs who reported that their lawyer did not bring expert power to their case, eight also offered an explicit evaluative assessment of their representation. Of these, five reported solely negative attitudes toward their lawyers overall, and three reported some form of dissatisfaction.

Plaintiffs are aware, too, of the power imbalance between their lawyer and opposing counsel. Several respondents observed how stratification within the legal profession affected the outcomes of their cases. They believed undesirable outcomes derived not from the material facts of the case or the competence of their lawyer, but from the disproportionate power of defense counsel. Annie Daley (P18), an African American manager in her forties whom we will feature at the beginning of chapter 7, said,

> I think, you know, getting the attorney, I think all that was good. I mean, because here's like this David and Goliath case. . . . They have whole offices and teams of lawyers, you know. Here I am . . . pulling my little pennies together for this one attorney.

Some plaintiffs expressed empathy for their lawyers, whom they saw as generally competent and well-meaning yet completely outmatched by powerful corporate defense firms. Plaintiffs said their lawyers were overwhelmed by the paper avalanche and blitzkrieg litigation styles of the larger, better-resourced defense firms. Many plaintiffs recognized that the formula for success in litigation includes more than just the merits of the case. It requires representation that can match defense firms' legal teams. Debra Leonard (P26), a white administrator in her forties, described the defense counsel and their relationship with the judge in even more formidable terms:

> The lead defendants . . . hired a firm that everyone affectionately referred to as "Gestapo," "Nazi," and "Hitler," and then the subsequent employer hired "Mussolini and Associates," and they buried my attorney. . . . And I must say that the perspective that I got from my attorney was this, kind of like a good old boys network, like [the judge] really liked these lifelong attorneys that came in from [a large city] to put on this big defense.

Emotional and Psychological Stress Produced by Lawyer-Client Interactions

Numerous respondents reported overall positive experiences with their lawyers, but six told us that their lawyers' behaviors caused them emotional or psychological hardship. Recall the pain that Pamela Richardson suffered when her lawyer—"the one person that I trusted to help [me]"—joked with the judge about her case. Not surprisingly, these six plaintiffs were the most likely to express decisively negative attitudes about their representation overall. Respondents characterized their reactions to their lawyers' offending behaviors with such adjectives as "upset," "angry," "scared," and "depressed."

Our systematic analysis of plaintiffs' comments about their lawyers reveals variation in plaintiffs' positive and negative views of their lawyers. Yet it is clear that a majority of plaintiffs saw serious problems in their legal representation and could offer assessments that were ambivalent, at best. Just as often, they provided a negative assessment of the quality of their legal representation. Some scholars have referred to the difficulties facing employment civil rights plaintiffs in obtaining competent counsel as a kind of market failure.[12] In this formulation, there are not a sufficient number of qualified plaintiffs' attorneys to handle employment civil rights case, there are no effective mechanisms for matching plaintiffs with appropriate counsel, and there is not enough financial return for many plaintiffs' lawyers to meet plaintiffs' expectations.

Plaintiff Lawyers' Relationships with Their Clients

Our analysis reveals variation in plaintiffs' perceptions of their lawyers, with the weight of the evidence suggesting considerable dissatisfaction. When we examine the relationship from the perspectives of their *lawyers*, we also see variation.[13] Plaintiffs' lawyers speak from the perspective of professional experts. At least implicitly, they hold themselves out as ethical and reasonable in the performance of their role. Yet many of the same tensions plaintiffs identified appear in the lawyers' accounts of working with plaintiffs. The central issue plaintiffs' lawyers noted in their relationships with clients is reconciling the ideal of deference to clients' preferences with navigating an adversarial process on their clients' behalf.

Plaintiffs' Attorneys' Techniques for Controlling Clients

Plaintiffs' counsel employ several techniques to control their clients. Some involve the management of expectations. Mr. Kovac (PL8), a Latino attorney in his fifties, asserted that "one of the cardinal rules is that you never oversell a case to a client, you undersell." He continued,

> You want the client's expectations to be very low, so that when you get the result, the client thinks that there should be parades in your honor. I mean, from a business standpoint, to do it any other way would be crazy. If you told the client they had a great case that was worth millions and then . . . suddenly you are asking them to accept a $100,000 settlement, there's a huge credibility problem, and oftentimes it's not pleasant for the lawyer.

Commonly, in settlements, the employer makes no admission of liability. Plaintiffs' counsel must explain this to clients before they accept the settlement, and it can be a moral sticking point. Joseph Shapiro (PL12), a white attorney in his fifties, reported that clients "have to understand that [an employer's] willingness to pay significant amounts of money represents sort of an admission" but that the defendant organization is not going to "roll over and say 'I did it, I'm wrong.' It's just never going to happen." But this routine part of legal settlements, in which moral dispute is transformed into monetary exchange, is surely an affront to plaintiffs who feel they have been wronged.[14] Recall, for Kristin Baker, an apology in front of other coworkers (if off the record) was part of the settlement. Most plaintiffs do not receive this kind of moral affirmation.

In addition to explaining the "realities" of settlement, lawyers sometimes exert pressure on clients to pursue other employment opportunities so as to mitigate the damages they have experienced from the alleged discrimination. Kara Morrison (PL35), a white attorney in her fifties, explained that she works with clients to ask for their job back and to seek other jobs, because "she had gotten burned early in her career on people not mitigating their damages." In this way, however, the lawyer is imposing the expectations of law—the requirement to mitigate damages—on the plaintiff.

Plaintiffs' counsellors are aware of the influence they have in guiding client decisions, especially around settlements. Mr. Shapiro prepared his client to see multiple settlement offers:

> I tell them, "There's going to be a number that's going to be offered that I'll give to you. . . . Sometimes, I don't even want to tell you about it . . . but I'm not going to expect you to take it. There's going to be a number where I'm going to say, 'You really, definitely should consider it.' There's going to be a number that I'm going to say, 'You definitely have to take it. I'm going to kill you if you don't!'" And I explain to them "I'm kidding," that it's their choice, but I am going to tell them my two cents.

Even when plaintiffs' counsel is not shy about offering direct advice, some plaintiffs will reject that advice. But as Mr. Shapiro told us, "I had many times where people will say, 'I don't want this now,' but you get closer to the trial date and suddenly they're willing to take that original offer." And that's not unreasonable, he added: "Sometimes they even get less." Here the legal process itself enhances plaintiffs' counsel's leverage. As time goes by and tension builds in a case, the client may become more accepting of the lawyer's advice (even as, in many instances, they become more dissatisfied with the lawyer).

As we saw in chapter 5, one of the defining characteristics of a good client, according to attorneys, is that they follow counsel's directions. Mr. Shapiro characterized a good client as "somebody who will trust you and you can communicate with, but also someone who's responsible and follows instructions, whether it's depo prep or . . . responding to document requests." Lawyers apparently do not like to be pushed to an ultimatum, but they will suggest to noncompliant clients that they may need to seek other counsel. Margaret Cottle (PL51), a white lawyer in her thirties, denies ever having "fired a client," but describes having had to put such a decision to clients:

> We've had people I guess where we've started representing them, and we felt, if, for instance, they wouldn't agree to a settlement that we thought was fair . . . that we've said to them, "Maybe I think you need to find a different attorney." And it'll go either one of two ways. They'll ultimately agree with you and do what you want, or else they'll go and find someone else. I've had that happen, but we would never leave someone without some kind of resolution.

In practice plaintiffs' counsel is constantly framing issues, educating clients about what is possible, offering advice, and laying down subtle ultimatums. Lawyer-client relationships in employment civil rights are fraught with tension on both sides. Lawyers with experience may begin to take this tension for granted, but for plaintiffs, who generally have little experience with the legal system, tensions with their own counsel is one of the inherent costs of exercising their rights.

Deference to Client Wishes

Some attorneys articulated a personal commitment to the professional norm that the client make critical decisions, including whether to accept a settlement offer. As Mr. Kovac explained, "The bottom line is that I've never lost my sense that there are employees out there who do get screwed [by their employers]. . . . I pick a case with the attitude that if I have to go to trial, I'm going to trial. . . . It's the client's call, not my call." He recalled telling his client, Maureen Sands (P8), that the settlement offer the defense presented was "the best they'll do" and "their last, final, and best offer," but if she wanted to go to trial, "then we'll try the case." Ms. Sands chose to take the settlement.

Here Mr. Kovac equates his willingness to go to trial with the fact that some employees "get screwed" and deserve their day in court. Although he talks about Ms. Sands's decision to accept the settlement offer as her own decision, he is also clearly presenting "facts" that may sway that decision (it is the "final, and best offer")—and presumably he presented these as facts to Ms. Sands personally. Elsewhere in the interview, Mr. Kovac notes that Ms. Sands had, by this point, taken another, better-paying job, which may have further undercut her demand for damages and desire to go to trial.

We turned to our interview with Ms. Sands (P8) to see if she saw her decision in the same way. Indeed, Ms. Sands reported that she felt her lawyers had explained the situation and provided "their opinion" but had left the choice to her. She reiterated that she did not feel her lawyer pressured her to forego trial. Other plaintiffs' lawyers claim that they "take as many options to the client as possible" (PL22) and were concerned about running afoul of disciplinary rules if they, "instead of the client," settled the case (PL40).

Yet we also found cases in which the client felt the lawyer had strongly influenced, if not dictated, the decision, even when the plaintiff's counsel recalled the decision as entirely the client's. A striking instance of such divergence was reported in the case of Kristin Hamilton (P15), a forty-three-year-old African American supervisor suing for sex discrimination. Her lawyer (PL15), an established, senior African American attorney, recalled his advice to Ms. Hamilton about the settlement offer: "We pretty much left it up to her. The question of taking the settlement is the client's decision." The offer in question came at the end of an intensive mediation session, with the defendant organization offering a settlement of $500,000. Ms. Hamilton declined the offer, only to lose on summary judgment and walk away empty-handed. We asked Ms. Hamilton her attorney's role in deciding to decline the settlement:

> Well, basically he was calling the shots. Even though he would constantly say, "We're going to do whatever you want." . . . You're sitting there with two attorneys. . . . It's like, "Oh no, they can't do this to her." He's going on the backbone, he got all this information from quote "these people who are judges who said I'm going to win this case." And he said, "Oh no, you don't need that. What they've done to you," and just on and on and on. So, I'm like, okay! [But then] I lost it.

This kind of dramatic miscalculation, as Ms. Hamilton reconstructed it, might well lead lawyer and client to remember a different version of who was in control of rejecting a significant offer. Both lawyer and client acknowledge the lawyers said "we are going to do whatever you want." But the client, who lacked sophistication in law, heard her lawyers saying she would win much more than what was offered in settlement and believed, at least retrospectively, she was following her lawyer's advice.

Ms. Sands's and Ms. Hamilton's cases demonstrate that lawyers believe and articulate the norm of deference to client wishes. In practice, however, the capacity of individual clients to make judgments that run counter to the advice of counsel may be quite limited.

The Range of Client Involvement: From Passive to Assertive to Heroic

Plaintiffs' involvement in the lawyer-client relationship exists along a continuum, from passive to actively engaged. Through interviews with both plaintiffs and plaintiffs' lawyers, we learned that some clients seem completely passive in the handling of their case. Jack Stern (P22), a young white police officer with a chemical imbalance, filed a claim of disability discrimination after being terminated during his probationary period. Officer Stern seemed dissociated from his case at the time of his interview, unsure if his lawyers had talked to him about filing a complaint anywhere other than in federal court. He told our team, "I just let them, you know, run the whole thing." Answering more questions, Officer Stern recalled no discussion about settlement and expressed surprise because "I thought at some point, someone would talk to me, I guess." Yet he still felt confident his lawyers were representing his side of the story.

Additionally, in class actions such as Ms. Slayton's case at the opening of this chapter, it is clear that class action lawyers know what to ask for in settlement and clients do not. Lawyers know, for instance, to seek injunctive relief and the monitoring of progress on remedial plans. Such technical aspects of many cases leave little room for meaningful client participation.

Some plaintiffs' lawyers said they needed to go beyond what their clients understood in negotiations for settlement. The lawyer for Kristin Baker, whose case appears in the opening chapter of this book, described the protracted settlement negotiations in her case:

> 🎧 It's not the first or last time this [sexual harassment] has happened [to her], so she had a list of demands: one, two, three, four, five. Well, now [it's] "I want six, seven, eight, nine, and ten." She was working on anger and a need for some kind of retribution. . . . That's one of the things you deal with as a

> lawyer. . . . And I went back [to the defense] and asked for six, seven, eight, nine, and ten, and I think we got six and seven. And Kristin and I sat down and talked about it. (PL34)

In Ms. Baker's interview, she was very positive about her lawyer and described her own involvement in the case as highly engaged. She affirmed that settlement negotiations were extended (when the defendant employer offered $10,000 if she left the company, she refused, insisting on keeping her job and receiving an apology) and that her final settlement was trivial (one dollar) after a painful litigation. But she believed she had gotten what was most important to her.

Lawyers who specialize in plaintiffs' employment civil rights work are required to scrutinize, evaluate, and control clients—work that may seem removed from the ideals of pursuing workplace justice through law. At least occasionally, these lawyers report working with "heroic clients" who exhibit both extraordinary personal courage and commitment in a case that makes new law. Perhaps the clearest example was Cliff Wavel (P30), a white senior executive approaching sixty years of age who was terminated due to his deteriorating health shortly after the ADA became applicable to his employer. As an early case involving a jury trial under the ADA, Mr. Wavel's claim was legally significant. He filed the claim after being told by his doctor that he had six to twelve months to live. One of his attorneys (PL30, 1) spoke in reverential tones, "The man was . . . a true visionary. A human being with frailties and faults, but a remarkable visionary with respect to his place in the world. . . . When it came to his place in history and legal history, [he] had a very clear vision." Mr. Wavel gave a videotaped deposition a few months after filing his claim but died prior to trial. His heroism may have bolstered his case. The jury awarded his family over $300,000, and the award was upheld on appeal.

Problems with Clients

One of the realities of the employment civil rights practice from the standpoint of plaintiffs' attorneys are problems they inevitably encounter in representing plaintiffs. The plaintiffs' lawyers we interviewed described plaintiffs' confusion, defiance, and unrealistic expectations.

CONFUSION ABOUT WHAT IS UNFAIR AND WHAT IS ILLEGAL. According to the plaintiffs' lawyers, a central part of the screening process in selecting clients and initially handling their cases revolves around explaining to a potential plaintiff the difference between treatment that is *unfair* and treatment that is *illegal*, which they commonly misunderstand. Aaron Erlington (PL24), a white attorney with a small firm, described his approach:

> I usually don't suggest discrimination. I want to know if they'll come up with that on their own, and many times they do. If they think it's strictly a personality conflict or "They said I didn't do a good job, but I really did do a good job"—it's simply a difference of opinion. . . . I'd say far and away the majority of cases I cannot do anything about. I use the term: "It may be unfair, but unfair is not illegal." . . . I might go to the "at will" doctrine.

The at will doctrine, in most states, gives the employer the right to terminate an employee "at will"—that is, for any reason or no reason at all, so long as the reason is not illegal. A central challenge in employment civil rights cases is to prove the claim that the employer behavior was illegal discrimination, not just unfair treatment. Potential clients who do not see the distinction may find themselves frustrated with lawyers they believe just do not understand their situation.

MANIPULATING THE ATTORNEY AND DEFYING ADVICE. Occasionally plaintiffs' lawyers will learn that their client has not told the truth about some aspects of their claim. Mr. Kovac, the experienced attorney quoted earlier, noted that sometimes clients have consulted several attorneys about whether they have a viable claim. In the process, they learn what parts of their story to emphasize in order to interest an attorney in taking the case. He described, for example, a client making a sexual harassment claim involving her supervisor, who allegedly "was after her for sexual favors." After deposing her coworkers, it became clear to Mr. Kovac that the client had engaged in provocative behavior toward the supervisor. Mr. Kovac remembered "taking her aside and saying, 'Why did you lie to me?' Her response was, 'Well, he's lying too.' . . . She wanted to play the litigation lottery and told me a story." Mr. Kovac described for us how he took control of the situation by saying to her, "You know what we are going to do now? We're going to settle your case, and you're going to take whatever I can get, or you're going find another lawyer."

Plaintiffs' lawyers report they sometimes begin to encounter more tension with clients as a case proceeds, to the point that they may believe they are "being worked" by the client. Doug Schwartz (PL52), a white, small-firm attorney in his early sixties, described how after two years of "fighting with the damn employer and the employer's lawyers . . . you want your client to love you, and instead they start thinking you are trying to sell them out like everyone else. And then they start to play you." He described one client who was not straightforward about what she would settle for. After extensive negotiations with opposing counsel and the client's initial inflexibility about her demands, it became clear to Mr. Schwartz that his client was planning, all along, to take the employer's final offer. "She didn't want to share that [information] with us, because she thought we wouldn't work hard enough for her."

As plaintiffs enter the adversarial process, their attorneys commonly advise them on how to behave as credible claimants. Even the best preparation does not always work, though, as attorneys recounted the ways that plaintiffs fail to follow advice on how to approach the proceedings. One experienced attorney (PL15) suggested that his African American client lost on summary judgment because, against his advice, she appeared at a videotaped deposition in a black leather jacket, which he feared would evoke an image of "the Black Panther party" or "being militant." Worse, though, were her answers to very basic questions about discrimination:

> [Defense counsel] would ask . . ."Do you believe 'X' discriminated against you because of your race?" and she would say, "No." . . ."Do you believe 'X' retaliated against you?" "No." Well, what the hell am I here for? This is the precise thing that we told her not to say. . . . Once you give those answers . . . you take the bat out of your lawyer's hands.

Other attorneys noted that plaintiffs who come across as "a know-it-all" or "too arrogant" would predispose the courtroom players against the client.

CLIENTS' UNREALISTIC EXPECTATIONS AND BAD DECISIONS. Plaintiffs' lawyers must constantly manage clients' emotional needs. In some cases, this may make it difficult for the lawyer to, in their view, rationally resolve the case. Ms. Cottle spoke about the challenge of settling a case "if the person really feels they were mistreated . . . because they have a lot of emotional distress and anger and frustration, but not a lot of monetary damages." Other attorneys recalled clients determined to go to trial no matter what. In one story, a lawyer thought his client might have been offered a token settlement, but "she'd never have taken it. She was on a mission."

Plaintiffs' lawyers believe some clients will never be satisfied with the outcome of their case. Mr. Shapiro said, "We have a joke, 'How much does your client want?' 'A dollar more than [the defendants] are willing to pay.'" In the case he discussed with us, Mr. Shapiro believed there were some weaknesses. When the client was offered a substantial settlement offer, he and other attorneys advised her to accept it. Though she eventually did take the settlement, she often was resistant:

> One moment [the client] would listen to the whole spiel and agree, and then one moment she wouldn't. Then she did agree, and then, after she agreed, while we were working on the paperwork, she claimed she didn't understand it. I didn't really think that was accurate, because I knew we'd been very careful, and I also knew . . . she's a smart, sophisticated person. . . . Another old saying around here is, "By the time you get to the end of a case, you understand why the client was fired."

Plaintiffs' counsel also occasionally encounter clients with inflated estimates of the damages they might win in their case, just as they encounter clients with realistic, even low estimates of possible damages.

Some of the declined settlement decisions we have described thus far followed the advice of counsel, and yet, in retrospect, the plaintiff would have been better off accepting. Other bad decisions on settlement offers were made even in the face of strong legal advice to the contrary. One horror story involved a case in which the plaintiff had lost on summary judgment in the trial court, had filed and argued an appeal in the appellate court, and, while waiting for the appellate decision, was offered a significant settlement by the employer:

> They put $300,000 on the table to settle the case. . . . I told the client, "You want to roll the dice, it's your call." The client would have wound up with $180,000. . . ."If you want to take it, it's over, done with. And remember, the trial judge threw it out of court . . ." He wanted to roll the dice, and the appeals court affirmed. He wound up with nothing. (PL8)

These accounts of plaintiffs' attorneys and their clients provide new insights into how the system of employment civil rights litigation functions. Both plaintiffs and their lawyers recognize that, despite lip service to the notion that plaintiffs control their cases, plaintiffs' lawyers largely call the shots. Interviews from each side of the relationship also show that lawyer-client relationships in this arena are fraught with tension. Plaintiffs' lawyers struggle to control their clients and deal with opposing counsel, while clients struggle to understand their case and assert their rights. Many of these tensions are created in the workplace and exacerbated in the litigation process. As employees attempt to mobilize their rights and turn to law and lawyers, they confront a harsh set of realities. Plaintiffs' lawyers seek to encourage valid legal claims, while often translating harsh realities for clients.

Our interviews reveal the variations in cases, clients, and lawyer-client relationships. Just as clients range from passive to assertive to heroic to problematic, lawyers range from insensitive and selfish to caring and competent. These variations and tensions give rise to predominantly ambivalent or negative evaluations of lawyers by plaintiffs in our sample.

Defendant Employers' Perspectives on Their Legal Representation

Our interviews with the twenty defendant representatives—sixteen of whom are inside counsel, the remainder HR officers—stand in stark contrast to the reports of plaintiffs about their lawyers.[15] Defendant organizations report being in control of or at least working very closely with outside counsel, making decisions based on strategic (mostly cost-based and managerial) considerations, and having long-standing relationships with outside counsel. Unlike plaintiffs, who often express ambivalence or downright distaste for their lawyers, defendant representatives—namely, inside counsel and HR personnel who are part of management—expressed no ambivalence about outside counsel. In fact, they generally characterized the relationship without any kind of expressive comment.

Yet one realization that comes through the defendant representative interviews, from their perspective from inside the employing organization, is that outside counsel are not the center of the workplace employment civil rights universe. Outside lawyers are but one kind of resource. For most defendant employers in most cases we discussed, outside counsel is seen as playing a relatively minor role (the smaller the organization and the fewer their cases, the more important outside counsel will appear). Outside attorneys are far more likely to be involved in the upper levels of the employment civil rights dispute pyramid—at the level of filing with the EEOC or in court. In the much larger base of the pyramid, at the level of *potential* disputes, HR departments are more likely to be the central actors.

Given this backdrop, we organize the analysis of interview material in two main sections. First, we report the internal perspectives of defendant representatives in employment civil rights matters, where the emphasis is on the strategies used by internal counsel and HR executives to handle and prevent claims. Second, we consider how defendant organizations characterize their agreeable relationships with outside counsel.

From the Inside: Handling and Preventing Claims

Inside counsel and HR personnel are part of management. Although our interviews focused on how employer organizations deal with lawsuits, the defendant representatives discussed how they deal with potential claims as one aspect of managing an organizational personnel system. Krista Hewick (D36), a white inside counsel in a manufacturing company, explained how her department pursued broader personnel goals in handling potential cases:

> I would say the general strategy would be to figure, to early on sort out the problem and understand that these are real people. . . . As a result, the problem is not only legal. You know? You just can't solve the legal problem. It's not really litigation. You're trying to solve the whole problem. The personalities, the job structure, you know, whatever is going on that is causing these issues. We're trying to resolve all of that, because, essentially, what we're looking for is productivity, and productivity comes from people understanding what they are being asked to do and doing it together and not undermining each other. . . . Now, we still get sued. We still have a number of EEO charges, for example, and eventually a certain number of them become lawsuits. . . . Most of the time, [these cases arise] when [inside counsel is not] involved at the early stage. Either somebody didn't recognize it, or the employee didn't give us a warning that there was a problem, and all of a sudden, there you go: now we're sued.

Law is integrated into several standard personnel processes.

One inside counsel (D71) consistently got signed waivers in exchange for a generous severance pay plan:

> We like to think of it as sort of a transition pay, to kind of help them through the next month until they can maybe land on their feet and kind of get things settled, but we also look at it as resolving a lot of disputes early on. [It] puts things to rest.

Such a practice is not just to be humane but also to gain some legal protection. One inside counsel mentioned an omnibus phone line that allowed employees to complain about any company matter: "The hope is that sometimes, if you've got areas where we have potential exposure . . . it gives you an opportunity to make changes that you need to make" (D62-2). According to this lawyer, sometimes counsel must persuade a manager that the company will settle, rather than litigate, because the "case is not winnable because of something stupid they said." In these instances, inside counsel routinely seeks to help employers to learn from mistakes and prevent future cases. Yet the overwhelming pattern reported by these insider interviewees was of a very small number of instances that led to formal legal complaints, and, of those, a tendency for making the smallest settlements possible.

The internal perspective we provide here casts more direct light on the organizational politics that may be at work in decisions on employment civil rights cases. Informants discussed the tensions between the law department and operational department managers over whether and for how much to settle cases. This sometimes concerned who was going to pay, as most defendant organizations seem to have a centralized legal risk budget, so that the department involved would not have a cost imposed on it (D63). Other informants reported that HR was the lead department on employment civil rights claims, both in terms of when they became involved and who within the organization had the authority to make decisions on settlement offers.

These observations provide a distinct perspective on how defendant organizations deal with employment civil rights in the workplace prior to the resolution of cases. While, in some sense, we can think of these inside counsel and HR professionals as representatives of equal employment opportunity, they deploy law in the service of management. Our informants' accounts include some stories of political conflict around litigation strategy between those two teams, but the accounts are mostly about different strategies within law, not conflicts about legality itself or about the autonomy of professional judgment.

Deploying Outside Counsel

Some employers rarely use outside counsel in employment cases. Nicole Price (D64), a white inside counsel with a healthcare nonprofit having 1,300 employees, reported that her company typically had two or three claims pending with the EEOC or the state Department of Human Rights at any given time: "We actually handle things in house here, so we actually do the entire process. We've found that that tends to be much more effective than farming it to outside counsel." At her company, it was more common to use outside counsel for "strategy purposes." Another inside counsel reported handling "95% in house" (D11). At the EEOC charge stage, outside counsel is only brought in under unique conditions. Susan O'Hoone (D62-1), a white inside counsel for an energy corporation, described those conditions: "There is something extremely unusual . . . or there's multiple plaintiffs, or . . . we're confident it's going to turn into a lawsuit. . . . In all the ones I handled, I maybe had outside counsel on an EEOC charge once or twice."

In smaller companies, the HR department and outside counsel may take primary responsibility even at the early stages of an EEOC charge. Don Gale (D61), a white inside counsel to a research corporation, told us that HR handles EEOC matters, which was his preference. "They have a much larger office, they have more resources. . . . I do get a copy of [the EEOC charge], but it's also referred immediately to our outside counsel." Mr. Gale went on to discuss how the company relies on outside counsel rather than add internal staff, both because the EEO cases were so rare and because the timing of demands for this extra work are sufficiently unpredictable that one more staff person might not be able to handle all the demands at once.

When employers hire outside counsel, they typically use lawyers and law firms with whom they have a long-standing and, often, "preferred provider" relationship (which typically entails a discount for fees). One vice president described using the same law firm for "at least thirty years" (D61). He said he had used the same lawyer for more than fifteen years, even though the lawyer had been with three different law firms over that period: "For me, it's just simpler."

Nonetheless, inside counsel may work closely with outside counsel over the course of litigation. Sara Ramsden (D31), a white inside counsel, edited pretrial briefs, participated in witness preparation, and would have been second chair to outside counsel had the case not settled:

> This particular case, we had lived and breathed it before it went out [to outside counsel]. Not always do we do that. It is more typical that a whole case will go out, rather than we have it and then, on the eve of trial or when the trial date's been set, we hand it out. On those cases where they really work on it start to finish, it's more typical that outside counsel will be more directly involved, although we almost always review and edit briefs before they go out.

In this case, Ms. Ramsden selected a trusted outside counsel "that a lot of people at the company know and whom I knew, that if he went to trial, they would trust. . . . But further, that he needed to tell them to settle the case." She confirmed that the outside counsel was primarily retained to reinforce her decision.

This is an interesting illustration of how sophisticated clients deal with employment civil rights cases. Ms. Ramsden's choice of counsel reflected her strategy for resolving the case in a way that optimized the outcome for her employer. She was also sensitive to the political context within her company: no one would second-guess her choice of counsel or the litigation strategy that person would recommend. The case presented some substantial risk to her employer. After losing on motion for summary judgment, she and the outside counsel worked together to settle the case. The settlement was substantial in monetary terms, but the plaintiff was not allowed to return to work. As Ms. Ramsden recalled, "The client's goals were to continue doing business in the way that they wanted to do business, and their goals were definitely achieved."

While inside counsel and HR officials have a distinctive insider perspective on how to deal with actual and potential civil rights claims, they did not describe for us any significant tensions with outside counsel. As resourceful clients, inside counsel and HR managers control the decisions about whom to retain for outside counsel and how to use them. Depending on outside counsel for their expertise and their capacity to handle the demands of cases that proceed to litigation, inside counsel and outside counsel share a commitment to advance the interests of the employer—in the case at hand *and* in the long run.

Defense Lawyers' Perspectives on Employer Defendants

Defense counsel in employment civil rights cases have amicable professional relationships with their clients—much more so than plaintiffs' lawyers do with their clients. However, due to the nature of the adversarial system, some of the same tensions arise. The most basic difference is that defense attorneys are representing organizations with which they have an ongoing relationship or with whom they are *trying* to cultivate an ongoing relationship. While individuals are not infrequently named as parties to these cases, most cases involve the defense of a business or a governmental unit. Employer defendants vary considerably in terms of organization size, but most large companies in particular are repeat players in employment civil rights cases. To paraphrase one informant, they have been sued before and they will be sued again.

In this section, we examine the significance of ongoing relationships between outside counsel and employer clients for the system of employment civil rights.[16] Then, we turn to a central issue in the literature: what is the power of defense counsel with respect to their clients? Do they enjoy professional autonomy, allowing them to set the terms of their professional engagement and act as mediators of social conflict? Or are their approaches dictated by clients, relegating them to the narrow role of "hired gun"? Finally, we discuss some of the problems and positive experiences defense counsel report about their relationships with clients.

The Significance of Ongoing Relationships with Defendant Employers

Most defense counsel we interviewed primarily represent one side in employment civil rights cases—employers.[17] Most of these attorneys are specialists in employment law (employment civil rights, in particular). These outside counsel to defendant employers typically have been representing their clients for several years. Perhaps at the upper end of the distribution for duration of a client relationship, Jim Schultz (DL22) reported that he had been representing his clients for more than forty years. Mr. Schultz and other defense counselors we spoke with strongly identified with their clients and took an employer perspective on discrimination claims. Mr. Schultz stated:

> We don't discriminate anywhere, let me hasten to add. None of my municipalities, and I hope I can get some [credit] for that. Because the Civil Rights Act came after I was employed in all these municipalities, and we take it very seriously. Those three towns I think are the best three towns in the United States and we try to promote diversity, tolerance, to reach out.

Later, Mr. Schultz reported that his clients seldom settle claims because "we never make mistakes."

Defense counsel learn the distinctive preferences of clients for handling discrimination claims and adapt their representation to suit those preferences. James Kohner (D52), a white lawyer for a large retail chain, was asked whether the particular company and case that he discussed or any of his other clients had a standard strategy:

> Yes, they do. . . . Some take frivolous cases to the mat, like you say, and I think [this large retail chain] is one of those. The case we are discussing . . . after litigating that matter for a year, that particular case settled for three figures. . . . So we were like, "Congratulations." . . . But other clients . . . look at it more from a "cost of business" standpoint. . . . In a retail setting, word gets out. Because everybody knows everybody and . . . each little store is like a little town. . . . If you start settling cases for the cost of defense . . . then you are . . . more likely to be sued more often. Whereas someone who is not in that business, where people aren't turning over all the time, the cost of defense makes more sense.

With ongoing relationships between inside counsel and outside law firms, defendant organizations have considerable control over the nature of their representation.

Outside counsel routinely had capacity to build an intimate, ongoing relationship with the employer organization and their employment matters. Several defense counsel reported providing advice on employment manuals and other practices to reduce the likelihood that their clients would be sued again. Many became involved in terminations before they occurred, further committing those lawyers to defending management's behavior if litigation ensued. For example, Trond Davies (DL72), an experienced white counsel with a small firm, described how he steered management away from their initial plan to not rehire a disabled employee after a reduction in force, advising, instead, that an outside expert document the man's underperformance. The employee sued after losing his job, but the client organization was well prepared to respond. That is unlikely to be the experience of the employee.

Defense counsel were able to pick and choose and strategize among a stable of their own lawyers to satisfy their clients' needs—in sharp contrast to the uncertainties plaintiffs faced in their search for appropriate counsel and the resources plaintiffs' lawyers have at their disposal. Defense counsel also report that they determine and tailor their defense strategy based on the politics of the workplace and the personalities involved. Preston Gibbon (DL2), a white middle-aged attorney in a medium-sized law firm, explained:

> One of the things that's different . . . in employment cases as opposed to other types of cases is they're very emotional. Someone is accusing someone of discriminating or sexually harassing someone. That becomes very, very personal. . . . How that plays into the politics of the organization will, in some measure, determine how or what you're willing to settle a case for.

A particularly profound difference we see when we compare the relationships between defense counsel and their clients with the relationships between plaintiffs' counsel and their clients is the role of money. In chapter 5, we detailed how money is often a barrier to plaintiff obtaining and keeping representation and has a determinative effect on how plaintiffs' lawyers conduct cases. For defense counsel, money is also a central consideration, although money is not a barrier to representation. Instead, cost shapes how defendant employers determine their legal strategies. Our interviews with defense counsel are replete with references to whether it is "worth it" to clients to pursue the defense of a claim, though it may be technically more expensive than settling. Some defense lawyers talk about how their high hourly rates make clients take their advice seriously. And there is discussion of what policies and practices can be put in place to minimize potential exposure to major liability and its attendant costs.

The Power of Defense Counsel?

The relationships between defense counsel and defendant organizations shape the treatment of employment civil rights claims. Employers of significant size typically have inside counsel to manage the relationships with outside counsel. Large employers also have HR professionals who are involved with employment matters and sometimes interact with outside counsel. One question relevant to the study of the legal profession concerns the consequences of the relationship between these professionals and management. Our interviews support Rosen and Nelson and Nielsen's assertions that it is more valuable to analyze how defense counsel use their repertoire of professional skills and resources to advance the interests of their clients than to search for ways in which they are autonomous from clients.[18] We find that defense counsel prioritize those interests with a philosophy that the clients' concerns are foremost and by avoiding conflict with their clients.

THE CLIENT IS ALWAYS IN CONTROL. Like their counterparts in the plaintiffs' bar, outside defense counsel consistently state that the client is always in control of key decisions about litigation. Coming from plaintiffs' lawyers, this sometimes seemed like lip service. However, it is part of the business model of defense representation. Mary Hill (DL18), the defense attorney in the case brought by Annie Daley, said of corporate clients:

> 🎧 You really always have to start with asking them about what their business concerns are associated with a case, what their business objectives are. Because if you start trying to tell them what their philosophy ought to be, that usually doesn't work. And it seems presumptuous, because the lawyers always have to ultimately serve the business.

As defense counsel work with a client, they listen to and learn about how their clients want to handle the case. Donald Bryant (DL71), a white partner in a nationally prominent employment firm, explained, 🎧 "It's not like I barge in and say, 'Here's how we're going to do this case, and it's my way or the highway.' . . . It's a very collaborative process. I listen to what the client wants early on in the case."

Defense counsel clearly see that part of their role in employment civil rights litigation is to gain an understanding of the client's objectives and tailor their actions to achieve those objectives, in the case before them and on their employment civil rights cases in general.

Government attorneys echoed this observation. Despite the fact that when the government is a defendant in a civil case the decision makers do not suffer a monetary consequence in the same way a private business does, the agency being sued controls decisions about the litigation. Gary

Littlejohn (DL74), an African American defense lawyer who worked with city government, said, "They're not paying us, but we'll yield to them because . . . it comes from their budget line. . . . They are the client, and we respect that." Another government attorney bemoaned the fact that some of the cases she believed should have been settled had not been, because "one of the problems working for a state agency is there's no cost-benefit analysis" (DL39). Whether by conscious design or bureaucratic mandate, defense counsel accept that clients control key decisions in litigating employment claims.

ABSENCE OF CONFLICTS WITH CLIENTS OVER LITIGATION DECISIONS. As defense counsel apply their expertise, it is conceivable that there will be occasional tactical disagreements. With the exception of the government attorney immediately above, we find a remarkable lack of such conflict. We asked Lilly Evans (DL51), a white senior attorney in a large law firm, if a major difference of opinion with a client had given her qualms about proceeding with representation. She reported that she always deferred to the client: "That's part of the way it works." This demonstrates how outside counsel, through their reported attitude and actions, avoid conflict. Likewise, none of the private defense counsel respondents reported an irreconcilable conflict with a client. Mr. Gibbon was asked whether a disagreement led to severing a client relationship: "I've been practicing for thirty years, and maybe I'm fortunate. I've never had a situation where . . . I hadn't been able to go to a client and say 'We're wrong, you need to fix this.' Never."

DYNAMICS OF DEFERENCE AND THE CONSEQUENCES Defense counsel still give their clients advice. And given the context of the client-attorney relationship on the defense side—characterized by the outside counsel's strong identification with client goals and its active participation in advancing the clients' broader interests in adversarial conflicts—the advice offered by outside defense counsel often shapes how matters are handled. Glenda Klondike (DL54), a white attorney in a large law firm, described the variation in how much clients defer to her:

> We deal either with in-house attorneys—in large companies sometimes it will be an in-house attorney who handles only employment cases—and then we have smaller clients, where we're dealing directly with an HR person and maybe a company president making the call. I think they rely on us to tell

> them . . . an objective assessment of the credibility of their witnesses. We can tell them what our experience has been in similar cases, we can give them information about typical verdicts, we can scare them, or we can give them great confidence about the case. I think we have quite a bit of [influence] in terms of whether it settles.

Ms. Klondike went on to say that division heads are "very responsive" to advice. The "only exception," she said, is when the allegations come against someone "fairly high up the food chain." In those situations, the client is likely to fight the case by taking the position that they will not defend someone who has engaged "in the conduct that [that person is] alleged to have engaged in." As these interviews reveal, even sophisticated and powerful actors in the defendant organization will defer to the technical expertise of their outside counsel. Still, if push comes to shove, as in a case involving someone "high up the food chain," the client may be reluctant to follow the tactical advice.

Outside attorneys may exercise their authority in subtle ways, as well. Ms. Hill articulates about how she takes control of the construction of her client's case:

> I don't actually depend on my client to tell me the plaintiff's side of the story, because I assume that my client actually does not know the plaintiff's side of the story. That's kind of my job, so I try to construct the plaintiff's side of the story from whatever data is available before the deposition . . . and try to take the plaintiff's deposition . . . very early in the case.

As an outsider to the defendant organization, Ms. Hill had a representational repertoire that included learning the plaintiff's account directly from them in the course of a deposition. This process of learning the plaintiff's story already is inherently adversarial. The defense counsel will attempt to elicit a plaintiff's narrative that undermines the plaintiff's legal case. We know in the case of Annie Daley, who was deposed by Ms. Hill, that the deposition was a stressful experience in which her character, competence, and veracity were challenged.

When it comes to weighing whether to offer a settlement to avoid legal costs or to litigate fully despite the legal costs, defense attorneys could be very deferential to their clients' preferences. Trent Watkins (DL25), a white middle-aged attorney in a large law firm, commented on one client that preferred litigating to settling:

> The particular client took a very hard line on a lot of these things. If [the company] . . . went through the process and reached the conclusion that it had done no wrong, it really was a client who said, "Hey, we'd rather spend a lot more money to vindicate ourselves than spend less money . . . to get rid of it." . . . I don't know from a business point of view whether it's prudent or not prudent, but their view was, "Once we decide we did it right and our people were right, we will back it to the hilt. . . . We won't give them a dime."

Yet outside counsel frequently reported having considerable influence over the design and execution of strategy. Sometimes it is the defense counsel who suggests forging ahead. Ms. Hill recounted her advice to clients to take cases to trial rather than settle if plaintiffs' lawyers began bringing a series of cases against them:

> I have, on occasion, where a client has a plaintiffs' lawyer who seems to specialize in the client or you are getting the fourth, fifth, sixth case or the same plaintiffs' lawyer . . . I've gone to the company and said, "Look, this guy is making a living on you. . . . You've got to destroy his business plan, and there is only one way to destroy his business plan. You have to take him to trial, and you have to beat him. And then you have to let everybody know about it."

These instances again drive home the importance of the fact that outside counsel are a key resource that employer defendants, as repeat players, can rely on when employees mobilize their rights in the asymmetrical, unequal system of employment civil rights litigation. Their attorneys are litigating with the organization's broader interests in mind, not with regard to what might be seen as fair in an individual case.

Defense Attorneys' Problems with Clients

As some of the foregoing suggests, the fact that employer defendants have resources and often are repeat players in employment civil rights does not mean that defense lawyers do not encounter problematic client behavior. Defense counsel observed that the HR staff may not have been very effective in handling cases, sometimes by giving away too much in the early phases of a dispute.

One defense counsel working in government complained that some agencies "always" took a hard line in litigation regardless of what defense counsel advised. That made it hard for counsel to manage the cases. Just as plaintiffs' attorneys may be surprised by their client's behavior in depositions and at trial, despite their best efforts at coaching, defense attorneys can be taken off-guard. Allison Matsumi (DL73), a white attorney in her fifties with a mid-sized firm, said:

> Sometimes we have people who are totally innocent, and they're just awful witnesses, awful, awful, awful. And, I mean, you sit at depositions, and you go, "Why did I spend three hours with them? They just are terrible witnesses." I've had supervisors who sit there, and in front of the plaintiff, will completely change their story and be like really friendly to the plaintiff.

Some of the problems defense counsel run into stem from the organizational nature of their clients. Individuals who were centrally involved on the management side of these cases may have left the company, sometimes on less than favorable terms, but these named defendants may remain clients of the defense attorneys. Mr. Gibbon recounted: "It can happen and it can be a nightmare. . . . If you [tell them to get their own lawyer], then you lose control over that individual, and once that happens, you have less control over what they're going to say. And that could hurt your other client." Like plaintiffs, defendant organizations may sometimes change their goals over the course of litigation. These changes in objectives often come through interaction with outside counsel.

Mr. Bryant had a typology for how clients change approaches over the course of litigation:

> I like to say there are three types of clients. Client A is "I'll spend a million dollars to defend this suit and not a penny for tribute. I will not pay on a case that I don't have to. I am taking this to the mat." We like Client As, by the way. . . . Client B, everything is a business decision. "What will it cost to litigate this case? What will it cost to settle it? How cheap is it to settle it?" Everything is a business decision. We have very few, very, very few who are Client As. [We have a] fairly significant group of Client Bs. But the vast majority are Client Cs. Client Cs *think* they are Client As, but they are really Client Bs. . . . The less sophisticated the client is, the more likely they are to fall into level A or C.

In Mr. Bryant's account, most Client Cs eventually come around to a business calculus about disposing of the case. Such changes could present challenges for how defense counsel manage their relationships with clients and develop strategy.

Perhaps the most intractable problem for defense counsel is that, from their perspective, their clients are never fully satisfied with the outcome of their cases. Ms. Klondike said, "They feel horrible no matter what happens. . . . Never vindicated. The only time maybe is when some large company is splitting the bill with an individual manager. [Then, the leadership] feels that they've been vindicated." Even then, she remarked, the worry is that "somehow the company is going to hold it against me. I cost them this money. . . . We've had some great wins for clients, and they still are kind of like, 'Thanks, big huge bill.'"

There is little doubt that defense counsel in employment civil rights cases are strongly identified with the positions of their corporate clients and zealously advance their client's objectives. As we will see even more explicitly in the next chapter, part of their relationship with employer clients is that they embrace the importance of adherence to antidiscrimination laws, thus they must consistently attack the credibility of the plaintiffs who seek to invoke the law.

Simultaneously, as part of their function to minimize the legal risks and legal costs of clients, defense counsel become a voice for legality in the defendant organization's workplace. They warn clients not to engage in certain actions, and they urge clients to adopt policies that will minimize the threat of liability. Lawyers often bear the bad news that it would be wise for the client to settle a case rather than pay the mounting cost of representation. We could say: defense counsel are damned if they do and damned if they don't. If they pursue a full litigation strategy, they guarantee their client will pay some significant costs. If they urge a course of settlement, they leave their employer client feeling like they have paid money without vindication. Defense counsel may, therefore, be unhappy—if well-paid—participants in a system they help to sustain.

Conclusion

This chapter analyzed lawyer-client relationships in employment civil rights cases and contested constructions of such cases through the perspectives of plaintiffs on their lawyers, plaintiffs' lawyers on their clients, defendants on their lawyers, and outside defense counsel on their employer clients. The findings confirm the significant differences in lawyer-client relationships between individual plaintiffs and corporate defendants. As individuals, plaintiffs face the challenge of finding a lawyer on their own and often struggle in their efforts to work with their lawyers. They feel both dependent on and powerless to control their lawyers. Plaintiffs' lawyers face the challenge of selecting good cases and good clients and often struggle to control their clients in the face of attacks by defendants and defense counsel. It is not surprising that the pressures on both sides of the plaintiffs' attorney-client relationship result in plaintiffs' largely negative and ambivalent assessments of their legal representation.

In contrast, lawyer-client relationships for defendant organizations are far more positive. No defendants are unrepresented. Most have multiple professionals, inside the company and out, to assist in keeping them out of court and winning cases if they do end up in court. Defendant employers control their relationships with outside defense counsel, typically through the work of inside counsel (employees). While defendant representatives and outside defense counsel have complaints about each other, they both strongly identify with the interests of the employer defendant, share a commitment to advancing the client's interest, and can have significant influence on employer behavior as interpreters of legal risk (see chapter 4). Since their top priority is to minimize the legal risk to their client, they see no tension between ensuring that their client complies with EEO law and taking a tough, adversarial approach toward plaintiff employees.

Thus lawyer-client relationships reflect and reinforce the inequality we see at work elsewhere in the system of employment civil rights litigation. With the limited exception of class action litigation, wherein plaintiffs' attorneys can mobilize their clients to attack systemic practices of an employing organization, plaintiffs' lawyers, defendants, and defense counsel engage in the individualization of the civil rights claim. When plaintiffs' lawyers are deciding which clients to accept and how much to invest in various stages of litigation, they are analyzing the individual strengths and weaknesses of the case, including the strengths and weaknesses of the plaintiff. Similarly, defendants and their lawyers, having designed personnel systems to minimize legal risk, seek to discredit the individual plaintiff and their claim. We give closer attention to the adversarial dynamics of employment civil rights litigation in the next chapter.

CHAPTER SEVEN

Right Right, Wrong Plaintiff

Adversarial Conflict and the Disavowal of Discrimination

In this chapter, we analyze how opposing sides experience adversarial conflict in employment civil rights litigation. Employment discrimination law, like much American law writ large, is implemented through a system of adversarial legalism.[1] Lawyers and polarizing litigation prevail over the formation and implementation of policy and the resolution of disputes. As the cases we study proceed, zealous advocacy on both sides further polarizes an antagonistic conflict. This adversarialism informs each side's actions and perceptions. As our interviews reveal, plaintiffs see themselves as the proverbial little guy in a litigation system that favors the more resourceful party.

Meanwhile, defendant representatives and defense attorneys insist that discrimination law rightfully exists and that they lawfully abide by it, and yet they find fundamental flaws with virtually every individual case. They report that when "problem employees" become plaintiffs in a discrimination lawsuit, they are almost always unworthy, misinformed, or malicious adversaries.

We begin the chapter with the stories of two plaintiffs and other legal actors involved in their cases, including defense attorneys with critical assessments. While both plaintiffs saw racism throughout the process, from the workplace to the courtroom, and both faced physical threats, the first story illustrates the experience of a plaintiff who proceeded without counsel and his arguably questionable explanation of why his case resolved as it did. The second story highlights the contentious relationship between attorneys on each side.

Plaintiffs' Stories

Franklin Williams' Case against Railroad, Inc.

Franklin Williams (P11), a thirty-eight-year-old African American man, was a railroad laborer for fifteen years. According to Mr. Williams, his white supervisors became jealous after he was featured in a company film for developing new safety techniques. Then, when he scored the highest on a promotion test, he was not promoted. This led him to file a charge with the EEOC, which he did not pursue. Sometime later, on the job, a large crane hook struck Mr. Williams in the head, and he was seriously injured. He was given a period of leave and a cash payment of $25,000.

Soon after Mr. Williams returned to work, he was punished for two infractions and terminated for a third. First, management suspended him for five days for missing work while appearing in court, even though Mr. Williams claimed that he gave advance notice and that other employees who had taken similar leaves had not been punished. Then management suspended him for ten days for allegedly sleeping on the job. Finally, Mr. Williams's supervisor accused him of saying that he had his supervisor "in his sights" (which the supervisor took to mean his gun sights). At that point, Mr. Williams was fired and led out in handcuffs from the work site by security. In our interview, Mr. Williams denied the validity of all these disciplinary charges, particularly that he threatened his supervisor.

Mr. Williams filed a claim of race and disability discrimination with the EEOC and in federal court. He attempted to obtain a lawyer but ended up representing himself with the very substantial assistance of his wife, a paralegal. We interviewed Mr. and Mrs. Williams in their home. They were convinced that he had been strongly affected by the racism of his fellow workers and supervisors in the workplace. They suspected that the white coworker—one who "dressed like a skinhead"—who unleashed the crane that struck Mr. Williams in the head may have done so purposefully.

Mr. Williams's move to file a claim was the first formal step of transforming his workplace conflict into a legal fight. According to David Lever (D11-2), a white man in his fifties who was one of the railroad company's inside counsel and who tried the case, the charge brought by Mr. Williams was "completely bogus." Predictably, the railroad company worked with legal counsel to fight the case, although, somewhat surprisingly, it did not file a motion for summary judgment. Mr. Lever explained to us that filing such a motion is a "pain in the backside" because of the time investment required, which can be more burdensome than preparing a case and can predispose the judge against a company.

From the Williams's perspective, they were up against more than just the railroad. The judge became an adversary, too. The couple saw racism in the actions of the judge and lawyers and in the legal system writ large. As Mr. Williams remarked, "When it boils down, oh man, talk about racism." One indication of this bias, according to the Williamses, was the fact that the judge, a white man, repeatedly allowed defense counsel—led by a white man—to miss required dates for trial preparation. When Mr. Williams asked for sanctions, the court rejected his request. He described it this way:

> The judges wouldn't touch [the defense counsel] with a ten-foot pole. We asked that he be sanctioned. We asked for judgments by default. Had I been late one time, they'd have kicked it out: "You lose." With him? Nooo. Gave him all the time he needed.

Mr. Williams understood the judge's behavior as racialized, extremely derogatory, and flagrantly unlawful.

> I took it as though they were telling me straight up, and let me be candid, "Nigger, I'm not going to destroy his career for you. Okay, he doesn't follow civil rules of civil procedure. I'm not going to do it for you. I'm not going to sanction him. I'm not going to do one damn thing." And they didn't. I said, "Okay." And believe me, by law, we were right every time and on the money.

The case proceeded to a three-day bench trial. On the last day, the judge interrupted the proceedings to announce, from the bench, the verdict in a high profile, racially charged murder case: O. J. Simpson, a famous African American football player, had been found not guilty of killing his ex-wife, Nicole Brown, who was white. This was a polarizing case. At the time, and for the subsequent decade, the majority of white Americans insisted on O. J. Simpson's guilt, and substantial numbers of African Americans insisted on his innocence.[2]

Later that same day, the judge issued his ruling from the bench, denying all of Mr. Williams's claims. Certain that they had been winning all along, Mr. and Mrs. Williams became convinced that the O. J. Simpson verdict motivated the judge to rule against them "out of anger." Mr. and Mrs. Williams continue to believe that if the judge would reread the transcript of the trial, he would change his mind. Mr. Williams described how he felt about the outcome of the case:

> You know, if it wasn't for my wife and my children, I'd have did like this [mimes shooting himself in the head]. Because I lost everything, you know, and given the fact that, like I said, I've never been arrested for anything, I'm thinking the law exists for everybody. You know how they say it's, "justice?" It's "just us." Not justice for all. . . . "Just us."

In contrast, Mr. Lever, the railroad company's inside counsel, thought this was a clear case for the defendant organization. In his eyes, the case did not even merit a substantial settlement offer because the cause for termination—the alleged threats to the supervisor—were so evident. Mr. Lever said in our interview, "It was, you know, pretty clear . . . [Mr. Williams made] cracks . . . to supervisors about . . . what was it? 'From such and such a location I can see you in my gun sights.' It's like, okay, 'Goodbye.'"

Like Mr. Lever, the trial judge saw the case very differently than did Mr. Williams. In the trial transcript of the judge's ruling from the bench, he noted that it is difficult to prove racial discrimination by "so-called direct evidence" because:

> People usually don't announce their . . . discriminatory attitudes when they make employment decisions. . . . The issue is not whether the employer was right or wrong. . . . [The law] doesn't even guarantee a fair decision. What it does guarantee is that there will be no decision made on the basis of race. . . . I conclude that there is no evidence that Mr. Williams was treated less favorably than any [w]hite employee with a similar pattern of conduct. . . . Possible circumstantial evidence that would support a discrimination charge is simply nonexistent in this case.

In so many words, discrimination exists, according to the judge, but not *evidently* in this case. This was a refrain we heard over and again from defendant representatives.

Annie Daley's Case against Telecommunications, Inc.

Annie Daley (P18), a forty-year-old African American woman, supervised supervisors in a large telecommunications firm. Ms. Daley began to experience what she regarded as racial animus shortly after Judy Berman, a white woman, became her director and started overseeing her hiring decisions:

> I must have had about six or seven supervisors [under my supervision]. And I think I probably I had about four supervisors who just happened to be qualified African American supervisors. And it wasn't that I was specifically going out looking for African American supervisors. I hired the people that were best qualified. And so then I was accused by my director of hiring too many African Americans in my department and, like I said, once I got my team organized and that's when we began to really start pulling things together and we all started meeting our goals.

Ms. Daley later went to Ms. Berman to ask for support when the white supervisors she oversaw were underperforming and engaging in overtly hostile talk about race. Ms. Daley told us:

> And so and I'm telling my director, you know, "Hey, this person is not doing this. This person's not doing that." . . . But she does not support me in correcting them. . . . So there was one particular supervisor who, who made it very clear that she was not going to report to a black woman. . . . She even called me a black "B" [bitch]. . . . You know, I'm telling her all this stuff . . . But well, she's not supporting, my director is not supporting me at all.

When Ms. Berman did not provide assistance in disciplining the white supervisors, Ms. Daley went to the HR department to report these concerns. An HR manager talked to Ms. Berman. Then, two weeks later, Ms. Daley was terminated without warning.

Ms. Daley entered the adversarial legal conflict with counsel. After her termination, Ms. Daley approached a white male attorney, Ellis Barry (PL18), who had represented other plaintiffs against the telecommunications company. Mr. Barry told us he took the case despite the fact that, in his words, "there were no epithets" or other smoking gun evidence:

> I have a strong recollection of her, and she's somebody who I got a very quickly, got a sense of being a quality person who I'm sure—I was sure at that time and still am—you know, was good at her job and was somebody who seemed to me like a quality employee who gave me an explanation of how things happened to her that, I'm sure, based on my recollection now, involved the subtle kind of racial discrimination that you see a lot in the workplace.

Mr. Barry took Ms. Daley's case largely based on his impression that she was a "quality person" whose account would be credible, given circumstantial evidence.

The adversarialism was escalated by the contentious relationship between attorneys on each side. The telecommunications company retained outside counsel, Mary Hill (DL18), a white woman in her fifties, who had a very negative view of Ms. Daley's lawyer. She characterized him as a "bottom feeder" who was reaching to get a large award. According to her account, he tried several clearly unprofessional tactics at trial. Mr. Barry, in turn, voiced suspicion of both the defense and defendant lawyers in general. Offering a more general comment about defendant employers' willingness to lie, he said, "There is a moral relativism . . . that has certainly gotten worse in the last fifteen years. That your team needs to win, and if you've got to forget something or get rid of an email or whatever you need to do. . . . People are strongly motivated to make their team win."

On the defense side, Ms. Hill also had a negative view of Ms. Daley and her case. Interestingly, her description of Ms. Daley was precisely what Ms. Daley believed about how she was perceived and portrayed by her coworkers. Ms. Hill told us:

> I am pretty sure that Annie Daley's supervisors and all the people in that line—because there were some individual defendants in that case, too—um, felt pretty strongly that everything they had done was absolutely kosher. And Annie did not have a case. She had *not* been discriminated against. Uh and, my recollection is that the in-house lawyers supported that as well—both the lawyer and his boss. . . . And then I took her deposition, and I didn't think she was a very persuasive person in deposition. . . . She came across as rigid and sort of bitchy.

The narrative about the lawsuit and, implicitly, the working environment became characterized as Ms. Daley's individual personality problems. Years after the litigation, this characterization remained the one thing everyone could agree on: Ms. Daley was a bitch—a stereotype that we elaborate further in chapter 9. We also see Ms. Hill's subtle but crucial presumption that discrimination is real and that law addresses it—specifically, by setting parameters around what is a case and what is not.

Efforts at settlement were half-hearted from both sides, as the telecommunications company's posture in this period was to litigate rather than settle. Its position may have been hardened because Ms. Daley's attorney had represented other plaintiffs against the company. The company was interested in sending a message to their employees and this attorney that they would not simply settle.

The defendant organization filed a motion for summary judgment, which was denied. On the eve of jury selection, the defendant organization offered a settlement of $100,000. Both the trial judge and Ms. Daley's attorney recommended she accept the offer, although her attorney made it clear that it was her decision. Ms. Daley declined the offer, and the case proceeded to trial. The jury was largely white and included several older white males.

The interviewees each recounted different notable aspects of the trial. Ms. Daley's lawyer recalled learning that the general counsel for the defendant employer attempted to intimidate a witness outside the courtroom. He informed the judge, the trial was halted, the jury was removed, and the general counsel was placed under oath and questioned about the allegation.

For the defense attorney, what stood out about this litigation was that an African American woman who was particularly hostile and who had been Ms. Daley's director (before Ms. Daley's termination) was required to appear before court and give testimony. As the attorney recalled, this woman exuded anger in her appearance, but also admitted that she had given negative evaluations to Ms. Daley.

The night before closing arguments, Ms. Daley recalled, a brick was thrown through her window. She went to a friend's apartment and missed the last day of the trial. Ms. Daley thought that missing the final day of trial influenced the jury's decision. When the case went to the jury, it did not take them long to return a verdict for the defendant organization.

In retrospect, Ms. Daley wished she had accepted the settlement offer. Yet both she and her attorney said that money was a secondary matter in the case. The pursuit of justice was the most important goal. As Ms. Daley explained:

> I was hoping to let them know that this was something that they could not just continue to do to people. To let them know that they were being put on notice. To get justice and then, of course, after that, to get some sort of compensation. . . . You can try to prevent people from you know from mistreating people. . . . But you can't make them not be racist, but you can make them feel it if they choose to be.

Ms. Daley notes not only the difficulty of getting justice but also of changing how people think about race in the workplace. Her case is atypical in that it went to trial, but remarkably typical in other ways. When she pursued a legal claim, the company response was defensive. The defense attacked her competence and questioned her attorney's motives. And, ultimately, in pursuing the case to trial, Ms. Daley lost.

Introduction

Mr. Williams's and Ms. Daley's cases indicate a crucial point of common agreement among those involved in all sides of discrimination litigation: discrimination is wrong and appropriately forbidden by the law. The shared assumption is that employment decisions in the workplace should be colorblind (or otherwise difference-blind). The distinction across the participants lies in their perceptions of why, under law, a given particular case is or is not a case of discrimination. This fundamental issue is contested through an adversarial process that advantages the defense in numerous respects. As repeat players, defendant representatives understand how the adversarial process will play out. Plaintiffs are far less emotionally and financially prepared for litigation and are heavily dependent on their lawyer, if they have one. If, like Franklin Williams, they do not have counsel, they are overmatched and likely to lose. Even with counsel, plaintiffs often are shocked by how they are treated by their former employer and by the legal system.

Of course, plaintiffs bear the burden of proof in civil litigation. What may be less obvious are the emotional and financial burdens plaintiffs carry. As plaintiffs enter litigation they are subject to personal attacks on their competence and credibility. Representatives of the employer and individual named defendants also face financial burdens in litigation, but their experience of the adversarial process is qualitatively different from that of plaintiffs. Because employers have specialists for dealing with personnel disputes and their legal fallout, the stakes for their side are far less personal and far less consequential.

To explain in depth the parties' experiences of adversarial litigation, we first compare the survey data we gathered from plaintiffs, plaintiff lawyers, defendant representatives, and defense lawyers. These data document significant differences in the legal attitudes of plaintiffs and defendant representatives, but also reveal a surprising conservatism among plaintiffs about the civil justice system in general. Second, we examine how plaintiffs experience the litigation process, from dealing with the bureaucracy of the EEOC and the courts to the harsh realities of being subjected to attack by coworkers and defense lawyers. Third, we turn to the defendant representatives' perspective on litigation, which centers on their individualistic explanations for why there is litigation when they no longer discriminate. The fourth section of the chapter documents the often highly contentious, highly emotional character of litigated cases, with an emphasis on attorneys' perspectives on each side.

In a context in which defendant representatives subscribe to the belief of the "right right, wrong plaintiff," the adversarial process individualizes claims of discrimination. Allegations of discrimination are lifted from the complicated context of workplace relations, as we saw in chapter 4, and thrust into an arena of conflicting factual and legal claims. While the effects of this process are more obvious in the small percentage of cases that proceed to trial, adversarialism casts a shadow over all aspects of the cases, shaping the behavior and experiences of parties on both sides and reinscribing the very ascriptive hierarchies that plaintiffs challenge.

Divided Opinions on Civil Justice

As we demonstrated in previous work, plaintiffs and those representing defendant employers have a shared feeling of being unfairly treated in the litigation process.[3] Both parties believe that the litigation process disfavors them for a variety of reasons related to the situated, structural ways that law affects them in the workplace and in the courts. But parties disagree on the fundamental issue: whether discrimination occurred. Plaintiffs and their lawyers begin from a position of believing it did whereas HR executives and defense lawyers—while not completely dismissing the possibility that discrimination can happen—start off believing that discrimination is unlikely in general, unlikely in their specific workplace, and definitely has not happened to this particular individual.

Analysis of our closed-ended interview data on participants' perceptions of civil lawsuits demonstrates the dramatically divergent views that plaintiffs, defendant organizations, plaintiffs' attorneys, and defense attorneys have of the legal system. (All percentage differences reported below are statistically significant at .056 or lower, according to chi square tests.) Seventy-one percent of plaintiffs and 78% of plaintiffs' attorneys we interviewed agreed or strongly agreed with the statement, "Most people who sue others have legitimate grievances," whereas only 35% of defendant employer representatives and 50% of defense attorneys felt similarly. Not a single plaintiffs' attorney disagreed or strongly disagreed that most people who sue have legitimate grievances, whereas 25% of defense attorneys did.

To determine respondents' attitudes about litigation in general, we asked them to respond to the statement: "There are far too many frivolous lawsuits today." Predictably, 80% of defendant representatives and 70% of defense attorneys agreed or strongly agreed with this statement; only 11% of plaintiffs' attorneys did so. Interestingly, 63% of plaintiffs agreed or strongly agreed with this statement. On the one hand, this seems counterintuitive, because we might think plaintiffs, who have first-hand experience with the difficulties of even *getting* to the legal system, would be more sympathetic toward others in the same situation. On the other hand, Haltom and McCann teach us that ordinary citizens are subjected to very biased depictions of law.[4] Plaintiffs, as the only lay participants in the research, generally believe the litigation explosion story but see themselves as exceptions to this rule.

A second point of agreement among plaintiff and defense sides—that litigation brings justice—also is relevant. When we asked respondents to react to the statement "Civil lawsuits have made this a more fair society," all of the plaintiffs' attorneys strongly agreed or agreed, as did 75% of defense attorneys. Even defendant representatives acknowledge the power of the courts to affect justice in society, with 65% agreeing or strongly agreeing with the statement. Plaintiffs had more mixed responses; only 39% agreed or strongly agreed that civil lawsuits have made society more just and another 39% disagreed or strongly disagreed. Thus we see a general belief on the part of all the lawyers we interviewed about the positive social role of civil litigation, while plaintiffs reflect the general public's ambivalence on the issue.

We also see group differences when questions address specific actors within the civil justice system. When asked whether "judges are generally fair and impartial when hearing civil cases," between 83% and 90% of plaintiffs' attorneys, defense attorneys and defendant representatives agreed or strongly agreed. In contrast, only 41% of plaintiffs agreed and none strongly. Juries' ability to determine outcomes and assess damages drew more positive responses from strong majorities of plaintiffs (61%) and their lawyers (83%). Only 45% of defendant representatives and 50% of their lawyers indicate confidence in juries. Plaintiffs' positive view of juries may be explained by the fact that juries are the lay component of the civil justice system. Defendant representatives may fear juries in civil matters because of highly publicized cases in which juries have decided against business and because of inflated reports of large jury awards circulated by insurance companies.

These quantitative results provide a snapshot of the parties' and their attorneys' views of the legal system in the abstract. From our qualitative interviews, which we turn to next, we hear the voices of these participants as they describe their situated, lived experiences of the adversarial dynamics of litigation.

Plaintiffs' Experiences of Bureaucratized Justice

From most plaintiffs' perspectives, what begins as a fight for justice quickly turns into a grueling, frustrating, or tedious encounter with bureaucracy. Malcolm Feeley describes the experience that lay people have navigating bureaucratic hurdles in criminal courts as "the process is the punishment."[5] In employment discrimination litigation, plaintiffs confront myriad rules that must be followed "by the book" and detached legal authorities.[6] The organization of this legal bureaucracy shapes their experiences.[7] It informs their understanding of whether and how to be involved in litigation and the value of doing so (or lack thereof).[8] Plaintiffs routinely perceive legal bureaucracy as dehumanizing, inflexible, and an affront to their ambitions of justice. Those who are privileged, knowledgeable, or just lucky may be able to make sense of the system, identifying where formal rules are more flexible and working them to their advantage. These are the exceptions, however. Most plaintiffs are troubled to find that their case is not decided based on an assessment of merits, but is processed bureaucratically and decided based on rules of procedure.

Dashed Hopes and Lack of Control

Plaintiffs told us they turned to law with optimism. They believed independent authorities would step in, bringing rationalism and justice to the overwhelming, irrational, and unjust conflict in the workplace. Almost across the board, their narratives carry a rueful tinge: plaintiffs assumed the law would be an unbiased path to justice and turned to it as a venue of independent recourse, then learned otherwise as their case went through the bureaucratic process. Kristin Hamilton (P15), an African American woman in her forties who believed that a younger, white male with far less experience was promoted over her, recalled:

> I went [to the company's internal EEO office], and of course they said they were going to investigate, but how do you investigate yourself? . . . There's not an outside [agency] doing it. [The employer is] doing it. So then I did go to EEOC and filed a complaint, and then that's when they gave me the letter to sue.

Ms. Hamilton and other plaintiffs' dispassionate language about seeking legal help contrasts with their descriptions of the workplace problems that spurred the suits. "It was a terribly abusive environment," one plaintiff said. "I was just so appalled and mad," remembered another. "It got stupid; it got real stupid. It got ridiculous," said yet another. Going to a lawyer or filing a complaint seemed like a rational, pragmatic response to an unthinkable situation.

Narratives about the litigation experience transform from visceral and vivid descriptions of unjust treatment at work to a description of fading optimism in the face of the complexities and mundanities of the legal process.

When an individual files a legal claim, they must interact with low-level public sector employees—what Michael Lipsky calls street-level bureaucrats.[9] These employees are the face of the legal bureaucracy. Many plaintiffs remember their first encounters with EEOC and FEPA employees as sources of frustration and dashed hopes. Marjorie Turner (P25), an African American administrative assistant in her forties, is a typical example:

> I mean, I really did go [to the state Department of Human Rights] naively, thinking that they were going to do what I thought was their mission, and that was to protect the rights, your civil rights. And what I found is that

> consistently they don't do that. . . . In fact, I just wrote a letter to ACLU [American Civil Liberties Union] about the Department of Human Rights and the fact that they don't accept evidence that the victim wants to present to them. . . . They don't return calls. I had an investigator who was really rude to me on the phone [and] did not interview me at all before having the fact-finding conference.

Ms. Turner is among the nine plaintiffs we interviewed who report that they expected the EEOC or FEPA, as a gatekeeper of the legal system, to deliver far more than it did. Ten others reported disappointment with the agency. The sociological literature suggests that such dispiriting encounters with street-level bureaucrats are commonplace and consequential. Those employees' jobs are structured, as Lipsky shows, to focus on tasks such as rationing out resources and processing paperwork, while the people who turn to these employees hope for personal responsiveness.[10] Repeated over and again, such routinized tasks constitute the implementation of policy, often to the dismay of those looking to these offices for fairness.

Some plaintiffs initially believed that the EEOC or FEPA would issue a legally binding decision. Philip Jacobson (P21), the African American printing clerk whose story begins chapter 5, explained that, to his memory, the EEOC decided that he had experienced race discrimination and then it changed its position. "I got another letter from EEO saying 'The decision we rendered was erroneous but you have a right to go to federal court.' If the decision was erroneous, then why don't you adjudicate and grant me the things I asked, like my promotions and my back pay? And they didn't." With the federal filings, some plaintiffs run into clerical mistakes and other complications. These plaintiffs' eventual disappointment in law rests, in some part, on their assumption that law would treat them as more of an equal than did their employer and provide helpful recourse.

For other plaintiffs, registering a charge with the EEOC and filing a claim in federal court were non-events. Some who had attorneys did not even recall doing or filing this paperwork. One remarked, "I don't know where we filed." This held true for some *pro se* plaintiffs, in particular, who were quite confused about the technicalities of their cases. Disappointed with the initial reactions they received and unclear on the bureaucratic details, plaintiffs generally came to see their involvement with the litigation system as—in one person's words—"an uphill battle."

Plaintiffs' attorneys are crucially important for helping plaintiffs understand, navigate, and interpret these bureaucratic hurdles. Without a lawyer, plaintiffs struggle. Some benefit from the goodwill of a particularly helpful judge or court clerk, but, for the most part, these individuals face repeated obstacles in the adversarial process. As chronicled in chapter 5, *pro se* plaintiffs see the legal system as operating beyond their control and as degrading.[11] Chris Burns (P5), an African American machinist who, without a lawyer, filed a claim of race, disability, and age discrimination against the military, recalled, "I got so, you know, depressed with the whole bunch of, you know, they send you through all this red tape gobbledy goo, and they say these big twenty-five cents words, and you know without a lawyer degree that you don't understand a thing that they are telling you."

At the Behest of Legal Bureaucrats: Judges, Court Personnel, and Juries

For many plaintiffs, the most significant opportunity they had to make their case was in their interactions with legal actors. As they pursue a case, plaintiffs encounter legal bureaucrats beyond the EEOC and FEPA. Judges are the most important among them, as professionals with specialized training, elevated status, and, above all else, crucial decision-making power. When justice is bureaucratized, judges are supposed to follow the formal rules by making morally neutral decisions.

Plaintiffs' assessments of the judges involved in their cases were mixed among our respondents. Plaintiffs often did not fully comprehend the decision-making process at the level of the judge, magistrate, or appellate judge—other than sensing that that process was supposed to be neutral (as shown above, their assessments of impartiality varied). For most plaintiffs, the judges involved in their cases were distant; many had no face-to-face contact with their judge. Some found this inaccessibility troublesome, while others took it as a sign that the judges were impartial.

When assessing judges, plaintiffs took into account not just the judge's specific decision but also the judge's general role in reaching the decision. Many plaintiffs recounted how judges had intervened or provided assistance in one form or another. Sometimes the judge seemed to be acting to the plaintiffs' advantage, sometimes to the defense's advantage, and sometimes it was not entirely clear—quite likely, toward the judge's own objective of closing the case. Most often, this took the form of encouraging the employer to make a settlement offer or advising the plaintiff to accept such an offer. Maureen Sands (P8), a white product manager in her fifties whose disability case ultimately settled late, described how the judge intervened in her case. The trial date had been set, but he apparently wanted the parties to settle:

> The company didn't want to really settle. . . . And eventually . . . I don't remember why, but the judge asked if I would step out. My assumption is that the other side was not being reasonable . . . and I guess, what the judge wanted to say, he didn't want to say in front of me. I don't know, but it got to the point that he was just doing it between the attorneys.

Seven of the forty-one plaintiffs we interviewed (17%) took their cases to jury trial, which is much higher than the national average, in which just 5.5% of cases go to trial (of those, 68% are heard by a jury). The disparity is an artifact of how we selected the subsample precisely so we could learn about plaintiffs' interactions with judges and juries. As reported above, most plaintiffs had positive views about juries deciding cases when asked in the abstract, but their experiences in their own cases varied substantially. One white executive (P30) testified in court in his disability discrimination case about having been fired from his job when his illness progressed to a serious stage. At that time, his health was deteriorating considerably. His stepson, whom we interviewed, believed that his stepfather's presence in the courtroom "had a real significant impact on the jury," which took just forty-five minutes to award him more than $300,000. Ms. Daley, in contrast, lost her case to an all-white jury that took a few hours to deliberate. By and large, these seven plaintiffs had little to say about the jurors and, when describing the trial to us, were more focused on the outcome and the attorneys' behavior. For Ms. Daley, for instance, the real drama was the brick thrown through her window the night before closing arguments.

Again, having effective legal counsel made a difference for plaintiffs' experiences of facing a judge or jury. Good attorneys worked with plaintiffs to anticipate and make sense of judges' decisions. Ms. Hamilton (P15), who had filed a sex discrimination case and lost, described how her attorney, Harry Morgan (PL15), anticipated and interpreted the judge's decision. Mr. Morgan, she explained, was very optimistic about the prospects of her case:

> He thought Judge Klein was a pretty good judge. 'One of the best out there,' that's what he said. . . . We had our case, they had their case, and she ruled against me, and Mr. Morgan responded by saying, "She made her decision based on their summary judgment. She totally ignored ours."

In the adversarial process, plaintiffs' institutional support (if they had any) came from their attorney. Two had the assistance of non-profit organizations, one of which works on behalf of people with disabilities and the other on behalf of conservative causes. One other described their US senator's office as very helpful.

Not surprisingly, plaintiffs without legal counsel are the most confused about the role of the judge and his or her actions. As one *pro se* plaintiff told us (P13), "[The] judge was a nice lady, but she closed her eyes sometimes. Maybe she felt she had to, maybe she had to, I don't know." A number of plaintiffs complained that the judge decided on some of the charges they filed, but not others. This was an issue for Mr. Williams, who was troubled that the judge did not rule on his disability. Chuckling, Mr. Williams told us, "He didn't even address it at all, and it was in my motion. He just played around it." *Pro se* plaintiffs routinely look to, and depend upon, judges to break down and explain what was going on in their case, which judges did only some of the time. Mr. Burns, who described himself as having only a twelfth-grade education, recalled: "I stood up there before the judge, and he said something way over my head, and, man, I said, 'What?' . . . He didn't take time for me to really get an understanding of what they were doing."

Plaintiffs frequently conflated judicial fairness with favoritism toward their side and conflated judicial bias with favoritism for the defense (the defendants did much the same).[12] A handful of plaintiffs gave glowing comments about the fairness and empathy of the judge in their cases. In the disability discrimination case filed by Evan Oliver (P40), a white environmental scientist in his forties, he was awarded back pay and front pay by the judge; he described the judge working on his behalf in numerous ways, including after his case was closed, when the company refused to pay the full settlement. Mr. Oliver wrote to the judge and, three weeks later, received the money.

Even more meaningful for Mr. Oliver was the judge's final decision in his case. He brought a copy of it with him to the interview and read from it a number of times. Mr. Oliver saw the decision as affirming the fact that he was capable of doing his scientific job of reviewing files despite his disability. Mr. Oliver quoted for us the decision:

> "Specifically in light of Oliver's budding expertise in file reviews, his position could have been structured to make him a specialist in that area. In addition, the position could have been tailored so he would provide information to a senior permit advisor, therefore eliminating public contact. Oliver could have become more involved in compliance evaluation. In short, as far as Jackman, his boss and chief of the section where Oliver was employed, had testified, Oliver's disability could have been accommodated." Now that's the proof right here, that they could have done it.

At least five plaintiffs also described their judges as helpful and affirming.

Yet at least ten plaintiffs characterized a judge in their case as unfairly biased. One plaintiff was blunt, "Excuse my language, [the judge] was a dick. He was a real prick, you know. I mean, you could tell. I mean, he was just so prejudicial against my attorney." Some plaintiffs perceived the judge as colluding with their own attorneys, and even more perceived collusion with the defense. Debra Leonard (P26), a white worker's compensation analyst who lost her disability discrimination case on summary judgment, described the judge in her case as siding with the defense attorneys. Those attorneys, she said, operated as "a good old boys network," with as many as nine appearing in court from two firms. Explaining the outcome of her case, Ms. Leonard said, "The judge took their side. And my attorney was new, kind of new, and he, and he just didn't like my case, I guess." Especially distressing for plaintiffs were judges and juries who endorsed what plaintiffs believed were falsehoods repeated by the defense.

Co-opted Coworkers and Liar Lawyers

As plaintiffs talk through their experiences pursuing litigation, they gradually focus less on the offensive supervisor or the harassing coworker and more on the defense attorneys—and, in the background, upper management—as adversaries. Plaintiffs feel vilified by the defense in depositions and trial testimony. They believe the defense is otherwise favored in the legal system, but, as they see it, the defense side lies. Some plaintiffs told us that witnesses lied in court—some of whom (current or former coworkers) even privately admitted that they had lied. It seems obvious that a coworker who still works for the company has a lot to lose in taking the side of the former employee in court. And yet, plaintiffs were surprised when people who had been their friends and confidantes did not tell the plaintiff's truth. Catherine Harris (P12), whose story opens chapter 4, said:

> They brought that affirmative action/EEO guy on as a, to take a deposition . . . [and later] he says, "I work for the guy; what do you want me to do?" You know? So [in the deposition] he says, "Oh, I didn't see anything." But he used to come into my office and say, "Oh that was shameless what he said to you."

Many plaintiffs felt deeply betrayed by their colleagues' lies. Mr. Collins (P6), a white tradesman in his forties whose case was dismissed with prejudice, explained,

> The thing that upset me the most were the people that I thought were there—that I knew, that I personally knew and liked and I truly believe liked me, that I felt that were there to help me, turned their back on me like I had the plague, like I was nobody. That was probably the cruelest thing out of it all.

Plaintiffs, of course, also blame their employers. Marla Riteman (P32), an African American machine operator whose sex and race case settled early with prejudice, said that she received a troubling phone call at work from—supposedly—the judge in her case, who called with no prior warning. Ms. Riteman suspected that her employer was complicit in this call or fabricated it altogether. She described her reaction when a supervisor told her that the judge was on the phone,

> I kept telling them, "No, this isn't how I want to do it. I don't want to do it on a phone on a tape recorded line." And that's when basically they [the employer] told me if I didn't go along with this that, they would take it to federal court, and I would end up losing and paying all the fees. And I went in there, and I am trying to explain to them, you know, this person who is telling me he is the judge. I am like, "Well, you gotta understand, I don't know who you are,

and this is a tape recorded line." He said, "Well, your supervisor said he is not going to record it." [I said,] "Well, this is a person who is making false accusation. I don't really believe her." He said, "Well, we are going to settle this right now." So that was it.

As it would be highly unusual for a judge to call a plaintiff, Ms. Hamilton had good reason to think the call was fabricated.

Above all else, plaintiffs singled out defense lawyers to blame for negative experiences in the lawsuit. According to one plaintiff, "The defense attorney pulled a lot of crap" (P31). Interviewees said that defense lawyers lied and facilitated lying by witnesses. Lois Smith (P19), a white woman in her thirties who worked as a locomotive engineer, was typical in her surprise at how many people she believed the company convinced to come to court and lie under oath. Ms. Smith said that she lost her case because the defense side brought in two witnesses she had never seen before, and they lied for the company:

LS: They brought this witness in [who said] I was throwing a fit and this and that [scoffs]. . . .

I: So they brought a witness and you had no memory of this person?

LS: Person, incident, anything. Another one too. This conductor [who said] . . . that I was feeling him up in the elevator and I was in some slinky dress. I don't even *own* slinky dresses and I certainly don't bring 'em [to work] . . . I'm a grip on a locomotive! If I'm in Reno, I'm on a train. I came in on the engine, not in the dining car. You know what I mean?

I: Right. So they brought in witnesses that were just surprises to you?

LS: Yes. Friggin' lies. Bold-faced lies.

Even when plaintiffs were able to impeach the credibility of a witness they believed was lying, they said nothing changed. For example, Mr. Williams, the railroad laborer whose story opens this chapter, told us the manager's testimony about the alleged threat was a "bald-faced lie." He told us:

I was on the top of a locomotive washing, you know. We had to clean the roofs because all the soot get up there. And what happened was the supervisor . . . walked back and says, "I heard Franklin mumble a threat to me." Mind you, have you ever heard a locomotive run? . . . It all came out in court.

> How in the hell could you hear me mumble anything to you? We brung that out, we brung it out in the investigation. . . . How can you hear a mumble on a locomotive as high as this woodwork here [indicating about ten feet]?

The lie from the workplace continued to be the story in the litigation in Mr. Williams's estimation. Plaintiffs like Mr. Williams also expressed desperation for a moment in the adversarial process when they could counter these perceived lies, and yet the rigidity and formality of the courts left them little opportunity.

Defendants' Disavowal of Discrimination

A new truism has gained popularity in the United States in the latter twentieth and early twenty-first centuries: racism is a social ill.[13] High-profile figures who express outright racial prejudice can face public backlash and private punishment.[14] In the contemporary United States, hostility expressed explicitly at people of color for their racial status is generally understood to be unacceptable, especially in a work environment.[15] And yet, as the stories in this volume demonstrate, and other studies of discrimination confirm, both overt and subtle forms of discrimination in the workplace occur with regularity.

As such, when defendant HR professionals, their business partners, and outside counsel in private corporate law firms described the antidiscrimination law and the adversarial process, they never defended racial discrimination, or discrimination against any other protected class. They did not ideologically attack antidiscrimination law itself, either. None argued during our interviews that law should not prohibit employment discrimination on the basis of race, sex, disability, and age. Although antiregulatory activists and employers are routinely involved in political and legal activities that challenge the scope of the employment discrimination laws and the legal facts of whether some set of actions constitutes discrimination, our defendant interviewees went out of their way to insist their companies take discrimination very seriously, are morally opposed to it, and adhere to the shared abstract beliefs about workplace rights embodied in Title VII and similar statutes.

And yet, defendant employers and defense lawyers dismissed almost every real and hypothetical claim of discrimination we discussed.[16] They were remarkably similar in their approach and attitudes. They began with the firm and professedly genuine belief that discrimination did not occur in the cases we discussed, whether it was the individual case of interest or other discrimination cases in which they were involved. They spoke in great detail about how their company, their managers, and their HR practices do not tolerate discrimination. It does not *exist* in their company. Jim Schultz (DL22), a very experienced white defense attorney, articulated his thinking about why the cases against the city government he represented could not constitute discrimination:

> We do not discriminate. We do not discriminate for many reasons. First of all, it's against the law. Secondly, it's immoral. And third, we want diversity. The communities that we represent are all diverse. I mean we have substantial minority populations and we attempted to recruit women before anybody else was doing it and it just galls me when we're accused of doing things that we didn't do.

Defendant organizations and attorneys explain litigation trends by attributing the rise to meritless cases. As Don Gale (D61), a white, in-house counsel in his late forties, recounted, "Most cases, I don't say they're totally frivolous . . . [but] I really don't believe any of our cases [were cases] where the other side had sufficient merit." Although some cases *may* involve inappropriate behavior, the defendants and their attorneys are confident that such behavior is rare and managers properly address it. According to Mr. Gale, "The management's position is if the misconduct or the bad performance is established, whatever disciplinary action is appropriate will be taken." He and others depict their managers' proactive problem solving as evidence of a lack of discrimination.[17]

The defense offers two scapegoats: the plaintiffs themselves and their lawyers. We know from social psychology that coworkers and supervisors routinely deprecate those who make claims of discrimination, even when founded in facts.[18] Apparently, legal actors are not immune to such tendencies.

Ignorant, Malicious Plaintiffs

Defendant representatives and defense lawyers most frequently attempt to reshape a dispute by characterizing claimants as naïve about the legal system and ignorant about what constitutes actionable discrimination. Defense lawyers found various ways to make sense of what they saw as claimants' ignorance. Some went to great lengths to avoid loaded words. Thomas Howard (DL1), an African American defense attorney in his forties, said:

> I think most employment and discrimination, if it's race or gender, most of those cases at the end of the day, it would be overstating it to call them bogus, but generally the decisions I don't think have anything to do with race or gender, but oftentimes with personality or perceived, you know, view of the applicant.

This defense attorney wanted to ensure we knew he was not claiming the plaintiffs and the claims were fraudulent, but fundamentally, he told us, the claims were not about discrimination.

By far the most common explanation from the defense is that employees simply do not understand what constitutes discrimination. Nicole Price (D64), a white, in-house counsel in her forties, explained, "Yelling at an employee is not discrimination but, you know, some people believe it should be." Similarly, Cindy Abbott (DL12), a Latina defense lawyer in her forties, told us:

> In general, we get a lot of people that don't really have good understanding of what the basis for, you know, everybody's got their own definition of discrimination, harassment. As a consequence of that, I developed training courses not only for managers and employees, but basically I'm saying, "Let's understand what the city wrote as a definition of discrimination, harassment and what our obligations are and move along."

Ms. Abbott carefully manages (potential) plaintiffs' expectations. If they come to the workplace with unrealistic or incorrect assumptions about what constitutes discrimination, she wants to dissuade them from these ideas as early as possible.

For these lawyers, the best way to remedy the problem of employees who misunderstand their suffering as discrimination is training. Such trainings are meant to help workers understand their rights (or, from this perspective, that they do not have very many rights) so that management will not have to be bothered by ignorant inquiries from their workforce. Most succinctly, Gary Littlejohn (D74), an African American male attorney, told us the best solution to the problems of workplace discrimination would be "just to clarify the laws. I think a lot of the litigation is generated because people don't understand what it means, like the ADA."

In fact, Mr. Littlejohn exemplifies the thesis of this chapter. He sees people misperceiving discrimination while acknowledging that, as an African American man, he has been discriminated against, as have others in his community. He notes, "As an African American man growing up in an African American community it would be foolish of me to think it doesn't exist."

A related ideology is shared widely among defense lawyers and their clients: plaintiffs maliciously and knowingly manipulate the legal system. According to this reasoning, the plaintiffs might be trying to punish the employer for some bad (but not discriminatory) decision or just be looking for an easy way to get money. Such plaintiffs, they explain, are conniving, greedy, and lazy. Trent Watkins (DL25), a white defense attorney in his forties, described for us a plaintiff who "really did not believe that she had been terminated because of her pregnancy":

> The plaintiff's goal, in my somewhat cynical opinion, was to get money. I think that the plaintiff perceived that the organization would attempt to resolve the case fairly quickly. . . . I think in many, many employment discrimination cases—and this comes from a defense lawyer's standpoint—the individual does not sincerely believe they were discriminated against.

Attorneys such as Mr. Watkins do not just think that workers who file legal claims are ignorant. Rather, they see the workers as the problem—they brought the claim. Many had a story like this one, told by Mr. Howard (DL1):

> Then there are certain people that are just built to be plaintiffs in employment cases. I had one case where a woman on her first day in the office went during her lunch break to buy a little journal which she titled, "Journal of Discrimination, Harassment, Retaliation." First day, first day of work.

Mr. Howard intended to demonstrate that some people had a "litigious posture" and essentially only entered the workforce to await the day they could sue for discrimination.

Plaintiffs as Problem Employees

Another ideological move by defendant representatives and defense attorneys is to construct the plaintiff as a problem employee.[19] Their complaints about such employees are many: poor performance, inflated self-image, "difficult" disposition. They characterize such plaintiffs as emotionally unsound, even mentally ill. Such problem employees cannot sensibly evaluate what has happened in the workplace. On his desk, one HR executive has a jar engraved like a funeral urn: Ashes of Problem Employees (see fig. 7.1).

One way that the defense side rejects nearly every individual claim while disavowing discrimination is by painting the complaining employee as excessively angry. According to these attorneys and HR executives, the anger (while perhaps justified) blinds the plaintiffs to the "facts" and makes them irrationally pursue litigation. By this way of thinking, any time a worker admits to not liking an alleged discriminator or a decision, it provides evidence that the claim is illegitimate because it is based in anger. For example, Jordan Zarins (DL28), a white male attorney in his sixties, told us: "In this case I think this person, this plaintiff, was angry at her supervisor, and in her deposition she—although

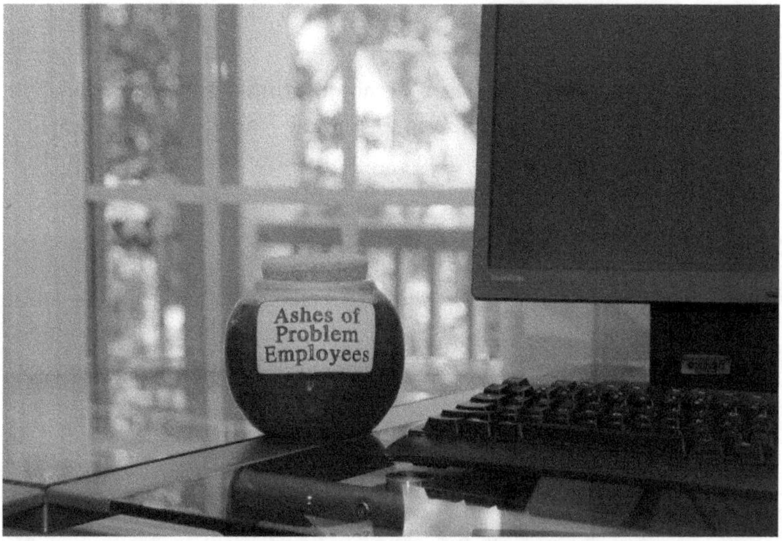

FIGURE 7.1. Ashes of problem employees jar. Source: Tumbleweed.

she was alleging age discrimination—she admitted that she didn't get along with him." From Mr. Zarin's perspective, anger was a sign of a malicious employee, and it caused some of these lawsuits (as opposed to being a result of real discrimination). Other defense attorneys discussed employees' anger or dissatisfaction with employment decisions. An African American, female, in-house counsel explained, "We get a lot of claims from employees, and basically, you know, just like anything else, they're unhappy with [it] when a decision has been made. They either got suspended or fired or didn't get hired or didn't get a promotion or something like that" (D74).

Defendant representatives and defense lawyers with whom we spoke almost universally characterized workers who brought complaints as lazy or unreliable. Using the basic characteristics of what constitutes a "good worker" allows defendant representatives and defense attorneys to both malign the individual employee and suggest a possible motivation for the lawsuit. After all, what could be lazier than wanting to not work while collecting money from the company? Mr. Zarins commented,

> One thing that's interesting is that sometimes you see the same problem that caused the employment difficulty sort of surface in the course of the litigation itself. For instance, you know, the charging party who was fired for tardiness and absenteeism who fails to show up for their fact-finding conference at HR or is a half an hour late or something.

Still other defense attorneys used the termination itself as evidence that the employee must have always been a bad worker. By this reasoning, if a problem employee is terminated, the employee *must* be lazy and unreliable, because the burden for termination is so incredibly high in these organizations. This argument was offered very strongly in government organizations, as Pam Girard (DL39), a white defense attorney for a state government, said:

> It's not that easy to get fired [by the state] or even disciplined in a lot of the agencies. And it seemed to me that a lot of people sued sort of on the basis of, "I never had to do that before, why do I have to do it now?" [Employees] get a new supervisor and all of a sudden the ways that they were doing things before were not being accepted, and mostly they weren't very good employees. And many, many times I find that they are not mentally ill, exactly, but certainly resistant to any sort of change or any sort of direction. Some-

body's been leaving them alone for a while because of this resistance to supervision, and then they change supervisors. You wouldn't believe how many times that is the pattern, and the new supervisor says, "Well, wait a minute, you know, you're not doing the work, your work isn't good, and what's the story here?" And they start the progressive discipline and then end up firing them.

Mr. Jain (D12), the EEO officer we quoted in chapter 4, summed up the basic characterization that many on the defense side share about most plaintiffs as unintelligent, belligerent, underperforming workers:

> Most of the people that bring complaints in here, I'm saying 3, 4, 5% of the workforce, we're not talking about the smartest, you know, nails in the box or anything. These are folks that sometimes they have attitude and/or conduct and/or behavioral problems. Sometimes they mix discrimination and stuff. They try and mask their performance issues.

One explanation, unique to sexual harassment lawsuits, is that the party complaining (typically a woman) had been in a relationship with the harasser (typically a man) for some time, and the lawsuit was a way of exacting revenge on a former romantic interest. Daniel Bryant (DL71), a white defense attorney, told us:

> What I see are cases that are either, that [laughing] the office romance gone awry, where everything was going great, and it was all, you know consensual for three years until they didn't get the promotion they wanted. Then all of a sudden it's been coerced the whole time, and you go through and you get their diary and you get their notes, and it's just ridiculous.

Mr. Bryant is basically claiming that most, some, or even all sexual harassment claims result from women being duplicitous or conniving for better jobs.

A related complaint is that plaintiffs are, in Mr. Bryant's words, "hypersensitive." Consider the story that Trond Davies (D72), a white defense attorney in his sixties, told about racial epithets in the workplace:

> A couple of Afro-American people felt that they were being the butt of jokes, the butt of language that shouldn't be used in terms of race. . . . [I've had] maybe four of those types of situations in seventeen years. What I do

> is try to sit with both sides and, in this particular instance, we warn people, to get, so, you know, [say to the white manager], "You're using terminology that shouldn't be used." . . . After [the employee] verbalizes those complaints and someone sits down with him from corporate and tells him everything is okay, [he keeps his job]. He's a little sensitive, I think, to some of the situations that occur . . . and he knows that the people who were at fault were saying the wrong thing. . . . And a lot of times you know it becomes a matter of him thinking, "I'm glad that the company thinks enough of coming out here or resolving the situation. So I'll put up with a little more because I know the company is concerned."

Mr. Davies went on to discuss how corporate management, by "taking the problem seriously," could result in helping African American employees be more tolerant of their (mis)treatment. He said that this may help workers understand that if they "hear one or two remarks [they will] say, 'Oh that's just old Clyde again,' instead of filing a complaint." So antidiscrimination training, instead of being used to reform "Clyde" from his racist or otherwise offensive comments, becomes about teaching African American workers to brush off Clyde's behavior.

Even though defendant employers and defense lawyers do not think most of the cases that come to them are legitimate, they tacitly endorse rights as a mechanism of protection against the harms of discrimination. Rights are not the problem; plaintiffs are.

Manipulated by Plaintiffs' Lawyers

The third broad justification that HR executives and defense lawyers give for the number of employment discrimination lawsuits is flaws among plaintiffs' lawyers. Sometimes the defense side casts plaintiffs' lawyers as uninformed, but more often the narrative is that they are greedy, unethical, or corrupt. For example, Preston Gibbon (DL2), a white defense attorney in his fifties, explained how he thinks lawyers transform workplace disputes into legal ones:

> When people say, "I want to be treated fairly," it means . . . "I want to be treated fairly as I perceive fairness." And a lot of what happens in these cases is people don't think they've been treated fairly . . . and they go to a [plaintiff's] lawyer and the lawyer says, "I got to have a hook because fairness is not a legal issue." So then they find race or something like that.

Despite his view that plaintiffs' lawyers invent claims, Mr. Gibbon shares the widely held (or stated) belief that plaintiffs are not necessarily evil, greedy liars. According to Mr. Gibbon, the plaintiff's lawyer persuasively reframes the issue for the plaintiff, transforming it from workplace "unfairness" into illegal discrimination. Mr. Gibbon continued this thought:

> In the vast majority of cases, people legitimately file these things. . . . [Lawsuits] are not pleasant to go through. [Plaintiffs] believe they have not been treated fairly. Now whether race actually plays a role or gender actually plays a role, I think is true in a lot fewer cases. [But] . . . one thing that happens in litigation is that people become entrenched in their positions, and whether they believe it or not at the beginning, by the time you get to trial, they believe with all their heart and their soul and their mind that they have been discriminated against, because that unfairness has now been successfully, in their own minds, transmuted into sex discrimination or race discrimination. Because otherwise, "Why was I treated this way? It couldn't be because of me. It couldn't be because I did something wrong, because I don't believe I did. So it must be race. It must be my sex. It must be my religion."

From this perspective, the unethical behavior comes from plaintiffs' attorneys. One white male defense lawyer explained it this way:

> I think [plaintiffs' attorneys] owe it to the clients to say . . ."I make my money representing people like you suing companies . . . for this type of thing. If you ask me to rank your case, you know, on a scale of one hundred . . . with one hundred the best and one the worst, you're at five. You're down at the bottom, and if you want to pursue it, it's your privilege. I don't think it's a very good case. I think you'll be disappointed at the end of the day." I don't think there [are] enough [plaintiffs' lawyers] who say that to clients. . . . I think the attitude is much more of . . ."I probably can, you know, get something for it, and I'll get [my client] something, and I'll get something just to make it go away," as opposed to, "This person really has a legitimate grievance." . . . Lawyers, I think, are more of a problem often than the clients because the lawyers should know better. (DL24)

By blaming plaintiffs' lawyers, defendant representatives are able to explain the number of lawsuits in the absence of actual discrimination.

This technique is the ultimate way to exonerate individual employees; the plaintiffs' lawyer is cast as the expert who should have known better.

Just as they disavow discrimination and, usually implicitly, revere rights, defendant representatives describe a broken system of litigation. From their perspective, the system of employment discrimination litigation is broken because it is too open.[20] They see their organization as being forced into court by misinformed, problematic, and misguided employees, regardless of the merits of their case.[21] The litigation system, they believe, is overrun with baseless claims.

Adversarialism across Party Lines: The Role of Attorneys

As cases progress in litigation, the actions and opposing worldviews of the plaintiffs and defendant organizations—in general and in the individual case—escalate the conflict between the parties. As we saw in chapters 4 and 6, on the defendant employer's side, professionals are involved in cases from early on, although this often is invisible to the potential plaintiff. When workers become plaintiffs, the employee-employer relationship changes fundamentally.

The plaintiff and defense attorneys' descriptions of the other side shed light on the adversarial dynamic. Mark Laramie (PL34), a white plaintiff's attorney who represented Kristen Baker, whose story helped open this book, told us about the problems that arise when plaintiffs involve a lawyer in the dispute (note that he typically represents corporate litigants):

> If there is any chance of the person staying there and sort of resuming a normal working relationship, it not only has to happen before there's an EEOC charge, 90-plus percent of the time it has to happen before the employer even receives the demand letter from a lawyer. . . . Look, you bring a lawyer into the situation, and they're going to get defensive, they're going to go to their lawyers as a buffer between you and the person who's making the decision. . . . If you've been a good employee . . . you have kind of a store of goodwill that you can use. The minute you bring in the lawyer, the lawyer doesn't have that goodwill.

Despite defendant representatives' assertion "if we are wrong, we will fix it," plaintiffs' lawyers reported surprise at the level of defensiveness shown by employers in seemingly very clear cases of discrimination. Mr. Laramie ordinarily represented business clients and took Ms. Baker's case only as a favor to a friend. Ms. Baker alleged that she was exposed to ongoing, flagrant sexual harassment, including having a photograph left on her desk depicting a woman having a watermelon inserted into her vagina. Mr. Laramie was in disbelief at how defense counsel handled the case:

> The company was represented by a very good firm, and a very good lawyer said, "We'll undertake to investigate." And my supposition was when you get high quality legal counsel on the defense side, and you go out and investigate, you're going to see the problem. . . . I remember being appalled . . . that the investigation was really an exercise in building a defense. . . . I guess the point comes in every case where the management has to decide, "Are we going to circle the wagons and try to protect this person, or are we going to get the facts on the table and, if we have a problem, fix it?" . . . I thought that she and that law firm would be more professional.

This attorney, who typically did not represent individuals, thought the defense lawyers' response was unprofessional. In a case we referred to earlier in this chapter, a jury returned a substantial verdict for the plaintiff after only forty-five minutes of deliberation. We asked the plaintiff's counsel his opinion on what the defense side had been thinking. He replied, "There was just an obstinance [*sic*] from early on. . . . I really wonder if the lawyers just had bad information from the client" (PL30-1). If defendant employers react to such extreme facts with an adversarial posture, it suggests they will have an adversarial response to every case.

From both plaintiff and defense lawyers, we often, but not always, heard disparaging remarks about opposing counsel. Some negative characterizations centered around personality conflicts, but others had a more partisan tone. Defense attorneys described their opponents in terms such as "an unpleasant woman" (DL39) and "a whack job" (DL54). Ms. Hill, who had called Ms. Daley's attorney a "bottom feeder," expressed dislike for plaintiffs' lawyers in generally. She characterized them as "zealots": "They think you are intrinsically evil because you represent a corporation. . . . They just have to fight you about everything and be as insulting as possible all the time."

This antagonism sometimes breaks into open, personal conflict. One plaintiffs' attorney described such a case:

> I'd get a letter every day threatening me with sanctions. . . . One of the things I learned during the course of that case, which has stood me well since then, is to realize that there are some things I don't have to deal with. Probably the twentieth insulting, five-page-long litany letter that I got, I realized I don't actually have to respond point-by-point. . . . It serves nobody's interest . . . to get into these personal things with opposing counsel. In fact, it's a chosen strategy on their side to suck you into that. (PL36-2)

Much of the tension between sides revolves around resources and tactics. One defense lawyer talked about a plaintiffs' lawyer he liked personally, but who had to keep a high volume of cases going. This person, the lawyer told us, was doing "the minimum necessary to get by and keep the case alive. . . . Our [approach] was sort of full-court press. . . . He couldn't possibly have devoted as much time to case as we did" (DL24).

Attorneys on both sides of these disputes also report instances of discovery abuse or wasteful motion practices by the other side's counsel, although plaintiffs' lawyers complained about it more than defense lawyers. One plaintiffs' lawyer described one case that "just exploded in discovery":

> In fact, at one point I think I got about a $28,000 fee award just because of the discovery nonsense. . . . It was all strategic. All I needed were the employee benefit plans, so I could say these two plans are different and this is what she is entitled to. . . . They wouldn't produce it. . . . But it's like every case with them. . . . It's just nutty. . . . They must go out and present themselves to clients by saying, "You're gonna pay us an absolute fortune. And if that's what you want to do, then we're your law firm." (PL26)

Summary judgment motions are particularly important in defendant representatives' strategies, because defendant organizations can exploit their resource advantage. Jeff Kovac (PL8), a Latino attorney in his fifties, was a lawyer we sampled for his role as a plaintiffs' lawyer, but who had been representing defendant employers for the last eight years. Mr. Kovac remarked:

> All defense lawyers, especially . . . large companies . . . represented by [large law firms] filed summary judgments whether they had merit or not . . . because many plaintiffs . . . don't put a lot of investment in their cases. They take the case and then they sit on them. The filing of the summary judgment

> motion tells them that they've got basically forty-five days to take whatever depositions and other things they want to take. If they're like most plaintiffs' lawyers in the region, they're inundated with other cases. So they'll push for an early mediation, because there is a summary judgment hanging over their heads. . . . They're inclined to just get rid of the case. . . . I have been doing defense work exclusively now for several years, and I can't think of a single case that I haven't filed a summary judgment motion.

This informant, who has been on both sides of cases, offers a somewhat cynical interpretation of the behavior of both sides in these cases. According to his interpretation, plaintiffs' lawyers have onerous caseloads and take no action on them until faced with a motion for summary judgment, defense counsel routinely file summary judgment motions to smoke them out, and neither side pays much attention to the merits as they jockey for position.

Employment civil rights litigation is fraught with suspicion among opposing lawyers and litigation tactics that exacerbate conflict without much regard for the merits of the case or, in some instances, the resources of the parties. One plaintiffs' counsel who had represented both sides in employment discrimination litigation described a case in which the plaintiff might have accepted a $25,000 settlement in mediation, but the defense would offer no more than $3,000. A trial produced an award over $200,000. This attorney saw the company's view as: "You can really beat down individuals" (DL72).

These reports hardly suggest that lawyers are operating, in this context, to mediate conflict and bring parties together in constructive ways. Yet we did hear lawyers recount instances in which they fought hard cases against other lawyers whom they now regard as friends. As one respondent said, if he saw the other lawyer going down the street, he would make a U-turn to talk to him or take him to dinner. Adversarial antagonism is not absolute.

Conclusion

The stories of Franklin Williams and Annie Daley are barely recorded in the files of federal records centers. Theirs are not the cases that appear in media accounts of discrimination litigation. Some stories like theirs are captured in the relatively small number of cases that produce an opinion on a motion for summary judgment or a trial court opinion. And in those documents, their stories appear in legally stylized form, as a reduction or refraction of the nature of their dispute with their employer.

And yet, our in-depth analysis of these cases brings to life the contentious nature of the adversarial process and the sharp divergence between plaintiffs and defendant organizations' perspectives on what happened in the workplace and its significance in law. The adversarial process reflects and magnifies the polarized interpretations of the parties. For the plaintiffs who go to the law seeking a fair adjudication of their claims, they find themselves isolated, their claim individualized, and their work ethic (if not their person) besmirched. Asymmetries in resources and experience exacerbate these problems for plaintiffs. Plaintiffs often are treated by EEOC and court bureaucrats, defendant organizations, defense lawyers, judges, and even their own lawyers as unworthy claimants. It should come as little surprise that they attribute negative outcomes to bias in the law.

The defendant employers reject the assertion that bias is driving employment decisions. Instead they see plaintiffs playing "the race card." In Franklin Williams's case, the trial judge—after earlier announcing the outcome of the O. J. Simpson verdict from the bench—ruled that Williams had not proved that adverse employment actions had been racially motivated. Likewise, Annie Daley's claims were rejected by a largely white jury. Thus, the law, like employers, embraced the right to a discrimination-free workplace—the "right right." But it rejected the claims of these plaintiffs—the "wrong plaintiff."

CHAPTER EIGHT

Win, Lose, or Draw

Perspectives on Case Outcomes

This chapter examines how parties to employment civil rights lawsuits understand the final resolutions of their cases. We know from earlier chapters that plaintiffs turn to employment civil rights law hoping to receive some measure of justice for a workplace injury, but they quickly confront the challenges of navigating litigation. Like our quantitative data on case outcomes presented earlier, our qualitative data here highlight the difficulties of defining what, exactly, counts as a "win" or a "loss" and who, exactly, is the "winner" and the "loser." Plaintiffs' understandings of their case resolutions are complex. The chapter begins with two stories that capture in depth plaintiffs' perspectives on the resolutions of their cases. One felt he lost despite gaining a substantial settlement. The other was disappointed with the outcome but satisfied in her belief that her voice was heard. The chapter moves on to discuss the range of ways that defendant representatives and plaintiffs make sense of case outcomes.

As the adversarial process comes to an end, the asymmetry of power between parties becomes clear. Plaintiffs often get little or nothing of material value as a result of litigation. They routinely experience grave nonmaterial costs, such as depression. Defendant employers, while not happy with paying a settlement or carrying litigation costs, very seldom have to acknowledge that they committed discrimination. In the vast majority of cases, law reinscribes ascriptive hierarchies by leaving untouched both those hierarchies and the alleged injustices that give rise to employment civil rights litigation in the first place. Indeed, in many cases the power of law is deployed to "seal" the outcome of a case, in that employees sign agreements not to disclose the terms of settlement.

Plaintiffs' Stories

Sam Grayson's Case against Center City

Sam Grayson (P4) had his dream job. He was a police officer in Center City, a racially homogenous (89% white), relatively wealthy (average household income around $90,000), family-oriented (69% of households include parents with related children) community with a population of about thirty thousand. Officer Grayson was regularly promoted over seven years as an officer and had the distinction of working as a School Resource Officer conducting D.A.R.E. training and helping school-age kids to stay off drugs. A physically fit, well over six feet tall, white man, Officer Grayson invited us to his suburban home in Center City to tell us his story—one that, on record, is a win in court. But that was not his experience.

On duty one night, years earlier, Officer Grayson began to feel dizzy. His immediate supervisor told him, "Just go to the hospital. Go see what's going on." The emergency room doctor discovered that Officer Grayson, dizzy and now with slurred speech, had a very low heart rate. Officer Grayson told us (and court records confirmed) that the doctor ordered light duty until he could be examined by a cardiologist. Instead, the police department placed him on leave. He "went from doctor to doctor to doctor. . . . No one could really explain what was going on." Officer Grayson saw multiple cardiologists before he ran out of sick and vacation time. "And then what happened is they then said 'We can no longer pay you,' and they could no longer provide health benefits." He said he had been "going through a pretty good time at work" before he was placed on leave: "I'd never been adversarial during that whole time." Eventually Officer Grayson was forced to resign so as to gain access to his pension funds (about $20,000) so that he could pay his mortgage and living expenses.

A few months after resigning, Officer Grayson was researching disability law and ran into some former colleagues, officers from Center City and a nearby town who had sued the city for failing to grant light duty under medical orders. Officer Grayson began to think that what happened to him might be illegal and began interviewing lawyers. He retained, on contingency, an attorney who had represented others who had sued Center City for disability discrimination in the early days of the Americans with Disabilities Act. His lawyer's first request was reinstatement without back pay. She argued that the two notes from the ER doctor and his general practitioner's recommendation for "light duty" amounted to a reasonable request for accommodation for a disability.

Center City rejected this request, so Officer Grayson's lawyer filed with the EEOC, was granted the default right-to-sue letter, and filed in federal court. The case was settled four years after it was filed. Meanwhile, Officer Grayson described the discovery process as "very frustrating" because he thought City Center was withholding information required by law: "We ha[d] copies of the same documentation that was released from other . . . police officers that had been sued or that were suing them." Officer Grayson reported similar dishonesty during depositions, saying it was "kind of heated and emotional for me because to have people—you know, if I treated people in law enforcement, and if I lied like that—and to have [police officers] say . . . 'We never saw that slip from that doctor.' I mean to go all the way and to say that's your defense?"

About a week before trial, the judge in the case told City Center that they should settle. The parties began negotiating in earnest. Since he was suing a city, Officer Grayson's settlement is a matter of public record; he received $100,000—an amount well above the median settlement in employment cases (about three times!). When we asked him about the settlement, he told us:

> SG: It wasn't anything big. It was $100,000. But, you know, obviously [one third of] it goes for the attorney . . . and like my attorney said if I hadn't quit and I had just sat, it could have been more. But it cost the City more than $100,000.00"
>
> I: . . . Did you think it was fair?
>
> SG: Well you know what, I didn't want any money. I wanted my job back. I didn't want the money. I wanted my job back. And I actually, to be completely honest with you, cried and left and felt like I lost because it wasn't about the money.

As he reflected on his case, he was not sure he would do the lawsuit again: "It's just that personally, it took its toll on my life." He explained that he eventually had to declare bankruptcy, despite the common perception that settlement money would be sufficient. "When you get a lump sum of twenty thousand dollars . . . it doesn't last long." One of the indignities was that he could no longer work as a police officer, and instead worked in a much lower wage position outside his area of expertise:

> I was working for a vet, as a vet assistant. It was my vet, he needed a person and I was working for like $8.00 an hour. . . . And that's another part of this whole process. Here you are in your own hometown that they've seen you in all the schools and the whole thing, and the next time I'm no longer a police officer. My stuff hits the paper. I'm working at my vet holding people's dogs you know and having people go, "What are you doing?" and they don't realize I have to make a living. I have to make a living. I have to do something! . . . The one savior for me is my work in the schools, and I was able to work as a dean's assistant and things like that in the high school because of my reputation at least with the school district.

Officer Grayson's case was one of losing while winning, and his losses were many.

Denise Anderson's Case against Truckers, Inc.

Denise Anderson (P23) was another of the many plaintiffs whose win felt like a loss. Ms. Anderson worked in one of many satellite offices scattered about the Midwest for a large trucking firm headquartered a few hundred miles away. Ms. Anderson was what she referred to as an "office girl," as she did data processing for many years at various satellite offices of Truckers, Inc. She coordinated trips and payroll but traditionally did not interact with the truck drivers. After many years, Ms. Anderson told us:

> We got this new fellow in. Steve . . . was fairly young; he was like barely in his thirties, I think. And for some reason or another, he and I just locked horns right off the bat. . . . It was like he didn't know what I was doing, and I did know what I was doing. And I didn't need his input that he was giving me.

Steve instituted a policy that workers in Ms. Anderson's position would handle "driver check-in" and supervise driving logs. It is unclear if the policy change was Steve's choice or if corporate management required the new rules, but the careful regulation of maximum driving and rest hours in the trucking industry increased the stakes of doing her job well. Ms. Anderson, in her early sixties at the time, found the new tasks challenging: "Everybody else that had been put in that position [the company] had sent to Detroit for, to be educated on it, you know. The [other workers] knew what they were doing." Ms. Anderson repeatedly requested the training or a computer at her workstation so she could try to learn the new system. As she recounted, Steve's refusal put additional burdens on her, as she struggled to devise manual work-arounds for tasks that should have been automated. Drivers got frustrated with her, and she became emotionally distraught.

Ms. Anderson took a leave of absence and made inquiries with the EEOC, which said she could likely get her job back. "I didn't want that. I was unhappy, you know. I couldn't handle it. I wasn't prepared for it at all." Even still, Ms. Anderson could not get Truckers, Inc. to restore her to her job, and she languished on disability leave. Still an employee, she filed with the EEOC for age discrimination. The lawsuit itself was remarkably simple from Ms. Anderson's point of view. The EEOC told her they thought she had a good age discrimination case and depositions were held. She relished the deposition because she had hours to address Steve directly:

> I didn't mince any words. In fact, I was sort of glad that my boss was there. He got his ear, he couldn't say anything. So I had the floor, so to speak, you know, and that made me feel good, to get it off my chest, because as long as he was my boss at work, I didn't feel at liberty to tell him exactly what I thought.

Steve's boss, Mike, was also at the deposition. Ms. Anderson liked Mike, and Mike knew her to be a good worker. During a break in depositions, he told her, "'This is not personal, this is company business, just part of a job that I have to do.' . . . That made me feel better, you know."

Shortly after the depositions, Truckers, Inc. was sold to Mega Truckers Inc., which made Ms. Anderson an offer to settle. Her attorney advised that she take the offer: "I was tired, I was sick, I had just had it. I had enough of it. So I took the [settlement]. They offered $15,000 and he got a third, so what did I get out of it?" Of the $10,000 remaining, she said, "I had to pay back the $8,000 that the Social Security had sort of doubled up on. . . . I ended up with nothing. The doctor bills." When we asked if she would have done anything differently, Ms. Anderson said, "I don't think I would have taken the settlement so quick. . . . But like I say, at the time, I was just glad to be rid of it. But I know I had a good case."

Introduction

The stories of Sam Grayson and Denise Anderson vividly demonstrate the disjuncture between what the law provides and how those who turn to the law for relief understand whether they won or lost in the lawsuit. Officer Grayson wanted nothing more than to be reinstated as a police officer. Neither a large sum of money nor a pronouncement by the court that came short of returning him to the police force would suffice. Denise Anderson received a small settlement. While she still believes her case was worth more than she was awarded, she seems more satisfied with the resolution of her case in part because she had the opportunity to tell her story during her deposition.

Because so many cases are settled and many of those settlements involve confidentiality agreements, the question of which side won or lost a case can be difficult to determine. From a plaintiff's perspective, winning might mean recovering an amount of money deemed "fair" or significant enough to make the organization change their behavior. As Officer Grayson's and Ms. Anderson's cases reveal, however, material outcome may bear little relation to the satisfaction of plaintiffs with the law. Some draw satisfaction from using law to give voice to their complaint. But some who receive large financial settlements feel disappointed in the outcome.

Defendants also have different definitions of a "win" or a "loss." They may take the view that a low cost (even a nuisance) settlement is a win, because it disposes of a potentially expensive matter at low cost. But occasionally defendants will not be satisfied unless they obtain vindication against a morally laden charge of discrimination. Such vindication may carry a high price in lawyers' fees.

After considering the three main goals that parties to employment civil rights litigation bring to the process, and how those goals may shift over the course of the litigation, we compare how defendants and plaintiffs assess the outcomes of cases. While neither side expresses enthusiasm for the outcomes of their cases, we find that plaintiffs experience serious personal harms over the course of litigation.

How Parties Assess Case Outcomes: Money, Vindication, and Organizational Change

The literature on procedural justice demonstrates that, for parties to a lawsuit, satisfaction with a case's outcome is distinct from winning. Legal participants often express more concern about the process of the legal encounter than about substantive legal outcome.[1] If participants do not see their case conducted with a fair process, they are likely to lose confidence in law and avoid legal institutions in the future.[2] The literature on procedural justice, as well as critiques of the approach,[3] suggest the importance of examining litigants' subjective interpretations of case outcomes as well as more objective aspects of outcomes such as settlement amounts or award amounts.

We asked both plaintiffs and defendant employers about the goals they pursued in litigation and how satisfied they were with the outcome. All of our plaintiff respondents told us they wanted similar things from their lawsuits: compensation, vindication, and organizational change. These three goals exist in an uneasy, changing, and complicated equation that is different for every individual plaintiff and changes over the course of the lawsuit, as plaintiffs and their lawyers come to understand what is possible. The goals might best be understood as existing in something resembling a pie chart, with each slice of the pie varying in size as it represents the relative importance of that component for the final resolution of the case. A case settles when the plaintiff and the defendant organization can agree on a distribution of these three components that satisfies both sides well enough. As the case progresses, plaintiffs come to understand that they must place more relative importance on money, because that is what defendant employers are willing to give. Vindication and organizational change are rarely part of a settlement or adjudicated outcome.

Defendant employers have parallel, if reversed, goals. They also are pursuing money (in the form of cost avoidance), vindication, and preservation of organizational patterns without legally mandated change. Although defendant employers in general are more sophisticated than plaintiffs at the outset of litigation, they also have different preferences among these three slices of the pie. And their preferences also will shift over the course of litigation. We begin with defendants' perspectives because the defense side typically takes the lead in determining the case outcome.

How Defendant Employers Understand Case Outcomes

We saw in chapters 6 and 7 that defendant employers and their representatives make calculated tactical decisions about how to respond to employment civil rights lawsuits. For example, one inside counsel said the company never offered settlements in reduction-in-force situations (D62). To make such decisions, the defense side weighs which of the three potentially competing goals is most important to them, although some sort of cost-benefit calculation is foremost.

We heard repeated comments from defendant representatives and defense attorneys about the need for a strong defense to avoid paying money to both plaintiffs and plaintiffs' attorneys, whom they described as undeserving (at best). Mary Hill (DL18), the defense attorney in Annie Daley's case, which opened chapter 7, indicated that her client was convinced of the correctness of its employment decision and also saw the value in a strenuous defense against a plaintiffs' attorney who "is making a living off you" by representing plaintiffs in several different cases against the company. Likewise, in Peter Nichelson's case against a city government, the inside counsel (DL1) cited the fact that several unions had signed off on the promotion process that Nichelson was contesting. This was cause for a vigorous defense. "To have to pay or to promote him, particularly when there was really no evidence that any of the people involved in the process were looking to discriminate against older white men, was something we were not prepared to do."

Part of the defense side's perspective is a concern with the possible signals that case resolutions send to other workers (i.e., potential claimants). Teresa Lewis (D74), an African American woman working as inside counsel in city government, indicated that the city would not settle with continuing employees, "The employees who we've settled with in the past, who continue to work here, tend to come back more than once. So we just don't [settle] . . . [unless] it's clear that we did something wrong." Occasionally employer organizations will "go to the mat" and mount an all-out defense despite the cost. They do so either for reasons of organizational politics or, more often, to discourage future litigation by sending the message that, in one interviewee's words, "we don't just roll over" (D65). Recall Harold Ward (D67), whom we quoted in chapter 4. He took great pride in his record of refusing to settle with claimants and discouraging claims from other employees, boasting that he held "two liens" on the houses of former employees who had sued his company, lost, and been charged litigation costs. He said, "My theory is every time you settle one [claim] . . . then I get five more."

Employers' preference for defending the organization and discouraging further litigation can conflict with cost-benefit analyses. Many defendant representatives were very direct in discussing these considerations, particularly regarding the question of whether to settle or to further litigate. Troy Pedlow (D9), a white general counsel for a product manufacturer, said: "I think settlement or not is based on an assessment of risk and costs. . . . If there's a lot of risk in a case, we're going to be much more likely to settle. If the operating people or legal had done the same things in a . . . case that presented no risk, you wouldn't settle."

Some respondents voiced concern that our interview discussions of their settlement strategies remain confidential—"Now again, I'm not going to be identified in this, because I don't want the message to get out there that we just roll over" (D71)—yet, over and again, we heard that prevailing strategy, after avoiding litigation and trying to get cases thrown out, was to make the smallest settlements possible.

The defendant organizations' goals—their definition of a win—can change over the course of a lawsuit, as the attorney's fees add up or as evidence that the company actually engaged in prohibited behavior emerges. We asked outside counsel how they understand their clients' goals and the consequences when organizational representatives (usually inside counsel) change strategies mid-case. Ms. Hill verbalized this thinking clearly:

> MH: Well, sometimes I don't agree with the change of goals, but it's not my decision. . . . Why do they change motivations? Probably the most common reason is money. You know, they're spending a lot of money on defending the case, and they're saying, "I just don't think it's worth it anymore. Make it go away." . . . The anger that they had about the case when it was first filed has evaporated. . . . They just want to make it go away.
>
> I: They get tired.
>
> MH: But mostly they get tired of spending the money. They get tired of the fight. [Or] sometimes it's a change internally. There'll be a change within the company.

Over time, defendant representatives and outside defense lawyers develop more realistic expectations about how cases can be resolved. Given that realism, several exuded pride in their track record of defeating plaintiffs. As representatives of defendant organizations present changing, contradictory, and contingent goals to their outside lawyers, those lawyers themselves attempt to reframe certain outcomes (usually settlements) into something palatable for their client. By emphasizing the positive or negative aspects of a settlement, defense lawyers are hoping that they can strike an appealing balance of company interests that also map on to the preferences of the plaintiff-employee.

Yet the employer-client has an underlying ambivalence about any case resolution. Even when lawyers "win" by having a case dismissed or winning on summary judgment, ultimately, the defendant organization is presented with a bill for attorney's services. Glenda Klondike (DL54), a white attorney for a state government, described employers' understanding of case resolutions:

> GK: They feel horrible no matter what happens.
>
> I: No matter what?
>
> GK: Never vindicated. . . . The only time maybe is when some large company is splitting the bill and an individual manager feels that they've been vindicated, their decision has been vindicated, but I think even then they worry. Somehow the company is going to hold it against me that I cost them this money . . . We've had some great wins for clients, and they still are kind of like, "Thanks. Big huge bill." [laughs].

The cost of the lawsuit is very important for defendant organizations, but "cost" can be difficult to calculate. One defense attorney explained the complexities that arise even when much of the lawyering is done in-house:

> Clients never say, "Well, I'm glad you lost for less money," you know. So you have to sort of dot the I's and cross the T's, and you may be able to make some strategic, you know, things that we could have done more or you could do less (if less is enough), but, boy, that's a difficult call to make. (DL28)

How Plaintiffs Understand Case Outcomes

Plaintiffs are largely disappointed with the final resolution of their cases. Plaintiffs express disappointment with the process itself, believing their case outcome had little or nothing to do with the substance of their claim and that they were unable to get a fair hearing in which they could tell their whole story. Some reported feeling pressured or even duped by their attorneys into accepting regrettable settlements. Only three plaintiff interviewees reported that they were "very satisfied" with the outcome. Twenty-three reported that they were "not at all satisfied," and fifteen expressed ambivalent feelings.

FINANCIAL COMPENSATION. Most of the plaintiffs we interviewed (indeed, most of the plaintiffs who file employment civil rights lawsuits) have been terminated from their job. Most of them are financially insecure. Between their perhaps unrealistic idea of what a case of discrimination is worth (in terms of an award or settlement) and a belief that justice would involve being reinstated in their job, plaintiffs told us that they were motivated by money in their lawsuits. Yet there are contingencies around which category a financial award falls into. For example, many plaintiffs told us they began their lawsuit seeking to return to their jobs. They considered that outcome to be one form of financial compensation and vindication. As it became clear that the more likely result was a financial payment, plaintiffs began to transform how they thought about money. In the absence of an apology or a return to their job, a settlement sometimes became adequate vindication.

Reinstatement. In many plaintiffs' minds, the most obvious way to right the economic harms associated with termination was for the organization to reinstate them or retain them in their job. Over 40% of plaintiffs we interviewed hoped to get their jobs back, and the importance of this desire cannot be overstated. It may seem counterintuitive to think that plaintiffs want to return to a job where they felt discriminated against, but in addition to the sense of identity that people gain from their jobs, the financial security of working is vitally important. Among what observers might think of as big winners *and* big losers, dissatisfaction about not being reinstated confirms prior findings that workers drastically misjudge the degree of job protection that law can provide.[4]

Indeed, some plaintiffs recognized the practical difficulties associated with returning to their job. They worried about how they would be received and how future workplace decisions would be made, but they still made plans for return. Floyd Kelly (P7) said, "I did have in my mind that if they offered [my job] back to me, I would go." He had, however, some stipulations in mind: there must be an agreement about retributive harassment, because he had seen another terminated employee return under scrutiny: "They were just waiting and watching every little move he made. If he blew his nose wrong, they were watching."

Other plaintiffs were reluctant to go back to their jobs, but it was less because they feared differential treatment and more because the lawsuit revealed that the company was not one they wanted to work within. Maureen Sands (P8) insisted: "I wouldn't have wanted to go back to work for the company period. I just didn't like how they did business anymore. I worked for that company for like fifteen years, and it wasn't the same company anymore." The experience of discrimination and litigation had altered her view of the organization.

Though these employees had reasonable reservations, for the most part, they wanted to settle the case with the option to return to their jobs. For Pamela Richardson (P13), meaningful financial compensation was more than just her salary. Like many employees, Ms. Richardson not only took personal satisfaction and a salary from her job, but also retirement benefits and health insurance coverage. She described her reaction when her lawyer encouraged her to settle for $15,000: "What they did to me was illegal. I didn't care about the money. I wanted my job. I had it for twelve and a half years. [When I lost that job] I lost my retirement, I lost my life insurance. And I had worked hard."

A number of interviewees told us that the job that led to the lawsuit was one of the best jobs—or the best job—they ever had. It may be that plaintiffs who lose their jobs come to reimagine those jobs as better than they were, but an equally plausible explanation is that people are only willing to fight this hard for a job they considered good. Work histories reveal that many plaintiff interviewees were at a pinnacle of their career before the lawsuit and either did not work again or never had as good a job again. Lois Smith (P19) said that she simply sought "some resolution and mediation" through the courts, because the job she worked in was her "dream job." She wanted to keep it "more than anything in the world."

Like most Americans, these plaintiffs identified with their jobs, whether those jobs were a way to pay the bills or a career that gave their lives structure and meaning. Losing that job (or fear of losing the job) was a significant disruption to their identity. As Laila Walter (P33) spoke about her and her husband's lawsuit: "I was hoping, by the way that me and my husband approached this, that they would actually have compassion and realize that we are not out trying to be mean, vindictive people. We are good people trying to support a family and just want to keep our jobs and do it well."

Lump Sum Compensation. Plaintiffs also could potentially achieve financial security through the more common lump sum payments generated by settling or, less often, winning a lawsuit. At least twenty-two of our plaintiff interviewees were awarded some kind of financial compensation, and half of these reported that they were at least somewhat satisfied with the outcome of their case—a far greater rate of satisfaction than for those who won no financial compensation. Yet most of these twenty-two reported regret and disappointment: they felt the financial compensation was inadequate, the offending individuals had not suffered adequately, or the discriminatory practices at the employing organization had continued. One said ruefully,

> I was going on fifty years old. . . . I don't know where they thought I was going to get another job, but like I say, they should have paid me at least up to my retirement age. . . . I did not get punitive damages, and I did not get the job back. (P40)

Officer Grayson, too, was bitter: "They don't settle for anything. They'll fight you until the very end and rather pay the attorneys the money than to give you any money."

The vast majority of plaintiffs we interviewed who accepted a settlement were not satisfied with at least some aspect of the settlement. This is not meant to say the outcomes we analyze were necessarily bad or unfair, but that respondents perceived them as such. Plaintiffs' dissatisfactions range from not having a clear idea of how much money they would actually receive, to wanting their job back and not getting it, to just feeling the pain of commensuration—a number placed on a harm to their dignity.

First, plaintiffs were unsatisfied with the amount of money that eventually came to them, whether the actual amount of the settlement or how little they actually recovered. Although those with legal representation knew that their lawyers were going to take one third of the settlement, plaintiffs were usually unprepared for the court costs, litigation expenses (if their attorneys had hired experts), and taxes. Although generally satisfied with his award, Mr. Nolls (P3) pinpointed an undercurrent we heard from many: "it's never enough." But other things matter, too. He continued, "But I still, one of the finest things I feel is that even the American [Disease] Association president called me to thank me. [He said], 'You've really helped [people with the disability] in the future, I want to thank you for all the work that you've done.'" For this plaintiff, it was a call from the professional association leading education and lobbying efforts on behalf of all of the people suffering the condition that Mr. Nolls suffers. At other points in the interview, Mr. Nolls said his settlement was enough for him to retire and to take an exotic vacation with his wife. It seems lingering dissatisfaction with the amount can be eclipsed by personal satisfaction.

Other plaintiffs accepted offers simply to end the unpleasantness of various aspects of litigation and the pressure from attorneys and judges. Consider the following, from Catherine Harris (P12), whose story opens chapter 4:

> I didn't want to tear people up like that, and I knew they'd try to tear me up. It was so unpleasant, it was just so unpleasant, and I think that's in the end why I did take the settlement. [My] attorney really wanted me to take it. He put a lot of pressure on me to take it.

Ms. Harris went on to explain that when the employer, a city government, made the settlement offer through the court, their attorney insisted it was the best offer she would get. She saw it as a bluff, but her own attorney said, "'Well, if you're going to blow off your attorney, maybe you should go see another attorney.' I said, 'Wow!' You know. I wanted a tough attorney to go after *them*, not *me!*"

Gerry Handley (P14), whose story opened this book, also told us that his lawyer advised him to accept a $50,000 settlement:

> No. I told him no. I told him no, I didn't want to do that, but my home had went into foreclosure and I was behind in my bills and stuff. . . . I really got the bitter end. I won, but sometimes you win, you lose.

Mr. Handley did not think the settlement was fair, but he needed the money.

Ms. Smith represents a different kind of dissatisfaction about settlement. When people retired from the railroad, they often were granted lifetime rail passes; one of Ms. Smith's primary goals in settlement included this pass, but she did not receive it. Ms. Smith told us that her settlement gave her:

> [A] really shitty feeling . . . because I thought the case was worth a whole lot more . . . like a half a mil. . . . I was treated unfairly, and to get $25,000, I mean, you know, that's about . . . four or five months of wages for me . . . But, I mean, I got what I needed and I won. . . . That's the bottom line. *They* paid *me*; I didn't pay them. And they spent an awful lot of money defending themselves. [My attorney] heard up to like $750,000, $800,000.

Still, being a train conductor had been her identity, and the railroad was the heart and soul of what she loved about the job. Without the lifetime rail pass, the settlement was, in her mind, just money.

One of the most complicated stories of settlement came from a class action in which the lead plaintiffs felt their share of the settlement should have been larger because of all the work they put in to keep the case moving forward. One of the named plaintiffs told us her portion, $275,000, did not feel fair. "They didn't even wanna give us [the four lead plaintiffs] that much! . . . And I told [the federal judge], 'Look, I've been doing this for ten years. . . . Who would do this again for the amount that they want to settle on me?'" (P36). The judge raised the amount, but it was still lower than what a male manager would have been paid over ten years. Two metrics disappoint her. First is the effort she put in so that all of the female plaintiffs in the class could be compensated. The second is her assessment of how much back pay she was owed. Because she was so involved with the case and her work history was one of the primary examples analyzed, she knew in far more detail than most plaintiffs the precise value of her case.

Occasionally plaintiffs reject settlement offers. As we noted in chapter 6, sometimes these decisions turn out to be miscalculations, as when plaintiffs lose at trial. But sometimes plaintiffs reject settlement amounts as insulting. As Arthur Zeman (P10), a stock broker who filed a disability claim, said after being offered a settlement "in the teens":

> I probably would not have taken it, only because . . . I'm not, nor was I, money hungry. I wasn't a person like that. I was just thinking that it is an insult to, you know, demean me and tell me that "You stink. You're out of here." Just like that, when I sacrificed to drive up here for three months. I didn't even have to work, period. I could have just stayed home and just been sick.

ACCOMPLISHING JUSTICE AND CHANGING THE ORGANIZATION. Many plaintiffs echoed the sentiment that it was "not about the money" and that they had other goals in mind in pursuing the lawsuit, such as achieving justice and holding their employer accountable. People who file lawsuits commonly hope for an opportunity to tell the whole story of their case to a legal authority. Some of the plaintiffs we interviewed (seven) felt they had the opportunity to tell their full story to a lawyer, a state fair employment agency, the EEOC, a judge, or a jury, and this experience bolstered their sense that law could be fair. Shelly Simmons (P31), a forty-five-year-old African American female lab technician, felt affirmed when the judge in her case sympathized with her:

> The trial vindicated me. Well, the process from where I started representing myself to the end of the trial vindicated me, as far as I was concerned. [The judge] made an open apology of what happened [earlier in the case]. . . . And believe you me, [when] I see her today, I hug her. She saved my life, because that really picked me up out of the dumps. It really did. It gave me motivation and courage.

Interestingly, Ms. Simmons lost at trial and on appeal. In recounting how she rejected a significant settlement offer, she spoke of refusing to be silenced. "You are not going to shut me up for $100,000." Despite her loss in court, the opportunity to express her claim at trial gave her significant satisfaction. Other plaintiffs derived a sense of exoneration during the depositions, when they told their version of the story, unencumbered, in front of their former employer.

For Ms. Harris, justice had not truly been achieved in her case: the organization had not changed. She described her $160,000 early settlement as a "victory" but recounted many reasons for disappointment in the outcome. One of the most salient was that the individual bad actor was not terminated from his job. She viewed this as an affront to the principle of public service and to her identity as a city employee and resident:

> As someone who is very proud of a public service career, I did not feel comfortable with this individual being in a leadership role in a city that, in any city, but one that I was proud of and one that I was associated with and my city that I lived in. . . . Basically, I think he was a golfing buddy of the city manager, and until the city manager was going to leave, he wasn't going to probably leave, and all that stuff was well out of my control.

Many plaintiffs enter litigation in an effort to vindicate their view that what the employer had done was wrong. For these plaintiffs, money—and even organizational change—are secondary goals. Robert Lester (P16), a white tour manager in his late forties who sued for age discrimination, but who lost on all counts of the employer's summary judgment motion, describes his motivation:

> I think the main thing I felt was I felt betrayed. I felt betrayed by the fact that I spent twenty years with an organization, and yet this is the way they're treating me. They're tossing me out and saying, "Hey, you're no good anymore." And the people they were bringing in just didn't have the knowledge, ability, or the talent. . . . I felt really angry at the same time knowing full well that, you know, I spent a lot of time away from my family, I spent a lot of time traveling, I spent a lot of time, you know, sitting in an empty airport waiting for the plane to come to get to the next meeting or get to the next sales conference.

When we asked Maureen Sands whether she felt satisfied with the settlement in her disability case, she replied: "It is okay. I would have liked more, but it was okay because it wasn't about money. I was more pleased that I made them have to admit that they were in the wrong, and that was most important to me."

BALANCING LIFE CONSEQUENCES. Plaintiffs' most significant calculation in assessing outcomes involved assessing whether the case was "worth it" given the toll on their personal and family lives. What started as a necessary quest for funds or an emotional desire to right an injustice often became an unbearable burden. None of the plaintiffs we interviewed described this as an easy time: the stress from being in conflict on the job, being terminated (usually), deciding to pursue a lawsuit, and the lawsuit itself had a variety of negative effects on plaintiffs. Almost universally, plaintiffs described bankruptcy, divorce, alcohol or drug problems, or depression as an important part of their story. Very often plaintiffs experienced several of these negative life outcomes. It is, of course, difficult to know if these life events would have occurred regardless of their workplace struggles and, in some instances, it is possible that these life circumstances may have started prior to and contributed to workplace failings. And yet, the sequence reported by respondents was that their personal troubles began after their professional ones.

Bankruptcy. One of the most common impacts of litigation was money troubles. As noted above and in chapter 3, a majority of employment civil rights plaintiffs have been fired from their job, so they already are dealing with loss of income. Further, lawsuits are expensive, especially if the plaintiff has an attorney. Because plaintiffs' lawyers are less and less likely to charge on a pure contingency-fee model, out-of-work plaintiffs are paying at least part of their attorney's fees, looking for work, *and* trying not to default on their routine expenses (mortgage, credit cards, monthly bills). Several plaintiffs mentioned financial stress, and at least five plaintiffs we interviewed (8%) told us that their lawsuit led to a bankruptcy declaration. And three of those plaintiffs technically won—meaning they settled their case. This does not include those who reported spending all or part of their retirement savings, using children's college funds to get by, or taking second mortgages on homes.

Loss of a job, litigation, and health issues can create a perfect financial storm for plaintiffs. When we discussed attorney's fees with Daris Barrett (P24), featured in chapter 4, she admitted somewhat shamefully that she had filed for bankruptcy, as she could not afford to pay her attorney and was threatened with an unrelated lawsuit. While Ms. Barrett's bankruptcy was partly strategic, it would not have been granted without proof of dire financial need. In fact, for many, bankruptcy is a bitterly ironic but frequent outcome, since the remedies for employment civil rights are explicitly designed to make up for lost earnings. But, like other kinds of lawsuits, these drag on and on, making any eventual recovery unlikely to help many litigants recover financially.

Divorce. Bankruptcy, while personally humiliating, did not compare to the grief of those plaintiffs who told us workplace and legal battles led to marital problems resulting in divorce or separation. Seven plaintiffs attributed such a breakup to the stress of the lawsuit. One of the most disturbing stories came from Mr. Handley. He told us he "lost his wife" because:

> I was like paranoid of everybody, I felt like I couldn't trust nobody. My wife was white, so I felt like white people was against me, and I couldn't trust her because her attitude was, "Why are you having these problems at work? . . . People are not racist against you. . . . You should be going to work and make this money and bring this money home. You have a good job. You are a blessed black man." . . . I was trying to tell her, you know, "These white peo-

ple are, like, prejudiced against me, and how they treat me at work and these things that happen." And she was saying, "Just forget it." Forget it? She didn't understand, so I became hostile toward her.

Peter Nichelson (P1), who worked closely with his attorney and drafted many of the documents in his case to save on lawyer's fees, explained that, with all the work of filing papers, meeting deadlines, exhausting internal appeals, and the like, his wife began to think that he was, "going . . . down the same road that I went back in '98 and flipping out again. She had it." She moved out with their two-year-old son.

Drugs and Alcohol. Other plaintiffs revealed that they attempted to manage the stress with drugs and alcohol. This sometimes played a role in disrupted relationships and occasionally led to a stint in rehabilitation. One of our exchanges with a plaintiff (P16) went as follows:

I: When you think back about this period in your life now, what kind of strain, if any, did it put on, did this process put on you and your family, and how did you deal with it?

R: [pause] It was easy; I guess it was easy to drink. [laughing]

Mrs. Burns, the wife of Chris Burns (P5), talked about worrying that her husband would "go postal":

Thank God, my husband was able to get a hold of himself. 'Cause he went through a drinking thing. I mean it was depression. I mean, a man that has been working and taking care of his family and then all of a sudden, health wise, and a whole bunch of things are against him.

It is probably not surprising that the effects of litigation included drug abuse and family difficulty, given the level of stress litigation places on individuals. Nonetheless, the consistency of the reports was astounding.

Physical Deterioration and Depression. The health impacts of racism and other forms of discrimination are well documented. People who perceive they are being discriminated against face a number of debilitating health issues.[5] In our sample, Lois Smith (P19), a white woman who suffered a very hostile sexually harassing work environment in the very masculinized field of railroad operations, told us that, as she looks back on it now, she should not have fought to keep the job as long as she did:

> I should have quit really. . . . It was a terribly abusive environment, but I'm not a quitter. I ultimately won. . . . Not a lot, but I won. [And yet there was a] toll on my marriage and my migraines and my body. I had Bell's Palsy and I had pneumonia and I had toxic hepatitis. I mean my body was crying out, and I hospitalized myself twice for depression. I was really suicidal. It was horrible.

Financial strain also put plaintiffs in a position of taking one or more jobs even if they led to further physical degradation. Philip Jacobson (P21), an African American printing clerk, told us:

> I also kept a second job. We got five kids; you got to have a second job. And so I just started doing more security, and then met this guy who was an iron worker, and they make very good money. . . . And so I took that job, and within two days I tore my knee up and tore some ligaments in my back. So I've been on disability since then. This whole experience caused my wife and I to fight all the time. I didn't spend as much time with my children, because I was sullen a lot. Eventually . . . they put me off on medical leave, a doctor did. And they started giving me depression medicine. And it just broke me down. I'm still . . . I've been trying to figure out—excuse me, I get emotional sometimes [crying]. . . . I couldn't believe they'd done this stuff to me. When you tell people, they don't believe you. They look at you like, "Well, what did you do?" I said, "I showed up for work!" [laughs] But . . . they wanted to fire me. . . . So it's just like, you just want me to die.

Depression—whether clinically diagnosed or referenced colloquially—was mentioned by numerous plaintiffs we interviewed. Matthew Brown (P9), an African American man who filed a racial discrimination case, talked of the lingering effects:

> Sometimes I still get depressed. You know, because I see how I was really jammed, and I'm just glad you guys are interested in what, you know, what's done. In other words, after all these years, I'm able to just tell some non-blacks. You know, I'm serious, actually what happened. And from you reading it, you can see I'm not lying. It happened exactly like that.

And yet, there were still plaintiffs who survived the ordeal in remarkable health, both psychologically and physically. When asked if the lawsuit was stressful and took a toll, Floyd Kelly said:

> No, it didn't, because I was always taught that Christ and God watch over. . . . I was drafted and went to Vietnam, and this shoulder here was tore off, my friend died in my arms, and all of the stuff I went through, even the discrimination over there. . . . These kind of things? That lawsuit? That was nothing. Emotional, no.

Conclusion

Seldom can plaintiffs or the defendant organizations clearly articulate whether they won or lost a case. At different points in time, both plaintiffs and defendant employers report having very different goals than those they had at prior moments in the litigation process. While both plaintiffs and defendant spokespeople express ambivalence about the outcomes of these cases, the litigation process takes a much higher emotional, physical, and financial toll on plaintiffs than it does on defendants and their representatives.

One of the most striking instances of the difficulty of assessing winning and losing came from Gerry Handley, who was racially harassed at work and even asked by coworkers whether he had sex with his daughter. At one point in our interview Mr. Handley said that he would "have took it" rather than file because "the justice it isn't there." Yet he also told us:

> It's probably been ten years since I even talked about it. I have a sometimes decent relationship with my wife now. I can talk to her, you know, I talk to my kids, and I try to put closure to it. She's like, "Well, that's gone, and the money is all gone, so don't even talk to me about it now." So, then, for a long time, but I was getting beyond that, you know, and I got like some really nice daughters, you know. I have two of the greatest daughters in the world, you know. When I look back at it, it was worth it, just for them.

With Mr. Handley, as with other plaintiffs, we hear his anguish over the injustice he experienced in both his workplace and the legal system. We also hear his shifting and polyvocal understanding of what happened, as he retrospectively makes sense of the many losses he suffered.

PART III

Conclusion

CHAPTER NINE

Stereotyping and the Reinscription of Race, Sex, Disability, and Age Hierarchies

Laws prohibiting employment discrimination were created to remove the invidious effects of race, sex, disability, and age discrimination in the workplace. Yet when plaintiffs invoke their rights through a formal complaint to a fair employment agency or the EEOC, the responses of employers, agencies, and courts often operate to reinscribe the very hierarchies the law was designed to attack.

In chapters 4 through 8, we showed legal reinscription processes in different stages of litigation, from the early workplace conflict to the final case outcome. Whether the plaintiffs were alleging racial, sex, disability, or age discrimination, they experienced many similar challenges. These processes include employees' lack of familiarity with antidiscrimination law, unresponsive plaintiffs' lawyers, and unsatisfactory legal resolutions. In approaching all four types of claims, employers also responded similarly and mounted similar defenses. They denied discrimination, asserted managerial prerogatives, individualized the problem, and denigrated the plaintiff. They offered small monetary awards, minimizing and monetizing the harm asserted by the plaintiff. They isolated the discrimination dispute from the workplace by refusing to reinstate the complainant. They required that plaintiffs sign confidentiality agreements concerning settlements. The federal courts presiding over these processes effectively legitimized these practices. For in applying standard rules for litigation and taking a position as neutral arbiters of rights claims, they ignored the asymmetry of power between plaintiffs and employers in the workplace and in litigation.

In this chapter we turn our attention to the unique ways that hierarchies of race, sex, disability, and age are reinforced in employment discrimination litigation through one particularly noteworthy mechanism of reinscription: stereotypes. Stereotypes are arbitrary, superficial assumptions and beliefs about the traits, actions, and roles of the individuals identified with a certain social category.[1] They are not rooted in accurate assessments of individuals' skills and accomplishments.[2] Men, for example, are stereotyped as more committed to their careers and women as more committed to family, despite scientific evidence that they share similar orientations toward both career and family.[3] Stereotypes fuel discrimination against those who have been negatively stereotyped in favor of those who are positively typed.[4] They serve as cultural constructs that seem to describe social reality and, therein, justify unequal social relations. Thus, when people in positions of power—for the purposes of our study, employers, lawyers, or judges—rely on stereotypes, they degrade members of a subordinate group—for our purposes, people of color, women, people with disabilities, and older workers—while protecting the privileges of already dominant groups.[5]

We find that plaintiffs confront certain stereotypes based on their social identities and related to the bases of discrimination they allege. These stereotypes express and reinforce hierarchies of race, gender, disability, and age. They are relevant in the workplace and in court. The legal reinscription process is dynamic; it occurs both through employers' and legal actors' active reliance on stereotypes and through the legal system's neglect of these stereotypes, when it fails to address or remediate them.

Stereotypes at Work and in the Courts

Intergroup stereotypes can be impactful in the workplace. They influence whether people are able to attain jobs, advance to well-compensated middle- and upper-managerial and professional jobs, support themselves financially, and achieve career goals.[6] For example, women's employment is routinely structured by horizontal segregation: employers channel women into positions that are predominantly occupied by women and typed as feminine and inferior.[7] Meanwhile, men occupy higher-status positions with substantially higher pay, validated by stereotypes of men as more competent and better suited to the demands of competitive work.[8] In other words, stereotypes are a mechanism by which employers maintain existing regimes of inequality.[9] They come to be self-referential justifications for inequality, perpetuating ascriptive hierarchies that are central to social inequality.

Legal actors in the US courts, too, rely on stereotypes, with severe consequences. Many observers note that stereotypes of African American and Latino men as dangerous are pervasive in the criminal justice system, which contributes to the disproportionate criminalization and penalization of those groups.[10] Although the courts interpret employment discrimination law to prohibit stereotyping in cases such as *Price Waterhouse v. Hopkins*, antidiscrimination law can also rest upon and reinforce social stereotypes.[11] Sexual harassment law, for instance, conceptualizes harassment primarily as a matter of sexual desire, rather than one of male domination. That construction of the problem reinforces the stereotype of women as sex objects. Our analysis reveals the relevance of stereotypes in the social process of pursuing litigation.

Analytic Schema: The Legal Reinscription of Inequality through Stereotyping

Ascriptive hierarchies and their associated stereotypes shape workplace hierarchies, which include distinctions based on race, sex, disability, and age. Discrimination based on these statuses is illegal, and those who believe they have experienced discrimination can pursue legal redress. Yet these same inequalities—along with pervasive class-based inequalities, such as occupational status and access to managerial power—infuse the legal process. Through law, they gain legitimacy. In many cases, managers rely on stereotypes to degrade and discriminate against employees. Sometimes attorneys adopt those same stereotypes. Plaintiffs' attorneys may turn aside cases or make decisions about how they handle cases based on similar stereotypes, but stereotyping is particularly common among defense attorneys as they question plaintiffs' motives and attack their competence.

Under limited circumstances, a win for the plaintiff can upset insidious workplace stereotypes. But in most cases, plaintiffs' claims are dismissed or denied by legal actors, most evidently in the final decision in a given case. Although the courts' denial of claims is not tailored to stereotypes per se, litigation outcomes such as modest settlements and dismissals against plaintiffs typically leave alleged acts of discrimination—and managers' stereotyped interpretations of those plaintiffs—unaddressed. That is, the legal process does not disrupt managers' authority over discriminatory behavior at work. Such outcomes reinforce the defense's construction of plaintiffs' claims as invalid and their characterizations of plaintiffs as problems. The link from case outcomes to the broader set of societal attitudes that make up stereotypes and ascriptive hierarchies, while far more complicated than presented here, may also reinforce negative stereotypes, as plaintiffs are denigrated for bringing claims and participating in what public commentators refer to as "the excuse factory."

Empirically, stereotypes are observable in what people say and their actions at work and in the courts. They are identifiable indicators that we can document with interview data. To begin our analysis of stereotyping and reinscription, we categorized, for each major category of discrimination (race, sex, disability, age), all the plaintiff interviewees for whom that type of discrimination was salient. For example, a plaintiff may have filed a race, sex, and disability case, but, for her, disability discrimination was the most meaningful issue during the interview. Then we did in-depth analysis of interviews with plaintiffs in each of the four categories, with a preference toward those cases for which we had multiple perspectives. For that analysis, we built definitions of race, sex, disability, and age stereotypes by deductively drawing from relevant literature, then refined those definitions inductively as patterns emerged while coding the interview data.

In addition to our analysis of plaintiffs' narratives, we counted the prevalence of the main race, sex, disability, and age stereotypes across the plaintiffs. We included an intercoder reliability check of those counts by assigning two research assistants the task of coding two interviews from each of the four categories, to ensure consistency in how they interpreted the stereotype definitions. Then each coder was assigned two stereotype categories to review in the full sample of interviews. The coders also flagged and counted common experiences in each category, such as overt racial and sexual hostility, problems with medical evidence, and emotional trauma.

As we show, stereotypes can be more or less salient in different moments of these disputes and may be invoked in subtle and not-so-subtle ways. In many cases, the stereotypes are most evident in the workplace, yet plaintiffs' accounts of their employment experiences are refracted through law, as the legal process frames or describes the workplace. Stereotypes surface in the courts, too—often the same stereotypes that were prevalent at work, sometimes different ones. However, because most cases settle and may settle early and are not even recalled by anyone other than the plaintiff, our information about stereotypes is not equally available across cases.

Further, the stereotypes and the intensity of their expression vary according to the social category an individual occupies. In plaintiffs' accounts, race and sex stereotypes are front and center in their conflicts. Stereotypes about disability are present, as well, and frequently are mediated through medical documents and experts. Age stereotypes are the most complex and, simultaneously, the least pronounced in our interviews with plaintiffs. Such stereotypes may be less prominent because they can work either in favor of or against older workers; age is often a trait of the powerful in the workplace and correlates of age, such as experience and knowledge, often are seen as positive attributes at work. Age stereotypes also can be made salient by layoffs and other business decisions. We turn first to racial stereotypes and the reinscription of racial discrimination.

Racial Stereotypes and the Reinscription of Racial Discrimination

Out of the twenty-one cases in our interview sample that included a race discrimination claim, there were fifteen cases in which race discrimination was salient for the plaintiff—in all cases, African Americans. These cases are part of the 40% of the cases in our national sample claiming race discrimination. Our interviews with those plaintiffs reveal four primary stereotypes that are highlighted, reinforced, and reinstitutionalized in the employment discrimination litigation process for African Americans: that African Americans are *uppity*, *lazy or stupid*, *dangerous* or *violent* (for males) and *bitchy* (for women). All of these stereotypes have long histories in American society, and all have received significant scholarly attention.

The uppity theme (experienced by nine plaintiffs) and lazy theme (experienced by ten) were among the most prevalent. Being uppity was raised thirty-four times. The dangerous or violent theme (five plaintiffs) and bitchy theme (four plaintiffs) saw lower frequencies, likely resulting from the gender-specific quality of these stereotypes. While many plaintiffs reported that a particular stereotype figured prominently in their experiences with the legal process, five of the plaintiff interviewees described being victimized by three racial stereotypes. It is also worth pointing out that a majority (nine) of these fifteen interviewees experienced overt racial harassment in the workplace, including racial epithets and open intimidation. For these plaintiffs, efforts to assert their rights were frequently met with hostility; eight reported retaliation during their cases.

AFRICAN AMERICANS AS UPPITY. The view of African Americans as uppity is based in a widespread but generally unspoken racist perception that African American people should be subservient to white people.[12] This is a stereotype with deep historical roots in the power relations of African American slavery, in which subordinated African American slaves were abused or killed by white slaveholders for minor infractions or the appearance of insurrection. This stereotype also reflects how, in interpersonal interactions, white people frequently respond negatively to people who strongly identify as African American.[13]

The story of Floyd Kelly (P7) began as an attempt to gain racial justice in the workplace but devolved into one in which he was perceived as an uppity African American on the job. A Vietnam War veteran, Mr. Kelly was one of the few African American workers hired at a transportation company in the early 1970s. He developed strong friendships with coworkers over the years. By the early 1980s, as information technology changed, the nature of jobs in the department began to change. Mr. Kelly and others began to notice that the company was training new white employees who were quickly promoted, while the African American workers who had trained them (and who had seniority) were not. When African American employees seeking to understand what was happening formed a group, Mr. Kelly's seniority, as well as his age, military service, and long-standing friendships with management, made him the obvious choice as their informal leader. Mr. Kelly told us:

> I wanted to make sure that it wasn't a . . . militant type thing. . . . I didn't want it to look like we were trying to overthrow anybody. . . . I suggested we . . . write a letter . . . asking [management] if we could just have a meeting and sit down and just kind of go over some things and, as I said, find out

which direction they were going, what direction they wanted us to go, what they wanted us to do to move forward with the company.

Proceeding with this plan, the group sent the letter requesting a meeting. Apparently with the encouragement of Mr. Kelly's friend in management, the department head met with some thirty African American workers. In the meeting, the department head promised to do more to promote African Americans and to meet again in six months to review progress.

In the succeeding months, Mr. Kelly observed that virtually all the white workers in his group had been sent to training, but he had not. Mr. Kelly asked the assistant department head when he would be sent to training and was told, "We send who we want to send." Mr. Kelly recalled this as the first time he was met with this kind of hostility from the executives at the company and that this seemed particularly pointed.

About five months after the meeting between the department head and the group of African American workers and very shortly after he received a very positive evaluation from his direct supervisor, Mr. Kelly was called into the office of the assistant department head, his supervisor's manager. Expecting a promotion or an acknowledgment of his positive evaluation, Mr. Kelly was instead given a letter explaining that the company "was downsizing" and that "[his] services will no longer be needed." Mr. Kelly said: "Now I'm getting emotional. I said, 'Can't you transfer me? Can I transfer to another . . . ?' And, he said, 'Don't you get it? We don't want you here.'"

Mr. Kelly signed a release form and received severance pay in an amount less than $1,000 per year for his sixteen years of service. He later learned that the African American employee who recorded the notes from management meeting also had been terminated. Two white workers were also terminated, which Kelly interpreted as management's attempt to cover any retaliation against the African American group. Devastated, Mr. Kelly hid in his house and kept his car in his garage for a week so that neighbors did not know he had lost his job. He asked a friend at the company to keep an eye out for information that might be relevant if he brought a case. Three months later, the friend sent Mr. Kelly a list of ten new hires in the department, all of whom were white. Mr. Kelly now perceived and had documentary support that the downsizing was a pretext for firing him as the acting leader of a group dedicated to advancing the situation of African American workers. He believed management was following the adage, "If you cut off the head of the snake . . . you kill the snake."

Mr. Kelly was seen as uppity not only because he challenged managerial prerogatives (true in all of the cases in this research), but also because he represented others who sought to question promotion and training decisions. Although he explained that he had been very careful to couch his questions to management in a way that would not seem like he was leading a revolt, when he questioned his station and the station of other African American employees, he went from a respected worker in the organization who felt comfortable with management to someone that management "didn't want here."

AFRICAN AMERICANS AS LAZY OR STUPID. In the courts, Mr. Kelly encountered a different stereotype: the unintelligent African American. The view of African Americans as lazy draws from notions of self-improvement, personal responsibility, and work ethic.[14] This couching of antiblack sentiment in the ideology of work is representative of "symbolic racism," which claims that the persistent socioeconomic status gap separating whites and African Americans is traceable to a lack of effort on the part of African Americans.[15] This idea is exacerbated by the widespread perceptions among white people that African Americans are unjustly favored by social policies at the expense of white Americans and that those policies allow otherwise capable individuals to not work.[16] Similarly, the lazy stereotype also motivates resistance to race-targeted redistributive social policies.[17]

When employees are terminated discriminatorily, they are not *told* they are being fired due to their race, sex, disability, or age. Rather, they are routinely terminated for "failure to perform." In the context of race, this often comes in the form of accusations of laziness and incompetence. For example, one of the disputed allegations made against Franklin Williams (P11), the thirty-eight-year-old African American railroad laborer, was that he had fallen asleep on the job.

The idea of African Americans as "lazy" or "stupid" is carried out in the legal system as well. Floyd Kelly believed that his lawyers conspired against him; even as they told him he was "smart," it was in a way that implied he was stupid. Mr. Kelly's understanding that he represented an uppity African American who was being beaten back for it was reinvigorated by his court experience. He reported feeling suspicious when his lawyers asked him to leave a meeting about his case. He recalled that, after a few minutes, he was called back into the room, where his lawyers, the defendant employer (including his former supervisor) and its lawyers, and the mediator were present. According to Mr. Kelly, the defense attorney referred to the release he had signed:

> And one of them said, "Mr. [Kelly] you're . . . a very intelligent young man and we feel something, something, something," I don't remember what it was, but that kind of threw me for a loop. What does that have to do with anything? What? Am I supposed to be stupid? And then I got, again, I would say this—now I'm getting offended, because am I supposed to be stupid because I'm black? That's my next thing in my mind. I didn't say that.

As negotiations came to an impasse, Mr. Kelly told the lawyers, "We'll just go to court." The opposing attorneys commented that the judge in the case would not be sympathetic to the plaintiff. Mr. Kelly's lawyer then suggested a settlement. Mr. Kelly relented, effectively leaving intact stereotypes about him and other African American employees.

The "lazy" trope is one of the most commonly used in discrediting descriptions of African Americans because it goes to the heart of the reason a person could be legitimately terminated.[18] No organization wants "lazy" workers, and no court would condemn termination for failure to perform. Unfortunately, given the stereotype, this racialized, derogatory description is more likely to be believed by lawyers and courts when deployed against African American workers than against their white counterparts, thereby justifying terminations that may be, at least in part, due to race, not incompetence.

AFRICAN AMERICAN MALES AS DANGEROUS OR VIOLENT. The perception of African American men as dangerous or criminally violent is one of the most durable stereotypes about African Americans.[19] While survey evidence shows a decline in other negative racial attitudes, the racialized view of violent crime is widely held, even among those who profess tolerant beliefs.[20] This stereotype of African American men underlies whites' support for harsh policing and penal sanctions.[21] It also informs perceptions of African American neighborhoods as dangerous and undesirable.[22] The pervasiveness of these views is maintained, in part, by the outsized proportion of media attention given to African American violence, in which African American males are depicted as physically threatening more often than their white criminal counterparts.[23] The hyper-racialized criminal justice system provides an important source of support for the stereotype, which is, in turn, reinforced by its use as a political tool for stoking racial resentments.[24]

This stereotype was made most clear in the experience of Franklin Williams, as featured in the opening of chapter 7. Mr. Williams complained of racial (and disability) discrimination at his employer for not being promoted and filed, but did not pursue, an EEOC claim. After suffering a serious injury on the job, receiving a cash award, and returning to work, he was terminated after a series of three disputed infractions. In one allegation, Mr. Williams was standing atop a locomotive when his supervisor walked by and indicated that he had the supervisor in his "sight." The supervisor understood this comment to mean Mr. Williams had him in his "sights"—gun sights. The supervisor claimed he felt threatened, terminated Mr. Williams, and contacted security. As Mr. Williams told us, he was removed from the workplace in handcuffs. Mr. Williams's subsequent lawsuit proceeded to trial, where he represented himself, went to bench trial, and lost.

Years later, the railroad's lawyer, David Lever (DL11), was still just as certain of the supervisor's interpretation of the events and his decision to terminate Mr. Williams as he was when he defended the railroad in the lawsuit, saying to us that the case was "pretty clear." He suggested Mr. Williams's purported "got you in my [gun] sights" comment was "a cultural thing" or simply one of those things that "don't to me make any sense."

Mr. Williams, on the other hand, experienced the event as fraught with racial stereotypes. He felt his firing was a "racial thing" with "racial overtones," in part because there was no investigation or chance for him to describe his side of the story. "After the 'threat,' they had me handcuffed, and the thing of it is, I've never been arrested in my life. I don't even have damn parking tickets."

The stereotype of African American men as dangerous sometimes dovetailed with a stereotype of African Americans as hypersexual and sexual predators (five interviewees). We began this book with an egregious story of the deployment of the hypersexualization stereotype in the workplace: the story of Gerry Handley (P14). Mr. Handley was the computer operator subjected to intense racial harassment by his lead coworker, including his coworker's discussion of slaves from the Caribbean committing incest and questions to Mr. Handley about whether he had sex with his daughter. Such statements made Mr. Handley out to be a sexual predator. While Mr. Handley ultimately succeeded in settling his case and kept his job, he endured significant personal costs in raising his discrimination claim. He became divorced and homeless as a result of tensions growing out of the lawsuit. He felt that he and his coworkers were persecuted during the course of the litigation. And he was laid off a year after his settlement during company-wide reductions in force.

AFRICAN AMERICAN WOMEN AS BITCHES. Like the uppity stereotype, elements of the stereotype that African American women are bitchy or overbearing matriarchs originate in African American slavery. Stereotypes of the feminine as delicate, good, and modest were limited to white women, while black womanhood meant masculinized strength and hard labor in combination with attributes of promiscuity.[25] In modern America, the matriarchy stereotype also is rooted in the reality of high unemployment among African American men and the imperative that African American women fulfill the breadwinner role (in turn, this economic reality clearly contributes to the stereotype of male laziness).[26] The stereotype of the "angry African American woman" caricatures African American women as possessive, nagging, and always irate. The stereotype has structural origins in the "shortage" of available African American men through incarceration, homicide, and unemployment in the United States.[27]

Annie Daley (P18), the forty-year-old African American supervisor featured near the beginning of chapter 7, filed a race discrimination claim against her employer, a telecommunications firm. Her director, a white woman, had accused Ms. Daley of hiring too many African Americans. Then, the employees under Ms. Daley's charge began performing at a subpar level and expressed open racial hostility. Ms. Daley told us: "There was one particular supervisor who, who made it very clear that she was not going to report to a black woman. . . . She even called me a black 'B' [bitch]." Soon after Ms. Daley looked to her own supervisor and the HR department for assistance in disciplining these white employees, she was fired.

While Ms. Daley's attorney, Ellis Barry (PL18), a white man, praised her character and noted "a pattern of somebody who clearly was not in favor, not in management's favor or never had been," her employer's attorney, a white woman, Mary Hill (DL18), described Ms. Daley exactly as Ms. Daley anticipated. Ms. Hill told us: "She came across as not terribly sharp and really kind of cold. . . . Not someone you would warm up to and feel sympathy for. She came across as rigid and sort of bitchy."

Ms. Daley refused the last-minute settlement offer of $100,000, and the case went to trial. The jury, which was comprised largely of white people and included several older white males, decided in favor of the telecommunications company—neglecting the problematic characterization of her as bitchy. In retrospect, Ms. Daley assesses her case in terms of the difficulty of achieving justice and the challenges of confronting racism at work: "You can try to prevent people from, you know, from mistreating people. . . . But you can't make them not be racist." Stereotypes that occur at the intersection of identity categories like the "black bitch" are especially pernicious for workers who receive the message that they are not performing their race or their gender well.

Gender-Based Stereotypes and the Reinscription of Gender Inequality

Our analysis of sex discrimination cases reveals other stereotypes of women, in addition to the black bitch, that underlie discrimination in the workplace and surface again in legal processes, when the target of these stereotypes exercises her legal rights and finds the reinscription of those stereotypes in the institution she looks to for remedy. Drawing from the thirteen sex discrimination cases in our interview sample, we examined the eight cases in which the plaintiffs (all women) spoke in detail about sex discrimination and sexual harassment. These cases are among the 37% of those in our national study that allege sex discrimination and sexual harassment.

These plaintiffs, in their stories of workplace discrimination and experiences in court, mention sex-based stereotypes of women as *hysterical persons*, *sex objects*, and *inferior workers*. The frequencies for the three sex stereotypes are identical, with seven plaintiffs experiencing each. In terms of the total number of times that a plaintiff referenced a stereotype, however, hysterical was by far the most common theme, mentioned a total of thirty-one times. This stereotype may be especially prominent because it allows employers to belittle or dismiss the grievances of women. Among plaintiff interviewees in sex discrimination cases, six women reported some instance of overt sexual harassment in the workplace, whether in the form of sexual advances from male coworkers or inappropriate sexualized language. This pattern is indicative of the pervasive sexual harassment that women face in employment in the form of threats, advancements, and hostile comments.[28]

WOMEN AS EMOTIONALLY HYSTERICAL AND IRRATIONAL. One pervasive stereotype is that women are emotionally weak or hysterical. The core assumption here is that women are overly emotional and irrational—as if their actions were not guided by reason and their perceptions were not grounded in reality.[29] This stereotype was invoked most completely in the case of Pamela Richardson (P13), the white clerk featured in chapter 6 who claimed that her employer failed to accommodate her health problems of premenstrual syndrome. She alleged discrimination on the basis of her disability, race, sex, disability, and age. However, for her, a combination of disability and sex discrimination together was most salient. The gendered nature of her disability claim seems to have made it particularly unlikely that her claim would be adequately addressed under antidiscrimination law, which fails to account for the intersectionality of multiple social identities.[30]

Suffering from extreme premenstrual syndrome (PMS) diagnosed as premenstrual dysphoria (PMDD) and anemia, Ms. Richardson sought vacation days, sick days, and ultimately unpaid leave via the Family and Medical Leave Act. Her serious and well-documented medical problem was met with skepticism, at best. In the workplace, the gendered hysterical trope was routinely assigned to her. One manager told Ms. Richardson that the federal government agency for which she worked "did not give sympathy at that level." According to such a perspective, accommodation is what people with actual disabilities get, while sympathy is what an irrational woman is asking for—and notably, does not receive. By framing the issue as such, the manager denied the extreme physical condition Ms. Richardson was suffering.

The stakes were high for Ms. Richardson, as she ultimately lost her job and had a child to support. She suspected that her employer never took her medical condition seriously because of the social stigma associated with PMS and because employers in general had a significant interest in thwarting claims about PMS, as a substantial proportion of employees could potentially suffer from it. (Of course, this would belie the fact that Ms. Richardson's health condition was apparently much more severe than the typical experience of PMS among women of childbearing age.)

In the legal system, the narrative of Ms. Richardson as out-of-control and mentally ill continued. As part of the process to officially verify she had a disability, she had to endure repeated medical examinations across multiple doctors, including psychiatrists. This medical attention cast doubt on her status and further branded her as hysterical.

Moreover, this stereotype animated her own attorney's perception of Ms. Richardson and his ultimate decision to drop her case. Ms. Richardson had difficulty finding a lawyer at all, but she was represented by Theodore Wilde (PL13), a white male in his early eighties, for a short period. In our interview, Mr. Wilde said things such as "I remember I didn't like the case from the get-go. I said, 'She ain't going to win.' I felt that she would have been hysterical. Imagine! I get these people, I take them in, and listen to them." Just as he derided Ms. Richardson for feminine distress, he also denigrated his other clients and people who consulted him about potentially becoming a client. He seemed to want recognition and sympathy from us, the interviewers, for his perceptions: "You know, I liked her as a person, but you find so many people with [a] syndrome who take advantage where they can. Use a doctor, get a report, and play it for all it's worth. That was my impression of Ms. Richardson. I thought, 'We are not going to win this case.'" Indeed, the primary reason Mr. Wilde "fired" her as a client, he said, was her "delusions" about her health.

So the trope of the lazy employee exaggerating symptoms is not just one applied to African Americans or, as we will soon see, people with disabilities, nor is it only espoused by businesses and their lawyers. Ms. Richardson encountered it as she tried to access the legal system. Hoping for an advocate and willing to pay for one, she instead found a lawyer who expressed the same kind of skepticism about her medical condition that she had faced in the workplace—and, as we noted in chapter 6, who could not recall her name. It is not surprising that Ms. Richardson felt dehumanized by her only advocate—she told us she "had met heroin addicts with better manners"—in what she described to us as the most difficult challenge of her life.

Ms. Richardson's case did not fare well. She was not accommodated in her workplace, as she understood it, and then was fired. Her attorney abandoned her mid-case. Finally, without counsel, Ms. Richardson lost at trial. Ultimately, Mr. Wilde was correct or created a self-fulfilling prophecy: the idea of accommodating a woman who suffered from PMS or PMDD was not taken seriously by the federal government employer or by the courts.

Stereotyping of women as hysterical and weak also worked against

Denise Slayton (P36), whose experience joining a sex and race class action lawsuit is chronicled in chapter 6. The central claim was that the company failed to promote women to store manager positions. The case resulted in major late settlement funds for different groups of plaintiffs. Ms. Slayton, a forty-five-year-old white retail clerk, described for us a meeting that the management called at a point when a lawsuit may have been possible to avoid. At that meeting, managers cited a variety of reasons for not promoting women, among them the assertion that women too easily become emotional and out-of-hand. As Ms. Slayton told us:

> They had a meeting of all their managers and human resources and another company they brought in. And it was like a little get-together to discuss all of this stuff. . . . The store manager said: "Women cry . . . you know, that women get upset and they cry. Do you know that? Well, men can't handle that. We can't have a store manager that gets upset and cries."

Women's alleged irrationality comes in many forms: they may be hysterical from menstruation, delusional about their health and their competencies as employees, or emotionally weak as revealed by (actual or imagined) crying at work. This stereotyping often overlaps with treatment of women as sex objects.

WOMEN AS SEX OBJECTS. One of the most pervasive stereotypes of women in the workplace is that they are not so much workers as available sex objects for men. This stereotype reveals the dual power dynamics of "male sexual dominance over women and employers' control over workers."[31] Of course, sexual harassment has been recognized as a cognizable claim under Title VII since the late 1970s (thank you, Catharine MacKinnon), and yet blatant sexual harassment persists.

The most egregious case in our sample is Kristen Baker (P34), the thirty-three-year-old white senior buyer whose story is detailed in the introduction to this book. As she told us, she was subjected to an environment in which "rough language" turned into sex jokes, which morphed into a culture in which it was permitted for some men to use the conference room to watch pornographic movies at lunchtime. Ms. Baker was personally objectified when Daniel, her manager and the vice president of purchasing, showed their colleagues a photo of a woman in stiletto heels with a watermelon rammed into her vagina and said "'Oh look, Kristen, we would recognize you anywhere with those heels on.'"

Not only was Ms. Baker being subjected to sexualized talk in the workplace; she also was the *object* of the sexualized talk. Her boss regularly projected her into the pornography he shared in the workplace. She also was told that she would get a promotion if she gave her boss oral sex. And finally, as she explained it, there was a horrific lunch she attended with this supervisor at which he stuck a chocolate dildo in her face and said, "'Suck on this.'" Ultimately, here, her supervisor tried to enlist her in a quasi-sexual act.

Unlike Ms. Richardson's lawyer, Ms. Baker's lawyer was sympathetic and believed her claims of sexual harassment. He did not further exacerbate the problem by reinscribing sexual objectification into the lawyer-client relationship. Rather, it was the attorney on the other side who did that. A white man in his forties, Donald Bryant (DL71) was reluctant to think women are *ever* sexually harassed. He told us that women are unrealistic about what they can expect in terms of damages should they bring a sexual harassment lawsuit:

> You don't get the $7.4 million dollar jury verdict for someone dropping a couple of M&M's down your blouse, and you've been there forty-five days. . . . I'm not suggesting by any means that what happened to her was appropriate or right or that she didn't deserve something. That's not my point. My point is that . . . I mean, you see cases where people are intentionally mowed down in a car. Quadriplegics—they don't get that kind of money.

Although empirically correct (that is to say, women do not get very much for sexual harassment claims), the cavalier manner in which Mr. Bryant discussed sexual harassment is striking. Isolating one incident that received popular media attention in a case we were not even discussing belittles sexual harassment.[32] And while this attorney admitted that what happened to Ms. Baker was not "appropriate or right," in the next breath he told us:

> I've been doing this [defense side employment discrimination litigation] for twenty years and, in sex harassment cases, out of all of the cases I've seen throughout the years, I have yet to see a legitimate sex harassment case. . . . What I see are cases that are either [laughing] the office romance gone awry, where everything was going great, and it was all, you know, consensual for three years until they didn't get the promotion they wanted. Then all of a sudden it's been coerced the whole time and you go through and you get their

> diary and you get their notes and it's just ridiculous. Or you get the hypersensitive claimant, which is very common, where somebody's really trying to make a harassment claim out of nothing.

This comment vividly illustrates how gendered stereotypes of women as sex objects *and* irrational can be mutually reinforcing. Women are either hypersexualized (as in the "office romance") or "overly sensitive."

The same is true in the case of Lois Smith (P19), first introduced in chapter 4, a trailblazer as a young female locomotive engineer in an overwhelmingly male occupation. At work, Ms. Smith was alternatively portrayed as weak and feminine and as irrational for not sleeping with her boss when he propositioned her. She explained that her male coworkers had treated her poorly, and she tolerated it until the situation escalated:

> Then the boss that everybody loved . . . propositioned me. . . . [This] led to my EEO complaint because, you know, he propositioned me, and then he didn't talk to me for six months. . . . [He said], "You know you want it. . . . You know we're going to do it eventually. I do it with everybody . . . who works for me."

Ms. Smith is simultaneously treated as an available sex object and also as a delusional woman who simply does not know what is expected of her. Just as her boss treats Ms. Smith as though she is irrational for spurning his advances, he also normalizes the sexualized work environment.

WOMEN AS INFERIOR WORKERS. A number of female plaintiffs cited being treated as inferior workers. This stereotype is pervasive in the evaluative biases at work that code men and male dominance in the seemingly neutral vocabulary of merit, competence, and effectiveness.[33] Among these plaintiffs was Ms. Slayton. In her company's "good old boy system," she said, "they kept the women in the check stands" while men did work that led to promotions and full-time positions. According to Ms. Slayton, the women who did get promoted were somehow related to somebody in management. Those few women in management were in "that bottom position" and would not get promoted further: "They ended up getting jobs someplace else because they said, 'We'll never go anywhere here.'" Ms. Slayton's was one of the relatively few cases in which a judge found the defendant organization at fault and awarded her and other plaintiffs a sizable settlement. Here, women were channeled into lower-tier jobs that were overwhelmingly occupied by women, and this segregation and discrimination created the organizational foundation for the stereotype of women as less valuable and less capable.

The experience of another plaintiff, Marla Riteman (P39), another African American plaintiff labeled a bitch, further shows how different forms of discrimination can combine. Not only was she seen as a bitch, her story shows how African American female employees are treated as inferior to their white female counterparts. After twenty years of employment, Ms. Riteman charged the manufacturing company for which she worked with racial discrimination and sexual harassment. She said the problems were there from the very beginning. She had a "packing level four" position, which she described as "women's work. . . . That's taking the boxes off the line and putting them in the bigger boxes." Then she moved up to a packing level five position—"men's work"—which involved pushing heavy boxes around the factory floor. As she recounted, management would hire white women to level five positions, but not expect them to do some of the heavy work:

> So they would say "Marla, you gotta go do that, because this girl here, she can't do it." . . . And I would say, "Well, if she can't push these bins, then you better find somebody else to do this job, because I am not going to do this part of her job just because she is white."

Ms. Riteman said, "I was viewed as sort of a work horse, and the white women were viewed more delicately." Here, an African American woman is counterintuitively treated as physically stronger yet less of a woman than a white woman, an inferior but more capable worker.[34] She and other African American women also were targeted by a white male foreman who "used to tell nasty jokes in front of us, you know sexual jokes and stuff like that." This is illustrative of the ways in which African American women are stereotyped as hypersexual and deviant, in contrast to the common stereotype of white women as innocent and pure.[35]

Although Ms. Riteman received a settlement, the litigation did not succeed in punishing the man who harassed her most—whose behavior involved calling her "bitch" from across the room. He was apparently suspended with pay but never lost his job. Meanwhile, a settlement agreement in her separate worker's compensation case, which involved a disability, required that she not work again despite wishing to. In the end, the law implicitly sanctioned the discriminatory treatment and stereotyping of her as both a workhorse and overly sexualized.

Stereotypes of People with Disabilities and the Reinscription of Disability Discrimination

Seventeen of our plaintiff interviewees filed disability discrimination claims, and for twelve of those, disability discrimination was a salient concern. They claimed that the employer discriminated against them based on the legal definition of a disability: a physical or mental impairment that substantially limits a major life activity. They are part of our national sample, in which 20% of cases included a disability claim.

The unfair treatment of people with disabilities—a phenomenon that disability scholars and activists call ableism or disableism—follows from the belief that able-bodied people are the norm and people with disabilities are deficient and inferior.[36] Research shows that people are evaluated differently and face varying degrees of discrimination in access depending on their disability type.[37] Likewise, there are different stereotypes associated with different disabilities, such as blindness or mental retardation.[38] Such assumptions are codified in behaviors, organizational policy, cultural norms, law, and the built environment itself.

Our analysis identified three stereotypes of people with disabilities: *faking it* or *not really disabled*, *unable to work*, and *abnormal*. The faking-it stereotype was the most commonly cited (nine plaintiffs). Plaintiffs reported that employers often used this "it's all in your head" trope while also using the disability as a mechanism for marginalizing these workers. Five plaintiffs were caught between two seemingly contradictory types of mistreatment: they were stereotyped as faking it and either were treated by their employer as unable to meet their employer's performance expectations or as abnormal. The prevalence of the stereotypes of unable (six plaintiffs) and abnormal (four) keys into the implicit otherness that stigmatizes employees with disabilities.

The dynamics of reinscription and stereotyping around disability discrimination cases diverge somewhat from other employment discrimination cases, given the unique challenges that workers with disabilities confront, the wide variation in the types of disabilities that workers have, and the expectations of medical documentation of disability. There are two distinctive ways that disableism is legally reinscribed. First, in both the workplaces and in the law, there is a widespread presumption that a disability is a medical condition or impairment caused by biological factors and requiring medical treatment.[39] This medical model assumes the disability itself is the problem, because it prevents individuals from meeting the norm and being full members of society.[40] Our interviewees confronted this medical model in the form of harassment and mistreatment and as they sought to fulfill the requirements of medical documentation. Of the twelve plaintiff interviewees with disability cases that we analyzed in depth, a number found difficulty with medical evidence (five), documentation (three), and doctors and insurance (four). This *medical mediation* of a disability case, and the troubles involved, reinforced the notion that they did not legitimately fit under the legally sanctioned medical model of disability. Medical mediation also tends to individualize the problem to the singular plaintiff and his or her unique condition.

Second, and related, in disability discrimination cases, the law is mediated specifically through the doctor's office. These legal cases frequently hinge on requirements for medical documentation to confirm that an employee's condition fits the legal definition of a disability. Disability discrimination is reinstitutionalized and—for plaintiffs—lived through their quests for medical documentation, disputes over medical paperwork, and disagreements between the plaintiffs' doctors and the employers' doctors. Many plaintiffs interviewed for this study, regardless of their (dis)ability, reported problems with their employer's paperwork: their positive performance evaluations went missing, or negative reviews were put into their personnel files without their knowledge. These issues with paperwork became consequential in court, because paperwork is (or, where it is missing, is not) part of the legal record and because parties make claims about it. For people with disabilities, paperwork issues reinscribe disability discrimination in particularly impactful ways, because written medical documentation is so important to their experiences at work and in court. The challenges of figuring out and paying for their medical care and medical documentation, along with simply managing their disabilities, further complicate their cases. Yet doctors can serve the converse role by challenging disableism. For many of our interviewees, doctors' diagnoses and affirmation of their health conditions provided substantive resources to pursue their cases as well as a satisfying sense of validation.

There is an alternative to the medical model: the environment—not the individual—may be treated as the problem for employees with disabilities.[41] From this social constructionist perspective, the disability is created by social, cultural, and environmental barriers, not by an individual's impairment. This model is institutionalized in legal prescriptions for employers. The ADA, for instance, requires that employers provide "reasonable accommodation" to qualified employees with disabilities to enable them to perform equally at their job. Plaintiff interviewees encountered this model when their doctors recommended workplace accommodation and when legal authorities insisted that the employer provide such accommodation. The stereotypes we discuss here all assume that the plaintiff's medicalized disability—rather than the employer's failure to environmentally accommodate it—is the essential problem.

MEDICAL MEDIATION AND THE STEREOTYPE OF FAKING IT. The stereotype of faking it implies that the person with the disability is disingenuously representing a problem where none really exists.[42] The presumption is that the problem is "all in their head" or that they are purposely feigning it. This stereotype presumes that, with a fictional disability, an employee could receive preferential treatment—in one plaintiff's words, "special privileges"—or be able to avoid work or responsibility, thus there is an incentive for workers to falsely claim disability. This stereotype of faking it is reinforced by the popular assumption that a legitimate disability is one that is visible, diagnosed, and easily understood by people who are not medical experts. The prototypical example is someone in a wheelchair because of, say, cerebral palsy. Both in the workplace and in the legal system, employees have difficulty establishing the legitimacy of their disability when it diverges from these assumptions.

Sam Grayson (P4), whose story led off chapter 8, is a case in point. Officer Grayson ultimately quit his job on the police force because of circumstances involving his disability. A white man in his early forties at the time of our interview, Officer Grayson had a doctor who ordered he be placed on light duty after he came to the hospital feeling dizzy and with a very low heart rate. Officer Grayson brought the doctor's note to his supervisor and, the following day, was put on a leave of absence. He used up his vacation and sick leave as he saw doctors, trying to determine what was going on. The city kept him as an employee, but stopped paying him and stopped providing health benefits. Humiliated, financially strapped, and not knowing that he would have had a stronger legal case had he stayed an employee, Officer Grayson resigned. He drew down his pension and later found another job.

Officer Grayson's employer had no formal policy for accommodating police officers for light duty. According to Officer Grayson, only some employees got light duty—namely, those with the right connections within the city or the union. He immediately encountered problems of medical mediation, as he lacked a definitive diagnosis of his medical condition: "We had an idea what [the medical problem] was," he told us, "but it hadn't really been pegged at this time." And though his doctor had written a note suggesting light duty, he refused to provide Officer Grayson with written confirmation of a disability, as his condition had not yet been confirmed. Officer Grayson's supervisor used this lack of medical diagnosis against him, telling him, "'I'm not bringing you back because we don't know what's wrong with you.'" Without medical documentation, Officer Grayson was treated as not really disabled. We see here the popular stereotype that people with disabilities are making up their problems or blowing things out of proportion.

Officer Grayson's case went to court, received a mixed summary judgment, and ended in a late settlement. In court, Officer Grayson recalled, the city tried to use his paperwork to disparage his legal case. He described the "lying" he heard at deposition: "'We never saw that slip from that doctor'" and "'Well, he never asked for accommodation.'" He explained that none of this was true: "There was a handwritten thing that I brought specifically to my supervisor, which is how they placed me on leave in the first place. If I hadn't of brought that [paperwork] there, it wouldn't have happened." In such ways, his claims rested on medical documentation—the use and misuse of which reinforced the pernicious stereotype of the misguided, manipulative employee who falsely claims a disability.

PEOPLE WITH DISABILITIES AS ABNORMAL. A pervasive social stereotype of people with disabilities is that they are abnormal—peculiar, freakish, even repulsive.[43] This stereotype stems from the hegemonic notion of normalcy, which emerged in the historical period of industrialization when high-speed factory production made it more difficult for people with disabilities to be incorporated productively into work activity.[44] The abnormal stereotype rationalizes the marginalization of employees with disabilities; it justifies coworkers' and supervisors' practices of isolating people with disabilities, excluding them from mundane routines, and even staring at them.[45]

Rick Nolls (P3) was stereotyped as abnormal at work and, initially, in court. A sixty-four-year-old white warehouse manager who suffered a chemical imbalance, Mr. Nolls filed a disability and age discrimination suit against the large food corporation for which he worked. While on the job, Mr. Nolls was stigmatized. It began when he went out on leave to get his blood levels under control. While he was absent, someone at work started a rumor that he was on medical leave for psychological evaluation. As he recalled, coworkers said he was "'in the nuthouse'" and branded him as "'crazy.'" After he requested accommodation, his employer would only refer him to the employee assistance program, typically reserved for people with drug and alcohol problems. One day, he had a chemical imbalance reaction at work and would not shake a new employee's hand. This event further reinforced the idea that he was abnormal; soon thereafter, he received a disciplinary letter warning against inappropriate behavior. Mr. Nolls recalled that, when he was fired, he was "escorted out of the plant like a nut, you know, considered criminal."

Employers discriminate against people with disabilities by deploying this stereotype of abnormality. Our other interviewees described managers who spread rumors, intentionally misinterpreted disability-related behaviors, and preyed on other employees' misunderstandings of disabilities. In Mr. Nolls's case, the employer manipulated people's misunderstanding of his chemical imbalance to frame him as a problem employee and as mentally ill, unstable and unpredictable, or drug addicted. His case was one of four (of seventeen) in which the employer turned the disability into a psychological stigma—thus fueling other people's feelings of discomfort, disgust, or fear regarding individuals with disabilities.[46]

For Mr. Nolls, disableism was reinscribed in other ways at work. The rumors that Mr. Nolls was mentally unstable and acting inappropriately further undermined his authority as a supervisor. When he was fired, his employer claimed that he was no longer a credible supervisor capable of managing his employees. Mr. Nolls wanted to file a suit against his employer for defamation of character. He got signatures from twelve employees who affirmed that their employer had told them that Mr. Nolls was on leave for psychiatric reasons, when, in fact, he was on leave to better manage his chemical imbalance. His lawyer, however, said that such a defamation case would be too difficult to pursue.

His workplace experience and the process of litigation, together with complications related to his chemical imbalance, put Mr. Nolls under considerable stress. He had become depressed, which is common with his health condition, and was taking psychiatric medication. The discrimination was reinscribed through the physical effects on his body, as the complications of his chemical imbalance were exacerbated by the situation at work and by the stress of the lawsuit.

Again, when a judge initially threw out his case on summary judgment, Mr. Nolls encountered the stereotype that disabilities are not real or meaningful. The judge reasoned that his chemical imbalance was not a disability. Ultimately, however, Mr. Nolls's story was one in which law helped *undermine* stereotypes and hierarchies of disableism. On appeal, another judge overruled the earlier decision, and Mr. Nolls won a late settlement for his disability claim. Further, his case was historically and legally significant, as it legally established his form of chemical imbalance as a disability. Mr. Nolls got tremendous satisfaction from the fact that his case had far-reaching implications and would help others.

PEOPLE WITH DISABILITIES AS UNABLE (TO WORK). There is a stereotypical notion that people with disabilities are incapable of working or doing other activities independently. Employers make this stereotype consequential when they label a person with disabilities as incompetent and incapable of performing on par with coworkers in similar positions.[47] Evan Oliver (P40), a white man who was hired as a chemist by a government agency soon after finishing college, was labeled unable after almost a year on the job. The person who managed Mr. Oliver, Ben Carter, had hired him through a program specifically for people with disabilities, so he knew that Mr. Oliver had a psychological condition that qualified him as disabled. Mr. Carter was sympathetic—in Mr. Oliver's words, "he kind of took me under his wing"—but left the organization soon thereafter. The new supervisor, Verna Jackman, was not sympathetic and was much less accommodating. Mr. Oliver perceived that Ms. Jackman disliked him for many reasons: because he was a chemist and she wanted a team of only geologists, because he was white and she was African American, because he had a disability, and perhaps because he was older. "She was bound and determined to get me out of there," he said. Her superiors, he believed, agreed: "Not only did Jackman do what she did out of meanness, apparently everybody above her backed her up. . . . They were just plain hell bent on getting me out of there."

There was no debate in Mr. Oliver's case over whether he had a disability. The dispute was over whether or not he could work. Mr. Oliver had difficulty with social interaction, particularly with people he did not know. When Ms. Jackman became his supervisor, he said, "she just put me aside and had me sit there and not do anything. . . . She didn't want to deal with me." Then she assigned him to do file reviews—what he described as "a dirty job that nobody else wanted to do." He was able to do the job, but he had difficulty with the requirement of making phone calls. He was fired seven days before the end of his one-year trial period. Mr. Oliver described for us his discouraging experiences of trying, and failing, to get accommodation:

> No one would step in and say, "This guy's a scientist, you know. We could use scientists. If it doesn't work out in the permit unit or Jackman doesn't like it, we could either change his job around so he doesn't have that much public contact or move him somewhere else."

In Mr. Oliver's disability discrimination case, the first judge decided on summary judgment in favor of the government agency. Mr. Oliver appealed, though, and the decision was reversed and remanded. He was awarded about $200,000 in adjusted back pay and three years of front wages. Yet Mr. Oliver was deeply disappointed in the outcome of his case. He, like so many other plaintiffs, wanted his job back. He was insistent that he was able to work and to make valuable contributions. He felt that the government agency, by discriminating against him and then fighting him in court, made him *less* able to work: "They made me unemployable. Not only did they smear me, they dragged me through the mud. They made a bad record of me and every other damn thing."

After paying the lawyer, taxes, and social security, Mr. Oliver had about $88,000 left to live on. He applied for many jobs unsuccessfully; he told us he had files full of letters of rejections from other employers. He became extremely depressed, to the point of being nearly dysfunctional. Once he was on Social Security and Medicare, he was afraid to apply for another job: he feared being fired again and then not being able to access those entitlements. He felt he should have been given his job back or else he should have received front wages up to retirement as well as punitive damages. When asked why he felt he should have received punitive damages, he said, "Because they ruined me spiritually." His court case, in effect, rendered him further disabled.

Issues of disability and age discrimination were often intertwined at work in salient ways for the plaintiff. Like people with disabilities, older workers are presumed to be unable to work. For example, Mr. Nolls—whose initial filing included an age discrimination claim—initially hid his chemical imbalance at work because he did not want to be seen as "weak." He explained that the company he worked for had a philosophy of "'Get rid of these old guys. If he's disabled he can't work, get rid of him. We're not running a nursing home here.'" After revealing his chemical imbalance to his managers, they tried aggressively to get rid of him: "I was fifty-seven, but because of the chemical imbalance and being sick and weakened—'Here's an old guy who's already sick and shouldn't be here.'" At one point, the employer told him they wanted to transfer him to a job that is "safer for you" in a unit that was about to be shut down.

Age Stereotypes and the Reinscription of Age Discrimination

The workplace is fraught with conflict among age groups, whether it concerns battles for leadership and succession at the top of an organization or tensions between newer (typically younger) and more senior (typically older) workers arrayed in different positions throughout a workforce. And conflicts often are made salient by technological and organizational change, which can upend the traditional age hierarchy of the organization by putting members of an aging workforce under the supervision of younger managers.

In our national study, 22% of plaintiffs charged age discrimination. Among the twelve plaintiff-interviewees who charged age discrimination, nine discussed it in depth in the interviews. Three stereotypes were evident in their cases: *less competent and less productive* (eight plaintiffs), *resistant to change* (four), and *out of touch* with the current state of the organization and with coworkers (three).

In our study, the pattern of stereotyping of older workers diverged from other stereotyping discussed thus far because it seemed less noticeable overall. We believe there are two plausible explanations for this finding. First, the phenomenon of age stereotyping at work is complicated and mixed: being older is sometimes seen as better than being younger. Perceptions of older workers' productivity and adaptability are decidedly negative, yet stereotypes about age and interpersonal skills are uniquely positive. This set of views holds that older workers are more sociable, friendly, and honest than their younger counterparts.[48] In terms of responsibilities at work, older employees are also viewed as more stable and less likely to be absent than younger workers.[49] On measures of loyalty, trustworthiness, and dedication to their work and to their organization, older workers are also held in a more favorable light than young employees.[50] Hence, an older worker might be simultaneously typed in positive and negative ways. Fiske and colleagues, for example, identify the "doddering but dear" stereotype, in which older people are viewed as good-natured but incompetent.[51] Of course, even seemingly positive stereotypes propagate an undesirably homogenous view of these workers, but these positive stereotypes may mitigate the sting of age-based stereotypes. A second explanation for the lack of salience of age stereotyping among the plaintiff interviewees concerns the confluence of age discrimination and business decisions—a dynamic that we elaborate below as deference to management decisions in organizational restructuring.

Although stereotypes were less salient in the age discrimination cases, they were nonetheless present. In our cases for in-depth study, we found multiple stereotypes in play for the same plaintiff—specifically, the stereotype of being incompetent in tandem with the stereotype of being out of touch or resistant to change.

OLDER WORKERS AS LESS COMPETENT AND RESISTANT TO CHANGE. A common stereotype of older workers is that they are incompetent. This is based on perceptions of older workers' relatively poorer health, lower energy, and weaker mental and physical abilities.[52] It draws from prevalent and general negative views toward aging itself.[53] Wrenn and Maurer, for example, find that peoples' theories of age-related declines in mental ability are positively associated with perceptions of older workers' ineffectiveness.[54] Likewise, employers sometimes view older workers as less productive, slower in performing tasks, lower in motivation, and less capable of meeting production deadlines than younger workers.[55] The stereotype of incompetence manifests itself in prominent mechanisms of job discrimination, including layoffs, barriers to mobility, and forced retirement.[56]

The incompetent stereotype runs throughout the case of Denise Anderson (P23), the white woman in her early sixties at the time of her claim whose story was featured near the beginning of chapter 8. As an operations supervisor for a transportation firm, Ms. Anderson felt she began to be mistreated by her new supervisor, a man "barely in his thirties." She recalled that from the very start of their relationship, "We just didn't see eye to eye. . . . It was like he didn't know what I was doing, and I did know what I was doing." At the same time, Ms. Anderson saw a dispatch operator whom she believed wanted her job becoming friends with the new supervisor. They were close in age and would spend time together socially. This was not an unusual experience. Of the plaintiff interviewees who filed complaints of age discrimination, nine described the problems of being replaced by a younger worker.

The gravamen of Ms. Anderson's complaint was that she was the only employee in her group who was not retrained when her company adopted new procedures for coordinating the flow of traffic. Other employees were sent out of state for the training, but she was not. She told us, "I asked [the supervisor] a few times, you know, 'When are you going to send me so I know what I'm doing back here?'" In addition, a coworker was provided a computer for their work, but she was not. She told us:

> I asked him to get me [a computer] so that I could speed up what I was doing. I was having to do it manually and didn't really know what I was doing. And a few of the drivers got a little irate because I was slow at it, and that hurt my feelings since I had been so efficient in my other job. . . . So I did the best I could, but eventually it got to me, and I almost had a nervous breakdown.

There are a few ways to interpret Ms. Anderson's experience. Here, we see that the stereotype of incompetent older workers can be self-reinforcing. Older workers are frequently regarded as more difficult to train and having lower potential for professional development.[57] This is based on an assumption of older workers' lack of ability and motivation. It may also be connected to a cost-benefit calculation on the part of employees; because older employees are necessarily closer to retirement, managers may be reluctant to invest in training them. (This, however, runs counter to the fact that younger workers are more likely to change jobs.)

Another interpretation is that Ms. Anderson was being typed as resistant to change, another widely held social stereotype.[58] Under this version of the "you can't teach an old dog new tricks" cliché, employers and coworkers assume older employees are resistant to updating their skills or lack the motivation and ability to work with computers or participate in training and career development.[59]

Ms. Anderson seems to have been driven from her job by a young manager who saw her as an unproductive older worker not worthy of training or a computer, despite her requests for both and despite these resources having been provided to her younger coworkers. Her employer defended against her charges of age discrimination, then settled for less than the median settlement amount in employment civil rights cases. Ms. Anderson did not even break even financially. Her immediate supervisor was not disciplined during the litigation, but lost his job six months later. It is plausible to see the employer defendant closing ranks during the litigation, only to terminate the responsible manager for showing a lack of judgment and exposing the company to needless risk.

OLDER WORKERS AS INCOMPETENT AND OUT OF TOUCH. Another stereotype of older workers is that, in addition to being incompetent, they are out of touch with the workplace and their coworkers. They may be accused of not participating in social activities at work, and they can feel unease with the ways in which socializing among younger employees overlaps with and influences workplace culture.

The case of Joanne Frankel (P28) exemplifies these stereotypes of being inept and disconnected. Ms. Frankel, a white woman, was in her mid-fifties when she completed an undergraduate degree and became a middle manager at a high-end guest services organization. As a new employee but an older person, Ms. Frankel perceived double standards: that the older workers in the organization were unfairly expected to work harder and take more responsibility than younger workers. Before she reached the end of a six-month probationary period, she was terminated by her boss, a man who was roughly the same age as her. She was replaced by a woman in her thirties.

After consulting with an attorney friend, Ms. Frankel sued, representing herself. She lost on a motion for summary judgment and lost on appeal. A critical weakness in her case was the fact that she was hired by the same manager who fired her and that they were the same age. Moreover, she was terminated within the first six months of her employment, while still on a probationary status.

The employer's lawyer, a white man named Jordan Zarins (DL28), explicitly characterized Ms. Frankel as incompetent. In our interview, he denied the possibility that her termination entailed ageism:

> Her supervisor who made the decision was older than she was, another relevant factor. And it was kind of a mid-level management position where you get, you know, where your productivity is important. It's not just that you

> did something wrong or not. It's how well you were able to perform the job. Are you able to sort of meet the objectives of the position? And part of the criticism of her performance was that she wasn't getting that done, you know. So that, those were all factors that led us to think that this was you know a reasonable decision.

Mr. Zarins went on to portray Ms. Frankel as acting arrogant and out of sync with a workplace culture in which older workers did not completely monopolize authority:

> It's amazing, these characteristics just carry through, and this is a person who, in her correspondence assessment, was kind of haughty—you know, used a lot of sarcasm and that was part of the problem in the case. She treated younger people like they were, you know, below her, younger managers. That was one of the supervisor's complaints is that she walked around criticizing these people as though they're just immature kids.

Perhaps it is easy to dismiss Ms. Frankel's effort to frame her firing as age discrimination as the behavior of someone out of touch with reality. She asked for $1 million in damages—a ludicrous amount. She had no money for a lawyer and represented herself. Hence she was unequipped to argue against a motion for summary judgment or for appellate review of the summary judgment decision. Ms. Frankel's lawsuit ultimately reaffirmed the authority of management to dismiss whomever they perceive as troublesome employees, even if the trouble they cause has to do with age. The message for potential plaintiffs is that assertions of age discrimination may be treated as a product of one's age and one's inability to fit in with a younger workforce.

AGE DISCRIMINATION AND DEFERENCE TO MANAGEMENT DECISIONS IN BUSINESS RESTRUCTURING AND LAYOFFS. As employers seek to downsize, economize, or modernize, older workers may be the most likely to feel the negative effects, either because of the disproportionate effect of new policies on older workers (who may be more expensive and/or segregated within certain positions or units) or as a result of overt animosity toward older employees. But when employers decide to close a plant or eliminate a division, we expect that they do so in the name of efficiency and the bottom line. Justifying stereotypes simply are less necessary, although age discrimination may be reinscribed nonetheless.

Litigation challenging layoffs often claims that the layoffs are aimed invidiously at older employees or disproportionately hurt those employees. Take, for example, the case brought by Sal DeLuca (P39) and his coworkers, who were terminated as a result of the closing of a state government unit—what the agency characterized as a budget-driven reduction in force. Mr. DeLuca, a white policy analyst who then was in his early forties, along with a coworker in his early sixties, charged that their termination and the agency's failure to rehire them were due to age discrimination. They also alleged that the failure to rehire them was in retaliation for filing an EEOC claim. As documented in the court records, their claims revolved in large part around the uncontested fact that an employee under the age of forty had been allowed to transfer to an opening before the layoffs took place, even though the reduction in force had supposedly eliminated all vacant positions. The retaliation claim rested on the fact that the agency hired younger workers into openings for lower-level positions some eleven months after the plaintiffs were terminated.

Mr. DeLuca and his coplaintiff lost on summary judgment on their claims concerning failure to rehire and retaliation, but they prevailed on the question of wrongful termination. The case went to a jury trial, where they lost. They lost again in the court of appeals. Asked about the jury trial, Mr. DeLuca said that in three and a half days, there was a lot of testimony, but "it could not really talk about the group of persons, the whole seven or eight or ten people that were laid off and it got really narrowly focused." Mr. DeLuca acknowledged that if they could litigate the case today, they might have tried to show the terminations were improper because they were based on political patronage, not merit. But, at the time, "the best we had going at that point was age." The opinion of the jury, as he recalled, was similar: "'What occurred was not correct. What occurred was not fair.' But [the jury didn't] believe it was age."

Age cases may be particularly vulnerable to the alternative view that the adverse actions are driven by organizational politics or budget pressures, not ageism. The defense attorney in Mr. DeLuca's case, Pam Girard (DL39), a white woman in her sixties who was a government attorney at the time, characterized the case as not really about age:

> Even though it was presented as an age discrimination case, it really was a layoff case. Then you want to know from the plaintiffs if they have any evidence that anybody ever said anything to them regarding their age. And one

of the guys who ended up going to trial was in his mid to late forties, like forty-five, forty-eight, or something. The other guy was older.

Here, by rejecting the age discrimination frame, the defense attorney, trial court, jury, and appellate court all refrained from challenging a managerial decision that seemed to have adversely affected older workers. Management decisions to lay off employees, close plants, or otherwise restructure the organization often will have a disproportionate effect on older workers, yet they are more readily explained based on a business logic than are decisions about individual workers.

In the three age discrimination cases discussed in this section, the law left managerial prerogatives for dealing with workers despite their arguably protected status based on age undisturbed. The settlement in Ms. Anderson's case shielded management from liability due to the apparently ageist behavior of a young manager directed at an older worker. In the other two cases, law authoritatively rejected the plaintiffs' efforts to make age discrimination claims as a way of challenging management decisions. For Ms. Frankel, law upheld the employer's decision to fire her for cause while still in a period of probationary employment. For Mr. DeLuca, law upheld a state agency's decision to lay off a set of older workers while showing favoritism to a younger worker. In those two cases, law ruled that the management decisions with adverse effects on older workers were not really about age. By taking jurisdiction over these claims, and rejecting them, and leaving ageist stereotypes intact, law can legitimate age hierarchies in the workplace.

Does Race, Sex, Disability, or Age Matter (More) in Court?

Does the basis of discrimination a plaintiff experiences—whether race, sex, disability and age—matter in their encounter with law? We considered this question by examining the similarities in case processing across the four major bases of discrimination in our national dataset. The Appendix (tables A.4, A.5, A.6) presents three sets of cross-classifications of those bases of discrimination by three measures we found were critical in the quantitative analyses reported in chapters 2 and 3: collective representation, case outcome, and type of legal representation. We made these comparisons in two ways: a "pure" classification of the basis of discrimination which included only cases that asserted one type of discrimination (72.3% of cases) and an "inclusive" classification that included all cases that asserted a basis of discrimination. (The latter approach is referred to as a dummy variable analysis because it creates a binary distinction between cases that have the trait of interest versus all other cases.) All cases analyzed here are closed cases.

What is most striking across the tables is the relative similarity on these quantitative measures, whether the claim is based on race, sex, disability, or age—with just a few exceptions. The four bases of discrimination cases have very similar patterns of collective representation. Plaintiffs alleging sex discrimination are slightly more likely to gain collective representation than other types of claimants (13% vs. 11% overall). But all four allegations predominantly consist of individual claims without collective representation. As reported in chapter 5, we again see a greater likelihood that race plaintiffs lack legal representation compared to other claimants (26% vs. 17% overall). The pattern for case outcomes is very similar across discrimination allegations. All four categories of cases are typically disposed of by settlement, dismissal, and loss on summary judgment. Only a small fraction goes to trial, where plaintiffs fare poorly (losing two times out of three).

Thus while the qualitative data we presented in this chapter clearly demonstrate that distinctive ascriptive hierarchies organized around race, sex, disability, and age operate in the workplace and give rise to distinctive claims and reactions in the legal process, for the most part these differences do not affect the contours of case processing in employment civil rights litigation. It is as though the system of employment discrimination litigation homogenizes the cases and then disposes of them in similar ways.

This similarity in case processing characteristics might not surprise students of litigation tactics, who would explain the result in terms of the probabilities of obtaining a given result at a certain cost for litigation. Nor would it necessarily surprise repeat players in the employment discrimination litigation system. Yet for scholars of inequality, social categorization, and power—who see significant differences in the four kinds of inequalities at issue here—it is remarkable that law seems to play the same role in absorbing claims about these hierarchies, with little difference in how those challenges to hierarchy are carried back into the work organization.[60]

Conclusion

Stereotypes in American society are widely shared, both consciously and unconsciously. And yet, we have a shared social goal that discrimination—often built upon these stereotypes—should not operate in employment decisions. The fact that stereotypes persist and shape workplaces may not be surprising, but that they persist even in the legal process designed to be aware of and remedy discrimination is eye-opening. The racist, sexist, ableist, and ageist stereotypes at the root of these cases reappear in the legal process or are left unchallenged by the legal process. This is a crucial mechanism by which law reinscribes ascriptive hierarchies. By silencing plaintiffs' assertions that these stereotypes and hierarchies exist and are pernicious, the litigation system serves to reinforce them. Even when plaintiffs have succeeded in law, as evidenced by a positive disposition at summary judgment, a substantial settlement, or a favorable trial outcome, the effect on the workplace has been minimal. And in most cases, plaintiffs flat-out lose—with a small settlement, a loss on summary judgment, or a loss at trial. In those losses, plaintiffs are punished for challenging the workplace ascriptive hierarchy.

The process of reinscription goes beyond what law and society scholars commonly assert about the advantages of repeat players in the legal system. The *law* is doing the cultural work of reinscribing inequality in the workplace. This may be similar to what many have observed as the "constitutive" effect of law. Yet in this context, the law effectively legitimates the very hierarchies it was designed to ameliorate.

CHAPTER TEN

The Voices of Employment Civil Rights

Since the 1964 passage of the Civil Rights Act, American law has mandated that employees have a right to be free from workplace discrimination based on their race, sex, religion, and national origin. In succeeding decades, that right was extended to discrimination based on age and disability. The definition of "on the basis of sex" has come to include sexual harassment, and there is debate about whether it now includes transgender. Protections for gay, lesbian, bisexual, and transgender individuals have been created in some locales. Targets of discrimination could use the law to enforce that right, first by complaining to the EEOC and then by filing a lawsuit in federal court. If successful, those plaintiffs could obtain damages, injunctive relief, and attorneys' fees. Over the course of fifty years, employment civil rights litigation has developed into a distinct legal field and a significant presence on the federal docket.

We introduced this book with the voices of two plaintiffs who took advantage of this system of rights to challenge workplace discrimination—Gerry Handley, a computer operator in a large manufacturing company, and Kristen Baker, an assistant buyer in the sales division of a mid-size auto parts manufacturer. Mr. Handley was the target of offensive racial harassment by coworkers; Ms. Baker was the target of extreme sexual harassment by a salesman in her division. Both turned to employment civil rights litigation as a last resort to redress these problems. Despite the apparent strength of their claims, both were subjected to hostile treatment by the legal process. They found themselves put on trial in the course of asserting their rights. We argued at the outset that the trials and triumphs of Mr. Handley and Ms. Baker, while unique in some respects, were in fact typical of both the liberating potential and practical costs of using law to assert rights to a discrimination-free workplace.

Although our project uses social science research to analyze employment civil rights, our findings resonate with studies of other arenas of law and social life. We argue that it is imperative for socio-legal research to give voice to participants in the legal system. In this project, we have literally done so, not just in this text, but also in providing as supplements digital recordings of portions of their interviews. In these recordings, we hear the stories of individuals who felt they experienced discrimination and sought to use law to gain justice. True to our multiperspectival approach, we also hear the perspectives of their lawyers, defendants, and defense lawyers.

In this concluding chapter we return to the fundamental question that motivated this study. How effective is the American rights-based system of employment civil rights litigation in providing justice to the targets of discrimination and in eliminating unlawful discrimination in the workplace? We have pursued that question by putting this rights-based system on trial through theoretically driven analyses of comprehensive quantitative and qualitative data on how the system operates. Although the focus of analysis has been on litigated cases, we have examined the relationship between litigation and the workplace hierarchies from which cases emerge, as well as the likely effect of case outcomes on workplace hierarchies going forward. These analyses reveal deep contradictions in the American system of employment civil rights regulation and enforcement. For while there is shared commitment to nondiscrimination in the workplace, the system of employment civil rights litigation may in fact perpetuate, even exacerbate, workplace discrimination.

In this final chapter we review and weigh the evidence about how employment civil rights litigation operates and its likely impact on workplace discrimination. We then consider the theoretical and policy implications of our results. We examine prospects for change in the adversarial system of employment civil rights, given the evidence of the continuing commitment of change agents to a rights-based, adversarial legal model, and the prospects for increasing levels of collective action within law. We also pose pragmatic policy suggestions for improvements within the current system, taking into consideration the suggestions offered by the plaintiffs and defense lawyers we interviewed. We then discuss the possibilities for a new *politics* of employment civil rights that might more fundamentally redefine the terms of debate over the relationship between law and workplace inequality. We close by returning to the central paradox of antidiscrimination law: it perpetuates inequality even as it purports to remedy it.

Putting Rights on Trial: Major Findings

The major empirical findings of this book align with the major themes we introduced in chapter 1—rights, law, and hierarchy—and provide insight into how the system of employment civil rights operates, and with what effects.

On Rights

RESPECT FOR RIGHTS. Both sides of employment civil rights litigation express a respect for the principle that workers have the right to be free of illegal discrimination. Many of the plaintiffs we interviewed did not seem to have thought about their rights until they began to experience a workplace conflict. Some were shocked into realizing that they were the target of discrimination; for others, the perception that they were being discriminated against evolved over the course of many interactions and employment decisions.[1] Interestingly, plaintiffs' attitudes about litigation are similar to the attitudes of Americans generally about civil litigation. That is, they are skeptical about lawsuits and think people too often turn to the courts.[2] Nonetheless, no plaintiff questioned the validity or value of employment civil rights.

Defendant representatives self-consciously embrace employment rights, often expressing a stated commitment to creating discrimination-free workplaces, recalling career accomplishments in preventing discrimination, and applauding the antidiscriminatory values of their employers and clients. When defendant representatives complain about antidiscrimination law, it relates to the ambiguity of the law or the perceived misuse or misinterpretation of the law by the EEOC, plaintiffs, and plaintiffs' attorneys.

THE LEGALIZED WORKPLACE. Legal participants' understanding of workplace rights is shaped not just by law or popular culture, but also by modern personnel systems. As Edelman, Dobbin, and others have demonstrated, a cadre of human resource and equal opportunity professionals has developed the modern personnel system based on principles of rationality and merit-based rewards. They have established policies and procedures that articulate equal opportunity as the standard for the organization.[3] This organizational personnel system socializes workers about their rights, trains managers in how to manage with respect to those rights, and provides the first line of defense against potential discrimination claims. It has been legitimated by the courts, which interpret diversity structures as an effort by employers to prevent discrimination.[4]

We see abundant evidence for the prevalence of these systems, at least in larger organizations, both at the origin of potential discrimination grievances in the workplace and in the deployment of the personnel/EEO bureaucracy to limit legal risk as a grievance threatens to become a legal complaint. First, personnel professionals and defense lawyers (commonly working behind the scenes) attempt to defuse the conflict by explaining the situation to the aggrieved employee. Defendant representatives may attempt to work out a severance package that includes the waiver of a lawsuit. If they see a dispute brewing, they may prepare the employment file to limit potential liability in the event the employee is terminated. At a growing number of companies, employees are required, at hiring, to sign agreements that they will forsake legal action for arbitration, in which conflict resolution differs from what happens in the courts and can involve destruction of evidence and other questionable actions by the employer.[5] If a dispute does proceed to the filing of a charge or a lawsuit, the employer's personnel bureaucracy may be deployed as part of the defense to the litigation claim—namely, in demonstrating that the employer has EEO structures in place that should limit its liability and actual instances of discrimination.

We also have seen that, within these personnel systems, discrimination takes place. And the alleged discrimination is not just the result of subtle bias, but sometimes egregious forms of racial and sexual harassment. The reaction of personnel professionals and defense lawyers to instances of discrimination is most often to deny that discrimination took place, minimize the legal risk faced by the employer, and, in the process, demonize the rights-claimant.

These structures and processes represent the double-edged sword of employment rights in the modern workplace. The personnel system at least pays lip service to employee rights, but it controls or "managerializes" the exercise of those rights to reduce legal risks to the organization.[6]

THE INDIVIDUALIZATION OF RIGHTS CLAIMS. The system of employment civil rights litigation is dominated by individual rights claims. In simple, numerical terms, we found from our large random sample of case filings that 93% of cases are brought by a sole plaintiff. In only 4% of cases do plaintiffs assert claims based on a theory of disparate impact that may affect a group of employees, in only 3% of cases does the EEOC become directly involved, and only 1% of cases are certified as class actions.

This statistical reality sets up the individualized treatment of rights claims, in which defendants are likely to treat the claim of one individual as not credible or as an aberration within the organization. In individual cases, defendant representatives tend to see the filing as the product of a problem employee or a greedy plaintiffs' lawyer. But it is also true that the predominance of individual claims means that most plaintiffs do not conceive of their discrimination claim as a group problem.

Trends in court decisions will further entrench the tendency for courts and employers to address discrimination as a set of individualized claims rather than as a systemic problem. There is a growing literature on procedural attacks on civil rights, which undercut the prospects for class actions and facilitate the disposal of individual claims at the motion stage of litigation.

Thus we find that disputes over employment civil rights—inherently legal issues—are recast as individual problems or issues of personality (mis)fit. This finding is consistent with theories of the managerialization of law, but goes beyond them. This tendency places the blame on the victim of discrimination rather than on a failed managerial relationship. The recasting of rights disputes as individual personality defects allows workplace actors to maintain general commitment to the ideals of civil rights laws while delegitimizing workers' claims. This process dilutes the law, undermines rights, and contributes to the reproduction of hierarchy.

On Law

MYTHS ABOUT EMPLOYMENT CIVIL RIGHTS LITIGATION. Our research disproves some widely held beliefs. First, contrary to the assertions of some prominent scholars, considerable social science research indicates that employment discrimination remains a significant source of workplace inequalities along the dimensions of race, sex, age, and disability.

Recent literature has given much attention to implicit bias as the more common and more difficult to detect form of discrimination. Yet most of the instances of discrimination reported by the subsample of plaintiffs we interviewed were not subtle.

Second, contrary to the image of a highly litigious American workforce projected in popular critiques of discrimination litigation, both quantitative and qualitative data suggest that the vast majority of potential grievants do not file with the EEOC or in federal court. In an analytic exercise based on a combination of survey data on the prevalence of discrimination, employment data on the number of full-time African American workers, and charging and filing data from the EEOC and the federal courts, respectively, we estimate that only one in one hundred potential African American grievants file a charge with the EEOC and thirteen in ten thousand potential African American grievants file a federal lawsuit. Our interviews with plaintiffs' attorneys reveal that they take only about one in ten cases for which they are approached. These data run counter to the frequent suggestions of defendant representatives that plaintiffs' lawyers do not screen effectively for weak cases.

Third, despite assertions about large numbers of class actions by defense counsel in professional publications, only 1% of filings are certified as a class action. We cannot know how many cases class actions represent (or potentially represent) because so few are certified and the enumeration of plaintiffs is not completed. Finally, although the media tend to report cases in which plaintiffs win large judgments or settlements, the typical case outcome for plaintiffs is far more modest. A large percentage of filings are dismissed early on or after a motion for summary judgment. A majority of cases settle and result in modest recoveries (with an estimated mean of $30,000). Only 6% of cases go to trial, where the plaintiff wins one-third of the time. When plaintiffs do win at trial, the award is typically about $150,000.

THE ADVERSARIAL PROCESS IN EMPLOYMENT CIVIL RIGHTS LITIGATION. When an employee files a charge with the EEOC or a lawsuit in federal court, they become a legal adversary of their employer. This act fundamentally alters the nature of their (already troubled) relationship and calls forth the American adversarial process. While a small percentage of EEOC charges reach successful conciliation, in most cases the die is cast. The employer is no longer interested in the welfare of an employee, but is concerned with minimizing damage to the organization. The case moves from HR to the legal department. As advocates, the lawyers' professional obligation is to engage in the zealous representation of their client—to win through whatever means is available in law. Together with defense lawyers' strong identification with their clients, the employee-plaintiff is subject to critical scrutiny. If there are technical weaknesses in the plaintiffs' case, defense lawyers will argue to throw it out of court (something that happens in more than one-third of cases). Plaintiffs experience the shift to the adversarial process as a personal attack. Many recount being shunned, even lied about, by former coworkers. For opposing lawyers, this is business as usual.

The cost of litigation exerts considerable pressure to settle. Neither plaintiffs nor defendants are satisfied with settlements, due to the lack of an authoritative resolution of a morally weighted claim of discrimination. For plaintiffs, there typically is a bigger gap between what they were hoping to achieve through litigation than for defendants, who, as repeat players in the legal system, may know the general ballpark of settlements but also are frustrated by the idea of "paying off" a frivolous claim. In contrast to plaintiffs, who continue to perceive the dispute as justice-centered, employers recognize that settlements are a cost of the modern legalized workplace.

THE DENIGRATION OF PLAINTIFFS. The adversarial process amplifies a well-documented finding from the psychological literature: management and coworkers devalue workers who complain of discrimination in the workplace, even when they also are presented with evidence that the claim of discrimination is true.[7] Thus, even though defendants respect rights in the abstract, in the context of an organizational hierarchy challenged in litigation, they denigrate plaintiffs. In virtually none of the cases we examined through interviews did defendants acknowledge that a specific plaintiff had a valid claim. We refer to this phenomenon as "the right right, the wrong plaintiff."

REPEAT PLAYER ADVANTAGES FOR DEFENDANTS. A consistent thread through the original empirical chapters of *Rights on Trial* are the advantages accrued to defendant employers as repeat players in employment civil rights litigation. Some aspects of this field of law might lead one to expect that it would defy or at least minimize the effect of this classical finding in the law and society literature: (1) there are state and federal enforcement agencies that monitor data on equal opportunity, promulgate regulatory guidelines, can foster litigation support structures, and can intervene directly in selected cases; (2) plaintiffs have access to federal court; (3) successful plaintiffs can receive attorneys' fees; and (4) class actions are available to promote impact litigation. Yet we find that plaintiffs often do not obtain legal representation, sometimes receive poor legal representation, face a difficult emotional challenge in litigation, bring cases by themselves, and often do not have the resources to continue through extensive discovery and trial preparation. Consistent with Galanter's core proposition, these disadvantages largely revolve around the social organization of litigation and are directly connected to patterns of legal representation.[8] The pressures on the "one-shotter," who experiences but one run-through with employment discrimination law, result in plaintiffs expressing profound ambivalence about their lawyers and the legal system. As their attorneys urge settlement in light of the realities of the case, plaintiffs feel shortchanged.

CASE OUTCOMES AND PERCEPTIONS OF FAIRNESS. Our quantitative data reveal the outcomes of these cases, as well as what determines whether a plaintiff wins or loses. Many plaintiffs win nothing from litigation, and most receive modest monetary settlements. Most important for a successful case is having a lawyer and being joined by at least one other plaintiff. Interestingly, both our own efforts at coding the strength of the case and the EEOC priority coding scheme for the strength of cases *could not predict* the outcome of cases. The difficulty of predicting case outcomes is consistent with what we observe of this type of litigation. Discrimination is a contested event. It is subject to many interpretations. Whose interpretation prevails depends on who is telling the story, in what venue, with what support.

What is not shown in the coded case files is what we learned from plaintiffs about the high personal cost of litigation. Many plaintiffs experienced joblessness, depression, alcoholism, and divorce as a result of the experience of litigation. Many more concluded that they were not treated fairly in the legal process. Defendant representatives also often expressed the view that their employer or client was not treated fairly during litigation, but no defendant representatives spoke of being harmed personally by litigation. Indeed, some relished the fact that this is merely their job—they can leave the cases behind when they are finished.

THE VALUE OF COLLECTIVE ACTION BY PLAINTIFFS. Our data document the value of collective action. The quantitative results show statistically significantly better outcomes for class actions, cases that involve representation by the EEOC or a public interest law firm, and cases with more than one plaintiff. The attorneys who represented plaintiffs in class actions could point to the transformation of whole industries as a result of successful litigation. Yet, these cases are exceedingly rare within the population of employment civil rights claims.

On Hierarchy

SUPPORT FOR MANAGERIAL AUTHORITY. A recurrent theme in interviews by defendant representatives and in the case law is that antidiscrimination law is not intended to disrupt the authority of managers in running the employer organization. Human resources professionals and lawyers (both within and outside the employer organization) spoke of giving priority to the organization's business needs. The courts have made clear that they will not sit as a "super human resource department" over businesses; they hold that their role is to penalize illegal discrimination, not to correct the judgments (even very bad judgments) of managers.[9] Thus, the formal hierarchy of employing organizations is legitimate under the antidiscrimination laws. It is only when that hierarchy is itself infected with illegal discrimination or practices illegal discrimination that it will be subject to legal liability. As we noted in chapter 2, however, those organizational hierarchies are overwhelmingly managed by the traditionally advantaged social group in American society: white men.

THE RACIAL DIVIDE IN EMPLOYMENT CIVIL RIGHTS LITIGATION. The racial disparities in the treatment and experience of African American plaintiffs are striking and disheartening, especially given that this system was created with a primary mandate to dismantle barriers to equal opportunity in the workplace for racial and ethnic minorities. African American plaintiffs are more likely to have their cases dismissed or to lose on a motion for summary judgment, in part because they are less likely than other groups to obtain legal representation. They are also more likely to lose a motion for summary judgment, especially when the presiding judge is white.[10] (Minority judges show no difference in disposition across race of plaintiff.) Our interviews with African American plaintiffs reveal that they viewed the legal system as operating in racialized terms. Franklin Williams perceived that the white judge in his case would not sanction opposing counsel because that counsel was white. Mr. Williams believed that the judge in his case ruled against him out of anger over the O. J. Simpson verdict (which the judge announced from the bench during the trial of Williams's case). Floyd Kelly became upset during settlement negotiations in his case, when he thought his white lawyer was talking down to him and keeping him out of discussions with opposing counsel.

THE REINSCRIPTION OF ASCRIPTIVE HIERARCHY THROUGH LAW. The process of legal reinscription is evident throughout the pages of this book. The litigation system tends to reinforce the same illegitimate ascriptive hierarchies it was designed to eliminate. Reinscription occurs in various parts of the system, such as plaintiffs' reliance on the private market for counsel. As we illustrate in chapter 9, stereotypes are one prominent mechanism of reinscription through cultural meaning-making in the workplace and in court. In the context of litigation, we see both plaintiff and defense lawyers sometimes invoke negative stereotypes about target groups. A white defense attorney characterized an African American female plaintiff as "bitchy," echoing the words of white subordinates to the plaintiff. A male attorney characterized the plaintiff in a gender discrimination and disability case as "hysterical." A white attorney characterized an African American plaintiff as "trying to hold us up," a phrase that conjures up stereotypes about African American criminality. The treatment of plaintiffs in law, in this way, corresponds to how they were stereotyped at work. Based either on comments by opposing counsel or on their own self-report, we found evidence that all but two plaintiffs believed they were treated according to a negative stereotype.

Reinscription also notably takes place when law functions to insulate the workplace from complaints about allegedly racist, sexist, ageist, and ableist behavior. The most common outcome in these cases is a settlement that includes a confidentiality provision about the outcome of the case. Such agreements effectively remove and silence potential critics of workplace discrimination and reduce the likelihood that taking legal action will, in turn, create fundamental change at the level of the organization.

Rights on Trial: The Judgment

These findings on the interaction of rights, law, and hierarchy offer a critical and realistic conception of the system of employment civil rights in the United States. The findings suggest that, while rights play an important role motivating plaintiffs to pursue justice in court and in the responses of defendant employers to their claims, the law limits the realization of rights and may even contribute to greater workplace inequality. These findings reveal a central paradox in American law: Americans cherish rights and sometimes revere individuals who press for the realization of rights. Yet the adversarial process in employment civil rights cases often individualizes and denigrates employees who claim they have been the targets of discrimination.

Our in-depth analysis of employment civil rights litigation uncovers serious problems with the system, offers insights into how those problems have emerged and why they persist, and suggests that the system may reinforce the very hierarchies it was intended to attack. Despite these significant problems, we do not advocate dismantling or weakening this system for a variety of reasons. First, we hope our findings can inform how this system could be made more effective. Second, despite the current system's problems, it is unclear that better alternatives can be achieved in the current political and regulatory environment. Third, the limitations of the current system should not blind us to the contributions the system makes to greater workplace justice. One such contribution is that it gives voice to targets of discrimination who might otherwise have no voice in the workplace.

Prospects for Change in the Adversarial System of Employment Civil Rights

Despite the problems with the rights-based adversarial approach to employment civil rights in the United States, many civil rights groups continue to advocate for the expansion and strengthening of this model as a primary means of advancing social change. Farhang reports that civil rights organizations coalesced around a strategy to strengthen Title VII litigation in the Civil Rights Act of 1991 and rejected less litigious approaches.[11] For more than a decade, gay and lesbian rights groups have campaigned for federal legislation patterned on Title VII that would make discrimination against LGBTQ individuals illegal and provide for enforcement by the EEOC and through private litigation.[12] Changes to, rather than an overhaul of, the litigation model remain central in policy debates about the future of employment civil rights.

It is clear from our data and from the research of other scholars that cases involving larger classes of plaintiffs and which aim at systemic discrimination are far more likely to succeed in court and to impact the employing-organization defendants.[13] They may even have radiating effects on other litigation-fearing businesses that see and hear the reporting about such cases. Yet only a tiny fraction of employment civil rights cases is collective in character. If the number of systemic cases could be increased, it would advance efforts to eliminate employment discrimination. Under the Obama administration, the EEOC has sought to do this in its own litigation activity. The EEOC Strategic Plan called for raising the percentage of systemic cases in its active litigation docket to 19–21% by 2014 and 22–24% by 2016. Its 2014 performance report indicated that the agency had exceeded the current year target with fifty-seven of 228 cases, or 25% of its docket, in systemic cases.[14] Important as this strategy is, we should keep it in perspective. As we saw in chapter 2, in 2013 the EEOC received 93,727 charges. The fifty-seven systemic cases it reported for the following year represents .06 of one percent or six in 10,000 charges.

As Schlanger and Kim point out, the EEOC may litigate on behalf of a group of workers without being subject to the new limits on class actions imposed by the *Wal-Mart* case.[15] Systemic cases under EEOC may become more important as a source of collective litigation. Yet it seems that more EEOC systemic litigation will not have enough capacity to meet the potential demand for systemic cases. Even before *Wal-Mart*, class actions were rare, amounting to 1% of the cases we sampled between 1988 and 2003. If 1% of the 16,000 employment civil rights cases filed in 2014 were class actions, it would amount to only 160 class action lawsuits.

Even within the new limitations contained in *Wal-Mart*, it may be possible to increase class action activity. Perhaps most effective would be to increase the amount of information available about workplace inequality. As Bob Siegel (PL36-2), the public interest lawyer, told us, the one thing that would make his practice more efficient is:

> Access to data without having to go to litigation. The biggest problem right now, I have to sue an employer without having statistical data. At best, I could get some primitive data through the EEOC. But what it means is, to some extent it's luck. To some extent, it means that there's a risk for me and for the employer that on imperfect data, I'm making the wrong choice [in bringing a lawsuit].

Employers with one hundred or more employees and federal contractors with fifty or more employees currently must submit EEO-1 reports indicating the gender and racial make-up of broad occupational categories of their workforce. If these data were made public, it would allow potential plaintiffs and their attorneys an opportunity to assess the likelihood that illegal discrimination is playing a role in the reward structures of employers.

Making de-identified wage and salary data available by protected category in certain companies also may have an impact on litigation prospects. While it may reveal equity and relieve some perceptions about discrimination in the workplace, in many cases it could reveal disparities that employers could voluntarily remedy or allow workers to file suit.

Expanding the infrastructure of public interest lawyering might also contribute to more systemic litigation. For decades, the Legal Services Corporation has been prohibited from engaging in class action litigation. Some public interest law organizations provide representation on employment civil rights cases, but relatively few emphasize employment rights.[16] If these organizations could obtain more support for systemic employment civil rights litigation from government, labor, community organizing, or philanthropic sources it might increase the overall level of collective legal action in this field. Again, we need to understand the relatively limited capacity of public interest law firms in employment civil rights. Less than 1% of our random sample of case filings entailed representation by a public interest law firm.

Given the relatively small presence of the EEOC, class actions, and public interest law firms, we are brought back to the importance of the private market for legal representation in employment civil rights cases. The same issues that arise for civil justice claimants generally are central to the quality of civil justice in employment discrimination cases. Civil justice reform would benefit employment civil rights litigation, yet the problems of the civil justice system are deeply entrenched. Efforts to expand access to civil justice for plaintiffs face powerful opposition from business and insurance companies.[17] Even after the passage of legislation that expands potential remedies, such as the Civil Rights Act of 1991, court decisions and the imbalance of power between plaintiffs and defendants limit the benefits of the new laws for plaintiffs.

If there were the requisite political support, it is not difficult to list practical changes that would benefit plaintiffs in pursuing their employment civil rights:

1) *Provide more access to legal representation.* In 23% of the cases contained in our sample, plaintiffs were unrepresented. Judges have the discretion to appoint counsel to the unrepresented, but seldom do. If the United States had a legal aid system that subsidized the cost of civil legal representation, plaintiffs could receive legal advice from the outset of their cases.
2) *Provide more resources to the EEOC and state fair employment agencies (FEPAs),* to provide for more thorough and effective case investigations. Currently, the vast majority of discrimination charges receives scant processing from these agencies and simply provides a right to sue letter.
3) As a corollary, *the EEOC and FEPAs could develop better forms of communication to and support of charging parties.* In our interviews, we encountered several plaintiffs who did not understand the communications they received from the EEOC or in court. Mitchell Collins (P6), for example, did not understand that the right to sue letter from the EEOC meant he could proceed in court. Instead, he thought it meant the agency found he did *not* have a case.
4) *Increase the amount of information available to employees about the demographic composition and earnings of their employer's workforce.* EEO-1 reports prepared by employers that show the race/ethnicity and gender of occupational groups are considered confidential by the EEOC. Further, employers are not required to prepare reports on earnings by race/ethnicity or gender, and many private employers have rules that prohibit employees from revealing their pay to other workers. If such information were made available, it would provide employees with an opportunity to assess fair treatment. The Paycheck Fairness Act proposed in Congress would provide some of these measures.[18] California has already passed the Fair Pay Act, which took effect in January 2016, and protects the rights of workers to ask about the compensation of coworkers in similar jobs.[19]
5) *Address racial disparities in legal representation and case dispositions.* Our research has uncovered racial disparities in obtaining a lawyer and in the ju-

dicial treatment of cases brought by African Americans, even after controlling for case characteristics. The legal profession and the judiciary could develop programs to raise awareness about this problem, even systematically collecting data on these disparities and publishing the results. Granted, there are complex dynamics that determine whether a plaintiff obtains a lawyer and how a judge deals with motions for summary judgment. Yet it would be instructive to analyze overall patterns and, if disparities are substantiated, consider ways to eliminate these disparities.

Given the adversarial character of the field, in which lawyers typically work exclusively for plaintiffs or defendants, we see a division of opinion about how to improve the field. In our interviews with lawyers, we asked what changes they would make to employment civil rights law. Although interviewees were not guided to answer any particular way, both plaintiffs' and defendants' lawyers overwhelmingly made suggestions that would work to the advantage of their clients. We already have noted some of the recommendations of plaintiffs' lawyers for providing information that would facilitate systemic litigation. For their part, defense lawyers emphasized ways of reducing litigation and eliminating frivolous cases. These included public education to clarify the law (so that people would know they did not have a case); reining in the EEOC; strengthening internal complaint processing and the use of other alternatives to litigation, such as mediation; discouraging *pro se* litigants; encouraging judges to grant motions for summary judgment; and shifting fees and costs onto unsuccessful plaintiffs to deter frivolous claims.

The deeply held and opposing views of plaintiffs' lawyers and defense lawyers indicate that the prospects for finding win-win, commonsensical ways to improve the system of employment civil rights litigation will likely prove elusive. In policy, as in court, we can expect structured antagonism between plaintiffs and defendants to continue.

Possibilities for a New Politics of Employment Civil Rights

As we confront the difficulties of reforming the system of employment civil rights litigation, we can see that the effort to eliminate workplace discrimination raises the fundamental conflict between a rights-based legal order in employment and the managerial and social hierarchies that control workplace relationships. This is an ongoing contest in which rights-claimants sometimes win, sometimes lose, and often settle with no authoritative decision on the merits of their claims. Our assessment is that litigation imposes relatively modest, relatively easily managed costs on employers. Defense lawyers and the media may inflate these risks, which could spur efforts at compliance with the law. But given the relative weakness of the threat of litigation, it will not be effective in eliminating discrimination.

Can we think of more fundamental changes, within law or without, that might transform workplace rights and reduce discrimination? Within law, the revitalization of affirmative action would allow employers to set goals for increasing the diversity of their workforce and foster programs to achieve those goals. As we noted in chapter 2, the courts have become increasingly hostile to affirmative action in employment and in education. While we cannot gloss over the gravity of the constitutional and statutory debate that revolves around affirmative action, if employers were given the flexibility to set numerical goals for qualified workers from historically underrepresented groups, it could have a significant impact on workplace inequality. We see evidence of this progressive impulse in some employers, although we also see the dilution of an inequality focus in existing diversity programs.[20]

The future of employment civil rights is tied up with worker rights more generally. Unions provide workers with employment rights that management must respect. As we have presented our results concerning the difficulties with litigation, we often are asked about unions as an alternative channel for protecting civil rights. But in our own sample of cases, unions did not prove very helpful to our plaintiffs. Some unions have a history of discriminating against minorities and women, although some unions have taken the lead in organizing women and minorities to press for rights through litigation.[21] Further, as unions decline as representatives of workers, with less than 10% of the American workforce currently belonging to unions, they may become less influential as enforcers and guarantors of workplace rights.

Short of unionization, other forms of worker mobilization within workplaces might strengthen a rights-based order at work. Although we have expressed skepticism about the commitment and power of personnel professionals to eliminate discrimination, if a new generation of diversity officers can make the case to management that it is in the best interest of the organization to adopt personnel policies and practices that are less subject to bias, it might promote opportunities for traditionally disadvantaged groups. Sturm and others advocate problem-solving approaches within organizations, rather than only pursuing court-mandated remedies, to redress barriers to equal opportunity.[22] Epp asserts that the combination of the threat of litigation, activist campaigns, and the leadership of professionals inside organizations can "make rights real."[23] And, as McCann illustrates, these processes could be aided by employee campaigns, for instance in the form of women employees demanding fair pay.[24]

Broader social and political changes may support a new framework for civil rights in the workplace. As the workplace becomes increasingly heterogeneous demographically and employers seek to maintain a committed workforce, employers may turn to rights-based personnel systems. In part, this may be propelled by the growing power of new groups within the organization and may reflect an effort to develop personnel systems that can coordinate a diverse workforce.

Another avenue for change seems to be opening through contemporary social movements that focus on economic inequality as a social problem, including efforts to raise the minimum wage. These movements may encourage workers to organize to address inequality within their work organization and, as a form of external threat, persuade employers to develop personnel systems that afford workers new rights.

Finally, some commentators suggest examining the practices of other countries in antidiscrimination law for ways to improve our own. In some respects, the European Union's commitment to nondiscrimination is broader in scope and more progressive than that of the United States. Title III of the Charter of Fundamental Rights of the European Union bans "any" discrimination on the basis of characteristics such as sex, race, color, ethnic or social origin, genetic features, language, religion or belief, political or any other opinion, membership of a national minority, property, birth, disability, age, or sexual orientation. In practice, as in the United States, systems of hierarchy and discrimination in the European Union are local, national, and international in character, rooted in the specific histories of European societies. Although there are interesting models of antidiscrimination law in the European context, by American standards these systems are less than robust.[25] To take one example, studies of efforts to combat sexual harassment in France[26] and Germany reveal that cultural norms about sex, sexuality, gender, politics, social movements, and labor relations produce very different definitions of discrimination than in the American case.[27]

While the United States has pursued nondiscrimination based on an individual rights approach, other societies approach employment law with a more collectivist orientation. In some countries this results in more worker-friendly outcomes.[28] Antidiscrimination law in the United States reflects its unique history, from slavery, through Jim Crow, through the civil rights movement, through the passage of the Civil Rights Act, and up to the current era of colorblindness. The differences across national histories and national contexts make it unlikely that we can borrow more effective models of antidiscrimination law from other countries.

As we reflect on prospects for change within the current system of employment civil rights law and on possibilities for a fundamental revision of employment civil rights, it appears that the current system is likely to persist with its attendant strengths and weaknesses. We close with some theoretical observations on the role of a rights-based model of employment civil rights law in American society.

The Voices of Employment Civil Rights

We can conceive of this project and this book as an examination of the voices of employment civil rights. This book is organized around voices in several ways. First, voice is a fundamental aspect of fair systems of law. Tyler identifies the ability to tell one's story and be heard as an important element of procedural justice (and this was borne out in our interviews with plaintiffs, particularly when they felt denied this redress).[29] Similarly, O'Barr and Conley discovered that even when litigants in court lose, they are satisfied with the proceedings and the judge if they have had the opportunity to give their version of what happened.[30] When an employee files a discrimination lawsuit, they are exercising a voice the employer cannot ignore. The employer must answer the claim of discrimination or risk legal liability. When a lawsuit is filed, the law further requires that both sides to the case have an opportunity to express their version of the facts and the law. We know, in fact, that within litigation the opportunity for parties to tell their story is quite limited, except in the stylized communications contained in court pleadings, depositions, and questions and answers in the trial if it gets that far. Because many cases settle early, the parties never receive an authoritative resolution of their case. This is a source of considerable frustration for litigants.

Second is the voice of popular conceptions of employment civil rights litigation as articulated by politically conservative critics. These critics suggest that contemporary antidiscrimination law has become an "excuse factory," in which incompetent employees attempt to use the law to receive unwarranted monetary gains and job protection.[31] This notion is supplemented by media coverage of employment civil rights cases—the media dramatically over-reports cases in which plaintiffs win significant settlements or trial awards.[32] This narrative was often reported in the interviews of defendant representatives in our sample, who asserted that most plaintiff lawsuits are frivolous. The broader narrative of which this is a part—the excesses of the American civil justice system—is even reflected in the attitudes of the plaintiffs in our sample. The plaintiffs to whom we presented survey items about the civil justice system expressed the view that too many people sue without a valid claim. Haltom and McCann and Ewick and Silbey refer to this narrative as hegemonic in American popular culture, in that it forms the taken-for-granted view of law as used by plaintiffs in civil cases.[33]

A third voice is that of management, which maintains that the workplace is (or at least should be) a meritocracy. The legal dimension of this meritocracy is what we have referred to as the legalized workplace. As sociologists of work have long observed, work organizations are not effective without the dedicated commitment of the workforce.[34] In the modern United States, the call for commitment to the organization is premised on a concept of fair treatment and fair rewards, according to the contribution each employee makes. Fair treatment includes rights guaranteed by law. Our interviews with defendant representatives express a management perspective. The role of these individuals is to assist management in achieving the goals of the organization, be they public or private. From the voices of defendant representatives, as representatives of law, we hear some concern about the legality of management's decisions as well as almost universal agreement with management decisions. Thus, the management view of workplace justice is also hegemonic, in the sense that workers and managers understand who defines the terms of the employment relationship. There are aspects of this relationship that are consciously negotiated, but there is no doubt that management ultimately is in charge.

Fourth are the voices of researchers. We have developed what Haltom and McCann refer to as a realist account of the system of employment civil rights litigation.[35] This differs from the popular account of how the system operates, as well as the accounts offered by the parties and management. In addition to objective facts about employment civil rights litigation, we have explicitly brought into the analysis the multiple, often conflicting interpretations of participants in the system. What these different perspectives suggest is that there are multiple lived experiences of workplace grievances and the steps in the process of filing and litigating a claim of discrimination. We see no contradiction in analyzing these different perspectives on the same cases and processes, or in the systematic analysis of quantitative and qualitative data. The use of multiple methods and the inclusion of multiple perspectives enriches our understanding of this regime.

Finally, and perhaps most importantly, we have given voice to the plaintiffs who have pursued their rights, as well as the lawyers who represented them and the defendant representatives who opposed them. The interview phase of this project was organized around plaintiffs. We began by sampling plaintiffs from the four major types of discrimination cross-classified by outcome, and, if successful in finding the plaintiff, we interviewed other participants in the case. Through this straightforward process of random sampling, we uncovered extraordinary stories. We opened this book and the five chapters in Part II with lengthy accounts from plaintiffs. These stories reveal workplace injustices and plaintiffs' challenges in using law to seek remedy. Because interviewees agreed to the use of digital recordings of their interviews, we can hear the emotion and strain in their voices, as well as make inferences about their race, age, gender, and class status. Ironically, social science research does not always capture the human element when examining social processes. The digital recordings of the interviews bring these informants to life.

The stories told by the plaintiffs are oftentimes sad, but sometimes triumphant. It is shocking, for instance, to hear Gerry Handley describe his lead coworker's questions about whether he engaged in incest with his daughter. And it is sad when he describes how he lost everything during the lawsuit—his marriage, his home, his health—and says that if he had to do it over again, he would have "just took it, when they said those things about my daughter, I would have just took it, because I lost everything." And it is shocking to hear Kristin Baker describe how her manager shoved a chocolate dildo in her mouth in front of her business customers, that the president of the company refused to believe the story until he heard it from a man who did not work for the company, and that the company's defense lawyers sought a settlement in which Ms. Baker would have received a small amount of money but would have had to leave the company. And yet it is inspiring to learn that Ms. Baker stood her ground, insisting that she had done nothing wrong and that she largely achieved her goals: a one dollar settlement, an apology in front of others, a promise that the company would conduct sexual harassment training, and a promise that her harasser would not be promoted above her.

Interviews with plaintiffs' lawyers and defendant representatives are also compelling. A main contribution of these interviews is an understanding of how the lawyers see the system of employment civil rights and what strategies they adopt within it. It is also striking to hear a white female defense attorney refer to a plaintiff as "kind of bitchy" and to hear a plaintiffs' attorney who had been "fired" by one of the plaintiffs in our sample use sexist language to describe the client (she was "hysterical") and other female attorneys (who were "beautiful but brilliant"). It is interesting to interview the vice president for human resources who had a jar labeled "ashes of problem employees" on his desk, who took pride in claiming that he had won liens on several employees' homes due to judgments for fees (see fig. 7.1).

These are the real-life stories of rights on trial. We believe that one of the responsibilities of social science research is to communicate our findings to broader publics outside the academy—to policymakers, judges, lawyers, ordinary citizens. We have attempted to do so by bringing together comprehensive empirical techniques and the personal narratives of those we studied. While we have benefited enormously from the resources provided by our funding organizations, we think this approach is possible through less expensive but still comprehensive research designs.

Employment Civil Rights and Inequality American Style

Our analysis makes clear that the current version of a rights-based approach to employment civil rights has many limitations for eliminating discrimination and providing a meaningful remedy for the targets of discrimination. Perhaps its most important contribution is that it provides a venue for voices challenging illegal discrimination, even if it does not often provide significant remedies and even if plaintiffs bear a heavy burden when they proceed through the legal process. It may be this potential for gaining the voice of law that continues to attract new social movements to the use of litigation for promoting rights.

Despite these limitations, in the American context there seem to be few alternatives to a rights-based litigation model. This reality reflects an important feature of American law and American inequality. The United States both embraces and reviles claims based on rights. This pattern may help explain why we have seen a growth in inequality between traditionally advantaged and traditionally disadvantaged groups. Despite the theoretical availability of a right not to be discriminated against, women and minorities are reluctant to exercise these rights. As opportunities have expanded at the top ranks of firms (ranks dominated by white men), women and minorities have remained reluctant to challenge the dominant group in the organization.

Antidiscrimination law helps to legitimate growing substantive inequality in American society. As inequality increases, the beneficiaries of the current system can point to antidiscrimination law as guaranteeing equal opportunity. Thus one of the paradoxes of American law is that as it provides for more rights, it accommodates greater inequality.

Acknowledgments

Legal rights are supposed to play a role in redressing inequality in American society. A centerpiece of law's efforts to eliminate invidious discrimination from American life are laws that prohibit discrimination in the workplace along the axes of race, gender, age, disability, national origin, and religion. The right to be free of discrimination at work primarily is enforced through the ability of plaintiffs to bring a lawsuit in court. While employment civil rights litigation has developed into a major field within law, making discrimination lawsuits among the most frequent types of cases on the federal civil docket, it has not been subjected to comprehensive social scientific analysis. This book seeks to offer a more in-depth understanding of this system through a combination of large-scale quantitative data on case filings and their outcomes and systematically collected and analyzed interviews with parties and lawyers on both sides. Our data put this system in a new light and raise fundamental questions about the relationship between employment civil rights and ascriptive hierarchies of race, gender, age, and disability that persist in the American workplace.

This project grew out of our individual and overlapping intellectual interests over the course of more than a decade. Ellen Berrey has a long-standing curiosity about the ability of law and other powerful institutions to ameliorate inequality, particularly law's constitutive role and cultural significance in people's everyday lives. This project builds on Robert Nelson's earlier research on the relationship between antidiscrimination law and gender inequality in organizations. This book extends Laura Beth Nielsen's research about the role of law in dismantling hierarchies of unearned privilege. Her work began with the study of speech on the streets, where law is very circumscribed due to first-amendment principles. *Rights on Trial* examines law's capacity to dismantle such hierarchies in the workplace, a domain in which law is seen as having a legitimate role to prevent discrimination. We all share a belief that mixed methods research provides fruitful tools for documenting the implementation, expression, and experience of law in society.

This book is a product of our relationships with a broad network of scholars and students. It began as a collaboration with John J. Donohue III and Peter Siegelman, who were coprincipal investigators on the quantitative data collection phase of the study. Steve Hoffman, Ryon Lancaster, Amy Myrick, Nick Pedriana, and Jill Weinberg collaborated on publications using these data in ways that advanced the project tremendously.

We have been fortunate to have a superb research team over the various phases of data collection, analysis, and writing. Our team was first headed by Ellen Berrey and later by Spencer Headworth. The team tirelessly visited federal records centers and courthouses all around the country, cajoling clerks to pull cases and then coding the cases meticulously. We thank Aaron Beim, Eric Bennett, Paul Durlak, David Harrington, Adriene Hill, Steve Hoffman, Kate Kindleberger, Evan Lowney, David McElhattan, Amy Myrick, Brent Nakamura, Talia Schiff, Aaron Smyth, Jill Weinberg, and Diana Yoon.

Several undergraduate research assistants worked on the project, many through the Montgomery Summer Research Diversity Fellowship Program of the American Bar Foundation. These include Alvita Akiboh, Pedro Alfonso, Larissa Davis, Mark Davis, Pauline Esman, and Simone Rivera.

Lucinda Underwood and Katy Harris of the American Bar Foundation provided different kinds of administrative and moral support throughout the years of this research. Thank you so much.

We thank our colleagues who provided helpful comments, including Catherine (KT) Albiston, Mario Barnes, William Bielby, William Bridges, Tom Burke, Pamela Coukos, Frank Dobbin, Laurie Edelman, Theodore Eisenberg, Scott Eliason, Charles Epp, Jeremy Freese, Lawrence Friedman, Bryant Garth, Jon Goldberg-Hiller, Laura Gomez, Valerie Hans, Christine Harrington, Wolf Heydebrand, Cheryl Kaiser, Linda Krieger, Sam Lucas, Catharine MacKinnon, Brenda Major, Michael McCann, Ajay Mehrotra, Elizabeth Mertz, Osagie Obasagie, David Oppenheimer, Shannon Portillo, Barbara Reskin, Mary Rose, Rebecca Sandefur, Robin Stryker, and Susan Sturm.

We received helpful advice and suggestions at various points in the project. In addition to the guidance of anonymous reviewers for *Law & Society Review*, the *Journal of Empirical Legal Studies*, and the University of Chicago Press, the work was aided by Laura Beth Nielsen's participation in the Sociolegal Justice Project (SJP), a joint effort of the American Bar Foundation, the National Science Foundation, and George Mason University.

We have been fortunate to have intellectual homes that provide opportunities to present our work at various stages of progress and receive critical feedback. Foremost is the American Bar Foundation, where two of the authors have been on the research faculty throughout this project, and where one author was first a doctoral fellow and then an affiliated scholar. The ABF not only provided sustained funding for this project, but an interdisciplinary environment that supported the very best in social science theory and method in research on law. We received intellectual support for our work from our colleagues in the Department of Sociology at Northwestern University, the Department of Sociology and Criminology at University of Denver, the Department of Sociology at the University of Toronto, and the University at Buffalo-SUNY Baldy Center on Law and Social Policy.

The book benefited from presentations at the Law and Society Association annual meetings (2009, 2010, 2012), the American Sociological Association meeting (2009), and workshops hosted by Cornell University Law School, Cornell University School of Industrial and Labor Relations, Emory University School of Law, the Center for Advanced Study in the Behavioral Sciences, Northwestern University Department of Sociology, Northwestern University Law School, the School of Public Policy at the University of Kansas, Stanford University Law School, University of Buffalo-SUNY Baldy Center, University of California, Berkeley, Jurisprudence and Social Policy, the University of Illinois at Chicago, Harvard Law School, the New Legal Realism Conference at University of California Irvine, and the Conference on Empirical Critical Race Theory.

This research was funded by the American Bar Foundation, the National Science Foundation (#SES-0417389), and the Searle Foundation. The research benefited from participation in the Discrimination Research Group, a joint effort funded by the American Bar Foundation, the Center for Advanced Study in the Behavioral Sciences, and the Ford Foundation (#1045–0189).

We are grateful to reprint some materials published in part in previous publications. Portions of chapter 3 originally appeared in Laura Beth Nielsen, Robert L. Nelson, and Ryon Lancaster, "Individual Justice or Collective Legal Mobilization? Employment Discrimination Litigation in the Post-Civil Rights United States," *Journal of Empirical Legal Studies* 7 (2010):175–201; copyright 2010, the authors; reprinted by permission. Portions of chapter 5 originally appeared in Amy Myrick, Robert L. Nelson, and Laura Beth Nielsen, "Race and Representation: Racial Disparities in Legal Representation for Employment Civil Rights Plaintiffs," *New York University Journal of Legislation and Social Policy* 15 (2012):705–59; copyright 2012 New York University Journal of Legislation and Social Policy; 2013 the authors; reprinted with permission of authors. Thanks also to Tumbleweed for permission to use the photograph in chapter 7; copyright 2016 Tumbleweed, reprinted by permission.

Some of the findings reported in the book were published in previous articles and chapters, but are not reprinted from those sources. These sources are cited as appropriate throughout the book, but we acknowledge them here as well. Ellen C. Berrey, Steve G. Hoffman, and Laura Beth Nielsen (2012), "Situated Justice: Plaintiffs' and Defendants' Perceptions of Fairness in Employment Civil Rights Cases," *Law and Society Review* 46 (1): 1–36; Laura Beth Nielsen (2010), "The Need for Multi–Method Approaches in Empirical Legal Research," in *The Oxford Handbook of Empirical Legal Research*, 951–75, edited by Peter Cane and Herbert M. Kritzer New York: Oxford University Press; Robert L. Nelson, Ellen C. Berrey, and Laura Beth Nielsen (2008), "Diverging Paths: Changing Conceptions of Employment Discrimination in Law and the Social Sciences," *Annual Review of Law and Social Science* 4:103–22; Laura Beth Nielsen and Robert L. Nelson (2005), "Scaling the Pyramid: A Sociolegal Model of Employment Discrimination Litigation," in *Handbook of Employment Discrimination Research: Rights and Realities*, edited by Laura Beth Nielsen and Robert L. Nelson, 3–35, Dorecht, Amsterdam: Springer; Laura Beth Nielsen and Robert L. Nelson (2005), "Rights Realized? An Empirical Analysis of Employment Discrimination Litigation as a Claiming System," *Wisconsin Law Review* 2005:663–711; Laura Beth Nielsen and Aaron Beim (2004), "Media Misrepresentation: Title VII, Print Media, and Public Perceptions of Discrimination Litigation," *Stanford Law & Policy Review* 15:101–30; Jill Weinberg and Laura Beth Nielsen (2012), "Examining Empathy: Experience, Discrimination, and Judicial Decisionmaking," *University of Southern California Law Review* 85:313–51.

John Tryneski of the University of Chicago Press was an unending source of encouragement for this project. We received expert help from Holly Smith and Jo Ann Kiser.

The very long process of conducting and writing up this kind of research simply is not possible without the love, support, and perspective that our family and close friends give us.

For Ellen Berrey, this important support came from my loved ones who value books and appreciate the challenges of writing them. Dalia Muller, Camilo Trumper, Ana Mariella Bacigalupo, and my dad, Robert Berrey, cheered me along through this process. My deepest gratitude goes to Team Berrey Hoffman: Steve and our children, Adela and Eli. We are in it together. I love you no matter what.

For Robert Nelson, this important support came from my kids: Hannah, Ben, Willy, and Ian, and daughter-in-law Kate. To you and the rest of the Sunday night dinner crew, including Juan Gil, I say thank you and stay thirsty my friends.

For Laura Beth Nielsen, this important support came from Melissa Bennis, Christine Carter, Paula Fitzgibbons, Robert V. Thompson, Steve van Kuiken, Betsy Wilson, the Sunday night dinner crew, the Mom's group moms (and dads), and especially my family. Thank you to Harry Connick Jr, Peet's Coffee, and especially Ellen and Bob for providing the soundtrack, caffeine, and collaborative friendship I require to undertake a project like *Rights on Trial.* I have deep appreciation for my parents, Judy and Dave Nielsen, and my *three* brothers and their families: Eric and Krista Nielsen, Chris and Dana Nielsen, and Dee and Linda Parsons. Toward the end of this project my nieces and nephews have grown up enough to understand what my work is all about, which has been really fun (but not as fun as staying up late and boogying to Blondie in Paris). I love you Dylan, Tyler, Karl, Jessie, Hannah, and Maya. And of course, my life would not be the same without the loves of my life, my favorite people in the world: Eric (yes Pat, I said I blacksmith and skateboard) Sorensen; Zach (Camaro lover and son of a sociologist) Sorensen-Nielsen; and Skyler (I'll just build a computer) Nielsen-Sorensen.

Our biggest debt of gratitude is to all the respondents whose stories provide the empirical basis of *Rights on Trial.* We are forever grateful for their willingness to spend time with us. Lawyers and business executives kindly invited us to their offices to help us understand the complexities of their work. Plaintiffs invited us to their homes and answered our questions even though revisiting these conflicts was profoundly painful for all of them. They participated in the hope that some good would come from participating in this research. We sincerely hope we have done their experiences justice. Theirs are the voices of *Rights on Trial.*

The authors contributed equally and appear in alphabetical order.

Appendix

TABLE A.1 **Pseudonym List for Interviewees**

	Pseudonym	Race/Ethnicity	Age
Plaintiffs			*Age at Time of Filing*
P1	Peter Nichelson	White	56
P2	Billy Deeds	African American	49
P3	Rick Nolls	White	64
P4	Sam Grayson	White	41
P5	Chris Burns	African American	60
P6	Mitchell Collins	White	47
P7	Floyd Kelly	African American	57
P8	Maureen Sands	White	53
P9	Matthew Brown	African American	47
P10	Arthur Zeman	White	45
P11	Franklin Williams	African American	38
P12	Catherine Harris	White	50
P13	Pamela Richardson	White	51
P14	Gerry Handley	African American	34
P15	Kristin Hamilton	African American	43
P16	Robert Lester	White	49
P17	Terry Lazio	White	67
P18	Annie Daley	African American	40
P19	Lois Smith	White	36
P20	Joseph Palmer	African American	45
P21	Philip Jacobson	African American	34
P22	Jack Stern	White	26
P23	Denise Anderson	White	64
P24	Daris Barrett	African American	45
P25	Marjorie Turner	African American	46
P26	Debra Leonard	White	41
P27	Christoper Coker	African American	51
P28	Joanne Frankel	White	59
P29	John Bloom	White	60
P30	Roger Wavel[a]	White	51

(*continued*)

TABLE A.1 ***(continued)***

	Pseudonym	Race/Ethnicity	Age
P31	Shelly Simmons	African American	45
P32	Marla Riteman	African American	50
P33	Laila Walter	White	40
P34	Kristen Baker	White	33
P35	Ron Reynolds	White	64
P36	Denise Slayton	White	45
P37	Murielle Byrd	African American	40
P38	Travis Winters	African American	56
P39	Sal DeLuca	White	46
P40	Evan Oliver	White	44
P41	Sharon Blake	White	33
Defendants			*Age in 2007*
D5	Bill Williamson	White	52
D9	Troy Pedlow	White	53
D11-1	Heath Cornwall	White	54
D11-2	David Lever	White	57
D12	Daniel Jain	African American	55
D18	Hank Rymiller	White	51
D21	Elena Mendoza	Latina	54
D31	Sara Ramsden	White	42
D36	Krista Hewick	White	54
D61	Don Gale	White	47
D62-1	Susan O'Hoone	White	47
D62-2	Joyce Mason	White	48
D63	Kate Duffy	White	52
D64	Nicole Price	White	47
D65	Alexandra Parker	White	50
D66	Emily Jones	White	27
D67	Harold Ward	White	62
D71	Marilyn Cole	White	55
D72	Bernard Farkas	White	71
D74	Teresa Lewis	African American	47
Plaintiff Lawyers			*Age in 2007*
PL8	Jeff Kovac	Latino	55
PL12	Joseph Shapiro	White	56
PL13	Theodore Wilde	White	82
PL15	Harry Morgan	African American	75
PL18	Ellis Barry	White	50
PL22	Dan Franco	White	46
PL24	Aaron Erlington	White	48
PL26	Leonard Phillips	White	54
PL30-1	Timothy George	White	54
PL30-2	Josephine King-Hickmann	White	62
PL34	Mark Laramie	White	56
PL36-1	Damon Beim	White	55
PL36-2	Bob Siegel	White	56
PL37	Valerie Lane	White	58

(continued)

TABLE A.1 ***(continued)***

	Pseudonym	Race/Ethnicity	Age
PL40	Karen Green	White	62
PL51	Margaret Cottle	White	38
PL52	Doug Schwartz	White	62
PL53	Kara Morrison	White	51
PL54	Juan Blanco	Latino	42
Defense Lawyers			*Age in 2007*
DL1	Thomas Howard	African American	44
DL2	Preston Gibbon	White	55
DL5	Gillian Kinsey	White	54
DL9	Michael Edwards	White	59
DL12	Cindy Abbott	Latina	43
DL13	Alan Chin	Asian American	40
DL18	Mary Hill	White	57
DL22	Jim Schultz	White	81
DL24	Mitch Weis	White	56
DL25	Trent Watkins	White	47
DL28	Jordan Zarins	White	60
DL30	Walter Hoffman	White	76
DL39	Pam Girard	White	62
DL51	Lilly Evans	White	61
DL52	James Kohner	White	40
DL54	Glenda Klondike	White	45
DL71	Donald Bryant	White	47
DL72	Trond Davies	White	60
DL73	Allison Matsumi	White	56
DL74	Gary Littlejohn	African American	40

[a] Roger Wavel is the son of plaintiff Cliff Wavel. His age is reported at the time of the interview in 2007.

TABLE A.2 **Demographic and Political Characteristics of Interview Respondents by Percent**

	Defendant	Defense Lawyer	Plaintiff	Plaintiff Lawyer
Race (*N*)	20	20	41	18
White	85	80	58.5	88.9
Black	10	10	41.5	5.6
Hispanic	5	0	0	5.6
Other	0	10	0	0
Education (*N*)	20	20	41	18
High school diploma, GED	0	0	12.2	0
Some college	0	0	29.3	0
Bachelor's degree	15	0	43.9	0
Master's degree	0	0	12.2	0
Professional degree, doctorate	85	100	2.4	100
Gender (*N*)	20	20	41	18
Male	45	70	56.1	72.2
Female	55	30	43.9	27.8
Political Ideology (*N*)	20	20	41	18
Conservative	25	10	22	5.7
Moderate	45	35	34.2	0
Liberal	10	50	26.8	77.8
Other	20	5	17.1	16.7
Income in $ (*N*)	17	16	37	16
0–50,000	0	6.3	64.9	6.3
50,001–100,000	11.8	12.5	32.4	6.3
100,001–150,000	35.3	18.8	2.7	25
150,001–200,000	23.5	6.3	0	18.8
More than 200,001	29.4	56.3	0	43.8

TABLE A.3 **Descriptive Statistics and Independent Variables for Model of Litigation Outcomes**

Variable	Mean	Std. Dev.	Min.	Max.
White	0.286	0.452	0	1
Black	0.380	0.486	0	1
Other nonwhite	0.334	0.472	0	1
Male	0.489	0.500	0	1
Manager, professional	0.304	0.460	0	1
Sales, service, office	0.447	0.497	0	1
Blue collar and other	0.249	0.432	0	1
Age	38.48	10.874	18	76
Job tenure	6.46	8.330	0	48
Member of union	0.091	0.288	0	1
Private defendant	0.755	0.430	0	1
Title VII – race	0.401	0.490	0	1
Title VII – sex	0.364	0.481	0	1

(*continued*)

TABLE A.3 ***(continued)***

Variable	Mean	Std. Dev.	Min.	Max.
Title VII – retaliation	0.336	0.473	0	1
Title VII – other	0.166	0.372	0	1
ADEA – age	0.224	0.418	0	1
ADEA – retaliation	0.061	0.241	0	1
ADA disability	0.191	0.394	0	1
ADA retaliation	0.050	0.219	0	1
42 USC §1981	0.188	0.391	0	1
42 USC §1983	0.074	0.263	0	1
Constitutional case	0.050	0.220	0	1
Other statute	0.352	0.478	0	1
Hiring	0.086	0.282	0	1
Firing	0.605	0.489	0	1
Sexual harassment	0.171	0.377	0	1
Conditions of employment	0.599	0.490	0	1
Pay	0.136	0.343	0	1
Index of legal effort	1.436	0.671	0	2
Specific individual perp	0.566	0.496	0	1
Disparate impact theory	0.040	0.196	0	1
EEOC A categorization	0.097	0.400	0	1
EEOC B categorization	0.233	0.500	0	1
EEOC C categorization	0.156	0.467	0	1
EEOC no categorization	0.513	0.500	0	1
EEOC supported	0.043	0.204	0	1
EEOC not supported	0.162	0.369	0	1
EEOC no finding	0.795	0.404	0	1
Only *Pro se*	0.148	0.355	0	1
Gained counsel	0.077	0.267	0	1
Lawyer throughout	0.775	0.418	0	1
Collective actor	0.090	0.288	0	1
Republican judge	0.521	0.500	0	1
y1989	0.025	0.158	0	1
y1990	0.038	0.192	0	1
y1991	0.034	0.182	0	1
y1992	0.050	0.220	0	1
y1993	0.050	0.220	0	1
y1994	0.061	0.240	0	1
y1995	0.091	0.288	0	1
y1996	0.092	0.290	0	1
y1997	0.087	0.283	0	1
y1998	0.082	0.275	0	1
y1999	0.083	0.276	0	1
y2000	0.067	0.251	0	1
y2001	0.077	0.268	0	1
y2002	0.062	0.243	0	1
y2003	0.034	0.182	0	1

Note: $N = 1672$; Index of Legal Effort only computed for Summary Judgment Loss and Late Settlement.

TABLE A.4 **Collective Representation by Major Types of Discrimination**

Pure Claims		
Claim Type	Percent Involved in Collective Representation (PILF, EEOC, multiple plaintiffs, or class action)	Total Claims
Race	9.49 (n = 39)	411
Sex	13.32 (n = 49)	368
Age	9.90 (n = 20)	202
Disability	7.11 (n = 14)	197
All	10.49 (n = 122)	1,178

Dummies (type of discrimination alleged alone or in conjunction with other types of discrimination)		
Claim Type	Percent Involved in Collective Representation (PILF, EEOC, multiple plaintiffs, or class action)	Total Claims
Race	9.34 (n = 62)	664
Sex	11.48 (n = 69)	601
Age	8.72 (n = 32)	367
Disability	7.23 (n = 24)	332
All	9.87 (n = 163)	1,651

TABLE A.5 **Case Outcomes by Major Types of Discrimination**

Pure Claims

Claim Type	% Dismissed	% Settled Early	% Plaintiff Loss on SJ	% Settled Late	% Plaintiff Trial Win	% Plaintiff Trial Loss	Total Claims
Race	16.58 (n = 63)	50.53 (n = 192)	17.11 (n = 65)	8.16 (n = 31)	1.58 (n = 6)	6.05 (n = 23)	380
Sex	19.89 (n = 70)	46.88 (n = 165)	19.89 (n = 70)	7.39 (n = 26)	2.56 (n = 9)	3.41 (n = 12)	352
Age	23.30 (n = 48)	44.66 (n = 92)	16.50 (n = 34)	8.25 (n = 17)	1.94 (n = 4)	5.34 (n = 11)	206
Disability	18.48 (n = 34)	48.37 (n = 89)	16.85 (n = 31)	11.41 (n = 21)	2.72 (n = 5)	2.17 (n = 4)	184
All	19.16 (n = 215)	47.95 (n = 538)	17.83 (n = 200)	8.47 (n = 95)	2.14 (n = 24)	4.46 (n = 50)	1,122

Dummies (type of discrimination alleged alone or in conjunction with other types of discrimination)

Claim Type	% Dismissed	% Settled Early	% Plaintiff Loss on SJ	% Settled Late	% Plaintiff Trial Win	% Plaintiff Trial Loss	Total Claims
Race	19.19 (n = 119)	50.00 (n = 310)	17.26 (n = 107)	8.23 (n = 51)	1.13 (n = 7)	4.19 (n = 26)	620
Sex	20.31 (n = 117)	48.78 (n = 281)	19.27 (n = 111)	7.29 (n = 42)	1.91 (n = 11)	2.43 (n = 14)	576
Age	22.22 (n = 82)	46.61 (n = 172)	18.16 (n = 67)	7.05 (n = 26)	1.36 (n = 5)	4.61 (n = 17)	369
Disability	19.16 (n = 59)	50.32 (n = 155)	15.91 (n = 49)	9.09 (n = 28)	2.27 (n = 7)	3.25 (n = 10)	308
All	19.43 (n = 305)	48.98 (n = 769)	17.71 (n = 278)	7.96 (n = 125)	1.85 (n = 29)	4.08 (n = 64)	1,570

TABLE A.6 **Representation Status by Major Types of Discrimination**

Pure Claims

Claim Type	% with Lawyer Throughout	% Pro se Throughout	% Gained Counsel Midway	Total Claims
Race	66.11 (*n* = 275)	25.96 (*n* = 108)	7.93 (*n* = 33)	416
Sex	85.79 (*n* = 320)	9.65 (*n* = 36)	4.56 (*n* = 17)	373
Age	76.10 (*n* = 156)	14.15 (*n* = 29)	9.76 (*n* = 20)	205
Disability	74.11 (*n* = 146)	18.78 (*n* = 37)	7.11 (*n* = 14)	197
All	75.31 (*n* = 897)	17.63 (*n* = 210)	7.05 (*n* = 84)	1,191

Dummies (type of discrimination alleged alone or in conjunction with other types of discrimination)

Claim Type	% with Lawyer Throughout	% Pro se Throughout	% Gained Counsel Midway	Total Claims
Race	63.19 (*n* = 424)	29.51 (*n* = 198)	7.30 (*n* = 49)	671
Sex	77.67 (*n* = 473)	17.08 (*n* = 104)	5.25 (*n* = 32)	609
Age	71.39 (*n* = 267)	20.59 (*n* = 77)	8.02 (*n* = 30)	374
Disability	70.06 (*n* = 234)	23.95 (*n* = 80)	5.99 (*n* = 20)	334
All	72.51 (*n* = 1,211)	20.66 (*n* = 345)	6.83 (*n* = 114)	1,670

Notes

Chapter One

1. The names of individuals and organizations contained in interviews are pseudonyms.

2. Berrey (2015), Dobbin (2013), Skrentny (2014).

3. Olson (1997). See also Institute for Legal Reform, http://www.instituteforlegalreform.com/issues/lawsuit-abuse-impact, accessed May 16, 2016.

4. Kaiser and Miller (2001), Major and Kaiser (2005).

5. Stainback and Tomaskovic-Devey (2012).

6. Burke (2002), Burke (2003), Epp (1998).

7. Nielsen (2004), Scheingold (1974), Williams (1991).

8. Galanter (1974), Merry (1990), Miller and Sarat (1981), Kairys (1998), Nielsen (2004).

9. McCann (1994).

10. McCann (1994).

11. Albiston (2010).

12. Epp (2009), Edelman (2016).

13. Engel and Munger (2003), Bumiller (1988), Ewick and Silbey (1998).

14. Bumiller (1988).

15. Lucas (2009).

16. Lucas (2009), Schultz (2003).

17. Green (2016).

18. Galanter (1974), Miller and Sarat (1981).

19. *Meritor Savings Bank v. Vinson*, 477 US 57 (1986).

20. *Wards Cove Packing Co. v. Antonio*, 490 US 642 (1989).

21. Lilly Ledbetter Fair Pay Act of 2009, 123 Stat. 5 (2009). *Ledbetter v. Goodyear Tire and Rubber Co.*, 550 US 618 (2007).

22. Burbank and Farhang (2015a).

23. *Wal-Mart v. Dukes*, 131 S.Ct. 2541 (2011)

24. Edelman et al. (2011).

25. Nelson, Berrey, and Nielsen (2008).

26. Ibid. See also Green (2016).

27. Jenkins (2000).

28. Bourdieu (1984), Gramsci (1971).

29. Lamont and Fournier (1992).

30. Loury (2002).

31. Loury (2002), Obasogie (2014).

32. Davis and Greenstein (2009), MacKinnon (1979).

33. Oliver (1990).

34. Santuzzi et al. (2014).

35. Fiske et al. (2002).

36. Harris (1990).

37. On institutional practices that attempt to minimize hierarchy, see Berrey (2015).

38. Baldez, Epstein, and Martin (2006).

39. On the racialization of jobs, see Grodsky and Pager (2001). On wage inequality, see US Bureau of Labor Statistics (2014).

40. England (1992).

41. See Heckman (1998).

42. Fryer, Pager, and Spenkuch (2013), Pager, Western, and Bonikowski (2009), Quillian (2006).

43. Banaji, Hardin, and Rothman (1993).

44. Acker (1990), Acker (2006), Correll, Benard, and Paik (2007), Crenshaw (1989), MacKinnon (1979), Harris (1993), Kang and Banaji (2006), Carbado and Gulati (2003).

45. Krieger (1995), Sturm (2001).

46. Berrey (2015), Dobbin (2009), Nelson and Bridges (1999), Reskin (2012), Roscigno (2011), Stainback and Tomaskovic-Devey (2012).

47. Berrey, Hoffman, and Nielsen (2012).

48. But see Hirsh (2008), Roscigno (2007).

49. Donohue and Siegelman (1991), Donohue and Siegelman (1993), Donohue and Siegelman (1995).

50. Early settlement refers to cases that settle before a ruling on a motion for summary judgment. We expected that these would be cases in which one of the parties wants to "get over with," i.e., cases with no merit or cases that are particularly egregious. Late settlement refers to cases that settle following a ruling on summary judgment; we expected that these cases would involve a longer period of discovery and other legal activity.

51. See Laub and Sampson (2004), Small (2009). Focusing on race and sex discrimination cases also was congruent with our initial research plans and per-

sonal research interests. We anticipated that some of the age discrimination cases could provide an indicator of perceived discrimination against traditionally privileged groups, i.e., whites and men. We predicted that disability cases could provide an example of legislation that was enacted relatively recently and was still open to greater interpretation by the courts and legal professionals.

52. Hans (2000), Nielsen (2004).

53. Miles and Huberman (1994).

54. Lofland and Lofland (1995).

55. Delgado (1989).

56. Polletta (2006).

57. See Berrey and Nielsen (2007), Engel and Munger (2003), Ewick and Silbey (1998), Fleury-Steiner (2004), McCann (2006), Nielsen (2000).

58. But see Mather, McEwen, and Maiman (2001), Sarat and Felstiner (1995).

59. On relational approaches, see, e.g., Emirbayer (1997).

60. The headphone symbol is the work of StudioIcon/Shutterstock.com.

61. Nielsen, Nelson, and Lancaster (2010).

62. Nielsen and Beim (2004).

63. Hirsh (2014), Roscigno and Wilson (2014), Wilson and Roscigno (2014).

64. Nielsen (2010).

65. Nielsen (2010), p. 969.

66. Jerolmack and Khan (2014).

Chapter Two

1. Siegelman and Donohue (1990).

2. Felstiner, Abel, and Sarat (1980), Sandefur (2014).

3. Merry (1990), Engel (1984), Galanter (1983).

4. Heckman and Payner (1989).

5. Pedriana and Abraham (2006).

6. Stainback and Tomaskovic-Devey (2012), p. 52.

7. Ibid., p. 61.

8. Dobbin (2009).

9. MacKinnon (1979).

10. Stainback and Tomaskovic-Devey (2012: 121), Woodward (2015).

11. Stainback and Tomaskovic-Devey (2012), pp. 33–36.

12. See Epstein and Rowland (1991).

13. Heckman and Payner (1989); more generally see Donohue and Heckman (1991).

14. Donohue and Siegelman (1991).

15. Carneiro, Heckman, and Masterov (2005a, 2005b), Heckman (2011).

16. Heckman (1998), pp. 101–2.

17. Neckerman and Kirschenman (1991), Neumark (1996).

18. Quillian and Hexel (2016).

19. Ibid., p. 23.

20. On offers, see Pager (2003). On willingness, see Pager and Quillian (2005).

21. Tilesik (2011).

22. Fryer, Pager, and Spenkuch (2013).

23. Blasi and Jost (2006), Kang and Lane (2010), Krieger (1995), Krieger and Fiske (2006).

24. Dixon, Storen, and Horn (2002).

25. Stainback and Tomaskovic-Devey (2012), pp. 33–35.

26. All percentages in this paragraph are calculations by authors from "Job Patterns for Minorities and Women in Private Industry," (EEO-1), 2013 National Aggregate Report, https://www1.eeoc.gov/eeoc/statistics/employment/jobpat-ee01/2013/index.cfm#select_label. Accessed May 24, 2016.

27. US Bureau of Labor Statistics (2014).

28. Jordan and Zitek (2012), Miller (2015), Williams, Blair-Loy, and Berdahl (2013).

29. Bagenstos (2004), Cox and Beier (2014), Rupp, Vodanovich, and Crede (2006).

30. Freeman (1982).

31. Albiston and Nielsen (2007); see also Burbank and Farhang (2015), Staszak (2015). Each of the legislative and jurisprudential changes noted here are their own areas of constitutional law, statutory interpretation, or legislative action with voluminous scholarly treatment. We summarize them briefly here as an overview.

32. *Griggs v. Duke Power Co.*, 401 US 424 (1971).

33. *McDonnell Douglas v. Green*, 411 US 792 (1973).

34. *Corning Glass Works v. Brennan*, 417 US 188 (1974).

35. *Albemarle Paper Co. v. Moody*, 422 US 405 (1975).

36. *Franks v. Bowman Transportation Co.*, 424 US 747 (1976).

37. *Hazelwood School District v. United States*, 433 US 299 (1977).

38. *Meritor Savings Bank v. Vinson*, 477 US 57 (1986).

39. *Martin v. Wilkes*, 490 US 755 (1989), *Price-Waterhouse v. Hopkins*, 490 US 228 (1989), *Ward's Cove Packing Co. v. Atonio*, 490 US 642 (1989).

40. Cox (1991).

41. 42 U.S.C.A. 1981.

42. U.S. CONST. amend. VII; Estreicher and Harper (2000).

43. Americans with Disabilities Act of 1990, 42 U.S.C. 12101–12213 (1994).

44. Burke (2003).

45. Family and Medical Leave Act of 1993, 29 U.S.C. 2601 et seq.

46. 29 U.S.C. 2601.

47. For a more comprehensive discussion of this trend, see Post and Siegel (2000). See also *United States v. Lopez*, 514 US 549 (1995), and *U.S. v. Morrison,* 120 S.Ct. 1740 (2000).

48. *Kimel v. Florida Board of Regents*, 528 US 62 (2000). For the commerce clause, see U.S. CONST. art. I, § 8, cl. 3. *Kimel v. Florida Board of Regents,* 528 US 62 (2000). For the ADEA, 29 U.S.C. 621–634 (1994 & Supp. I 1995). For section 5, U.S. CONST. amend. XIV, §5.

49. U.S. CONST. amend. IX; *Alabama v. Garrett*, 531 US 356, 360 (2001); *Alabama v. Garrett,* 531 US 356 (2001).

50. See *City of Richmond v. Croson*, 488 US 469 (1989). The standard of strict scrutiny also applies to race-conscious decision making in college admissions. See *Regents of the University of California v. Bakke,* 438 US 265 (1978); and *Grutter,* 539 US 306 (2003).

51. See *Wygant v. Jackson Board of Education*, 476 US 267 (1986).

52. See *Steelworkers v. Weber*, 443 US 193 (1979); *Johnson v. Santa Clara County,* 480 US 616 (1987).

53. See *Parents Involved in Community School v. Seattle School District*, 551 US 701 (2007), where the Court found unconstitutional race-based school assignment programs in Louisville and Seattle.

54. See Bagenstos (2004, 2006), Belanger (2000), Krieger (2000).

55. On restrictions, see Higgins and Rosenbury (2000), Rutherglen (1995), Shoben (2004). On more recent decision, see *Ricci v. Stefano* (2009), which holds that, in the absence of evidence of animus, the City of New Haven must honor the results of a firefighters' test even though it had a disparate impact on African American test takers. On show of animus, see *Ward's Cove* (1989), according to which employers should not be held liable for their actions unless the employee/plaintiffs could demonstrate individual animus on the part of the employer.

56. *Adams v. Florida Power*, 535 US 228 (2002).

57. *Alexander v. Sandoval*, 532 US 275 (2001).

58. Federal Rules of Civil Procedure, Rule 23 (a)(2); see *Wal-Mart Stores, Inc. v. Betty Dukes, et al.*, 564 US ___ (2011).

59. Burbank and Farhang (2015).

60. Ibid.

61. *Celotex Corporation v. Catrett*, 477 US (1986); *Anderson v. Liberty Lobby, Inc.*, 477 US 242 (1986); *Matsushita Electric Industrial Company v. Zenith Radio Corporation,* 475 US 574 (1986).

62. 550 US 544 (2007).

63. 556 US 662 (2009).

64. Eisenberg and Clermont (2015).

65. Edelman (2002), Edelman et al. (2011), Edelman, Uggen, and Erlanger (1999); 42 U.S.C. 2000e-1 to 2000e-16.

66. *Faragher v. City of Boca Raton*, 118 S.Ct. 2275 (1998).

67. Marks (2002)

68. See *Vance v. Ball State University*, 133 S.Ct. 2434 (2013).

69. Dobbin et al. (1993), Dobbin and Sutton (1998), Edelman (1990, 1992), Sutton et al. (1994), Sutton and Dobbin (1996).

70. Dobbin (2009), p. 222.

71. Edelman 2016.

72. Dobbin (2009), pp. 232–33.

73. Krieger, Best, and Edelman (2015).

74. Edelman (2002), Edelman et al. (2011), Edelman, Uggen, and Erlanger (1999).

75. Edelman 2016.

76. Woodward (2015).

77. Mulroy (2011).

78. Sturm (2001).

79. For a discussion, see Green (2003). Green (2016) argues in favor of addressing structural conditions within organizations that enable multiple forms of discrimination while also using law to hold employers strictly liable for proven discrimination.

80. For a debate over structural approaches and cooptation, see the exchange between Sturm and Edelman as reported in Berrey (2009). On unwillingness, see Bagenstos (2006).

81. Data on state agencies and courts are more fragmentary. In this book we focus on the federal cases. For more information on state court employment litigation see Oppenheimer (2003).

82. Donohue and Siegelman (1991), p. 989.

83. Administrative Office of the US Courts, Civil Master File, annual.

84. We thank Quinn Mulroy for providing us with archival material from the EEOC (charge tables and annual reports) used in constructing the time series shown in figs. 2.2 and 2.3.

85. Bales (2006), Bingham et al. (2009), Broome (2006), Drahozal (2007), Randall (2004), Rutledge and Drahozal (2014), Sternlight (2005).

86. Donohue and Siegelman (1991).

87. Ibid.

88. EEOC (2014a).

89. The analysis presented here is an updated and condensed version of Nielsen and Nelson (2005). See also Miller and Sarat (1981), Galanter (1983b), Felstiner, Abel, and Sarat (1980).

90. Felstiner, Abel, and Sarat (1980), Galanter (1983b), p. 13.

91. Felstiner, Abel, and Sarat (1980), p. 635, Galanter (1983b), p. 13.

92. Felstiner, Abel, and Sarat (1980), p. 635, Galanter (1983b), p. 13.

93. Felstiner, Abel, and Sarat (1980), p. 636, Galanter (1983b), p. 13.

94. Galanter (1983b), pp. 14–16, Miller and Sarat (1981).

95. It is important to note that these data are drawn from all civil cases and are not specific to antidiscrimination claims.

96. Smith (2002).

97. See Marshall (2003).

98. Harrell (2000), Lucas (1994).

99. On shame and rejection of victimhood, see Bobo and Suh (2000), Feagin (1991), Suh (2000). On social influences, see Suh (2000). On interpersonal costs, see Kaiser and Miller (2001, 2003).

100. See Smith (2002).

101. See Bobo and Suh (2000), Landrine and Klonoff (1996).

102. Smith (2000).

103. See Smith (2002), p. 16.

104. Ibid., p. 26.

105. Ibid., p. 28.

106. See Bobo and Suh (2000).

107. The Rutgers study is based on a nationwide sample of one thousand employed workers weighted to match the presence of selected groups in census data. The sample is 12% African American, 72% white, 5% Hispanic, 2% Asian, 1% Native American, 1% biracial, and 3% other. The response rate for the survey is not reported in the research report.

108. Dixon, Storen, and Van Horn (2002), p. 11.

109. Ibid.

110. Ibid.

111. Ibid., p. 14.

112. Ibid., p. 15.

113. As we demonstrate in what follows, if 3% of African American workers who thought they were treated unfairly on the basis of race or ethnicity in the past year in fact sued their employer, we would see vastly more lawsuits than are filed. The 3% figure in the Rutgers report may include EEOC complaints as well as state and federal lawsuits. It also may also be rounded up from a smaller fraction.

114. Recall the caveats about measuring perceived discrimination discussed above.

115. US Bureau of Labor Statistics (2014).

116. See, e.g., Litras (2000, 2002).

117. See Kaiser and Miller (2001, 2003), Major and Kaiser (2005).

118. See Bielby and Bourgeois (2002).

119. http://www.instituteforlegalreform.com/issues/lawsuit-abuse-impact, accessed May 16, 2016.

120. Seyfarth Shaw (2016).

121. Nielsen and Beim (2004).

122. Bisom-Rapp (1999).

123. Edelman, Abraham, and Erlanger (1992).

Chapter Three

1. Donohue and Siegelman (1991).

2. Donohue and Siegelman (1991, 1993), Siegelman and Donohue (1995).

3. A full report of descriptive findings appears in a report by Nielsen, Nelson, Lancaster, and Pedriana (2008).

4. Ibid., p. 5.

5. It is possible to allege systemic cases of disparate treatment against employers, in which statistical and other forms of evidence establish a "pattern or practice" of illegal discrimination. See *International Brotherhood of Teamsters v. United States*, 431 U.S. 324 (1977), and *Hazelwood School District v. United States,* 433 U.S. 299 (1977). And it is possible for a single plaintiff to allege discrimination based on disparate impact. Thus while there is not a strict binary distinction between the individual and collective character of disparate treatment and disparate impact theories, as we see below, very few cases include more than one plaintiff. The overwhelming proportion of cases are brought by a single plaintiff alleging disparate treatment.

6. Donohue and Siegelman (1991), pp. 1019–20.

7. We could determine the race of the plaintiff in 1,534 of the 1,788 cases.

8. An extended version of this analysis appears as Nielsen, Nelson, and Lancaster (2010). We express special thanks to Ryon Lancaster for his masterful work in creating the quantitative filings dataset and the statistical models contained in this book.

9. Cecil et al. (2007), Clermont and Schwab (2009), Eisenberg (2004), Eisenberg and Clermont (2015), Bagenstos (2004, 2006, 2014).

10. See Hirsh and Kornrich (2008), Nielsen, Nelson, and Lancaster (2010).

11. Rules 12 and 41, Federal Rules of Civil Procedure.

12. In a small fraction of these cases, the cases were dismissed "without prejudice," meaning the plaintiff could file again if he or she wished, typically when the plaintiff failed to first pursue administrative remedies with the EEOC or a FEPA.

13. Rule 56, Federal Rules of Civil Procedure.

14. Clermont and Eisenberg (2000), Clermont and Schwab (2004, 2009).

15. Albiston (1999), Albiston and Nielsen (2007). As noted in chapter 2, the *Twombly* and *Iqbal* decisions altered the legal test for granting a motion for summary judgment, making the test whether the plaintiffs' pleading was plausible even prior to the production of evidence through discovery.

16. Tyler (1990).

17. Our findings are consistent with research by Kotkin (2007), which examined a confidential dataset of nearly 500 employment discrimination cases settled by federal magistrates in Chicago between 1999 and 2005. That study revealed a median settlement award in employment discrimination lawsuits of

$30,000. At the extremes, 7% of the settled cases ended with the plaintiff receiving less than $5,000, and 2% of cases ended with the plaintiff receiving settlements over $300,000.

18. A limitation of discrete-time models is that they treat the occurrence of events as sequentially instantaneous without accounting for the real elapsed time and temporal dependence between events. The analysis could be further refined in future analyses by employing a competing risks model that accounts for the passage of real time.

19. We ended up using the discrete-time event-history model because it allowed us to control for case-specific variation, as well as simultaneously estimating the likelihood of a case ending at each stage. However, to test the robustness of our results, we also ran models that were specified as sequential logits, sequential probits, multinomial logits, multinomial probits, and conditional logits. In each of these specifications we observed the same patterns in direction and significance in our coefficients, indicating that our results are not due to the specific model.

20. R^2 is a measure of the percentage of variation in the dependent variable explained by the independent variables included in a model.

21. Kritzer (1990, 1997), Sandefur (2008, 2015), Seron et al. (2001).

22. Adding an interaction term for white people filing race claims did not change the significance level of the main race effects.

23. An analysis that included an interaction term for men claiming sex discrimination under Title VII found that these claims were significantly more likely to be dismissed. When that term was added to the model, the coefficient for Title VII sex discrimination claims was no longer statistically significant.

24. Hirsch (2008); Nielsen, Nelson, and Lancaster (2010).

25. Galanter (1974).

26. Nielsen and Beim (2004).

27. For example, Skaggs (2008).

28. Nelson and Bridges (1999), Nielsen (2004), Scheingold (1974).

Chapter Four

1. This is a conservative figure, as we identified this pattern inductively while we analyzed the interview transcripts. We did not ask about it directly during the interview.

2. Because our analysis started with lawsuits filed, we could predict that the interface with human resources departments in these stories was not going to resolve the problem. Here, we are describing what the HR process felt like for the plaintiffs and when they decided to escalate to a lawyer or to the EEOC.

3. Nelson and Nielsen (1999).

4. Scholars have used a range of descriptors in analyses of state-like bureaucratic structures in workplaces. Burawoy (1979) discusses the emergence of the "internal state," while Edwards (1979) and Baron, Devereaux-Jennings, and Dobbin (1988) investigate the proliferation of "bureaucratic control systems" and Bridges and Villemez (1994) analyze "bureaucratic personnel management" in organizations. Because many aspects of employment relationships in the United States are left unregulated by law and because antidiscrimination laws are themselves ambiguous (Edelman 1992, Dobbin and Sutton 1998), personnel managers have been responsible for creating the quasi-legal codes around which "firms have become states unto themselves" (Dobbin 2009, p. 2). These rule-driven internal "states" shape how social control is deployed in organizations (Selznick 1969, Burawoy 1979, Halaby 1986).

A range of variables may be used to measure the extent to which workplaces are "legalized." These include rationally designed compensation schemes (Nelson and Bridges 1999, p. 79), diversity and antiharassment training programs (Kalev, Dobbin, and Kelly 2006, Edelman et al. 2011), and formalized grievance processing and evaluation procedures (Edelman et al. 1999). For a thorough list of relevant organizational attributes, see Edelman et al. (2011), table 1. The simple presence of such organizational attributes has been shown to reduce firms' likelihoods of being found in violation of discrimination law in court, as judges tend to view the presence of these institutionalized structures as itself an indicator of nondiscrimination (Edelman et al. 1999, Edelman et al. 2011).

5. See also Silver-Greenberg and Gebeloff (2015).

Chapter Five

1. Collins (1997), Tomaskovic-Devey et al. (2005).
2. Dovido, Kawakami, and Gaertner (2002), Krieger (1995).
3. Bonilla-Silva (2003), Van Cleve (2016).
4. Seron, Ryzin, Frankel, and Kovath (2001), Sandefur (2015).
5. Nielsen, Nelson, and Lancaster (2010).
6. Ibid.
7. Myrick, Nelson, and Nielsen (2012).
8. Heckman and LaFontaine (2010).
9. Huffman and Cohen (2004).
10. Collins (1997), Tomaskovic-Devey et al. (2005).
11. Royster (2003), p. 102.
12. See Hofferth (1984), Miller-Cribbs and Farber (2008).
13. See Dombroski (2005).
14. Bruce and Thornton (2004).
15. When asked directly about their reasons for filing *pro se*, 45% of respon-

dents said their case was simple enough to handle alone; 22% said they had money available but chose not to spend it on a lawyer; 31% said they couldn't afford a lawyer, and 36% said they had contacted lawyers before deciding to appear alone, with an average of 2.3 consultations.

16. US Census Bureau (2015).

17. The average income for a full-time African American worker in 2010 was $28,964, whereas white, non-Hispanic full-time workers averaged an annual salary of $41,656 that year. U.S. Census Bureau (2011).

18. Hagan, Shedd, and Payne (2005).

19. Our sample of plaintiffs' lawyers is small, but has racial demographics similar to the American legal profession overall: 84% of our sample are white, 5% are African American, and 11% Latino. According to the After the JD Study, a national sample of lawyers in 2012 was 83% white, 6% Asian American, 4% African American, 3% Latino/a (Plickert et al. 2014).

20. As we noted above, work on how lawyers select clients is surprisingly limited and mostly focuses on torts. Generally, it finds that contingency lawyers are very selective and favor clients with high recovery prospects.

21. This is generally consistent with studies finding that plaintiffs' lawyers are highly selective. But, many show systematic variation in selectivity. *See* Kritzer (1997), Trautner (2006), Van Hoy (1999).

22. One study found that, depending on call volume, contingency firms rejected 59% to 83% of clients after the first phone call, with an average of 65% across all firms surveyed. See Kritzer (1997), p. 27.

23. Although many lawyers said they preferred clients who came to their meetings prepared with documents and having done background work, or those who framed their cases to include salient facts, some also cautioned that they often turned down clients who appeared to have visited several attorneys already and "ma[de] the case more interesting [through embellishment]" after being rejected (PL8). One said explicitly that he preferred clients who were *not* savvy about the legal process, noting that "what I feel more of an affinity for are people who really don't know what their rights are and they're generally lower in the food chain, lower in the corporate food chain" (PL18). Thus, attorneys seem to have perceived a line between clients who used knowledge to build a valid case and those who used knowledge to manipulate the system and its evaluative criteria. Lawyers referenced demeanor as a way to negotiate this line; clients who could articulate their rights and/or had assembled documentary evidence were preferred, but only if lawyers "believed" them based on their demeanor, and furthermore saw them as "reasonable" collaborators in the attorney-client relationship. For a mechanism linking listener beliefs to reduced facility, see sources above citing social-psychological research on how communicative performance suffers when people believe they are being evaluated for "stereotypical" group attributes.

24. We are aware of no major studies that consider cultural or social interactive practices that influence US lawyers' client selection. For an interesting international analysis, see Michelson (2006).

25. See Bisom-Rapp (1999).

26. Such criteria are perhaps surprising given that all the interviewed attorneys agreed that trials—bench or jury—were rare, and most cases were expected to settle based on an agreement between the parties.

27. Jacobs (1997: 363–64).

28. Dovidio et al. (2002), Kang (2005), Krieger and Fiske (2006).

29. Ibid.

30. Pew Research Center (2016).

31. McPherson et al. (2001), Rivera (2015).

32. Other studies have found similarly. See Kritzer (1993).

33. Still, most said they discouraged clients from proceeding when their cases appeared legally weak or their potential recovery was limited.

34. Other studies have found that elite lawyers feel increased pressure to take cases from friends and peers who are highly invested in the issues, even when the cases appear weak (Heinz and Laumann 1994, chapter 6).

35. Nielsen and Beim (2004).

Chapter Six

1. Mr. Siegel noted that class action cases require describing systemic problems with an employer, rather than discrimination against an individual. In Ms. Slayton's case, she was aware of systemic gender discrimination in promotion. However, in individual cases, a plaintiff may not be aware of the extent or character of systemic issues until it is revealed in discovery. For example, in most companies employees are prohibited from revealing their pay to other employees. It is when discovery yields evidence of statistical disparities in pay that it becomes an issue in the case.

2. On gate keeping, see Daniels and Martin (2015).

3. Kagan (2001). See also Mather, McEwen, and Maiman (2001) on the strategies that different types of lawyers use.

4. Galanter (1974).

5. Bisom-Rapp (1999).

6. 347 US 483 (1954). On litigation campaigns, see Galanter (1974).

7. Heinz and Laumann (1982).

8. Nelson (1988), Nelson and Nielsen (1999), Heinz and Laumann (1982).

9. Rosenthal (1974), Sarat and Felstiner (1995).

10. Edelman (1992), Edelman, Uggen, and Erlanger (1999).

11. The counts in table 6.1 represent the total counts of individuals who

made comments of a particular type, not the total number of times a particular comment was made. Thus, if respondent x mentioned her lawyer's dishonesty six times in her interview, we treated this as "1" in our category of "dishonest" comments.

12. Moss (2013).

13. We interviewed nineteen plaintiffs' attorneys. Fifteen were "linked," in that they represented plaintiffs we had interviewed. Due to the difficulty of tracking down specific plaintiffs' lawyers and the fact that some plaintiffs pursued their case without any representation, we added four randomly drawn plaintiffs' lawyers from cases that otherwise qualified for the subsample. For the linked interviewees, we asked lawyers about the specific case in which the plaintiff had been a party. For those who did not remember the plaintiff and for the randomly drawn lawyers, we asked them to select a closed employment case and to describe for us the evolution of that case.

14. For a similar dynamic around divorce settlements, see Sarat and Felstiner (1995).

15. We interviewed twenty defendant representatives. Nine of the defendant interviews were linked to a case in which we also interviewed the other side in the case. Eleven were chosen randomly from cases that met the criteria for our subsample but for which we did not possess a plaintiff interview.

16. We interviewed twenty defense attorneys (outside counsel). Thirteen were linked in that they represented the defense in the case involving a plaintiff we had interviewed. We added seven randomly drawn defense attorneys from cases that otherwise qualified for the subsample. For the linked interviewees, we asked lawyers about the specific case in which the plaintiff had been a party. For those who did not remember the plaintiff and for the randomly drawn lawyers, we asked them to select a closed employment case and to describe for us the evolution of that case.

17. A handful of the defense counsel in our sample also represent plaintiffs.

18. Rosen (1988), Nelson and Nielsen (1999).

Chapter Seven

1. Kagan (2001).
2. Gallup, Inc. (2004).
3. Berrey, Hoffman, and Nielsen (2012).
4. Haltom and McCann (2004). See also Nielsen and Beim (2004).
5. Feeley (1979).
6. Perrow (1986), p. 6.
7. Soss (1999).
8. Ibid.

9. Lipsky (2010 [1980]).

10. Ibid.

11. Myrick, Nelson, and Nielsen (2012).

12. See Berrey, Hoffman, and Nielsen (2012).

13. Bonilla-Silva (2003), Sears and Henry (2003).

14. See, e.g., Branch (2014).

15. Lucas (2009).

16. There are a few instances in which defense side respondents acknowledged that there was a gray area case, but none in which they conceded that their employer or client was contesting a valid claim.

17. See also, e.g., Edelman (1992).

18. Major and Kaiser (2005).

19. Berrey, Hoffman, and Nielsen (2012).

20. Ibid.

21. See also Abel (1997).

Chapter Eight

1. Lind et al. (1993), Lind and Tyler (1988), Tyler (1990).

2. Tyler (1990).

3. Berrey, Hoffman, and Nielsen (2012).

4. Kim (1997).

5. Mustillo et al. (2004).

Chapter Nine

1. Fiske (1998).

2. See, e.g., Bielby (2000).

3. Bielby (1992).

4. Dovidio et al. (1996).

5. See also Roscigno (2011).

6. Bielby (2005), Fiske and Lee (2008).

7. England (1992), Fiske (2011), Glick and Fiske (1996, 1997), MacKinnon (1979), Reskin (1993).

8. Ridgeway (1997, 2011, 2014), Swim and Sanna (1996).

9. Acker (2006).

10. See, e.g., Alexander (2010), Van Cleve and Mayes (2015), Van Cleve (2016).

11. 490 US 228 (1989).

12. Feagin (2010).

13. Kaiser and Pratt-Hyatt (2009), Lowery et. al. (2006). On perceptions of victimization, see Sellers and Shelton (2003).

14. Sears and Henry (2003).

15. Kinder and Sears (1981), Kluegel (1986), Sears, Henry, and Kosterman (2000).

16. Sears and Henry (2003).

17. Kluegel (1986), Kluegel and Bobo (2001), Reyna et al. (2005), Sniderman and Piazza (1993).

18. Roscigno and Hodson (2004).

19. Smith (1991), Sniderman and Piazza (1993).

20. Devine and Elliot (1995), Quillian and Pager (2001).

21. Duncan (1976), King and Wheelock (2007), Sweeney and Haney (1992).

22. Quillian and Pager (2001).

23. Entman (1992).

24. On the criminal justice system, see Hurwitz and Peffley (1997). On racial resentments, see Edsall and Edsall (1992).

25. On stereotypes of white women, see Alexander (1995). On stereotypes of black women, see Fenton (1998), King (1973).

26. Barnett et al. (1984), Staples (1986).

27. Blake and Darling (1994), Collins (2000), Harris-Perry (2011).

28. Welsh (1999).

29. Glick and Fiske (1996).

30. Crenshaw (1989).

31. MacKinnon (1979), p. 1.

32. Mr. Bryant was referencing a 1994 sexual harassment suit in which a jury awarded a former secretary of a major law firm $7.1 million. At the time, this was among the largest—if not the largest—punitive damage award ever in a sexual harassment case. Among the charges was the claim that the named defendant grabbed the plaintiff's breast while he dropped M&M candies into her blouse pocket.

33. Ridgeway (1997), Swim and Sanna (1996).

34. Joseph (1981).

35. Collins (2000).

36. Heyer (2007), Thomas (2004).

37. On evaluations of applicants, see Cesare et al. (1990). On discrimination, see Perry, Hendricks, and Broadbent (2000).

38. Stone and Colella (1996).

39. Heyer (2007), Oliver (1998), Thomas (2004).

40. Oliver (1998).

41. Heyer (2007). On the social constructionist model, see Heyer (2007), Oliver (1990), Thomas (2004). On the sociopolitical model, see Rembis (2010).

42. Mills (1993), Niemeyer (1991), Stone (1984).
43. Darke (1998), Davis (1995).
44. Davis (1995). See also Oliver (1990).
45. Robert and Harlan (2006).
46. Deal (2007).
47. Robert and Harlan (2006).
48. Doering, Rhodes, and Schuster (1983), Rosen and Jerdee (1976).
49. Hassell and Perrewe (1995), Rosen and Jerdee (1976).
50. Rosen and Jerdee (1976).
51. Fiske et al. (2002).
52. Duncan (2001).
53. Richeson and Shelton (2006).
54. Wrenn and Maurer (2004).
55. Britton and Thomas (1973), Fiske et al. (2002), Gordon and Arvey (2004)
56. Hutchens (1988), Johnson and Neumark (1997).
57. Rosen and Jerdee (1976).
58. Chiu et al. (2001).
59. Capowski (1994), Rosen and Jerdee (1976), Taylor and Walker (1998).
60. E.g., Loury (2002).

Chapter Ten

1. See chapter 4.
2. See chapter 7.
3. Edelman (2016), Dobbin (2009).
4. Edelman (2016), Edelman et al. (2011).
5. Silver-Greenberg and Gebeloff (2015).
6. Edelman (2016).
7. Kaiser and Miller (2001, 2003), Kaiser, Shatzki, and Bartholomew (2004).
8. Galanter (1974).
9. Bagenstos (2006), Edelman (2016).
10. Weinberg and Nielsen (2011)
11. Farhang (2010).
12. Feder and Brougher (2013).
13. Skaggs (2008), Schlanger and Kim (2014).
14. EEOC (2014b).
15. Schlanger and Kim (2014).
16. Albiston and Nielsen (2007).
17. Haltom and McCann (2004).
18. S. 862, H.R. 1619 (2015).
19. Zhou (2015).

20. Berrey (2015), Edelman, Fuller, and Mara-Drita (2001), Skrentny (2014).
21. Nelson and Bridges (1999), McCann (1994), McCann et al. (2015).
22. Sturm (2001).
23. Epp (2009).
24. McCann (1994).
25. Dobbin (2006).
26. Saguy (2003).
27. Zippel (2006).
28. Nielsen (1999).
29. Tyler (1984).
30. O'Barr and Conley (1985).
31. Olson (1997).
32. Nielsen and Beim (2004).
33. Haltom and McCann (2004), Ewick and Silbey (1998).
34. Burawoy (1979).
35. Haltom and McCann (2004).

References

Abel, Richard L., Ed. 1997. Lawyers: A Critical Reader. New York: The New Press.

Acker, Joan. 1990. "Hierarchies, Jobs, Bodies: A Theory of Gendered Organizations." *Gender & Society* 4(2):139–58.

——. 2006. "Inequality Regimes: Gender, Class, and Race in Organizations." *Gender & Society* 20(4):441–64.

Adler, Jane W., Deborah R. Hensler, and Charles E. Nelson. 1983. *Simple Justice.* Santa Monica, CA: RAND Corporation Institute for Social Justice.

Administrative Office of the US Courts. Annual. *Civil Master File.*

Albiston, Catherine R. 1999. "The Rule of Law and the Litigation Process: The Paradox of Losing by Winning." *Law and Society Review* 33(4):869–910.

——. 2000. "Legal Consciousness and the Mobilization of Civil Rights: Negotiating Family and Medical Leave Rights in the Workplace." Presentation at the 2000 Law and Society Association Annual Meeting. Miami, FL.

——. 2001. "The Institutional Context of Civil Rights: Mobilizing the Family and Medical Leave Act in the Courts and in the Workplace." PhD diss., University of California, Berkeley.

——. 2005. "Bargaining in the Shadow of Social Institutions: Competing Discourses and Social Change in Workplace Mobilization of Civil Rights." *Law and Society Review* 39(1):11–49.

——. 2010. *Rights on Leave: Institutional Inequality and the Mobilization of the Family and Medical Leave Act.* Cambridge: Cambridge University Press.

Albiston, Catherine R., and Laura Beth Nielsen. 2007. "The Procedural Attack on Civil Rights: The Empirical Reality of Buckhannon for Public Interest Litigation." *UCLA Law Review* 54:1087–134.

Alexander, Adele Logan. 1995. "She's No Lady, She's a Nigger: Abuses, Stereotypes, and Realities from the Middle Passage to Capitol (and Anita) Hill." In *Race, Gender, and Power in America: The Legacy of the Hill–Thompson*

Hearings, ed. Anita Faye Hill and Emma Coleman Jordan., 3–25. New York: Oxford University Press.

Alexander, Michelle. 2010. *The New Jim Crow: Mass Incarceration in the Age of Colorblindness*. New York: The New Press.

Ashenfelter, Orley, Theodore Eisenberg, and Stewart J. Schwab. 1995. "Politics and the Judiciary: The Influence of Judicial Background on Case Outcomes." *Journal of Legal Studies* 24(2):257–81.

Bagenstos, Samuel R. 2004. "The Future of Disability Law." *Yale Law Journal* 114(1):1–84.

———. 2006. "The Structural Turn and the Limits of Antidiscrimination Law." *California Law Review* 94:1–48.

———. 2014. "Formalism and Employer Liability under Title VII." *University of Chicago Legal Forum* 2014:145–76.

Baldez, Lisa, Lee Epstein, and Andrew D Martin. 2006. "Does the US Constitution Need an Equal Rights Amendment?" *Journal of Legal Studies* 35(1):243–83.

Bales, Richard A. 2006. "Normative Considerations of Employment Arbitration at Gilmer's Quinceanera." *Tulane Law Review* 81:331–94.

Banaji, Mahzarin R., Curtis Hardin, and Alexander J. Rothman. 1993. "Implicit Stereotyping in Person Judgment." *Journal of Personality and Social Psychology* 65:272–81.

Barnett, Bernice McNair, Ira E Robinson, Wilfred C Bailey, and John M Smith Jr. 1984. "The Status of Husband/Father as Perceived by the Wife/Mother in the Intact Lower-Class Urban Black Family." *Sociological Spectrum* 4(4):421–41.

Baron, James N., P. Devereaux-Jennings, and Frank R. Dobbin. 1988. "Mission Control? The Development of Personnel Systems in U.S. Industry." *American Sociological Review* 53:497–514.

Belanger, Nora. 2000. "The ADA—A Practitioner's Guide in the Aftermath of Sutton: Sutton v. United Air Lines." *Pace Law Review* 21(1):271–311.

Berrey, Ellen. 2009. "Sociology Finds Discrimination in the Law." *Contexts* 8(2): 28–31.

———. 2015. *The Enigma of Diversity: The Language of Race and the Limits of Racial Justice*. Chicago: University of Chicago Press.

Berrey, Ellen, and Laura Beth Nielsen. 2007. "Rights of Inclusion: Integrating Identity at the Bottom of the Dispute Pyramid." *Law and Social Inquiry* 32(1):233–60.

Berrey, Ellen C., Steve G. Hoffman, and Laura Beth Nielsen. 2012. "Situated Justice: A Contextual Analysis of Fairness and Inequality in Employment Discrimination Litigation." *Law and Society Review* 46(1):1–36.

Bertrand, Marianne, and Sendhil Mullainathan. 2004. "Are Emily and Greg

More Employable Than Lakisha and Jamal? A Field Experiment on Labor Market Discrimination." *American Economic Review* 94(4):991–1013.

Bielby, Denise D. 1992. "Commitment to Work and Family." *Annual Review of Sociology* 18:281–302.

Bielby, William T. 2000. "Minimizing Workplace Gender and Racial Bias." *Contemporary Sociology* 29(1):120–29.

——. 2005. "Applying Social Research on Stereotyping and Cognitive Bias to Employment Discrimination Litigation: The Case of Allegations of Systematic Gender Bias at Wal-Mart Stores." In *Handbook of Employment Discrimination Research: Rights and Realities*, ed. Laura Beth Nielsen and Robert Nelson, 395–408. Amsterdam: Springer.

Bielby, William T., and Michael Bourgeois. 2002. "Insuring Discrimination: Making a Market for Employment Practice Liability Insurance." Paper presented at the 2002 American Sociological Association Annual Meeting, Chicago, IL.

Bingham, Lisa B., Cynthia J. Hallberlin, Denise A. Walker, and Won–Tae Chung. 2009. "Dispute System Design and Justice in Employment Dispute Resolution: Mediation at the Workplace." *Harvard Negotiation Law Review* 14(1):1–50.

Bisom–Rapp, Susan. 1999. "Bulletproofing the Workplace: Symbol and Substance in Employment Discrimination Law in Practice." *Florida State University Law Review* 26:959–1047.

Blake, Wayne M, and Carol A. Darling. 1994. "The Dilemmas of the African American Male." *Journal of Black Studies* 24(4): 402–15.

Blasi, Gary, and John T. Jost. 2006. "System Justification Theory and Research: Implications for Law, Legal Advocacy, and Social Justice." *California Law Review* 94:1119–68.

Bobo, Lawrence. 1991. "Social Responsibility, Individualism, and Redistributive Policies." *Sociological Forum* 6(1):71–92.

Bobo, Lawrence, and Susan A. Suh. 2000. "Surveying Racial Discrimination: Analyses from a Multiethnic Labor Market." In *Prismatic Metropolis: Inequality in Los Angeles*, ed. Melvin L. Oliver, Lawrence D. Bobo, James H. Johnson, and Abel Valenzuela, 495–526. New York: Russell Sage Foundation.

Bonilla–Silva, Eduardo. 2003. *Racism without Racists: Color–Blind Racism and the Persistence of Racial Inequality in the United States.* Lanham, MD: Rowman & Littlefield.

Bourdieu, Pierre. 1984. *Distinction: A Social Critique of the Judgement of Taste.* Trans. Richard Nice. Cambridge, MA: Harvard University Press.

Brake, Deborah L., and Joanna L. Grossman. 2008. "The Failure of Title VII as a Rights–Claiming System." *North Carolina Law Review* 86:859–936.

Branch, John. 2014. "Clippers Owner Barred for Life over Racist Talk." *New York Times*, April 29.

Bridges, William P., and Wayne J. Villemez. 1994. *The Employment Relationship: Causes and Consequences of Modern Personnel Administration.* New York: Plenum Press.

Britton, Jean O., and Kenneth R. Thomas. 1973. "Age and Sex as Employment Variables: Views of Employment Service Interviewers." *Journal of Employment Counseling* 10(4):180–86.

Broome, Stephen A. 2006. "An Unconscionable Application of the Unconscionability Doctrine: How the California Courts Are Circumventing the Federal Arbitration Act." *Hastings Business Law Journal* 3(1):1–28.

Bruce, Marino, and Michael C. Thornton, 2004. "It's My World? Exploring Black and White Perceptions of Personal Control," *Sociological Quarterly* 45(3): 597–612.

Bumiller, Kristin. 1988. *The Civil Rights Society: The Social Construction of Victims.* Baltimore: John Hopkins University Press.

Burawoy, Michael. 1979. *Manufacturing Consent: Changes in the Labor Process under Monopoly Capitalism.* Chicago: University of Chicago Press.

Burbank, Stephen B., and Sean Farhang. 2015a. "The Subterranean Counterrevolution: The Supreme Court, the Media, and Litigation Reform." *Penn Law Legal Scholarship Repository* Paper 1544:1–32.

———. 2015b. "Class Actions and the Counterrevolution against Federal Litigation." *Penn Law Legal Scholarship Repository* Paper 1555:1–38.

Burke, Tom. 2003. "How Do Rights Work? The Case of the Americans with Disabilities Act." Paper presented at the Rights and Realities: Legal and Social Scientific Approaches to Employment Discrimination conference, Stanford Law School, Stanford, CA.

Burke, Thomas F. 2002. *Lawyers, Lawsuits, and Legal Rights.* Berkeley: University of California Press.

Burstein, Paul. 1991. "Legal Mobilization as a Social Movement Tactic: The Struggle for Equal Employment Opportunity." *American Journal of Sociology* 96(5):1201–25.

Capowski, Genevieve. 1994. "Ageism: The New Diversity Issue." *Management Review* 83(10):10.

Carbado, Devon W., and Mitu Gulati. 2003. "The Fifth Black Woman." *Journal of Contemporary Legal Issues* 11:701–29.

Carneiro, Pedro, James J. Heckman, and Dimitriy V. Masterov. 2005a. "Understanding the Sources of Ethnic and Racial Wage Gaps and Their Implications for Policy." In *Handbook of Employment Discrimination Research: Rights and Realities*, ed. Robert Nelson and Laura Beth Nielsen, 99–136. Amsterdam: Springer.

Carneiro, P., D. Masterov, and J. Heckman. 2005b. "Labor Market Discrimination and Racial Differences in Premarket Factors." *Journal of Law and Economics* 48(1):1–39.

Cecil, Joe S., Rebecca N. Eyre, Dean Miletich, and David Rindskopf. 2007. "A Quarter-Century of Summary Judgment Practice in Six Federal District Courts." *Journal of Empirical Legal Studies* 4(4):861–907.

Cesare, Steven J., Richard J Tannenbaum, and Anthony Dalessio. 1990. "Interviewers' Decisions Related to Applicant Handicap Type and Rater Empathy." *Human Performance* 3(3):157–71.

Childs, Erica Chito. 2005. "Looking behind the Stereotypes of the 'Angry Black Woman'": An Exploration of Black Women's Responses to Interracial Relationships." *Gender & Society* 19(4):544–61.

Chiu, Warren C. K., Andy W. Chan, Ed Snape, and Tom Redman. 2001. "Age Stereotypes and Discriminatory Attitudes towards Older Workers: An East-West Comparison." *Human Relations* 54(5):629–61.

Clermont, Kevin, and Theodore Eisenberg. 2000. "Appeal from Jury or Judge Trial: Defendant's Advantage." *American Law and Economics Review* 3: 125–64.

Clermont, Kevin M., and Stewart J. Schwab. 2004. "How Employment Discrimination Plaintiffs Fare in Federal Court." *Journal of Empirical Legal Studies* 1(2):429–58.

——. 2009. "Employment Discrimination Plaintiffs in Federal Court: From Bad to Worse?" *Harvard Law and Policy Review* 3:103–32.

Collins, Patricia Hill. 2000. *Black Feminist Thought: Knowledge, Consciousness, and the Politics of Empowerment*. New York: Routledge.

Collins, Sharon M. 1997. "Black Mobility in White Corporations: Up the Corporate Ladder but Out on a Limb." *Social Problems* 44(1):55–100.

Correll, Shelly J., Stephen Benard, and In Paik. 2007. "Getting a Job: Is There a Motherhood Penalty?" *American Journal of Sociology* 112:1297–1338.

Coscarelli, Joe. 2014. "Everything You Need to Know about V. Stiviano, the Woman Who Recorded Donald Sterling's Racism." *New York Magazine*, April 28. http://nymag.com/daily/intelligencer/2014/04/v–stiviano–donald–sterling–girlfriend–maria–perez.html. Accessed May 16, 2016.

Cox, Cody B., and Margaret E. Beier. 2014. "Too Old to Train or Reprimand: Evaluating the Effect of Intergroup Attribution Bias in the Evaluations of Older Workers." *Journal of Business Psychology* 29(1):61–70.

Cox, Paul N. 1991. *The Law of Employment Discrimination: Cases and Commentary*. Sterling Heights, MI: Lupus.

Crenshaw, Kimberlé Williams. 1989. "Demarginalizing the Intersection of Race and Sex: A Black Feminist Critique of Antidiscrimination Doctrine, Feminist Politics and Antiracist Politics," *University of Chicago Legal Forum* 1:139–67.

Curran, Barbara A. 1977. *The Legal Needs of the Public: The Final Report of a National Survey*. Chicago: American Bar Foundation.

Daniels, Stephen, and Joanne Martin. 2015. *Tort Reform, Plaintiffs' Lawyers, and Access to Justice*. Lawrence: University of Kansas Press.

Darke, Paul. 1998. "Understanding Cinematic Representations of Disability." In *Disability Reader: Social Science Perspectives*, ed. Tom Shakespeare, 181–200. New York: Continuum.

Davis, Lennard J. 1995. *Enforcing Normalcy: Disability, Deafness, and the Body*. New York: Verso.

Davis, Shannon N., and Theodore N. Greenstein. 2009. "Gender Ideology: Components, Predictors, and Consequences," *Annual Review of Sociology* 35:87–105.

Deal, Mark. 2007. "Aversive Disablism: Subtle Prejudice toward Disabled People." *Disability & Society* 22(1):93–107.

Delgado, Richard. 1989. "Storytelling by Oppositionists and Others: A Plea for Narrative." *Michigan Law Review* 87:2411–441.

Devine, Patricia G., and Andrew J. Elliot. 1995. "Are Racial Stereotypes Really Fading? The Princeton Trilogy Revisited." *Personality and Social Psychology Bulletin* 21(11):1139–50.

Dixon, K. A., Duke Storen, and Carl E. Van Horn. 2002. *A Workplace Divided: How Americans View Discrimination and Race on the Job*. New Brunswick, NJ: Rutgers, the State University of New Jersey, John J. Heldrich Center for Workplace Development.

Dobbin, Frank, and Alexandra Kalev. 2013. "The Origins and Effects of Corporate Diversity Programs." In *The Oxford Handbook of Diversity and Work*, ed. Quinetta M. Roberson, 253–79. Oxford: Oxford University Press.

Dobbin, Frank, and John R. Sutton. 1998. "The Strength of a Weak State: The Rights Revolution and the Rise of Human Resource Management Divisions." *American Journal of Sociology* 104(2):441–76.

Dobbin, Frank, John R. Sutton, John W. Meyer, and Richard Scott. 1993. "Equal Opportunity Law and the Construction of Internal Labor Markets." *American Journal of Sociology* 99(2):396–427.

Dobbin, Frank R. 2006. "Review: Sexual Harassment: The Global and the Local." *Sociological Inquiry*. 21(4):709–13

——. 2009. *Inventing Equal Opportunity*. Princeton, NJ: Princeton University Press.

Doering, Mildred, Susan Rhodes, and Michael Schuster. 1983. *The Aging Worker*. Beverly Hills, CA: Sage.

Dombroski, Matthew A. 2005. "Securing Access to Transportation for the Urban Poor." *Columbia Law Review* 105:503–36.

Donohue, John J., and James Heckman. 1991. "Continuous versus Episodic Change: The Impact of Civil Rights Policy on the Economic Status of Blacks." *Journal of Economic Literature* 29: 1603–643.

Donohue, John J., and Peter Siegelman. 1991. "The Changing Nature of Employment Discrimination Litigation." *Stanford Law Review* 43:983–1033.

——. 1993. "Law and Macroeconomics: Employment Discrimination over the Business Cycle." *Southern California Law Review* 66:709–65.

——. 2005. "The Evolution of Employment Discrimination Law in the 1990s: A Preliminary Empirical Investigation." In *The Handbook of Employment Discrimination Research: Rights and Realities*, ed. Laura Beth Nielsen and Robert L. Nelson, 261–84. Dordrecht, Netherlands: Springer.

Dovidio, John F., John C. Brigham, Blair T. Johnson, and Samuel L. Gaertner. 1996. "Stereotyping, Prejudice, and Discrimination: Another Look." In *Stereotypes and Stereotyping*, ed. C. Neil Macrae, Charles Stangor, and Miles Hewstone, 276–319. New York: Guilford.

Dovidio, John F., Kerry Kawakami, and Samuel L Gaertner. 2002. "Implicit and Explicit Prejudice and Interracial Interaction." *Journal of Personality and Social Psychology* 82(1):62–68.

Drahozal, Christopher R. 2007. "Arbitration Costs and Form Accessibility: Empirical Evidence." *University of Michigan Journal of Law Reform* 41:813–42.

Duncan, Birt L. 1976. "Differential Social Perception and Attribution of Intergroup Violence: Testing the Lower Limits of Stereotyping of Blacks." *Journal of Personality and Social Psychology* 34(4):590–98.

Duncan, Colin. 2001. "Ageism, Early Exit, and the Rationality of Age-Based Discrimination." In *Ageism in Work and Employment*, ed. Ian Golver and Mohamed Branine, 25–46. Burlington, VT: Ashgate.

Edelman, Lauren B. 1990. "Legal Environments and Organizational Governance: The Expansion of Due Process in the American Workplace." *American Journal of Sociology* 95(6):1401–40.

——. 1992. "Legal Ambiguity and Symbolic Structures: Organizational Mediation of Civil Rights Law." *American Journal of Sociology* 97(6):1531–76.

——. 2002. "Legality and the Endogeneity of Law." In *Legality and Community: On the Intellectual Legacy of Philip Selznick*, ed. Robert A. Kagan, Martin Krygier, and Kenneth Winston, 187–202. Lanham, MD: Rowman & Littlefield; Berkeley, CA: Berkeley Public Policy Press.

——. 2016. *Working Law: Courts, Corporations, and Symbolic Civil Rights*. Chicago: University of Chicago Press.

Edelman, Lauren B., Steven E. Abraham, and Howard S. Erlanger. 1992. "Professional Construction of Law: The Inflated Threat of Wrongful Discharge." *Law and Society Review* 26(1):47–83.

Edelman, Lauren B., Sally Riggs Fuller, and Iona Mara-Drita. 2001. "Diversity Rhetoric and the Managerialization of Law." *American Journal of Sociology* 106(6):1589–1641.

Edelman, Lauren B., Linda H. Krieger, Scott R. Eliason, Catherine R. Albiston, and Virginia Mellema. 2011. "When Organizations Rule: Judicial Deference to Institutionalized Employment Structures." *American Journal of Sociology* 117(3):888–954.

Edelman, Lauren B., Christopher Uggen, and Howard S. Erlanger. 1999. "The Endogeneity of Legal Regulation: Grievance Procedures as Rational Myth." *American Journal of Sociology* 105(2):406–54.

Edsall, Thomas Byrne. 1992. *Chain Reaction: The Impact of Race, Rights, and Taxes on American Politics*. New York: W. W. Norton.

Edwards, Richard. 1979. *Contested Terrain*. New York: Basic Books.

EEOC. 2013. *EEO-1 National Aggregate Report*. https://www.eeoc.gov/eeoc/statistics/employment/jobpat-ee01/index.cfm. Accessed May 16, 2016.

———. 2014a. *Enforcement Statistics 1992–2014*. https://www.eeoc.gov/eeoc/statistics/enforcement/index.cfm. Accessed May 16, 2016.

———. 2014b. *Strategic Plan*. http://www.eeoc.gov/eeoc/plan/2014par_performance.cfm. Accessed May 16, 2016.

Eigen, Zev J., David S. Sherwyn, and Nicholos F. Menillo. 2014. "When Rules Are Made to Be Broken." *Northwestern University Law Review* 109(1):109–72.

Eisenberg, Theodore. 2004. "Appeal Rates and Outcomes in Tried and Nontried Cases: Further Exploration of Anti-Plaintiff Appellate Outcomes." *Journal of Empirical Legal Studies* 1(3):659–88.

Eisenberg, Theodore, and Kevin M. Clermont. 2015. "Plaintiphobia in the Supreme Court." *Cornell Law Review* 100:193–212.

Emirbayer, Mustafa. 1997. "Manifesto for a Relational Sociology." *American Journal of Sociology* 103(2):281–317.

Engel, David M. 1984. "The Oven Bird's Song: Insiders, Outsiders, and Personal Injuries in an American Community." *Law and Society Review* 18(4):551–82.

Engel, David M., and Frank W. Munger. 2003. *Rights of Inclusion: Law and Identity in the Life Stories of Americans with Disabilities*. Chicago: University of Chicago Press.

England, Paula. 1992. *Comparable Worth: Theories and Evidence*. New York: Aldine de Gruyter.

Entman, Robert M. 1992. "Blacks in the News: Television, Modern Racism and Cultural Change." *Journalism and Mass Communication Quarterly* 69(2):341–61.

Epp, Charles R. 1998. *The Rights Revolution: Lawyers, Activists, and Supreme Courts in Comparative Perspective*. Chicago: University of Chicago Press.

———. 2009. *Making Rights Real: Activists, Bureaucrats, and the Creation of the Legalistic State*. Chicago: University of Chicago Press.

Epstein, Lee, and C. K. Rowland. 1991. "Debunking the Myth of Interest Group Invincibility in the Courts." *American Political Science Review* 85(1):205–17.

Estreicher, Samuel, and Michael C. Harper. 2000. *Cases and Materials on Employment Discrimination and Employment Law*. St. Paul, MN: West Group.

Ewick, Patricia, and Susan S. Silbey. 1998. *The Common Place of Law: Stories from Everyday Life*. Chicago: University of Chicago Press.

Farhang, Sean. 2010. *The Litigation State: Public Regulation and Private Lawsuits in the U.S.* Princeton, NJ: Princeton University Press.

Feagin, Joseph R. 1991. "The Continuing Significance of Race: Antiblack Discrimination in Public Places." *American Sociological Review* 56(1):101–16.

——. 2010. *The White Racial Frame: Centuries of Framing and Counter-Framing*. New York: Routledge.

Feder, Jody, and Cynthia Brougher. 2013. *Sexual Orientation and Gender Identity Discrimination in Employment: A Legislative Analysis of the Employment Nondiscrimination Act (ENDA)*. Washington, D.C.: Congressional Research Service.

Feeley, Malcolm M. 1979. *The Process Is the Punishment: Handling Cases in a Lower Criminal Court*. New York: Russell Sage Foundation.

Felstiner, William, Richard Abel, and Austin Sarat. 1980. "The Emergence and Transformation of Disputes: Naming, Blaming, and Claiming." *Law and Society Review* 15(3/4):631–55.

Fenton, Zanita E. 1998. "Domestic Violence in Black and White: Racialized Gender Stereotypes in Gender Violence." *Columbia Journal of Gender and Law* 8(1):1–42.

Fiske, Susan T. 1998. "Stereotyping, Prejudice, and Discrimination." In *Handbook of Social Psychology*, ed. D. T. Gilbert, Susan T. Fiske, and G. Lindzey, 357–411. New York: McGraw–Hill.

——. 2011. *Envy Up, Scorn Down. How Status Divides Us*. New York: Russell Sage Foundation.

Fiske, Susan T., A. J. Cuddy, P. Glick, and J. Xu. 2002. "A Model of (Often Mixed) Stereotype Content: Competence and Warmth Respectively Follow from Perceived Status and Competition." *Journal of Personality and Social Psychology* 82(6):878–902.

Fiske, Susan T., and Tiane L. Lee. 2008. "Stereotypes and Prejudice Create Workplace Discrimination." In *Diversity at Work*, ed. Arthur P. Brief. New York: Cambridge University Press.

Fleury–Steiner, Benjamin D. 2004. *Jurors' Stories of Death: How America's Death Penalty Invests in Inequality*. Ann Arbor: University of Michigan Press.

Freeman, Alan. 1998 [1982]. "Antidiscrimination Law from 1954 to 1989: Uncertainty, Contradiction, Rationalization, Denial." In *The Politics of Law: A Progressive Critique*, ed. David Kairys, 285–311. New York: Basic Books.

Fryer, Roland G., Devah Pager, and Jorg Spenkuch. 2013. "Racial Disparities in Job Finding and Offered Wages." *Journal of Law and Economics* 56:633–89.

Galanter, Marc S. 1974. "Why the 'Haves' Come Out Ahead: Speculations on the Limits of Legal Change." *Law and Society Review* 9(1):95–160.

——. 1983a. *The Radiating Effects of Courts*. New York: Longman.

——. 1983b. "Reading the Landscape of Disputes: What We Know and Don't Know (and Think We Know) about Our Allegedly Contentious and Litigious Society." *UCLA Law Review* 31(1):4–71.

Gallup, Inc. 2004. "Americans Still Believe O. J. Simpson Is Guilty."

Garland, David. 2001. "Introduction: The Meaning of Mass Imprisonment." In *Mass Imprisonment: Social Causes and Consequences*, ed. David Garland, 1–3. London: Sage.

Glick, Peter, and Susan T. Fiske. 1996. "The Ambivalent Sexism Inventory: Differentiating Hostile and Benevolent Sexism." *Journal of Personality and Social Psychology* 70(3):491–512.

——. 1997. "Hostile and Benevolent Sexism: Measuring Ambivalent Sexist Attitudes toward Women." *Psychology of Women Quarterly* 21(1):119–35.

Gomez, Laura. 2010. "Understanding Law and Race as Mutually Constitutive: An Invitation to Explore an Emerging Field." *Annual Review of Law and Social Science* 6:487–505.

Gordon, Randall A., and Richard D. Arvey. 2004. "Age Bias in Laboratory and Field Settings: A Meta-Analytic Investigation." *Journal of Applied Psychology* 34(3):468–92.

Gramsci, Antonio. 1971. *Selections from the Prison Notebooks*. Ed. and trans. by Quintin Hoare and Jeffrey Nowell Smith. New York: International Publishers.

Green, Tristin K. 2003. "Discrimination in Workplace Dynamics: Toward a Structural Account of Disparate Treatment Theory." *Harvard Civil Rights–Civil Liberties Law Review* 38:91–157.

Green, Tristin K. 2016. *Discrimination Laundering: The Rise of Organizational Innocence and the Crisis of Equal Opportunity Law*. Cambridge: Cambridge University Press.

Grodsky, Eric, and Devah Pager. 2001. "The Structure of Disadvantage: Individual and Occupational Determinants of the Black-White Wage Gap." *American Sociological Review* 66(4):542–67.

Gulati, Mitu, and Laura Beth Nielsen. 2006. "A New Legal Realist Perspective on Employment Discrimination." *Law and Social Inquiry* 31(4):797–800.

Hagan, John, Carla Shedd, and Monique R. Payne. 2005. "Race, Ethnicity, and Youth Perceptions of Criminal Injustice." *American Sociological Review* 70(3):381–407.

Halaby, Charles. 1986. "Worker Attachment and Workplace Authority." *American Sociological Review* 51(5):634–49.

Haltom, William, and Michael McCann. 2004. *Distorting the Law: Politics, Media, and the Litigation Crisis*. Chicago: University of Chicago Press.

Hans, Valerie P. 2000. *Business on Trial: The Civil Jury and Corporate Responsibility*. New Haven, CT: Yale University Press.

Harrell, Shelly P. 2000. "A Multidimensional Conceptualization of Racism-related Stress: Implications for Well-Being of People of Color." *American Journal of Orthopsychiatry* 70(1):42–57.

Harris, Angela P. 1990. "Race and Essentialism in Feminist Legal Theory." *Stanford Law Review* 42:581–616.

Harris-Perry, Melissa V. 2011. *Sister Citizen: Shame, Stereotypes, and Black Women in America*. New Haven, CT: Yale University Press.

Hassell, Barbara L., and Pamela L. Perrewe. 1995. "An Examination of Beliefs about Older Workers: Do Stereotypes Still Exist?" *Journal of Organizational Behavior* 16(5):457–68.

Heckman, James J. 1998. "Detecting Discrimination." *Journal of Economic Perspectives* 12(2):101–16.

——. 2011. "The American Family in Black & White: A Post-Racial Strategy for Improving Skills to Promote Equality." *Daedalus* 140(2):70–89.

Heckman, James J., and Paul LaFontaine. 2010. "The American High School Graduation Rate: Trends and Levels." *Review of Economics and Statistics* 92(2):244–62.

Heckman, James J., and Brook S. Payner. 1989. "Determining the Impact of Federal Antidiscrimination Policy on the Economic Status of Blacks: A Study of South Carolina." *American Economic Review* 79(1):138–77.

Heinz, John P., and Edward O. Laumann. 1982. *Chicago Lawyers: The Social Structure of the Bar*. New York: Russell Sage and Basic Books.

——. 1994. *Chicago Lawyers, Revised Edition: The Social Structure of the Bar*: Northwestern University Press.

Heyer, Katharina. 2007. "Review: A Disability Lens on Sociolegal Research: Reading Rights of Inclusion from a Disability Studies Perspective." *Law and Social Inquiry* 32(1):261–93.

Higgins, Tracy E., and Laura A. Rosenbury. 2000. "Agency, Equality, and Antidiscrimination Law." *Cornell Law Review* 85:1194–1220.

Hirsh, C. Elizabeth. 2008. "Settling for Less? Organizational Determinants of Discrimination-Charge Outcomes." *Law and Society Review* 42(2):239–74.

——. 2014. "Beyond Treatment and Impact: A Context-Oriented Approach to Employment Discrimination." *American Behavioral Scientist* 58(2):256–73.

Hirsh, C. Elizabeth, and Sabino Kornrich. 2008. "The Context of Discrimination: Workplace Conditions, Institutional Environments, and Sex and Race Discrimination Charges." *American Journal of Sociology* 113(5):1394–1432.

Hofferth, Sandra L. 1984. "Kin Networks, Race, and Family Structure." *Journal of Marriage and the Family* 46:791–806.

Huffman, Matt, and Philip Cohen. 2004. "Racial Wage Inequality: Job Segregation and Devaluation across U.S. Labor Markets." *American Journal of Sociology* 109(4):902–36.

Hurwitz, Jon, and Mark Peffley. 1997. "Public Perceptions of Race and Crime:

The Role of Racial Stereotypes." *American Journal of Political Science* 41(2):375–401.

Hutchens, Robert M. 1988. "Do Job Opportunities Decline with Age?" *Industrial & Labor Relations Review* 42(1):89–99.

Jacobs, Michelle S. 1997. "People from the Footnotes: The Missing Element in Client-Centered Counseling." *Golden Gate University Law Review* 27:345–422.

Jenkins, Richard. 2000. "Categorization: Identity: Social Process, and Epistemology." *Current Sociology* 48(3):7–25.

Jerolmack, Colin, and Shamus Khan. 2014. "Talk is Cheap: Ethnography and the Attitudinal Fallacy." *Sociological Methods and Research* 43:178–209.

Johnson, Richard W., and David Neumark. 1997. "Age Discrimination, Job Separations, and Employment Status of Older Workers: Evidence from Self-Reports." *Journal of Human Resources* 32(4):779–811.

Jordan, Alexander H., and Emily M. Zitek. 2012. "Marital Status Bias in Perceptions of Employees." *Basic and Applied Social Psychology* 34(5):474–81.

Joseph, Gloria I. 1981. "White Promotion, Black Survival." In *Common Differences: Conflicts in Black and White Feminist Perspectives*, ed. Gloria I. Joseph and Jill Lewis, 19–42. Garden City: Anchor–Doubleday.

Kagan, Robert A. 2001. *Adversarial Legalism: The American Way of Law.* Cambridge, MA: Harvard University Press.

Kairys, David. 1998. *The Politics of Law: A Progressive Critique.* New York: Basic Books.

Kaiser, Cheryl, and Carol Miller. 2001. "Stop Complaining! The Social Costs of Making Attributions of Discrimination." *Personality and Social Psychology Bulletin* 27(2):254–63.

Kaiser, Cheryl R., and Carol T. Miller. 2003. "Derogating the Victim: The Interpersonal Consequences of Blaming Events on Discrimination." *Group Processes & Intergroup Relations* 6(3):227–37.

Kaiser, Cheryl R, and Jennifer S Pratt-Hyatt. 2009. "Distributing Prejudice Unequally: Do Whites Direct Their Prejudice toward Strongly Identified Minorities?" *Journal of Personality and Social Psychology* 96(2):432–45.

Kaiser, Cheryl R., S. Shatzki, and M. Bartholomew. 2004. "Meritocracy Beliefs under Threat: Investigating the Interpersonal Consequences of Claiming Discrimination." Presented at the Fifth Annual Meeting of the Society for Personality and Social Psychology, Austin, TX.

Kalev, Alexandra, and Frank Dobbin. 2006. "Enforcement of Civil Rights Law in Private Workplaces: The Effects of Compliance Reviews and Lawsuits over Time." *Law and Social Inquiry* 31(4):855–903.

Kalev, Alexandra, Frank Dobbin, and Erin Kelly. 2006. "Best Practices or Best Guesses? Assessing the Efficacy of Corporate Affirmative Action Policies." *American Sociological Review* 71(4):589–617.

Kalman, Laura. 1986. *Legal Realism at Yale 1927–1960*. Chapel Hill: University of North Carolina Press.

Kang, Jerry. 2005. "Trojan Horses of Race." *Harvard Law Review* 118(5): 1489–593.

Kang, Jerry, and Mazarin R. Banaji. 2006. "Fair Measures: A Behavioral Realist Revision of "Affirmative Action." *California Law Review* 94:1063–1118.

Kang, Jerry, and Kristin Lane. 2010. "Seeing through Colorblindness: Implicit Bias and the Law." *UCLA Law Review* 58:465–520.

Katz, Jack. 1977. "Lawyers for the Poor in Transition." *Law and Society Review* 12(Winter):275–300.

Keele, Denise M., Robert W. Malmsheimer, Donald W. Floyd, and Lianjun Zhang. 2009. "An Analysis of Ideological Effects in Published versus Unpublished Judicial Opinions." *Journal of Empirical Legal Studies* 6(1):213–39.

Kim, Pauline T. 1997. "Bargaining with Imperfect Information: A Study of Worker Perceptions of Legal Protection in an At-Will World." *Cornell Law Review* 83:105–60.

Kinder, Donald R, and David O. Sears. 1981. "Prejudice and Politics: Symbolic Racism versus Racial Threats to the Good Life." *Journal of Personality and Social Psychology* 40(3):414–31.

King, Mae C. 1973. "The Politics of Sexual Stereotypes." *Black Scholar* 4(6–7): 12–23.

King, Ryan D., and Darren Wheelock. 2007. "Group Threat and Social Control: Race, Perceptions of Minorities and the Desire to Punish." *Social Forces* 85(3):1255–80.

Kluegel, James. 1990. "Trends in Whites' Explanations of the Black-White Gap in Socioeconomic Status, 1977–1989." *American Sociological Review* 55(4): 512–25.

Kluegel, James, and Lawrence D. Bobo. 2001. "Perceived Group Discrimination and Policy Attitudes: The Sources and Consequences of the Race and Gender Gaps." In *Urban Inequality: Evidence from Four Cities*, ed. Alice O'Connor, Chris Tilly, and Lawrence D. Bobo, 163–98. New York: Russell Sage Foundation.

Kluegel, James R. 1986. "If There Isn't a Problem, You Don't Need a Solution: The Bases of Contemporary Affirmative Action." *American Behavioral Scientist* 28(6):762.

Kotkin, Minna J. 2007. "Outing Outcomes: An Empirical Study of Confidential Employment Discrimination Settlements." *Washington and Lee Law Review* 64:111–64.

Krieger, Linda Hamilton. 1995. "The Content of Our Categories: A Cognitive Bias Approach to Discrimination and Equal Employment Opportunity." *Stanford Law Review* 47:1161–248.

——. 2000. "Foreword: Backlash against the ADA: Interdisciplinary Perspectives and Implications for Social Justice Strategies." *Berkeley Journal of Employment and Labor Law* 21(1):1–19.

Krieger, Linda Hamilton, Rachel Kahn Best, and Lauren B. Edelman. 2015. "When 'Best Practices' Win, Employees Lose: Symbolic Compliance and Judicial Inference in Federal Equal Employment Opportunity Cases." *Law and Social Inquiry* 40(4):843–79.

Krieger, Linda Hamilton, and Susan T. Fiske. 2006. "Behavioral Realism in Employment Discrimination and Law: Implicit Bias and Disparate Treatment." *California Law Review* 94(4):997–1062.

Kritzer, Herbert M. 1990. *The Justice Broker: Lawyers and Ordinary Litigation.* New York: Oxford University Press.

——. 1993. "Lawyer's Fees and the Holy Grail: Where Should Clients Search for Value." *Judicature* 77(4):187–90.

——. 1997. "Contingency Fee Lawyers as Gatekeepers in the Civil Justice System." *Judicature* 81(1):22–29.

Lamont, Michèle, and Marcel Fournier. 1992. *Cultivating Differences: Symbolic Boundaries and the Making of Inequality.* Chicago: University of Chicago Press.

Landrine, Hope, and Elizabeth A. Klonoff. 1996. "The Schedule of Racist Events: A Measure of Racial Discrimination and a Study of Its Negative Physical and Mental Health Consequences." *Journal of Black Psychology* 22(2):144–68.

Laub, John, and Robert Sampson. 2004. "Strategies for Bridging the Quantitative and Qualitative Divide: Studying Crime over the Life Course." *Research in Human Development* 1(1/2):81–99.

Lind, E. Allan, and Tom R. Tyler. 1988. *The Social Psychology of Procedural Justice.* New York: Plenum.

Lind, E. Allan, Carol T. Kulik, Maureen Ambrose, and Maria V. de Vera Park. 1993. "Individual and Corporate Dispute Resolution: Using Procedural Fairness as a Decision Heuristic." *Administrative Science Quarterly* 38(2):224–51.

Lipsky, Michael. 2010 [1980]. *Street-Level Bureaucracy: Dilemmas of the Individual in Public Services.* New York: Russell Sage Foundation.

Litras, Marika F. X. 2000. *Civil Rights Complaints in U.S. District Courts 1990–98.* US Department of Justice, Bureau of Justice Statistics, Federal Justice Statistics Program, NCJ 173427.

——. 2002. *Civil Rights Complaints in U.S. District Courts 2000.* US Department of Justice, Bureau of Justice Statistics, Federal Justice Statistics Program, NCJ 193979.

Llewellyn, Karl N. 1931. "Some Realism about Realism—Responding to Dean Pound." *Harvard Law Review* 44:1222.

——. 1950. "Remarks on the Theory of Appellate Decision and the Rules or

Canons about How Statutes Are to Be Construed." *Vanderbilt Law Review* 3:395–406.

Lofland, John, and Lyn H. Lofland. 1995. *Analyzing Social Settings: A Guide to Qualitative Research and Analysis.* Belmont, CA: Wadsworth.

Loury, Glenn. 2002. *The Anatomy of Racial Inequality.* Cambridge, MA: Harvard University Press.

Lowery, Brian S., Miguel M Unzueta, Eric D. Knowles, and Phillip Atiba Goff. 2006. "Concern for the In-Group and Opposition to Affirmative Action." *Journal of Personality and Social Psychology* 90(6):961–74.

Lucas, Samuel R. 1994. "Effects of Race and Gender Discrimination in the United States, 1940–1980." PhD diss. University of Wisconsin-Madison.

——. 2009. *Theorizing Discrimination in an Era of Contested Prejudice.* Philadelphia: Temple University Press.

MacKinnon, Catharine. 1979. *Sexual Harassment of Working Women: A Case of Sex Discrimination.* New Haven, CT: Yale University Press.

Major, Brenda, and Cheryl Kaiser. 2005. "Perceiving and Claiming Discrimination." In *Handbook of Employment Discrimination Research: Rights and Realities*, ed. Laura Beth Nielsen and Robert L. Nelson, 285–300. Amsterdam: Springer.

Marks, John H. 2002. "Smoke, Mirrors, and the Disappearance of 'Vicarious' Liability: The Emergence of a Dubious Summary-Judgement Safe Harbor for Employers Whose Supervisory Personnel Commit Hostile Environment Workplace Harassment." *Houston Law Review* 38:1401–62.

Marshall, Anna-Maria. 2003. "Injustice Frames, Legality, and the Everyday Construction of Sexual Harassment." *Law and Social Inquiry* 28(3):659–89.

Mather, Lynn A., Craig A. McEwen, and Richard J. Maiman. 2001. *Divorce Lawyers at Work: Varieties of Professionalism in Practice.* New York: Oxford University Press.

McCann, Michael. 1994. *Rights at Work: Pay Equity Reform and the Politics of Legal Mobilization.* Chicago: University of Chicago Press.

——. 2006. "Law and Social Movements: Contemporary Perspectives." *Annual Review of Law and Social Science* 2:17–38.

McCann, Michael, George Lovell, and Kirstine Taylor. 2015. "Covering Legal Mobilization: A Bottom-Up Analysis of *Wards Cove v. Atonio*." *Law and Social Inquiry* 41(1):61–99.

McPherson, Miller, Lynn Smith-Lovin, and James M Cook. 2001. "Birds of a Feather: Homophily in Social Networks." *Annual Review of Sociology* 27:415–44.

Merry, Sally E. 1990. *Getting Justice and Getting Even: Legal Consciousness among Working Class Americans.* Chicago: University of Chicago Press.

Michelson, Ethan. 2006. "The Practice of Law as an Obstacle to Justice: Chinese Lawyers at Work." *Law and Society Review* 40(1):1–38.

Miles, Matthew B., and Michael A. Huberman. 1994. *Qualitative Data Analysis: An Expanded Sourcebook*. Thousand Oaks, CA: SAGE.

Miller, Andrea. 2015. "The Separate Sphere Model of Family Responsibilities Discrimination in the Workplace." Unpublished manuscript on file with authors.

Miller, Richard E., and Austin Sarat. 1981. "Grievances, Claims, and Disputes: Assessing the Adversary Culture." *Law and Society Review* 15:525–66.

Miller–Cribbs, Julie E., and Naomi B. Farber. 2008. "Kin Networks and Poverty among African Americans: Past and Present." *Social Work* 53(1):43–51.

Mills, Linda G. 1993. "A Calculus for Bias: How Malingering Females and Dependent Housewives Fare in the Social Security Disability System." *Harvard Women's Law Journal* 16:211–32.

Morgan, Phoebe A. 1999. "Risking Relationships: Understanding the Litigation Choices of Sexually Harassed Women." *Law and Society Review* 33(1):67–92.

Moss, Scott A. 2013. "Bad Briefs, Bad Law, Bad Markets: Documenting the Poor Quality of Plaintiffs' Briefs, Its Impact on the Law, and the Market Failure It Reflects." *Emory Law Journal* 63(1):59–125.

Mulroy, Quinn. 2011. "Enforcing Rights Protections: The Regulatory Power of Private Litigation and the Equal Employment Opportunity Commission." Presented at the Annual Meeting of the American Political Science Association, Seattle, WA.

Mustillo, Sarah, Nancy Krieger, Erica P Gunderson, Stephen Sidney, Heather McCreath, and Catarina I Kiefe. 2004. "Self-Reported Experiences of Racial Discrimination and Black-White Differences in Preterm and Low-Birthweight Deliveries: The CARDIA Study." *American Journal of Public Health* 94(12):2125–31.

Myrick, Amy. 2013. "Facing Your Criminal Record: Expungement and the Collateral Problem of Wrongfully Represented Self." *Law and Society Review* 47(1):73–104.

Myrick, Amy, Robert L Nelson, and Laura Beth Nielsen. 2012. "Race and Representation: Racial Disparities in Legal Representation for Employment Civil Rights Plaintiffs." *New York University Journal of Legislation & Public Policy* 15:705–59.

Neckerman, Kathryn M., and Joleen Kirschenman. 1991. "Hiring Strategies, Racial Bias, and Inner–City Workers." *Social Problems* 38(4):433–47.

Nelson, Robert L. 1988. *Partners with Power: The Social Transformation of the Large Law Firm*. Berkeley: University of California Press.

Nelson, Robert L., Ellen Berrey, and Laura Beth Nielsen. 2008. "Divergent Paths: Conflicting Conceptions of Employment Discrimination in Law and the Social Sciences." *Annual Review of Law and Social Science* 4:103–22.

Nelson, Robert L., and William P. Bridges. 1999. *Legalizing Gender Inequality:*

Courts, Markets, and Unequal Pay for Women in America. Cambridge: Cambridge University Press.

Nelson, Robert L., and Laura Beth Nielsen. 1999. "Cops, Counsel and Entrepreneurs: Constructing the Role of Inside Counsel in Large Corporations." *Law and Society Review* 34(2): 457–94.

Neumark, David. 1996. "Sex Discrimination in the Restaurant Industry: An Audit Study." *Quarterly Journal of Economics* 111(3):915–41.

Nielsen, Laura Beth. 1999. "Paying Workers or Paying Lawyers: Employee Termination in the United States and Canada." *Law and Policy* 21(3):247–82.

——. 2000. "Situating Legal Consciousness: Experiences and Attitudes of Ordinary Citizens about Law and Street Harassment." *Law and Society Review* 34:1055–99.

——. 2004. "The Work of Rights and the Work Rights Do: A Critical Empirical Approach." In *The Blackwell Companion to Law and Society*, ed. Austin Sarat, 63–79. Oxford: Blackwell.

——. 2010. "The Need for Multi-Method Approaches in Empirical Legal Research." In *The Oxford Handbook of Empirical Legal Research*, ed. Peter Cane and Herbert M. Kritzer, 951–75. New York: Oxford University Press.

Nielsen, Laura Beth, and Aaron Beim. 2004. "Media Misrepresentation: Title VII, Print Media, and Public Perceptions of Discrimination Litigation." *Stanford Law and Policy Review* 15:237–365.

Nielsen, Laura Beth, Amy Myrick, and Jill D. Weinberg. 2011. "Siding with Science: In Defense of ASA's Dukes vs. Wal-Mart Amicus Brief." *Sociological Methods & Research* 40(4):646–67.

Nielsen, Laura Beth, and Robert L. Nelson. 2005. "Scaling the Pyramid: A Sociolegal Model of Employment Discrimination Litigation," In *Handbook of Employment Discrimination Research: Rights and Realities*, ed. Laura Beth Nielsen and Robert L. Nelson, 3–35. Amsterdam: Springer.

Nielsen, Laura Beth, Robert L. Nelson, and Ryon Lancaster. 2010. "Individual Justice or Collective Legal Mobilization? Employment Discrimination Litigation in the Post–Civil Rights United States." *Journal of Empirical Legal Studies* 7(2):175–201.

Nielsen, Laura Beth, Robert L. Nelson, Ryon Lancaster, and Nicholas Pedriana. 2008. *Characteristics and Outcomes of Federal Employment Discrimination Litigation, 1987–2003*. Chicago: American Bar Foundation.

Niemeyer, Linda Ogden. 1991. "Social Labeling, Stereotyping, and Observer Bias in Workers' Compensation: The Impact of Provider-Patient Interaction on Outcome." *Journal of Occupational Rehabilitation* 1(4):251–69.

O'Barr, William M., and John M. Conley. 1985. "Litigant Satisfaction versus Legal Adequacy in Small Claims Court Narratives." *Law and Society Review* 19(4):661–701.

Obasogie, Osagie K. 2014. *Blinded by Sight: Seeing Race through the Eyes of the Blind*. Palo Alto, CA: Stanford University Press.

Oliver, Michael. 1990. *The Politics of Disablement: A Sociological Approach*. New York: St. Martin Press.

——. 1998. "Theories of Disability in Health Practice and Research." *British Medical Journal* 317(7170):1446–49.

Olson, Walter K. 1997. *The Excuse Factory: How Employment Law Is Paralyzing the American Workplace*. New York: Martin Kessler Books.

Oppenheimer, David Benjamin. 2003. "Verdicts Matter: An Empirical Study of California Employment Discrimination and Wrongful Discharge Jury Verdicts Reveals Low Success Rates for Women and Minorities." *University of California Davis Law Review* 37:511–66.

Pager, Devah. 2003. "The Mark of a Criminal Record." *American Journal of Sociology* 108(5):937–75.

Pager, Devah, and Lincoln Quillian. 2005. "Walking the Talk? What Employers Say versus What They Do." *American Sociological Review* 70(3):355–80.

Pager, Devah, Bruce Western, and Bart Bonikowski. 2009. "Discrimination in a Low-Wage Labor Market: A Field Experiment." *American Sociological Review* 74(5):777–99.

Parsons, Talcott. 1951. *The Social System*. Glencoe, IL: Free Press.

Pedriana, Nicholas, and Amanda Abraham. 2006. "Now You See Them, Now You Don't: The Legal Field and Newspaper Desegregation of Sex-Segregated Help Wanted Ads 1965–75." *Law and Social Inquiry* 31(4):905–38.

Pedriana, Nicholas, and Robin Stryker. 2004. "The Strength of a Weak Agency: Enforcement of Title VII of the 1964 Civil Rights Act and the Expansion of State Capacity, 1965–1971." *American Journal of Sociology* 110(3):709–60.

Perrow, Charles. 1986. *Complex Organizations: A Critical Essay*. New York: McGraw–Hill.

Perry, Elissa L., Wallace Hendricks, and Emir Broadbent. 2000. "An Exploration of Access and Treatment Discrimination and Job Satisfaction among College Graduates with and without Physical Disabilities." *Human Relations* 53(7):923–55.

Pew Research Center. 2016. On Views of Race and Inequality, Blacks and Whites Are Worlds Apart. June 27. See http://www.pewsocialtrends.org/2016/06/27/on-views-of-race-and-inequality-blacks-and-whites-are-worlds-apart/. Accessed Oct. 4, 2016.

Plickert, Gabriele, and Ronit Dinovitzer, Bryant Garth, Robert Nelson, Rebecca Sandefur, Joyce Sterling, and David Wilkins. 2014. *After the JD III: Third Results from a National Study of Legal Careers*. Chicago: American Bar Foundation and NALP Foundation for Law Career Research and Education.

Polletta, Francesca. 2006. *It Was Like a Fever: Storytelling in Protest and Politics*. Chicago: University of Chicago Press.

Post, Robert C., and Reva B. Siegel. 2000. "Equal Protection by Law: Federal Antidiscrimination Legislation after Morrison and Kimel. *Yale Law Journal* 110:441–526.

Priest, George, and Benjamin Klein. 1984. "The Selection of Disputes for Litigation." *Journal of Legal Studies* 13(1):1–55.

Quillian, Lincoln. 2006. "New Approaches to Understanding Racial Prejudice and Discrimination." *Annual Review of Sociology* 32:299–328.

Quillian, Lincoln, and Ole Hexel. 2016. "Trends and Patterns in Racial Discrimination in Hiring in America, 1974–2015." Paper presented at the Meetings of the Population Association of America, Washington, DC.

Quillian, Lincoln, and Devah Pager. 2001. "Black Neighbors, Higher Crime? The Role of Racial Stereotypes in Evaluations of Neighborhood Crime." *American Journal of Sociology* 107(3):717–67.

Randall, Susan. 2004. "Judicial Attitudes toward Arbitration and the Resurgence of Unconscionability." *Buffalo Law Review* 52:185–224.

Rembis, Michael A. 2010. "Beyond the Binary: Rethinking the Social Model of Disabled Sexuality." *Sexuality and Disability* 28(1):51–60.

Reskin, Barbara. 1993. "Sex Segregation in the Workplace." *Annual Review of Sociology* 19:241–70.

——. 2012. "The Race Discrimination System." *Annual Review of Sociology* 38:17–35.

Reyna, Christine, P. J. Henry, William Korfmacher, and Amanda Tucker. 2005. "Examining the Principles of Principled Conservatism: The Role of Responsibility Stereotypes as Cues for Deservingness in Racial Policy Decisions." *Journal of Personality and Social Psychology* 90(1):109–28.

Richeson, Jennifer A., and J. Nicole Shelton. 2006. "A Social Psychological Perspective on the Stigmatization of Older Adults." In *When I'm 64*, ed. Laura L. Carstensen and Christine R. Hartel, 174–208. Washington, DC: National Academies Press.

Ridgeway, Cecilia L. 1997. "Interaction and the Conservation of Gender Inequality: Considering Employment." *American Sociological Review* 62(2): 218–35.

——. 2011. *Framed by Gender*. New York: Oxford University Press.

——. 2014. "Why Status Matters for Inequality." *American Sociological Review* 79(1):1–16.

Rivera, Lauren. 2015. *Pedigree: How Elite Students Get Elite Jobs*. Princeton, NJ: Princeton University Press.

Robert, Pamela M., and Sharon L. Harlan. 2006. "Mechanisms of Disability Discrimination in Large Bureaucratic Organizations: Ascriptive Inequalities in the Workplace." *Sociological Quarterly* 47(4):599–630.

Roscigno, Vincent J. 2007. *The Face of Discrimination: How Race and Gender Impact Work and Home Lives*. New York: Rowman & Littlefield.

——. 2011. "Power, Revisited." *Social Forces* 90(2):349–74.

Roscigno, Vincent J., and Randy Hodson. 2004. "The Organizational and Social Foundations of Worker Resistance." *American Sociological Review* 69(1):14–39.

Roscigno, Vincent J., and George Wilson. 2014. "The Relational Foundations of Inequality at Work I: Status, Interaction, and Culture." *American Behavioral Scientist* 58:219–27.

Rosen, Benson, and Thomas H. Jerdee. 1976. "The Nature of Job-Related Age Stereotypes." *Journal of Applied Psychology* 61(2):180–83.

Rosen, Robert Eli. 1988. "Inside Counsel Movement, Professional Judgement and Organizational Representation." *Indiana Law Journal* 64(3):479–553.

Rosenthal, Douglas E. 1974. *Lawyer and Client: Who's in Charge.* New York: Russell Sage Foundation.

Royster, Deirdre A. 2003. *Race and the Invisible Hand: How White Networks Exclude Black Men from Blue-Collar Jobs.* Berkeley: University of California Press.

Rupp, Deborah E., Stephan J. Vodanovich, and Marcus Crede. 2006. "Age Bias in the Workplace: The Impact of Ageism and Causal Attributions." *Journal of Applied Social Psychology* 36(6):1337–64.

Rutherglen, George. 1995. "Discrimination and Its Discontents." *Virginia Law Review* 81:117–47.

——. 1995. "Race to Age: The Expanding Scope of Employment Discrimination Law." *Journal of Legal Studies* 24(2):491–521.

Rutledge, Peter B., and Christopher R. Drahozal. 2014. "Sticky Arbitration Clauses—the Use of Arbitration Clauses after *Concepcion* and *Amex*." *Vanderbilt Law Review* 67(4):955–1014.

Saguy, Abigail. 2003. *What Is Sexual Harassment? From Capitol Hill to the Sorbonne.* Berkeley: University of California Press.

Sandefur, Rebecca L. 2008. "Access to Civil Justice and Race, Class, and Gender Inequality." *Annual Review of Sociology* 34:339–58.

——. 2014. *Accessing Justice in the Contemporary USA: Findings from the Community Needs and Services Study.* Chicago: American Bar Foundation.

——. 2015. "Elements of Professional Expertise: Understanding Relational and Substantive Expertise through Lawyers' Impact." *American Sociological Review* 80(5):909–33.

Santuzzi, Alecia M., Pamela R. Waltz, Lisa M. Finkelstein, and Deborah E. Rupp. 2014. "Invisible Disabilities: Unique Challenges for Employees and Organizations." *Industrial and Organizational Psychology* 7(2):204–19.

Sarat, Austin, and William Felstiner. 1995. *Divorce Lawyers and Their Clients: Power and Meaning in the Legal Process.* New York: Oxford University Press.

Sarat, Austin, and Thomas R. Kearns. 1995. *Law in Everyday Life*. Ann Arbor: University of Michigan Press.

Scheingold, Stuart. 1974. *The Politics of Rights: Lawyers, Public Policy, and Political Change*. New Haven, CT: Yale University Press.

Schlanger, Margo, and Pauline Kim. 2014. "The Equal Employment Opportunity Commission and Structural Reform of the American Workplace." *Washington University Law Review* 91:1519–663.

Schneiderman, David. 2013. "Judging in Secular Times: Max Weber and the Rise of Proportionality." *Supreme Court Law Review (2d)*.

Schultz, Vicki. 2003. "The Sanitized Workplace." *Yale Law Journal* 112: 2061–2193.

Sears, David O., and P. J. Henry. 2003. "The Origins of Symbolic Racism." *Journal of Personality and Social Psychology* 85(2):259–75.

Sears, David O., P. J. Henry, and Rick Kosterman. 2000. "Egalitarian Values and Contemporary Racial Politics." In *Racialized Politics: The Debate about Racism in America*, ed. David O. Sears, Jim Sidanius, and Lawrence Bobo, 75–117. Chicago: University of Chicago Press.

Sellers, Robert M., and J. Nicole Shelton. 2003. "The Role of Racial Identity in Perceived Racial Discrimination." *Journal of Personality and Social Psychology* 84(5):1079–92.

Selznick, Phillip. 1969. *Law, Society, and Industrial Justice*. New York: Russell Sage Foundation.

Seron, Carroll, Gregg Van Ryzin, Martin Frankel, and Jean Kovath. 2001. "The Impact of Legal Counsel on Outcomes for Poor Tenants in New York City's Housing Court: Results of a Randomized Experiment." *Law and Society Review* 35(2):419–34.

Seyfarth Shaw, LLP. 2016. *12th Annual Workplace Class Action Litigation Report*. Accessed at http://www.workplaceclassaction.com/2016/01/its-here-seyfarths-2016-workplace-class-action-report/.

Shavell, Steven. 1996. "Any Frequency of Plaintiff Victory at Trial Is Possible." *Journal of Legal Studies* 25(2):493–501.

Shoben, Elaine. 2004. "Disparate Impact Theory in Employment Discrimination: What's Griggs Still Good For?" *Brandeis Law Journal* 42:597–605.

Siegelman, Peter, and John J. Donohue. 1990. "Studying the Iceberg from Its Tip: A Comparison of Published and Unpublished Employment Discrimination Cases." *Law and Society Review* 24(1):165–74.

Siegelman, Peter, and John J. Donohue III. 1995. "The Selection of Employment Discrimination Disputes for Litigation: Using Business Cycle Effects to Test the Priest–Klein Hypothesis." *Journal of Legal Studies* 24(2):427–62.

Silver–Greenberg, Jessica, and Robert Gebeloff. 2015. "In Arbitration, a 'Privatization of the Justice System.'" *New York Times*. Oct. 31, 2015. http://www

.nytimes.com/2015/11/02/business/dealbook/in-arbitration-a-privatization-of-the-justice-system.html?_r=0. Accessed May 16, 2016.

Sisk, Gregory C., Michael Heise, and Andrew P. Morriss. 1998. "Charting the Influences on the Judicial Mind: An Empirical Study of Judicial Reasoning." *New York University Law Review* 73(5):1377–500.

Skaggs, Sheryl. 2008. "Producing Change or Bagging Opportunity? The Effects of Discrimination Litigation on Women in Supermarket Management." *American Journal of Sociology* 113(4):1148–82.

Skrentny, John. 2014. *After Civil Rights: Racial Realism and the Law in the New American Workplace.* Princeton, NJ: Princeton University Press.

Small, Mario Luis. 2009. "How Many Cases Do I Need? On Science and the Logic of Case Selection in Field-based Research." *Ethnography* 10:5–38.

Smith, Tom W. 1991. *What Americans Say about Jews.* New York: American Jewish Committee.

——. 2000. *Taking America's Pulse: NCCJ's 2000 Survey of Intergroup Relations in the United States.* New York: National Conference for Community and Justice.

——. 2002. *Measuring Racial and Ethnic Discrimination.* Chicago: National Opinion Research Center, University of Chicago.

Sniderman, Paul M., and Thomas Piazza. 1993. *The Scar of Race.* Cambridge, MA: Harvard University Press.

Soss, Joe. 1999. "Lessons of Welfare: Policy Design, Political Learning, and Political Action." *American Political Science Review* 93(2):363–80.

Stainback, Kevin, and Donald Tomaskovic-Devey. 2012. *Documenting Desegregation: Racial and Gender Segregation in Private-Sector Employment since the Civil Rights Act.* New York: Russell Sage Foundation.

Staples, Robert. 1986. "The Political Economy of Black Family Life." *Black Scholar* 17(5):2–11.

Staszak, Sarah. 2015. *No Day in Court: Access to Justice and the Politics of Judicial Retrenchment.* New York: Oxford University Press.

Sternlight, Jean R. 2005. "Creeping Mandatory Arbitration: Is It Just?" *Stanford Law Review* 57(5):1631–75.

Stone, Deborah A. 1984. *The Disabled State*: Temple University Press.

Stone, Dianna L., and Adrienne Colella. 1996. "A Model of Factors Affecting the Treatment of Disabled Individuals in Organizations." *Academy of Management Review* 21(2):352–401.

Stryker, Robin, Martha Scarpellino, and Mellisa Holtzman. 1999. "Political Culture Wars 1990s Style: The Drum Beat of Quotas in Media Framing of the Civil Rights Act of 1991." *Social Stratification and Mobility* 17:33–106.

Sturm, Susan. 2001. "Second Generation Employment Discrimination: A Structural Approach." *Columbia Law Review* 101:458–68.

Suh, Susan A. 2000. "Women's Perceptions of Workplace Discrimination: Impacts of Racial Group, Gender, and Class." In *Prismatic Metropolis: Inequality in Los Angeles*, ed. Melvin L. Oliver, Lawrence D. Bobo, James H. Johnson, and Abel Valenzuela, 561–96. New York: Russell Sage Foundation.

Sutton, John R., and Frank Dobbin. 1996. "The Two Faces of Governance: Responses to Legal Uncertainty in U.S. Firms, 1955 to 1985." *American Sociological Review* 61(5):796–811.

Sutton, John R., Frank Dobbin, John W. Meyer, and W. Richard Scott. 1994. "The Legalization of the Workplace." *American Journal of Sociology* 99(4):944–71.

Sweeney, Laura T., and Craig Haney. 1992. "The Influence of Race on Sentencing: A Meta-Analytic Review of Experimental Studies." *Behavioral Sciences & the Law* 10(2):179–95.

Swim, Janet K., and Laurie L. Cohen. 1997. "Overt, Covert, and Subtle Sexism." *Psychology of Women Quarterly* 21(1):103–18.

Swim, Janet K., and Lawrence J. Sanna. 1996. "He's Skilled, She's Lucky: A Meta-Analysis of Observers' Attributions for Women's and Men's Successes and Failures." *Personality and Social Psychology Bulletin* 22(5):507–19.

Taylor, Philip, and Alan Walker. 1998. "Employers and Older Workers: Attitudes and Employment Practices." *Aging and Society* 18(6):641–58.

Thomas, Carol. 2004. "How Is Disability Understood? An Examination of Sociological Approaches." *Disability & Society* 19(6):569–83.

Tilcsik, Andras. 2011. "Pride and Prejudice: Employment Discrimination against Openly Gay Men in the United States." *American Journal of Sociology* 117(2):586–626.

Tomaskovic-Devey, Donald, Melvin Thomas, and Kecia Johnson. 2005. "Race and the Accumulation of Human Capital across the Career: A Theoretical Model and Fixed-Effects Application." *American Journal of Sociology* 111(1):58–89.

Trautner, Mary Nell. 2006. "How Social Hierarchies Within the Personal Injury Bar Affect Case Screening Decisions." *New York Law School Law Review* 51(2):215–40.

Tyler, Tom R. 1984. "The Role of Perceived Injustice in Defendants' Evaluations of Their Courtroom Experience." *Law and Society Review* 18(1):51–74.

———. 1990. *Why People Obey the Law*. New Haven, CT: Yale University Press.

US Bureau of Labor Statistics. 2014. *Current Population Survey, Annual Social and Economic Supplements*. http://www.bls.gov/cps/earnings.htm#demographics. Accessed May 16, 2016.

US Census Bureau. 2011. "Selected Characteristics of People 15 Years Old and Over by Total Money Income in 2010, Work Experience in 2010." Online: http://www.census.gov/hhes/www/cpstables/032011/perinc/new01_005.htm. Accessed May 16, 2016.

———. 2015. *Income, Poverty and Health Insurance Coverage in the United States: 2014*. Washington, DC.

Van Cleve, Nicole Gonzalez. 2016. *Crook County: Racism and Injustice in America's Largest Criminal Court*. Stanford, CA: Stanford University Press.

Van Cleve, Nicole Gonzalez, and Lauren Mayes. 2015. "Criminal Justice through 'Colorblind' Lenses: A Call to Examine the Mutual Constitution of Race and Criminal Justice." *Law and Social Inquiry* 40(2):406–32.

Van Hoy, Jerry. 1999. "Markets and Contingency: How Client Markets Influence the Work of Plaintiffs' Personal Injury Lawyers." *International Journal of the Legal Profession* 6(3):345–66.

Weber, Max. 1978. *Economy and Society: An Outline of Interpretive Sociology*. Ed. Guenther Roth and Claus Wittich. Berkeley: University of California Press.

Weinberg, Jill D., and Laura Beth Nielsen. 2011. "Examining Empathy: Discrimination, Experience, and Judicial Decisionmaking." *Southern California Law Review* 85:313–52.

Welsh, Sandy. 1999. "Gender and Sexual Harassment." *Annual Review of Sociology* 25:169–90.

Williams, Joan C., M. Blair-Loy, and J. Berdahl. 2013. "Cultural Schemas, Social Class, and the Flexibility Stigma." *Journal of Social Issues* 69(2):209–34.

Williams, Patricia J. 1991. *The Alchemy of Race and Rights*. Cambridge, MA: Harvard University Press.

Wilson, George, and Vincent Roscigno. 2014. "The Relational Foundations of Inequality at Work II: Structure–Action Interplay." *American Behavioral Scientist* 58(3):375–78.

Woodward, Jennifer. 2015. "Making Rights Work: Legal Mobilization at the Agency Level." *Law and Society Review* 49(3):691–724.

Wrenn, Kimberly A., and Todd J. Maurer. 2004. "Beliefs about Older Workers' Learning and Development Behavior in Relation to Beliefs about Malleability of Skills, Age-Related Decline, and Control." *Journal of Applied Social Psychology* 34(2):223–42.

Yngvesson, Barbara. 1985. "Law, Private Governance, and Continuing Relationships." *Wisconsin Law Review* 1985:623–46.

——. 1988. "Making Law at the Doorway: The Clerk, the Court, and the Construction of Community in a New England Town." *Law and Society Review* 22(3):409–48.

Zemans, Frances Kahn. 1983. "Legal Mobilization: The Neglected Role of the Law in the Political System." *American Political Science Review* 77(3):690.

Zhou, Li. 2015. "Can California Prevent Wage Discrimination against Women?" *Atlantic*. Oct. 7. http://www.theatlantic.com/business/archive/2015/10/california-gender-wage-gap-fair-pay-act/409549/. Accessed May 16, 2016.

Zippel, Kathrin S. 2006. *The Politics of Sexual Harassment: A Comparative Study of the United States, the European Union, and Germany*. Cambridge: Cambridge University Press.

Index

Page numbers in italics indicate figures; page numbers followed by "t" indicate tables.

CPSIA information can be obtained
at www.ICGtesting.com
Printed in the USA
LVHW04s0727030918
588702LV00004B/4/P

9 780226 466859